The International Politics of the Red Sea

This pioneering book is the first comprehensive study of the Red Sea as a sub-region of the international system in its own right. Examining the international politics of the Red Sea region from the Cold War to the present day, it argues that the Red Sea area demonstrates the characteristics of a sub-regional system, given its increasing economic and social interdependence, greater regional integration, and flows of resources across it. It details how stronger regional powers – Egypt, Israel and Saudi Arabia – which co-habit the sub-region with much weaker, vulnerable and fragile states, are seeking to stamp their own authority on this dynamic sub-region. They have attempted to do so, the authors show, through extension of their military and economic influence wherever possible, while also forging regional partnerships aimed at protecting their interests or to fend off the possible encroachment of others.

The International Politics of the Red Sea discusses in great detail the security and military dynamics of the sub-region; the land and maritime borders; as well as economic issues, including trade, migration, capital flows and transport. It covers developments across the Red Sea and also within all the states of this newly-forming sub-region.

Anoushiravan Ehteshami is Dean of Internationalisation and Professor of International Relations at Durham University, UK. He was the founding Head of the School of Government and International Affairs at Durham, and also the Vice-President of the British Society for Middle Eastern Studies.

Emma C. Murphy is Professor of Political Economy in the School of Government and International Affairs at Durham University, UK. She is co-editor of *Mediterranean Politics* journal.

Durham Modern Middle East and Islamic World Series
Series Editor: Anoushiravan Ehteshami, *University of Durham, UK*

The International Politics of the Red Sea

Anoushiravan Ehteshami and
Emma C. Murphy

Routledge
Taylor & Francis Group

LONDON AND NEW YORK

First published 2012
by Routledge
711 Third Avenue, New York, NY 10017

Simultaneously published in the UK
by Routledge
2 Park Square, Milton Park, Abingdon, Oxon OX14 4RN

Routledge is an imprint of the Taylor & Francis Group, an informa business

First issued in paperback 2013

British Library Cataloguing in Publication Data
A catalogue record for this book is available from the British Library

Library of Congress Cataloging-in-Publication Data
A catalog record has been requested for this book

ISBN 978–0–415–67705–9 (hbk)
ISBN 978–0–415–72621–4 (pbk)
ISBN 978–0–203–80875–7 (ebk)

Typeset in Times New Roman by
Book Now Ltd, London

To Ardeshir and Kasra

Contents

Tables

Acknowledgements

We started thinking about the changing dynamics of the Red Sea area in the early 1990s, when we were engaged in separate research on the two recurring security dilemmas of the Middle East: the Arab–Israeli conflict and Persian Gulf stability. It struck us then that much of the research on Middle East regional security and politics had somehow tended to by-pass any serious discussion of the impact of regional developments on the Red Sea and yet our own research brought us back time and again to the significance of both the waterway and its littoral states. These states have tended to be viewed as members of sub-regional theatres (the Levant, the Persian Gulf, the Horn of Africa) that have little or nothing to do with their location on the sea itself, despite its tremendous strategic, military and economic importance for most of them. Moreover, the prolific evidence of interaction between Red Sea states is virtually ignored other than as part and parcel of greater regional or international activity.

Where the strategic character of the Red Sea has been considered, it has most frequently been as a variable in the superpower equations of the Cold War. With the onset of the post-Cold War era, it quickly became apparent to us that the tremendous sea changes at the international level and developments in the Middle East sub-system were having a direct impact on the Red Sea area and its states as well. This sea-way, we began to hypothesise, was slowly acquiring the characteristics of a sub-region in its own right.

We began exploring our ideas in discussions with friends, colleagues and policy advisers from Red Sea states and the wider world, whose perspectives and insights helped us enormously in our thinking about the Red Sea. Some of the early supporters of the project were based in our home institution, the University of Durham, however. We thank our colleagues across the university for their support and encouragement. Indeed, the project would never have got off the ground had it not been for the generous financial support of the Research Committee of the university, which provided us with the necessary finances to enable us to devote extra time and resources to the research. We hope that they will be pleased with the outcome.

In the course of the research, we relied heavily on the assistance and data resources of the University's Main Library, the Eric Watkins Papers collection, and the International Boundaries Research Unit. Three colleagues whose extensive assistance is particularly appreciated are Martin Pratt, Mamty Sunuodula and Avril Shields, all of whom aided us in hunting out the large amounts of data needed for the project.

The Canadian Board of Immigration was another institutional body which extended us generous support and provided us with many valuable documents and reports on contemporary developments in the Red Sea. In the same vein, we would also like to acknowledge the contribution that the excellent archives of Gulf 2000 and Jane's Information Group have made to our research. Each in its own way provides the researcher with a unique collection of materials. Without access to these considerable resources, the book would be that much poorer. We also benefited from the expertise of Rebecca Roland in compiling data on Red Sea transportation links.

Finally, we would like to take this opportunity to thank Peter Sowden, our Editor at Routledge, for his support and for his patience with us, and also to acknowledge the important contribution that the comments of the anonymous referees have made to this book. We found their comments and suggestions extremely valuable. Naturally, any outstanding flaws in the book remain the responsibility of the authors.

Abbreviations

ACC	Arab Co-operation Council
AFSED	Arab Fund for Economic and Social Development
AFTA	Arab Free Trade Area
AMF	Arab Monetary Fund
AMU	Arab Maghreb Union
ARC	Aqaba Railways Corporation
ASEZ	Aqaba Special Economic Zone
BOOT	Build-Own-Operate-Transfer
CENTCOM	Central Command
CNPC	China National Petroleum Company
DoP	Declaration of Principles
ELF	Eritrean Liberation Front
EPLF	Eritrean People's Liberation Front
FCiP	Five Countries Interconnection Project
FDI	foreign direct investment
GCC	Gulf Co-operation Council
GIA	Islamic Armed Group
GPC	General People's Congress
IDF	Israeli Defence Force
IGAD	InterGovernmental Authority on Development
IMF	International Monetary Fund
IOC	Islamic Conference Organisation
ISI	import-substitution industrialisation
LNG	liquefied natural gas
MCM	million cubic metres
MENA	Middle East and North Africa
NDA	National Democratic Alliance
OAU	Organisation of African Unity
OLF	Oromo Liberation Front
PA	Palestinian Authority
PDRY	People's Democratic Republic of Yemen
RDF	Rapid Deployment Force
REDWIG	Regional Economic Development Working Group

SCA	Suez Canal Authority
SPLA	Sudan People's Liberation Army
SPLM	Sudan People's Liberation Movement
SSM	surface-to-surface missile
SUMED	Suez-Mediterranean
TEAM	Taba-Eilat-Aqaba Macro area
TEU	twenty-foot equivalent unit
TPLF	Tigray People's Liberation Front
UAR	United Arab Emirates
VLCC	very large crude carrier
YSP	Yemen Socialist Party

Introduction

The seas and waterways of the Middle East have had a place in the complex weave of human affairs for thousands of years. Great civilisations have ebbed and flowed along their shorelines and international commerce found much of its early impetus in the trade which traversed their expanses. The region lies at the convergence of three continents, drawing in the resources and cultures of its peripheries, and conveying them out again to enrich and enliven the wider world. The Mediterranean, the Red and Arabian Seas, the Persian Gulf and the Indian Ocean have all played their part in this process. Communities have grown up around the extraction of resources from their waters. Conquerors, explorers, traders, migrants and slaves have crossed them. Naval fleets have fought over them for spheres of influence and control over trade routes.

In recent years, attention has been focused upon the Mediterranean basin and the Persian Gulf. The former represents the barrier, or the bridge, depending on one's perspective, between one of the world's most advanced regions and its developing neighbours. A sea which not so long ago nervously harboured the rival fleets of NATO and the Warsaw Pact, is today being pacified through the efforts of EU expansion, partnership programmes and association agreements. In the Persian Gulf, by contrast, the past decades have witnessed the end of the longest inter-state war in the twentieth century, only to see it replaced by an equally ferocious 'mother of all battles' over Kuwait in 1991 and forced regime change in Iraq in 2003 through the application of President Bush's 'shock and awe' military tactics. The Gulf's length is filled with warships and its significance in terms of hydrocarbon provision plain to see. Even the Indian Ocean is witnessing a revival of international attention as its littoral states develop their military might and rattle their economic swords.

The Red Sea, by contrast, is sometimes considered to have seen its greatest days. Today the name is synonymous with the steady flow of sea traffic through the Suez Canal, travellers to Mecca, piracy at one end of it, and snorkelling holidays along its coral reefs. Yet in the past, it rivalled all in terms of its strategic and economic importance. While the Mediterranean was the stomping ground of the classical civilisations of Rome, Greece and the Phoenicians, the Red Sea played a vital role in the power struggles of the Egyptian, Persian and later Ottoman

Empires among others. The Romans and Greeks too fought for access to and control over the sea, which represented the route between Asia and Africa as well as the conduit to the Indian Ocean and the wealth of the east beyond. The prophet Moses led the Hebrews across a mystically parted Red Sea, while the Nabateans placed their outposts southwards along the Arabian coast of the Red Sea in the third century AD. The Byzantines staved off the Persians through their monopoly over the waterway in the sixth century, drawing in the newly converted Christians of Ethiopia as their allies while their Persian rivals recruited Jewish convert communities residing at both ends of the sea. By the tenth century, trade between Europe and the East was opting for the Red Sea route rather than the Persian Gulf as Cairo grew in importance. By the twelfth century, the Fatimids of Egypt were drawing much of their power and revenue from Red Sea trade. Chinese textiles, glass and porcelain, spices from south and southeast Asia, gun powder and saltpetre all were brought to Cairo and from there distributed to Europe and the Middle East.[1]

The Seljuks were meanwhile lined up on the far side of the sea's shores, engaged in their own battles with the Crusaders, who were not above loading their dismantled ships onto camels to cross the desert, unloading them on the Gulf of Aqaba, and ultimately sailing down the coast of Arabia attacking coastal settlements. In one instance, Reynaud de Châtillon attempted to raid the Holy City of Mecca itself, inciting the ire of Muslim Egypt and causing the latter to send its own fleet in pursuit down the Red Sea. Throughout the fourteenth and fifteenth centuries, competition over Red Sea trade routes featured prominently in the conflict between Muslim provinces of the Horn of Africa and the southern march of Christianity. The Portuguese were to come to the rescue of Christian dynasties when the Muslims fought back, not least because they anticipated economic rewards for doing so.

By the sixteenth century, both sides of the sea had fallen to the Ottomans, whose naval forces spent much of their time defending the waterway from encroachment by the same Portuguese competitors who sought to extend their own influence into the hinterland of Syria, Egypt and the Hijaz.[2] Not only did these lands provide much of the Ottoman tax revenue, but control over Mecca in particular brought in pilgrimage income as well as a certain religious legitimacy for the empire. Once the Portuguese threat had diminished, the Ottomans were content to devolve authority over the Arabian provinces (which had little of their own wealth to recommend them).

By this time, however, the central role of the Near and Middle East in international trade was beginning to suffer from the effects of growing European maritime power. Not only did the Europeans open new trade routes westwards to the Americas, they also mastered the art of crossing the treacherous seas around the Cape of Good Hope. With Europe no longer dependent upon the land and sea trading routes that crossed the Arab world to Central Asia, India and China, the Ottoman Empire began to experience a decline that was to prove irresistible. Bernard Lewis has detailed, however, how it was not simply the circumnavigation of Africa which undermined the spice trade through the Red Sea, but rather the evolving power of the Dutch and British in Asia which allowed the Europeans to harness the productive and commercial potential of their colonies.[3] The Ottoman Empire was never really to recover from the loss of the monopoly on trade routes. Indeed, it became itself the target of European exports and the produce of European colonies elsewhere which were ultimately to undermine its own productive capacities and lead to the infamous capitulations.

That is not to say, however, that the region itself declined in strategic importance for the Europeans. Indeed, the French, British, Russians and later Germans and Italians, were to play out their rivalries in part through direct intervention in the area in the eighteenth century. The British in particular were concerned to develop their coaling stations on the coast of Arabia, Aden being occupied in 1839. For the most part, however, their concerns were concentrated in Egypt, Central Asia, the Caspian, the Black Sea and the Arabian Sea.

Yet in 1869, the Red Sea was to resurface as a waterway of vital strategic import for the colonial powers with the opening of the Suez Canal to international shipping. As early as the Pharoahnic times, efforts had been made to construct a water passage to link the Mediterranean to the Red Sea. Chroniclers of the ancient world such as Aristotle, Strabo and Pliny all believed that such a canal had been built during the reign of Sesostris I, who died in 1926 BC and an inscription in a temple at Karnak indicates that it may still have been in use during the reign of Set I, who died in 1290 BC.[4] Herodotus recounts how Pharoah Necho II attempted to reopen the canal, which had succumbed to drifting sands, a task completed, he claims, by the Persians under Darius the Great (522–485 BC). This canal was repaired and a new section added by the Roman Emperor Trajan (98–117 AD) when the eastern tributaries of the Nile, which had been used by the pharaohs, became too shallow for his ships. His canal subsequently became a busy route for traders between Rome and the East. The fact that successive rulers and conquerors prized such a waterway indicates the strategic importance attached to transport between the Mediterranean and Arabian seas by the powers of the past. Harun al-Rashid, then Caliph of Baghdad, reportedly considered reopening the canal in the eighth century but ultimately was warned off by advisors who pointed to the potential vulnerability of borders if enemies could travel so freely around his territory's periphery. In the event, any remains of a previous canal were swallowed in the sands and the laborious process of loading camel caravans to cross from Port Said to Suez became the common and not inexpensive practice until Napoleon Bonaparte arrived in Egypt in 1798. The opportunity then presented itself to open up new French markets in the Far East while simultaneously cutting off rival Britain from its Indian colonies. Under his leadership, the harbour at Suez was deepened but it took a diplomat, Ferdinand de Lessops, to make the dream of rebuilding the canal come true. When the canal was opened in 1869, the sea route between Europe and the Orient was shortened by 4,000 miles. It was no small wonder that the British came to call the canal 'the lifeline of the Empire' and the 'very spring of British trade, wealth and power',[5] with four-fifths of the traffic using it in 1875 being from that sea-faring nation. It was equally unsurprising then that, when the Egyptian king ran into financial difficulties, the British were eager to purchase 44 per cent of the shares in the canal company and with them to outmanoeuvre the French. In 1882, British troops entered the Canal zone and were subsequently to occupy Egypt itself. By the mid-1940s the Suez Canal zone had emerged as the 'largest British base in the region and was vital to the empire mostly because of the presence there of massive military depots ... [containing] base workshops, ammunition and medical supplies, petrol reserves and mobilization stores'.[6] There were around 200,000 British service personnel stationed in the Canal zone in 1946, the last of which was not to leave until May 1956. Even then, they were to re-invade in November under the phoney pretext of deterring an Israeli attack, demonstrating again the place of the Canal in the strategic thinking of great powers in Europe and the Middle East.

In subsequent decades it was the United States of America and the Soviet Union, together with their respective regional allies, who were to view the Red Sea and its littoral territories as part of a great and dangerous geopolitical game. There were four principal motivations behind the exertions of the superpowers: first, the post-Second World War era saw a vast growth in demand for oil, a resource found in greatest and most accessible abundance in the Arabian Peninsula. Second, the northern end of the Red Sea was bordered by the new state of Israel and two of its front-line enemies, Egypt and Jordan. The Gulf of Aqaba, the Suez Canal and the Straits of Tiran were prized possessions in the tactical military equations of a war which, while sometimes apparently dormant, was a running sore for regional and superpower politics. Third, the newly independent and mostly Arab states of the region were vulnerable to the expansionary tendencies of the Soviet Empire and equally important to NATO plans for containment of their own military and ideological enemy. It was in this context that Washington military planners soon after the end of the Second World War were to identify the British military facilities in the Suez Canal zone as 'a facility of vital importance' in case of any future confrontation with the Soviet Union.[7]

Finally, the Red Sea has continued to be a major world trading route. Who has control over the only two, narrow, points of access (the Suez Canal and the Bab el-Mandeb) is a major question for regional and international strategic thinkers alike, since – as the Israelis found to their cost – in a region as troubled by instability as the Middle East, it is as well to have as many and as accessible trade routes as possible. Equally, and most especially in the current climate of trade liberalisation, which for many Arab states represents the only available strategy to escape the trap of economic stagnation, low cost and accessible transport routes between the region, the markets of Europe and beyond are vital assets.

It seems strange then that, despite its strategic importance, the Red Sea has been under-valued and neglected by analysts of the wider Middle East and North Africa (MENA) region. The internal dynamics of littoral states have aroused interest when they are perceived to threaten external interests or regional balances (for example, the Free Officers revolution in Egypt, the coming to power of a pro-Islamist regime in Sudan, al-Qaeda activities in and from Yemen, or civil war in Somalia and extension of piracy from its territories, or Jordan's complex relationship with its neighbours). Likewise inter-state and multi-state conflicts, particularly those arising from hostility between Arabs and Israelis, have been prominent in international strategic thinking. Yet the dynamics of the Red Sea as a potentially distinct arena of activity have been virtually ignored. Relations between Red Sea states seem to be of little interest to the outside unless they impinge upon wider interests and spheres of influence. Changes in the balance of power between them, even an understanding of any such balance, have not featured in the literature of international relations.[8] The depth of this neglect is all the more ironic given that the history of relations between the sea's coastal entities is rich and varied. The population of the Horn of Africa includes Semitic peoples who originally came from Arabia, bringing with them both Islam and Judaism – and later Christianity – deriving from the Levantine lands at the northern end of the sea. Today that migration is annually reversed as Muslims from the Horn travel east to Mecca in pilgrimage, as Jews make aliya to Israel, and as labour migrants travel in search of work. Labour remittances combine with aid and capital flows that pass between the littoral states, supporting developmental and political agendas, shoring up domestic regime stability and international peace processes, Islamist opposition groups and weapons purchases. People, politics and finance flow today as easily across the waters as trade has always done, and the study of the interaction between Red Sea states can only serve to deepen our understanding of the role which these states, and the sea which joins them, play in the wider regional and international systems.

This book seeks to examine and unravel the complex web of relationships which tie the states of the Red Sea together with strands of common or collective destiny. It further seeks to place the collectivity of Red Sea states within a wider regional and international context, identifying linkages and influences which act to shape their characters and their own impact upon the wider environment.

The methodology of the study

Having begun with the observation that the Red Sea has by and large been neglected in post-war international relations literature on the Middle East and North Africa, and given that this project aims to rectify that inadequacy, it becomes necessary to define the unit of study more closely. It is, of course, not the body of water itself which is of interest, but rather the geographic location within which it sits. Specifically, this study will examine the littoral states which provide its coastline and, more critically, the parties most interested in activities taking place, on, around, above, within or because of that body of water.

If we are to assume that their location on the edge of the sea gives all such states some common interest, even some common basis around which to have a conflict of interests, then we may define the collectivity of such states as the principal unit of our discussion. Yet the states concerned do not belong to any single, common, institutional organisation which identifies that common interest or is founded upon it. Thus, we may ask, in what sense do they constitute any identifiable unit? Moreover, the states involved very definitely share identifiable common interests with other surrounding states on the basis of continental or regional proximity. Egypt, Sudan, Ethiopia, Eritrea and the Somali Republic are all African states. Egypt, Jordan, Saudi Arabia and Yemen are identifiably Arab states, with Sudan possessing a significant and dominant Arab population. Saudi Arabia and Yemen share a common Arabian Peninsula identity, while they join with Israel and Jordan in belonging to the Asian continent. We might then most conveniently start our journey of discovery by locating all the Red Sea states within a broadly defined Middle East and North Africa (MENA) region, that being their single common defining geographic feature. Although this starting point may initially seem questionable for various reasons, it becomes progressively more comfortable as we begin to unravel the relationships around the sea. We are not the first to conclude that the MENA region in a new millennium should be viewed in its wider sense, rather than in a narrower form that identifies only with the Mashreq or the Arab world. Geoffrey Kemp and Robert Harkavy, in their study of the strategic geography of the Middle East, have argued that a geo-strategic study of the region necessitates inclusion of peripheral states which nonetheless play a significant role in strategic developments. Their 'greater Middle East' includes Central Asia, the Caucasus, North Africa, Afghanistan, India, Pakistan and the Horn of Africa.[9] Our study does not require that the net is cast as wide as that, unless of course we explore the outer reaches of the piracy crisis off the coast of East Africa, but if all the relevant states whose actions impinge upon a region's coherence are to be included in its analysis, then the Middle East region must surely include those states on its geographic edge who nonetheless feature in the foreign policy decisions of core actors. Bassam Tibi has likewise recognised that peripheral states in what he terms the Red Sea conflict zone, specifically Ethiopia, Somalia and Djibouti, must be included as *de facto* members of a Middle Eastern sub-system, despite their subordinate roles relative to more regularly included member states. Tibi's analysis does, however, distinguish between sub-regions of the MENA sub-system (the Mashreq, the Maghreb and the Persian Gulf) and conflict zones (Arab–Israeli, Arab–Iranian, Lebanon, the Red Sea and the Western Sahara).

An identifiable MENA region has now been an accepted feature of international relations for many years.[10] In 1969, Michael Brecher, for example, pointed out that the Middle East was one of at least five definable subordinate state systems, a view also shared by prominent scholars such as Binder, Russet, Spiegel and Cantori. In more recent times, the term MENA has come to represent the collectivity of Arab states plus their non-Arab regional neighbours. Either way, by introducing this concept of a regional entity, we are introduced to the levels of analysis approach to international relations developed in the wake of the major works of Kenneth Waltz[11] and Morton Kaplan,[12] from which such regional conceptualisations derive notions of systemic dynamics which link the activities and alignment of individual states.[13] A levels of analysis approach allows us to see the MENA region as being subject not only to the whims and policies of its composite nation-state parts but also as having dynamics and momentum that derive from the systemic interaction of those parts.

Others have argued, and again with reference to a levels of analysis approach, that not only is the Middle East and North Africa a regional system, but that it is, in the words of Leonard Binder,[14] 'subordinate' to the international system. This perspective requires analysis of the region not only in terms of its constituent parts plus its systemic characteristics and dynamics, but also with reference to the penetration of the regional system by external powers and influences. In other words, a third 'level' is introduced, that of the international system itself.

Yet anyone familiar with the Middle East and North Africa will readily succumb to the argument that the region is not a single, homogeneous group of states acting in concert, but rather that – in spite of rather than because of – region-wide dynamics, there exist also smaller collectivities of states, what might be termed sub-regions. The very existence of sub-regional multi-state organisations such as the Gulf Co-operation Council (GCC) and the Arab Maghreb Union (AMU) indicates that some states share geographic locations which coincide with other commonly held economic, political or strategic interests. It is then possible to introduce still another 'level' to our analysis – that of the 'sub-region'. If a system equates with a simplistic definition of 'a set of units interacting within a structure',[15] there is no definitive reason why one system should not operate within, and as a sub-system of, another greater system at any given level. If regions may exist as sub-systems within an international system, why should not sub-regions act as sub-systems within regions?

We might ask ourselves at this point whether this approach is useful in itself, and for what facts its use might uncover, or whether its use is intended to demonstrate that it holds within it an ultimate truth. As Buzan has stated:

> It is not clear [for example], whether levels of analysis is more an epistemological construct (and thus about different approaches to knowledge) or whether it is ontological (and therefore about the number and type of entities that are thought to actually exist in the international system).[16]

Are 'levels' to be seen as units of analysis or variables that explain behaviour? For the purposes of our analysis it seems more appropriate to be inclusive of approaches rather than exclusive. Thus, the dimensions or axes of our analysis proceed simultaneously along a number of tracks.

First, we assume a simplistic series of levels – the state, the sub-region, the region (or sub-system) and the international system. However, we would reject rigid distinctions between these levels, given that any number of intermediary levels may be found to exist between any dyadic combination. The levels are more for the purposes of convenient exploration of the subject matter than to assert their inflexible and constant distinction. Therefore, we start our examination of the Red Sea states from a position which assumes they form some type of sub-regional configuration, with identifiable sub-regional tendencies, without intending to dogmatically assert the existence of any specific sub-regional character.

Second, and in common with the epistemological tradition, we recognise that systems can be examined not simply through reductionist fragmentation into their component parts, but also through sources of explanation. Buzan identifies three conceptual pegs which have developed within international relations theory and which are appropriate to systems analysis: interaction capacity, structure, and process.[17] Combining these 'pegs' within our framework of analysis allows us to benefit from both a reductionist and descriptive approach to the units within levels, and a holistic approach to the relations within and between levels.

It is not the intention of this book to assert a definitive method for analysis of the place of the Red Sea states in the international system. Rather, this composite utilisation of theoretical traditions enables us to view units and levels of analysis and their relationships with one another without committing ourselves to an exclusivist interpretation in advance.

Given the approach outlined above, the basic assumptions about levels of analysis which underlie this study are as follows. First, the unit at the bottom of our hierarchy of levels is the modern state. The state is an easily identifiable entity and is the determining or regulatory unit behind much of the activity which takes place upon, within or around the Red Sea. Yet the analysis would be incomplete if it did not take into account the internal ethnic, religious and political composition which has shaped those states and which has fed into much of their policy-making. Civil wars in Yemen, Somalia, Ethiopia and Sudan have in recent years all demonstrated that the nation-state is not a 'given' in the MENA region and that challenges to the integrity of states have implications for the region beyond their own geographic boundaries. Recent American intervention in Somalia, Iranian and Saudi meddling in Yemen, and Egyptian and Saudi involvement in the struggle for power in Sudan have all shown that sub-regional, regional and international actors perceive the internal security of sub-regional states to be sufficiently within their own interests as to merit not just interest but even direct intervention. The more general point being, 'superimposed on the regional level, and penetrating into it, is a powerful global level'.[18]

Our second level of analysis is the collectivity of the states bordering the Red Sea, which we believe justifies use of the category sub-region, albeit with reservations at this stage. There is nothing novel in this definition and the Red Sea states seem comfortably to wear its clothes. To qualify as a sub-region, the following conditions need to be satisfied among such a group:[19]

1 The actors must be geographically proximate states.
2 There must exist a minimum of two, but usually more than three, actors in the sub-region.
3 The actors' 'pattern of relations or interactions must exhibit a particular degree of regularity and intensity to the extent that a change at one point in the [sub-region] affects other points'.[20]
4 Local players and outside powers recognise the sub-region as a distinctive theatre of operations.
5 A substantial aspect of the proximate states' foreign policy will be dictated by the dynamics of the sub-region.

The first of these qualifications is most easily dealt with as a statement of the obvious. The second requires that we identify a number of 'actors', states which exert influence upon the system within which they exist and which can shape its characteristics and dynamics. Here our analysis points specifically at three emerging regional 'middle powers': Egypt, Israel and Saudi Arabia. If one measures power simply in terms of military capacity, then one can point out that the latter two possess a strategic capability (Israel's nuclear weapons and SSMs and Saudi Arabia's long-range SSMs), while all three boast a modern military machine. Since the late 1950s, all three have actively been seeking to cultivate their own 'zone of influence' and to demonstrate their regional presence, within the context of which their sub-regional activities become evident. Egypt and Saudi Arabia, for example, have at times sought to engage in a co-operative partnership for the purposes of securing regional order. At other times, however, it has become clear that they have competed to secure and maximise their own influence, even at the expense of regional harmony.

The Red Sea has featured prominently in this process. The Egyptian nationalisation of the Suez Canal, and its subsequent defence of that waterway in 1956, were only the beginning of Egyptian efforts to use its control over the canal as a way to exert influence over the northern end of the sea. The positioning of Egyptian troops in Sinai in 1967, the locating of shore batteries along, and subsequent closure of, the Straits of Tiran promoted an infamous Israeli response, indicating not least the importance attached by the latter country to free access to Red Sea trade routes.

It was in the mid-1970s, however, that the Red Sea truly emerged as a major strategic concern for the regional powers. First, the oil price hikes of the first half of the 1970s had increased the premium on reliable export routes to OECD markets. The Red Sea route had always been recognised as one of the cheapest and most efficient means of transit to Europe and the relaxation of tensions over the northern end of the waterway following the 1974 Egyptian–Israeli disengagement agreement allowed for renewed transport activity on the waterway. These were made possible by the re-opening of the Suez Canal in June 1975 after eight years of closure, opening up new commercial possibilities for the littoral and major powers alike, but equally raising the stakes in terms of secure access to the sea. For Saudi Arabia, the effort to secure an export route for oil which avoided the Straits of Hormuz or passage through another nation-state, led to the establishment of the Yanbu terminal on the Red Sea coast, reinforcing the strategic value of the Jeddah hinterland and the Suez and Bab el-Mandeb exit points. Inevitably, Saudi influence was more easily exerted over its neighbours, Jordan in the north and Yemen in the south, than over the western littoral states. Yet it has not been averse to intervening in Sudanese domestic affairs when necessary.

Israel, for its part, has been tightly constrained by its lack of diplomatic relations with any of its neighbours prior to 1979 and even afterwards by the 'coldness' of its peace with Egypt and Jordan. It is difficult to exert influence when one has no friends and when the only commonly held policy of one's neighbours is antipathy to oneself. Israel has thus resorted to one direct and three indirect methods of exerting regional influence. In direct terms, the development of an awesome strategic military capability which includes a non-conventional capability, has allowed Israel to at least exercise some deterrent influence. In regional terms, Israel has used its military muscle to put pressure on Jordan and Syria, to 'pacify' south Lebanon, to deter development of an Iraqi (and even Syrian) nuclear capability, to posture against an increasingly belligerent Iran, and to support regimes and movements that either put pressure on hostile regional actors or are prepared to countenance (unofficial) alliances with the Zionist state. At the less direct level, Israel has exerted influence across the region through its strategic alliance with the United States, through provision of technical and economic aid in some instances, and through efforts to 'sanction bust' prior to the 1990s and the lifting of the wider embargo after the 1993 Oslo Agreement with the Palestinians.

The emergence of these three regional powers, and the establishment of their influence over the Red Sea as a sub-region, can be traced through the Cold War and post-Cold War eras. As Chapters 2 and 3 will show, during the Cold War, their ability to project their influence over their neighbours was shaped and constrained by the superpowers' own interests and rivalries. As this competition has subsided, however, they have been able to take more proactive roles in asserting themselves around the Red Sea, contributing to the consolidation of the area as a sub-regional entity.

The third criteria for a sub-region, that changes at one point affect others, is also clearly evident around the Red Sea. The following chapters show how this has been evident during both the Cold War and post-Cold War periods. For example, the advent of the Nasserist regime in Egypt was a prerequisite for the development of republican tendencies in Yemen, which in turn drew in both Egyptian and Saudi involvement, as each perceived their relative power to be at stake. The establishment in that country of an Islamist-supported military regime in 1989, and more recent civil strife in Sudan, were equally of deep concern to Egypt, Israel and Saudi Arabia, and incited their political (and in some cases financial) intervention. The Arab–Israeli conflict at the northern end of the sea has touched the non-front-line states, as much in terms of domestic political impact as in foreign policy and regional alignment. Developments in the Arab world which followed the Camp David Accords had a direct effect on the Red Sea arena, where Egypt was keen to enhance its peace with Israel through closer co-operation over Red Sea/Sinai matters, while Syria and other Arab states were intent on punishing Egypt for its unilateral peace with Israel by isolating it politically and diplomatically (moving the headquarters of the Arab League from Cairo to Tunis, for instance) as well as economically (by severing virtually all financial assistance). In this phase, Arab pressures on Jordan not to join the US-orchestrated peace process increased immensely, leading King Hussein to reject President Sadat's overtures to join open dialogue with Israel in favour of closer co-operation with the opposition Arab states. As far as inter-Arab politics was concerned, Egypt remained in the cold until the latter half of the 1980s, when Jordan and Kuwait initiated the process of re-integrating Egypt into the Arab system.[21] Northern Red

Sea politics, therefore, had become hostage to inter-Arab divisions over the Egyptian-Israeli peace treaty and the scramble to fill Egypt's shoes as the political centre of the Arab world.

At the other end of the Red Sea, Arab competition for influence was running parallel with intense superpower interest in the Horn of Africa. While 'radical' Arab regimes, namely Libya, Iraq, Syria and South Yemen, had actively supported the Eritrean liberation movement in the mid-1970s, some Red Sea Arab littorals (Egypt and Sudan in particular) and others in the moderate Arab states camp had been supportive of the Ethiopian monarchy. Soon after the 1974 Ethiopian revolution, however, three Red Sea Arab states (Egypt, Saudi Arabia and Sudan), in addition to Bahrain and Kuwait, became close supporters of the Eritrean seccessionists. Libya and South Yemen, by contrast, found it prudent to drop their endorsement of the Eritrean liberation movements in favour of support for the new (Marxist) regime in Addis Ababa. Such strategic musical chairs has been a feature of this sub-system from its inception but what is striking is the dynamics of the Red Sea sub-region having an unsettling effect on inter-Arab politics, and also the wider balance of power in the Middle East sub-system.

This leads us to the fourth criteria for designation as a sub-region; that local and external states recognise it as a distinct arena of operations. In the 1970s, the sub-regional actors themselves identified the sub-region as an arena for their strategic and security-related concerns. At the initiative of King Khalid of Saudi Arabia, the three key Red Sea Arab countries, Egypt, Saudi Arabia and Sudan, met in Jeddah in 1976 to consider their collective development of a 'Red Sea-centrist consciousness', and the co-ordination of their Red Sea policies. Somalia's accession to the Arab League helped in provoking the Arab states' renewed interest in this area, with Saudi Arabia keen to put a distance between Mogadishu and its Soviet patron by asserting the 'Arab' character of the sea. Amidst closer co-operation between the Arab countries, marked by the Ta'izz Conference of March 1977 to discuss Red Sea security issues, Syria and other Arab states also began speaking of the Red Sea as an 'Arab lake' and a peace zone, which, through the co-ordinated efforts of its Arab littorals, should be kept free of 'international conflicts and pressures'.[22] Despite these moves, it soon became evident that inter-Arab rivalries would spill into the Red Sea sub-region and adversely affect its politics. Indeed, the 'Arabisation' of the Red Sea in the 1970s practically ensured such an outcome. Rivalries had two foci: Arab approaches to the Arab–Israeli conflict, and Arab intervention in the Horn of Africa. In the former theatre, by the end of the decade, the Cairo–Damascus–Riyadh 'triple alliance' of the 1970s had begun to strain under the pressure of Egypt's peace talks with Israel, thus forcing a closer convergence between Syria and Saudi Arabia. Evidently, the sub-system of the MENA region, and its Arab-system component, provide a greater environment within which the dynamics of the Red Sea sub-region have evolved. Red Sea states define their interests in, and policy towards, the Red Sea with due regard for their wider regional interests and dilemmas. Equally, regional events elsewhere have impacted upon policies of the Red Sea states and also policies towards these states.

At this point it becomes clear that our third level of analysis, the MENA region or sub-system has come into play. The Red Sea sub-region is only one of a number of sub-regions existing within the MENA sub-system, others include the Maghreb, the Levant, the GCC alignment and the Persian Gulf, each of which is equally an arena with both its own dynamics and its interlinkage with the larger sub-system. Weaving across them runs the so-called Arab system – the sum of the Arab states and some 350 million people who form the largest ethnic group in the area and inhabit lands from the Atlantic Ocean to the Indian Ocean.

Our fourth and final level of analysis, the international system, is also deeply relevant to discussion of the recognition by external actors that the Red Sea constitutes an arena of operations in its own right. The Middle East and North Africa sub-system can be viewed as a penetrated regional system which has been shaped in large part by the intervention of outside powers for at least two centuries. Within that context, and as this book will make clear, the Cold War era witnessed intense superpower interest and activity in and around a specific Red Sea geopolitical arena.

The Red Sea in the Cold War era

Following the Second World War, the process of penetration was dominated by superpower rivalry and their respective efforts to win influence over the region. Within this context, the Red Sea undoubtedly played a role in the strategic thinking of both the United States and the Soviet Union. The Red Sea itself, with its two choke points and several active players in the international system, was a strategic bridge linking several theatres – the Mediterranean theatre (southern flank), which enjoyed significant superpower military presence, the Asian theatre, the Horn of Africa and the wider East African zone – in a chain of global strategic interdependencies. Moreover, the Red Sea could be seen as the vital corridor which linked two significant international zones: the NATO-dominated Mediterranean region and the more diverse Indian Ocean arena, which has been host to a wide range of established and emerging naval powers, from the USA, Russia and India, to China, Malaysia, Thailand, Indonesia and the Philippines.

For the Soviet Navy, for example, the re-opening of the Suez Canal in 1975 provided a Red Sea passage linking the Black Sea Fleet with deployments in the Indian Ocean (Table 0.1). Thus one can see South Yemen beginning to feature more highly in the Soviet Union's military calculations thereafter. This aspect of the Cold War strategic game was built on Soviet concerns from the late 1960s that the United States had acquired (or was about to do so) the capability to launch nuclear missiles (Poseidon and Trident systems) on Soviet territory, or threaten Soviet shipping between its Pacific and Black Sea and Baltic ports, from submarines in the Indian Ocean. Not surprisingly, this Soviet fear and threat perception triggered a response in the 1970s, whose direct upshot was the strengthening of its military presence in the Red Sea and the deepening of its political links with Red Sea littoral states. While such contacts with pro-US Ethiopia, Saudi Arabia, Jordan and Israel were out of the question in the early 1970s, key countries like

Table 0.1 Soviet naval deployments in the Indian Ocean, 1977–82 (number of ship days)

Year					
1977	*1978*	*1979*	*1980*	*1981*	*1982*
6,700	8,500	7,600	11,000	10,700	10,200

Source: Blechman and Luttwak (1984, p. 151).

Egypt, South Yemen and Somalia were prepared to provide the Soviets with port visitation rights and some access to naval and air bases.

In the second half of the 1970s, however, new opportunities were presenting themselves to the Soviet Union. By 1973, of course, the Soviets had lost their most prized regional ally, Egypt, to their global rival, and in their search for new regional arrangements had dumped Somalia in favour of its neighbour, Ethiopia. Thus, having lost its footing in the northern Red Sea area, the Soviets expended much energy consolidating their position in the southern Red Sea countries of South Yemen and Ethiopia. All with devastating consequences for the sub-region and the balance of forces there.

Not surprisingly, the West displayed deep concern over this growing Soviet presence in the Middle East in general and the Red Sea area in particular, fearing that Soviet expansionary policies were part of a bigger design to test the West's two security vulnerabilities: access to the sub-system's sea lanes, and some control over the Persian Gulf/Arabian Peninsula's vast hydrocarbon resources. Soviet policy in the Red Sea area was interpreted as hostile to the Western world's legitimate interests in the Middle East region and potentially aggressive in posture. In particular, the Soviet military presence in Ethiopia and South Yemen (the Dahak, Perim, Socotra, etc.) agitated the USA greatly in the 1980s, particularly at the height of the so-called 'Second Cold War'.

A similar degree of reliance on the Red Sea is also evident in US behaviour towards the Middle East since 1980, stemming from the overthrow of the Shah of Iran and the new regional security threats following the commencement of hostilities between Iran and Iraq. US military dependence on the Red Sea was highlighted by two reactions to the Iran–Iraq war: first, its having to secure Egypt's consent to use its Red Sea port of Ras Banas in defence of Saudi Arabia and, second, having been able to dispatch its most effective amphibious response, a helicopter carrier, with 30 helicopters, 50 landing craft and 8,000 marines on board, to the war zone barely a month after the start of the war.[23]

The US Rapid Deployment Force (RDF) was born in the early 1980s in response to this perceived US strategic vulnerabilities in the area (the Iranian revolution, the Soviet invasion of Afghanistan in 1979, and the growing Soviet presence in South Yemen and Ethiopia), and its successor, Central Command (CENTCOM), has been dependent for success on unhindered access to the Red Sea. CENTCOM and its predecessor have been premised on 'access agreements' with countries such as Egypt, Somalia and Kenya to permit US forces to use bases in these countries. Apart from Kenya, the US Navy is wholly dependent on the Red Sea countries for access to these crucial bases. Indeed, the US connection with the Red Sea is even stronger than that; all Red Sea countries but one (Israel) fall within the CENTCOM's area of responsibility, and as such necessarily feature in Washington's security calculations. The Red Sea area is also significant for another reason: it is the artery through which easier access is facilitated between two other strategic US commands, the EUCOM (covering Europe and Africa) and the PACOM (covering the Pacific and Indian Oceans).

As can be gleaned from these observations, in purely military terms, US access to the Red Sea became an essential aspect of its global strategic planning during the Cold War. Two developments had encouraged this tendency in the 1980s in particular: Somalia's consent to allow the US Navy to stage P-3 anti-submarine flights out of Berbera to track Soviet submarines passing through the Bab el-Mandeb; and, when Egypt agreed in April 1986 to grant nuclear-powered US naval vessels permission to sail through the Suez Canal. For both superpowers, and other major powers for that matter, the Red Sea provided the vital maritime link between the continents. Without navigation through the Red Sea, distances can become prohibitive for military operations: 'the distance from the Black Sea to the Gulf of Aden is only 4,000 miles when the [Suez] canal is open, but is 12,000 miles if [it] is shut and the South Atlantic route is used'.[24] The distance between Norfolk (in the USA) and Dhahran increases from 8,600 miles to 12,000 miles if the Cape route is used.

Second, the growing reliance that both superpowers shared on naval power and deployment of advanced naval vessels in the 1980s merely underlined, in terms of access to ports and denial of territory to the enemy, the strategic significance of the Red Sea, where both the USA and the Soviet Union were busy building alliances with local powers. The superpowers' uneasy and shifting local alliances with southern Red Sea states, however, did not seem to affect their calculations and their strategic objectives. In a nutshell, 'Washington was determined to wage an anti-communist crusade and restrict Soviet-supported radicalism in the Horn and surrounding region, while the Soviet Union was determined to challenge the Western presence there'.[25] Put in these terms, the following seemed at the time to be a fair assessment of realities on the ground:

> Resolution of the many conflicts in the Middle East will not bring out a significant withdrawal of either superpower. Both west and east of Suez each will continue to maintain major maritime forces, because this part of the world encompasses the extended security spheres of the United States and ... those of the Soviet Union.[26]

According to Cold War strategists, of some 100 internationally significant choke points, there are a handful which can affect the course of a major conflict (see Table 0.2). Two of the three such choke points identified in the Middle East lie along the Red Sea. This reality has not changed with the passing of the Cold War and the blockage of Red Sea choke points remains as bad for business as it does

Table 0.2 Key strategic choke points in the world

Middle East	Far East	Europe	Africa	Americas
Suez Canal	Strait of Malaca	English Channel	Cape of Good Hope	Panama Canal
Bab el-Mandeb	Sunda Strait	Danish Straits		Florida Strait
Strait of Hormuz	Lombok Strait	Strait of Gibraltar Turkish Straits		Yucatan Strait

Source: Based on NATO documents and Faringdon (1989).

for the strategic well-being of interested actors; with over 10 per cent of the world's seaborne commerce passing through this waterway, equivalent to over 21,000 ships a year (or around 55 ships a day), its blockage could immediately disrupt international trade patterns. The ease with which shipping can be disrupted in this waterway was graphically demonstrated in July and August 1984, when some 18 vessels were damaged by sea mines laid near the Gulf of Suez. Almost immediately, Egypt was forced to seek outside assistance in dealing with the crisis. Thus, a mine-clearing operation was launched with direct Western support, involving the naval units of Britain, France, Italy and the United States, as well as Soviet co-operation. This short-lived crisis had a direct impact on the Egyptian economy as well as on the commercial interests of other countries, including the Soviet Union, one of whose container vessels was the first victim of the sea mines on 9 July 1984.

At the other end of the Red Sea, we have the Bab el-Mandeb, the natural sea lane in and out of the Red Sea, which provides the only entry point for several Red Sea countries. At the mouth of this choke point lie the strategically important Hanish islands, the control of which has already been the subject of considerable tension between Yemen and Eritrea. Just beyond the Bab el-Mandeb is the Yemeni island of Socotra, site of Yemeni military installations. Eritrea/Ethiopia, Israel, Jordan, Sudan and Yemen are all heavily dependent on the sea lanes of the Bab el-Mandeb, for some of whom it provides the only means of access to the high seas, and the only source of maritime trade. For Israel, which is always conscious of Egypt's grip on the Suez Canal, the Bab el-Mandeb is the only available route to Israel's increasingly important economic partners in Asia.

The post-Cold War Red Sea

With the Cold War behind us, it is interesting to note the importance that NATO and Russian military planners continue to attribute to the same choke points in their perceptions of international security. Navigability of the Red Sea, and the ways in which the domestic politics and regional policies of its littoral states affect regional stability, emerged as post-Cold War issues of the 1990s and beyond. Western security calculations in the Red Sea sub-region, for example, are today based largely on concerns for the stability of littoral states and their vulnerability to radical (particularly Islamist) forces. This is not least a result of America's continuing commitment to Israel's security, but it also reflects a more global American aspiration that regional states should define their foreign policy in line with the West's general interests. The Islamists who ruled Sudan in the 1990s were seen as a threat to such a 'world order', as indeed are Islamist players in Egypt and Jordan, and al-Qaeda terrorism in Yemen and Saudi Arabia. America's disastrous foray into Somalia in the early 1990s and its political support for regimes which tackle Islamist insurgency are indications of the concern which it feels at the prospect of 'rogue' players entering the game, a threat which seems exacerbated by Sudan's efforts to establish alliances with other Islamist regimes, and the subsequent alienation of its own North and East African neighbours.

While the sub-region no longer hosts the 'socialist-oriented' or Marxist regimes of Ethiopia and South Yemen which once incited American fears, it houses still a number of potentially destabilising elements other than politicised Islam. While Israel may have signed peace treaties with Egypt and Jordan, its relations with the Arab world remain hostile and untrusting (not least during the period of the Netanyahu governments between 1996 and 1999, and again after 2009). Israel's strategic alliance with the United States remains intact but Israeli intransigence in peace negotiations with Syria and the Palestinians during the Netanyahu governments has placed stress on American relations with its Arab allies, including Egypt, Jordan and Saudi Arabia. Meanwhile, in the absence of superpower containment, other sub-regional inter-state tensions remain buoyant: between Yemen and Eritrea; between Somalia and Ethiopia; between Eritrea and Ethiopia; between Eritrea and Djibouti; between Sudan and Egypt.

The domestic troubles of a number of Red Sea states also haunt American strategists: the civil wars in Sudan and Yemen, Jordan's perilous experiments with democratisation, popular uprisings in Egypt and Yemen, Saudi Arabia's efforts to suppress terrorist responses to government failures, and Somalia's feuding warlords all provide pertinent examples. The fear is that domestic and sub-regional tensions can all too easily escalate to encompass the entire sub-system. The breakup of Ethiopia into two sovereign territories in 1993 and the outbreak of hostilities between Eritrea and Yemen just two years later (in 1995) testify to the fragility of this sub-region; as does the bloody conflict between Eritrea and Ethiopia. It also points to the dearth of sub-regional mechanisms for conflict management, and, unlike the Persian Gulf sub-region, where the West remains engaged, the absence of outside powers' ability to contain Red Sea sub-regional tensions.

Not surprisingly then, and given the importance of the main Red Sea actors to the wider Middle East sub-system, the bulk of America's arms exports since the end of the Cold War have been to its allies in this region, with just two Arab countries (Egypt and Saudi Arabia) taking over 80 per cent of its arms deliveries to the entire Middle East region in the mid-1990s (Table 0.3), and Egypt, Israel and Saudi Arabia accounting for over 90 per cent of the same a decade later, at over $12 billion. Egypt remains politically the closest US Arab ally and the weightiest Arab state in military and political terms, while Saudi Arabia continues to be the country responsible for supplying the bulk of the Western world's oil

Table 0.3 US arms exports to the Middle East, 1990–95 ($ million)

Total	Country	1990	1991	1992	1993	1994	1995
World total		7,575	8,805	8,674	11,262	9,539	11,835
MENA total		2,999	4,862	5,270	6,791	4,062	6,899
	Red Sea countries	2,519	4,159	4,621	5,689	3,671	5,929
	Egypt and Saudi Arabia	1,899	3,751	3,890	4,877	3,187	5,550
	Other Middle East countries	141	236	327	926	275	542

Source: Calculated from CIA and ACDA data.

needs on a daily basis (to the tune of 8 million barrels per day since the second half of the 1990s) and the linchpin of its security relationships in the Persian Gulf and the Red Sea.

Similarly, and despite the Russian military presence now being at a minimum in the Red Sea sub-region, there remain three Western powers with sufficient naval strength to intervene in this part of the world (Britain, France and the United States). Indeed, France retains a garrison of around 4,000 troops in small but strategically placed Djibouti, whose role and presence have become even more significant since the growth of piracy off the coast of Somalia. The US military in the 2000s also secured access to the formerly French-controlled Camp Lemonnier in Djibouti, now stationing some 1,800 personnel there on a permanent basis.

The Red Sea in the revised MENA system

With superpower rivalry forming an increasingly distant memory, however, one can see evidence that a new era has dawned for the states of the Red Sea and the relations between them. Perhaps the most pertinent new feature is one which brings us back to our levels of analysis. In brief, one can see changes in the MENA sub-system which have arisen from the decline of an Arab sub-system. Yezid Sayigh has spoken[27] of the parallel existence during the Cold War era of an Arab states system and a Middle East strategic system, the latter allowing for consideration of the non-Arab Middle East players, notably Iran and Israel, whose interaction with the Arab world was confined to rivalry and strategic balancing.

With the end of the Cold War, and in the aftermath of the 1990/91 Kuwait crisis, Israel embarked on a process, however gradual and flawed, of peace-making with its Arab neighbours. However barren the reality of any peace agreements so far put on paper, the fact remains (as Sayigh points out) that Israel 'is in the process of becoming a full member of the Middle East state system, not just the strategic system'. One might equally point to the IOC conference in Tehran in December 1997 as evidence that Iran has made substantial inroads since the conclusion of its war with Iraq and in the immediate post-Cold War period in playing a greater role in Middle Eastern affairs beyond simply strategic considerations. In short, the decline of the Arab system has coincided with (and in some cases insti-gated) a deepening of the wider Middle East system to allow for a greater degree of inter-state relations on a number of levels other than simply strategic power-play. It is now being argued that there has been a blurring of the edges between the Arab system and the Middle East strategic system, even as each is changing and fragmenting. Since the 2000s, we have seen the former dissolving, and the latter restructuring. One consequence has been that Arab states seek not to assert themselves as leaders within the region but rather compete in the development of their relations with powerful non-Arab states: Syria competes with Lebanon, Egypt with Jordan in the definition of their relations with Israel; Syria's relation-ship with Iran is a matter of concern for Saudi Arabia as well as for Egypt. What is interesting is that despite continuing political tensions between Israel and its Arab counterparts, Israel has managed to emerge as the single most important 'partner' in any relationship for the Arab states.

Moreover, in some respects, the consolidation of the MENA sub-system poten-tially strengthens the position of its non-Arab actors, eventually weakening the 'Arab' character of the sub-system. A broader MENA sub-system offers the pos-sibility of the relative weakening of the Arab core states as Iran, Israel and Turkey are emboldened by their relations with the new non-Arab peripheries such as Central Asia (Iran, Israel, and Turkey) and by their relative economic strength and political proximity to Europe (Israel and Turkey). One might even view the con-vergence of the two systems as sounding the death-knell for the Arab unity scheme in which the core Arab states would have the opportunity to emerge as the dominant players in the Middle East sub-system. In today's regional order, where the 'national-territorial' interest prevails, Arab states appear to have come to terms with the fact that they must compete with each other with the same vig-our as with the region's non-Arab actors. In these circumstances, allies and alli-ances can be formed with any powerful force and from any part of the sub-system. The emergence of an even more divided and competitive Arab world can only mean a situation in which new alliances are likely to be built not on common Arab values and goals, but on the pursuit of interests derived from the state's own imperatives and its calculations about the regional balance of power. It is small wonder that, by the end of the 1970s, Salamé was able to argue that geography had become the main cause of change, replacing the pan-Arabist agenda of the post-1940s era.[28] The 'return' to geography, as he has put it, was one cause of the regionalisation of the Arab order, whose full effect did not surface until the Kuwait crisis of the early 1990s, which pitched Arab states against one another and fractured the Arab order beyond repair. 'Far from opening up new vistas of unity and cooperation', notes Fawcett, 'the post-Cold War Middle East revealed serious forces of fragmentation and division.'[29]

In such a situation, where power is more defused and alliances more fluid, hitherto peripheral regional zones such as the Red Sea acquire a new strategic importance. Arab regional powers, in seeking along with their non-Arab neigh-bours, to 'fill the superpower shoes', are keen to carve for themselves new spheres

Table 0.4 Red Sea countries among top 50 with largest population, 1999 and 2010

Country	Rank 1999	Rank 2010	Country	Rank 1999	Rank 2010	Country	Rank 1999	Rank 2010
Egypt	20	16	Ethiopia	22	14	Sudan	34	29
Saudi Arabia	51	41	Yemen	58	48			

Source: World Bank database and CIA, *The World Factbook* (various years).

of influence in such peripheries as the Red Sea sub-region and the countries of Central Asia and the Caucasus, in turn, both consolidating and raising the strategic profile of such sub-regions. Equally, non-Arab regional actors have exercised a freer hand in penetrating the sub-region. Iran, for example, has meddled in Sudanese Islamist and Yemen's sectarian Sunni-Shi'a divide; Israel, following peace treaties with Egypt and Jordan, has rapidly developed its courtship of Turkey and also the Red Sea states with offers of economic and technical co-operation. Amazingly, it has met with little opposition in its efforts to provide covert military support for Eritrea, and then later for being in a close relationship with Ethiopia.

It is worth noting that Arab Red Sea littoral countries figure prominently within the fragmenting Arab system. Of the Arab League's 22 members, for instance, seven are Red Sea littorals, comprising over 200 million people of Arab descent. Also in terms of population and territory, the Red Sea houses the largest Arab entities: Egypt in population terms, and Sudan and Saudi Arabia in terms of territory. Thus, where the Arab world seeks to retain its systemic features, and to play a role within the MENA regional system, it is led by the Red Sea Arab states. Furthermore, as Table 0.4 highlights, the five largest Red Sea states are all now in the top 50 most populous countries in the world, with a combined population of 264 million in 2010.

We are, as a consequence, witnessing, to borrow from Scott, the clustering of populations, as well as the clustering of economic activities, among the Red Sea states to merit closer consideration of a sub-regional mosaic.[30]

The structure of the study

If the brief analysis above justifies the initial use of the term 'sub-region', it also gives a clue as to how the following chapters are structured to develop this notion. The levels of analysis approach, and the need to understand the relative importance of state, sub-region, sub-system and international system, require that the historical analysis is divided into Cold War and post-Cold War periods. The first era witnessed the 'arrival' of the independent Red Sea states, their early efforts at institutional and national consolidation, the emergence of regional identities and formulations, and the penetration and subsequent shaping of the region by the two superpowers. During this period, the international, regional and state units in the levels of analysis approach predominated. The demise of the Soviet Union and the end of the Cold War, removed the element of superpower competition, if not American penetration, from the equation, allowing regional and sub-regional aspects to gain more pertinence. The first three chapters therefore analyse the international relations of the Red Sea from this perspective. Chapter 1 introduces the reader to the Red Sea states themselves, identifying the causes for structural weakness of most of these states, the reasons for their vulnerability to external interference, and the implications of these features for relations both between themselves and between them and the international community. One particularly important conclusion reached is that, while the states on the Horn of Africa remain most vulnerable to external penetration, three of the central MENA states (Israel, Egypt and Saudi Arabia) are significant actors in their own right in the waterway and are able therefore to exert their own influence across the water to the Horn.

Chapter 2 examines the international relations of the Red Sea in the Cold War era. It identifies the means by which the superpower competition at the international level was transmitted to the MENA region and more specifically to the states around the Red Sea. This transmission collided with developments within the region, such as the evolution of struggles for independence and Arab nationalism, with a combination of results. Domestic political weaknesses magnified sub-state and trans-state identities, inter-state instabilities evolved into two arenas of war (the Horn of Africa and the Arab–Israeli conflict), and the superpowers were increasingly drawn into the affairs of the region in their efforts to each contain the influence of the other. The result was an internationalisation of the affairs of the states around the Red Sea which obscured and even hindered any sub-regional identities from making their presence felt. Chapter 3 illustrates how the decline of the Soviet Union, and the end of the Cold War, profoundly altered this international dimension, creating the political space for regional actors to assume stronger regional roles, allowing for the intensification of regional conflicts and, as a result of both phenomena, consequently leading to new sub-regional identities, strategies and alliances. In short, the three chapters combine to show how the post-Second World War era has seen the gradual establishment of a sub-region (in terms of the criteria outlined earlier) which, while stunted and impeded in its development by the effects of superpower competition, has nonetheless and particularly since the end of the Cold War, experienced an accelerated period of consolidation in recent years. The Red Sea states may not as yet stand collectively as a distinct and separate entity in international relations; indeed, they may never do so given the strength of ties between individual states and other sub-regions and regions. But the potential for a distinguishable common identity is clearly there and significant steps have been taken to create a pattern of international relations around the Red Sea which justify the application of the term 'sub-region'.

The subsequent chapters attempt to provide supporting evidence for this argument through examination of four aspects of those international relations. Chapter 4 focuses on the security interests and policies of Red Sea states, and on the consequent militarisation of, and flow of arms into, the sub-region. Beginning with an assessment of the security dilemmas of the MENA region as a whole, it zooms in on the specific concerns of Red Sea states and the procurement strategies which they have pursued to win military security. In particular, it highlights the post-Cold War development of power projection capabilities by Egypt, Saudi Arabia and Israel within and over the Red Sea sub-region, explaining how this entity fits into their security assessments.

Chapter 5 moves the argument to the arena of land and maritime boundary disputes between Red Sea states. These have been at the heart of Red Sea relations as each state (and some non-state actors) has attempted to establish its own territorial integrity, legitimacy and security. The chapter surveys disputed boundaries between Red Sea states, arguing that the Cold War acted to either relegate them to the back burner of priorities for the states concerned, or alternatively shaped the ways in which they developed, led to armed conflict or, in some instances, were resolved. In the post-Cold War era, new dynamics have been generated which have propelled states to revive disputes. Broader regional and sub-regional dynamics have replaced superpower interests in shaping those disputes and Red Sea states are demonstrating an increasing awareness of the importance of resolving such disputes, either through armed conflict or through peaceful negotiation. The combination of their common need to claim the resources of the Red Sea, the threat faced by all states from sub-state and trans-state identities, the removal of the stabilising effect of superpower intervention and the efforts by regional actors to assert themselves over the sub-region, have led to a growing recognition of collective Red Sea interests in establishing internationally recognised borders. The challenge is to determine where those borders are and to whose advantage.

Chapters 6 and 7 re-focus the examination on the economic dimensions of Red Sea relations. Chapter 6 surveys the economies of the Red Sea states themselves; their relative strengths and weaknesses, their resource bases, the role of the state and their current performances. It further studies the linkages between them in terms of movement of goods, people and capital from within the context of their wider interaction with the international economy. The chapter concludes that there is a slowly emerging economic sub-region to consider, reinforcing sub-regional tendencies. The stronger economies, those of Egypt, Saudi Arabia and Israel, have integrated to a greater extent than their Red Sea neighbours into the global economy. The smaller states rely to a far greater extent on trade with, labour migration to and aid from, the regional powers. For them, sub-regional economic ties are a matter of survival, while for the regional powers they are economically less vital but strategically useful.

Chapter 7 looks at the actual processes of transporting goods and people around the Red Sea. Through a study of maritime, road, rail, aviation, canal, pipeline and energy networks, it demonstrates that the under-developed status of transport infrastructure is currently acting as a significant obstacle to sub-regional consolidation. However, there is evidence that most states (some more than others) have recognised the urgent need to invest in and develop that infrastructure with a view to advancing both sub-regional and international trade and personnel movement. The preference for economic liberalisation and integration into the global economy, through trade and investment both necessitates and facilitates this process, although there is still a tremendously long way to go.

Our final chapter seeks to draw some conclusions about the international politics of the Red Sea states, as well as more specifically about the usefulness of the concept of the sub-region in understanding those relations. Clearly, there are a number of dynamics within the international, regional and sub-regional systems which serve to increase the strategic, economic and political importance of the Red Sea. The states surrounding the sea do appear to have developed a sub-regional consciousness during the Cold War era as a result of the tensions surrounding inter-Arab, Arab–Israeli and superpower rivalries, all of which threatened the growing economic and strategic value of Red Sea transport routes for the littoral states. In the post-Cold War era, new tensions have arisen, or at least emerged at the forefront of the region's inter-state relations, which justify greater concern for the political, economic and strategic security of the sub-region. Equally, new forces are impelling regional actors to seek to extend their influence across the sea in ways which potentially threaten that stability. The dangers therein have drawn the attention of external powers, who seek to secure international goals through regional and sub-regional politics. The overall effect has been the consolidation of sub-regional tendencies, even if one must still use the term with reservation since there is not as yet a specific, identifiable and distinct Red Sea entity.

All of this is taking place within the context of major regional change. Economic reform programmes are opening the economies of the Middle East and North Africa to wider market forces; political Islam is enjoying a revival that challenges the legitimacy of regimes across the region; non-state actors (from al-Qaeda to Hezbollah) are growing in strategic significance, demands for political reform and recognition of sub-national identities are undermining established authorities; and international communications are being revolutionised by technological advances which carry subversive messages unwelcome to regimes and cultural conservatives alike. Globalisation is also impacting the sub-region, in both direct and indirect ways.

The Red Sea states are not only not immune to these winds of change, they are rather riding the waves. Through our study of the sub-region, we hope to shed light on both the forces which shape it today and those which are determining the future of the wider and still globally strategic MENA region.

1 Weakness and instability

National politics and their sub-regional impact

Introduction

For the Red Sea sub-region, as for the developing world in general, the nation-state is not a home-grown phenomenon. The states which can be seen today surrounding the Red Sea are, with the possible exception of Saudi Arabia, largely the product of the colonial experience and indeed of the competition between colonial powers that was still being played out in the aftermath of the Second World War. The legacies of colonial rule are manifold and have shaped not only the nation-states which were subsequently constructed, but also the relations among them, and between them and the wider world. Some of the features of the sub-region which have most characterised its post-war evolution can be traced to this colonial heritage. Similarly, the dilemmas of state-building after independence have left their mark. Revolutions and civil wars, inter-ethnic strife and disastrous development strategies that end in crisis – all have been born out of, and resulted in, the political instability that is the legacy of European rule and the fight for independence. For the most part, with Israel being the obvious exception, states have themselves been weak and fierce. Democratic experiments have faltered in the absence of national homogeneity, encouraging the failure to advance either or both economic growth and socio-economic justice, and the overlapping of interests that has caused ripples of cross-border interference and political activity.

This chapter seeks to unravel some of the chains of cause and effect which have resulted in the generally weak or unstable character of the Red Sea states. It goes further to identify the consequent implications for sub-regional relations and connections with the wider world. Most importantly for the purposes of this study, it seeks to discern those features of Red Sea state development which have left states vulnerable to the interference of their neighbours, which have made their domestic politics of concern to one another, and which have impelled them to take an active interest in manipulating political forces at a sub-regional rather than just a national level. The focus here is not on external involvement in the Red Sea states *per se*, since the interests of Cold War superpowers and other global and even MENA or African regional actors are dealt with elsewhere. Rather, we are concerned here specifically with the development and characteristics of, and relations between, Red Sea states themselves.

European colonial penetration of the Red Sea sub-region

Prior to the European penetration of Africa and West Asia, most of the Middle East and North Africa belonged to the Ottoman Empire, although the latter's reach never extended below the northern half of the sea itself. The Ottoman estates in Africa fell first to the European colonialists, who competed with one another to exploit the resources of the territories which they conquered. By the end of the nineteenth century, Britain and Italy had successfully carved up the North East and the Horn of Africa, leaving a scrap of Somaliland and a residue of influence in Egypt for the French. Egypt had repelled British and French efforts at military conquest in the first half of the century, only to fall foul of the debts of Mohammed Ali's grandsons and the Ottoman capitulations. The British and French attempted to exert strict controls over the Egyptian government's finances and, when this was resisted in 1882, the British landed troops at Ismailia, occupied Cairo and, in 1914, declared the country to be a protectorate. Despite the acknowledgement of Egypt's independence by treaty in 1922, Britain continued to effectively occupy the country until a 1954 agreement provided for the withdrawal of British troops from the Canal zone. The British presence and effective control over the Egyptian monarchy had been bitterly resented and the target of nationalist activity for over 60 years. Thus the successes of the new regime in negotiating their removal served as a bedrock in which it could ground its legitimacy in the new era. Table 1.1 shows the process of the gradual decolonisation of the Red Sea states.

As part of its occupation, Britain had also asserted historical Egyptian claims over Sudan, the northern, central and coastal areas of which had been conquered by Mohammed Ali in 1820–22 and Khedive Ismail in 1863–79. A rebellion led by Mohammed Ahmad ibn-Allah, better known as the Mahdi, expelled Egyptian forces in a series of battles through 1881–85, only to have the land reconquered by the British in 1896–98. An agreement between Egypt and Britain, signed in 1899, established the Anglo-Egyptian Condominium, giving Britain *de facto* control of a colonial regime. It was only when the Free Officers came to power in 1952, that Egypt agreed to Sudanese self-determination as a tactic for the removal of British forces and in the belief that Sudan would choose some form of federation with its northern neighbour. In the event, the Sudanese election in 1953 brought to power an administration which demanded the removal of both British and Egyptian troops and in 1956 the country declared its formal independence.

Ethiopia's occupation had been more short-lived. The country had been claimed as a protectorate by Italy in the 1880s, but the then-emperor, Menelik, led his armies to defeat the invading Italians at Adua. In 1935, Benito Mussolini determined to reverse that humiliation and sent his army into Ethiopia from Eritrea, having first heavily bombed Adua itself. By 1938, Italy occupied the country, only to be driven out again during the Second World War by the British Army. Ethiopia regained its official independence in 1941 and Emperor Haile Selassie was restored to his throne by the same powers who had ignored his appeals for help to the League of Nations in 1930s. Eritrea was not so fortunate, being the victim not least of Ethiopia's own imperialist ambitions. The colony of Eritrea was established by

Table 1.1 Decolonisation of the Red Sea states

Country	Colonial power	Date of European arrival	Independence
Djibouti	France	1884	1977
Egypt	Britain	1882	1922 (treaty)
			1953 (end of Condominium)
Eritrea	Italy	1883	1945 (WWII defeat)
	UN/Britain	1945	1952 (withdrew)
	Ethiopia federation	1962	1993
Ethiopia	Italy	1890s	1896 (Battle of Adua)
		1936	1941
Israel	Britain	1917	1948
		1920 San Remo Mandate	
		1922 came into force	
Jordan	Britain	1917	1946
		British forces entered	
		1920 San Remo	
Saudi Arabia			1932 (Kingdom formally established)
Sudan	Britain	1896–98	1956
Yemen	Britain	1839 (Aden)	1968

Italy in 1883 from coastal lands previously held by the Somalis. In 1945, after the Italians had been driven out, the British set up an administration at the behest of the United Nations. Not least as a result of American pressure, the British soon succumbed, however, to Haile Salassie's claims that Eritrea was in fact a part of the Ethiopian Empire which had been lost. In 1950, Eritrea was federated to Ethiopia by the United Nations and in 1952 the British withdrew. In 1962, a corrupt Eritrean national assembly voted to renounce Eritrea's autonomous status, and the territory was incorporated into the Ethiopian state.

The final Red Sea state on the Horn is Djibouti, the small corner of land which sits at the southern neck of the waterway. Originally named, 'The Overseas Territory of the Afars and the Issas', Djibouti's port facility was considered a strategic prize, sitting as it does at the mouth of the Red Sea. The French had claimed it as part of their efforts to link their African conquests with others elsewhere which could only be reached by sea. Frustrated by the British from being able to extend their control inland, they settled for a frontier within 100 kilometres of the sea and concentrated on developing the port itself. When France finally agreed to Djibouti's independence in 1977, it was reluctant to see the tiny state fall victim to Somali aspirations for a greater Somalia. It therefore maintained a garrison of 6,000 French troops, and left behind a neo-conservative colonial government which would support a continued French presence and influence in Djibouti.[1]

At the northern end of the Red Sea, Israel and Jordan share the legacy of the League of Nations mandates awarded to Britain at the end of the First World War. The mandates for Palestine and Transjordan were awarded at the 1920 San Remo Conference and approved by the League of Nations in 1922. For the native inhabitants of Palestine there was a double blow: the text of the mandate documents included a commitment to fulfilment of the terms of the infamous Balfour Declaration, the letter of British support for the establishment of a Jewish homeland in Palestine. Under British rule, the Jewish population of Palestine was allowed to swell rapidly, purchasing land from absentee landlords and the British authorities. The 1936–39 rebellion was fiercely quashed by the British. The Palestinian peasantry was disarmed and the leadership exiled. Following the Second World War, and spurred on by the atrocities of the Holocaust and their desire to accelerate immigration, elements of the Jewish settlers themselves took up arms against the British forces, with a bitter triangle of violence developing between native Arabs, Jewish settlers and British soldiers. When the British finally decided to withdraw in 1948, they abrogated responsibility for the mess which was their own creation, effectively leaving the key under the door mat for the victors of the ensuing military struggle to collect. On 14 May 1948, the State of Israel officially declared its independence, the armies of neighbouring Arab states invaded and the majority of the native (Arab) population were forced to flee as refugees. Palestine's fate was closely tied to that of Transjordan, where the British had installed the Hashemite Abdullah, son of Sherif Hussein of Mecca, as king. In 1923, the British recognised the independent constitutional state of Transjordan, although it remained under British tutelage until March 1946. Although Transjordan participated in the efforts of the Arab armies to wrest Palestine from the Jews in 1948, Abdullah's goal was itself one of territorial gain. By July, his troops had seized a sizeable rump of hilly land east of Jerusalem and, having secretly connived with the Israeli leadership, Abdullah held them there, renaming his enlarged state Jordan and annexing the so-called West Bank in 1950.

European involvement in Yemen and Saudi Arabia was more limited and generally less intrusive. The Ottoman hold over the Arabian Peninsula had been insecure and subject to fluctuation over time and European interest developed principally along the coastlines of the east and south. Portuguese, French and Dutch interests gave way by the nineteenth century to Britain's exclusive treaties with the various sultanates designed to counter French, Russian and German designs on India and the East. The Turks temporarily occupied the Hijaz from the 1850s, only to be expelled when the British allied themselves with the Hashemites in the Arab revolt. Yemen remained throughout an independent Imamate, although Aden was captured by British forces in 1839 and later was declared a protectorate. In the aftermath of the First World War, the Hashemites struggled to have their claim to Saudi Arabia and its northern peripheries recognised by the British. Britain, however, while awarding kingdoms in Transjordan and Iraq to Sherif Hussein's sons, refused to recognise his rights in Arabia. Instead, London ultimately chose to back Hussein's arch-rival, Abd al-Aziz Ibn Sa'ud who, under the banner of the fundamentalist Wahhabi sect of Islam, finally defeated Hussein's son Ali in 1926. In 1932, the Ibn Sa'ud's territories were united with the Hijaz provinces to form the Kingdom of Saudi Arabia. Britain had provided some financial and political support but never attempted either military occupation or colonisation.

Aden, meanwhile, had become a major British military base and port, protected by the British-occupied part of Somaliland on the other side of the Red Sea entrance. The British position was maintained through treaties with major tribes, although the Turkish presence in Yemen continued to be troublesome. In effect, the border between Aden and Yemen represented that between the British and Turkish empires, the legacy of which remains with us today. As David McClintock has observed:

> Britain's arrival not only checked the southern expansion of the Turks but, more importantly in terms of local political history, set the stage for mistrust and periodic conflict between Yemeni imams and a goodly number of sultans in the Aden Protectorates whose authority and territorial claims were supported by the British. While the southern border of modern Yemen thus became a dividing line between two nominally hostile imperial states, it also came to symbolise indigenous rivalries that have persisted to the present day.[2]

The Turkish presence in Yemen was removed by the events of the First World War, but the British remained in Aden until 1968. In the intervening half century, Britain played a major role in determining the sub-regional alliances which both grew out of, and contributed to, the Yemeni civil war and subsequent territorial division. The final British withdrawal signalled the end of the European colonial adventure in the Middle East but the subsequent decades have demonstrated only too clearly the instabilities which they left in their wake.

Nationalism, Arab nationalism and ideological contest

Perhaps the most immediate result of colonialism was the rise of nationalist responses in the Middle East and North Africa which were later to provide the ideological foundations of the independent nation-states. As Hisham Sharabi pointed out in 1969, the rejection of European rule by the Middle East and North Africa was to continue well after independence had been won, not simply as a political activity but as a cultural and economic struggle to reduce the West once more to an alien entity: 'In order that genuine autonomy be restored, the West must be extricated from the roots; it must be put on an equal level with the other cultural entities of the world.'[3] Thus, at least at the northern end of the Red Sea, the intellectual rediscovery of the Arab self, the rejection of alien impositions, and the need to develop political strategies and institutions to underpin independent nation-states, were synthesised in varying formuli to produce nationalist ideologies that were to shape the modern Middle East.

Resistance to foreign rule had been the principal mobilising factor in sub-regional politics since the Arab response to the Young Turks at the turn of the century. Initial satisfaction at the restoration of the Ottoman Constitution turned to dismay as it became clear that the Young Turks were seeking to centralise government further and to impose their own language and administration more systematically upon the Arab peoples of the empire. Thus, the early seeds of Arab nationalism were born in the small secret societies that sought to oppose Turkish-imposed inequality. Meanwhile British and French rule elsewhere in the Middle East was generating its own intellectual antithesis. In the nineteenth century, Arab intellectuals had sought a cultural renaissance as a way to counter the penetration of European language and behaviour, synthesising European literary forms with their own Arab consciousness and linguistic heritage. In the late nineteenth and early twentieth centuries, however, the baton of intellectual innovation was passed to Muslim thinkers like Jamal al-Din al-Afghani (1839–97), Mohammed Abduh (1849–1905) and Rashid Rida (1865–1935) in so far as they sought to reformulate Islam so as to demonstrate its compatibility with the modern world. Their ideas in turn stimulated new efforts to consider ways in which state and society should be organised, with Western political concepts being adapted and indigenised by religious and secular thinkers alike. The early seeds of Arab nationalism sown in the Ottoman Empire were cross-fertilised with intellectual responses to the political dilemmas presented by colonialism. The rediscovery of the Arab self became an essential part of the struggle for independence and the subsequent process of state-building. Its expression, however, was shaped by the particular circumstances of occupation and withdrawal, political and Islamic tradition, social structure and regional profile of each of the emerging nation-states. Thus, two principal variations on nationalism were to emerge: nationalisms born out of the experiences of newly-created nation-states and which were tied to territorial affiliations, on the one hand, and a more ephemeral Arab nationalism which denied the relevance of the colonially-imposed borders on the other. Arab nationalism had something of a head-start, given the shared linguistic and cultural heritage of Arab peoples across the region, and was to benefit from those features of modernisation which were equally transnational. Growing literacy and the expansion of the printing industry, films, international commerce and possibilities for foreign travel, all provided opportunities for the reinforcement of perceptions of the sharedness, rather than the uniqueness, of Arab culture.

The colonial experience, however, was also to simultaneously generate nationalisms that distinguished Arabs from one another and set apart their identities and interests. Principally, 'the boundaries of a colonial state and its administrative structures defined the area in which most of the political life now took place'.[4] Geographic areas which had previously been part of a larger political entity, namely the Ottoman Empire, became distinct from one another and found themselves separated by borders which had not previously existed and which now served to separate peoples, to reorganise them and to redefine their loyalties, identities and interests. As Yezid Sayigh has explained:

> while loyalties to clan, sect, or other local solidarity and to wider Islamic and Arab identity survived, they operated increasingly within the framework of the territorial state. The state was moreover cast as the repository of a new national identity, a process actively encouraged by the established elites that strove, with European support, to consolidate their social control within their new boundaries.[5]

While the struggle to win independence could accommodate both these territorially-based nationalist and wider Arab nationalist aspirations, the actual achievement of statehood witnessed the evolution of contradictions between the two.

For the states at the northern end of the Red Sea, this process held its own dynamics and was not always as straightforward as might have appeared. In Egypt's case, there was little new in the colonial borders, except for the formalised distinction of a border with Sudan. British rule brought with it in 1913 representative political institutions which, while they gave the Egyptian politicians little influence on the king and none at all on the occupying British forces, did facilitate the deepening institutionalisation of Egyptian political life. Secular nationalist aspirations were most significantly represented through the Wafd Party, but an alternative Islamist brand of resistance to British rule grew up in the form of the Muslim Brotherhood or Ikhwan, which had been founded in 1928 by Hassan al-Banna, and support for which spilled over into neighbouring Arab states. Arab nationalism was not to take hold of Egyptian politics until 1948 and the defeat of the Arab armies which had tried to expel the Zionists from Palestine. Following the coup by the Free Officers in 1952, Egypt was to become the banner-carrier for Arab nationalism, with tensions between the two forms of national identity rising to the fore repeatedly. With the creation of the United Arab Emirates (UAR) with Syria in 1958, for example, Egyptians expressed their dismay at the abandonment of the name of Egypt itself, while Syrians protested at the over-representation of Egyptians in the union's hierarchy and the subordination of Syrian interests to those of the Egyptian state. It seemed that there was no place in Nasser's pan-Arab vision for any leadership other than his own – and Egypt's. Equally, defeat in the 1967 War led to feelings that 'Egypt had suffered enough for the Arabs, and that Egyptians should rely predominantly on themselves for their salvation'.[6] Meanwhile, an African identity was simultaneously being fostered, with Egypt being promoted through the Horn of Africa: 'Nasser [thereby] hoped to prevent his Arab and western rivals from securing a position along Egypt's southern flank.'[7]

For Jordan, the dilemmas presented by competing nationalisms were to lead to civil war in 1970. More specifically, Palestinian and Arab nationalisms were inspiring political activities which threatened the state itself. As the Palestinian refugees sought to impose their own national agenda upon Jordanian politics, to replace the conservative regime with a radical regime sympathetic to both their revolutionary and nationalist ideals, and in such a way that Israel continually resorted to 'reprisal' raids against Jordanian citizens, the King was faced with little choice but to send his troops against their Arab brethren. The King was supported in this by the tribal forces of the East Bank, from which the army was drawn anyway and, in that instance, Jordanian national interests were placed solidly before Arab nationalist commitments. Too much emphasis should not, however, be placed on a distinct Jordanian nationalism in this instance. The issue was complicated by dynastic Hashemite claims to the land of Palestine, reduced upon Israeli statehood to claims on the West Bank. When King Hussein renounced those claims in 1988, he was in many ways finally clearing the way for consolidation of a distinctly Jordanian national identity. But loyalty to the

Hashemite throne, tribal affiliations located in the East Bank, and competition from Palestinians for ideological hegemony within the state, have consistently confused the dichotomy of Arab and Jordanian nationalism.

As Sayigh points out, the Palestinian case also presented something of a deviation from the rule. Although the mandate assigned borders to a new Palestinian political entity, carving it out from the Ottoman Empire in much the same way as Transjordan, Iraq, Syria and Lebanon had been, the policies of British authorities in support of Zionist colonisation and their efforts to prevent the emergence of a state-wide governing Palestinian political institution, directly undermined any emerging Palestinian affiliation with the mandate state. It was rather the struggle against the British and the Zionists, and finally the catastrophe which befell the Palestinians in 1948, which spawned a Palestinian national identity that associated itself with a territorial entity and distinguished itself from other localised identities. The struggle for Palestinian rights over their land and their lives gave the Palestinians an identity distinct from their Arab brethren yet simultaneously was to provide a common cause for the Arab nation. The frequently revolutionary nature of that Palestinian nationalism, and the demands which Arab nationalism correspondingly made on neighbouring regimes have, however, forced regimes to take pragmatic rather than ideologically consistent lines. Moreover, the congruence of Arab and Palestinian nationalism has been utilised by Arab leaders to serve their own particularist ends.

The dualism of state nationalism and Arab nationalism has been complicated further by a number of competing ideological influences, the most pertinent of which was the dichotomy between radical and conservative or traditional approaches to state-building. The classic example of this was the participation of Egypt and Saudi Arabia in the Yemeni civil war. Egyptian intervention had initially been inspired by the need to oust British influence from the peninsula. When the pro-British Imam Ahmad died in 1962, Yemeni officers, with Egyptian military help, bombarded the palace and (falsely it later turned out) announced the death of the new imam, Badr. Although Nasser himself was not implicated directly in the affair, the royalist supporters rallied around Badr's uncle, Hassan, and turned to Britain and Saudi Arabia for support in their efforts to eject the new military regime. In the subsequent fighting for control of the country, Egypt and Saudi Arabia were directly pitted against one another. While Nasser was nominally supporting an effort at republicanism, and Saudi Arabia defending the traditional ruling elite, the reality was that the two states were using Yemen as a pitch on which to play for leadership of the Arab world. While Syria, Iraq and Lebanon were ranged on Egypt's side, Jordan came in to bat for Saudi Arabia and the royalists. Malcolm Kerr has argued that not only was Nasser unconcerned by the division which this brought to the Arab world, but that he actually courted it. Kerr argues that Nasser used his revolutionary ideology

> to stimulate internal pressure on his rivals ... The Yemeni revolution initially seemed to him a golden opportunity: his army intervened as the champion of progress, while Saudi Arabia and Jordan, who felt compelled to support

the royalists out of dynastic solidarity, were put in an ultra-reactionary lights in the eyes of their own peoples.[8]

Moreover, while Syria and Iraq were bound to recognise the Yemeni revolutionaries, they did so at the expense of condoning Egyptian intervention in the affairs of another sovereign Arab state. Saudi Arabia, for its own part, found itself allied to the colonial enemy of the Arab world. Nasser's vision, therefore, of Arab unity was a vision of a united *revolutionary* Arab nation. More importantly, it was a nation led by *qualified* revolutionaries, notably himself. According to Kerr, at the heart of this aspect was the geopolitical reality of the Egyptian, Syrian, Iraqi and Saudi states muscling for status and power within an emerging regional Arab order. The episode raises two important issues: first, the interplay between Arabism and revolutionary socialism and, relatedly, the tensions which were created by the contradiction between Arab unity, on the one hand, and regime differentiation, on the other. Kerr has said of revolutionary socialism that after 1958 and again following the Iraqi Ba'athist coup of 1963, it tended increasingly 'to overshadow the anti-colonial spirit in ideological discourses and pronouncements'.[9] Those who opposed revolutionary reform were held to be reactionaries, in league with imperialist forces and obstructing Arab unity for their own purposes. It was no longer enough for regimes to be anti-colonial – what was being advocated now was a political blueprint for the greater united Arab state that was to emerge from the imperially divided multiplicity of Arab states. The variety of state forms, and the basic division between radical and traditional regimes, meant that this brand of Arab nationalism was as fiercely resisted as it was advocated, within the Arab world itself, and was viewed as a vehicle for Nasser's own promotion as much as a meaningful ideological proposition. Thus, Arab nationalism became as much a cause for suspicion and mistrust among Arabs as it aggravated the aspirations of another variety of nationalism on the shore of the Red Sea, that of Zionism.

The establishment of Israel in May 1948 united a territorial entity, its political institutions and a nationalist ideology that directly contravened the interests of the Arabs. Israel was, and continues to be, perceived by the Arabs as a colonial imposition, established with the assistance of Britain and the United States, and maintained through aid, military and diplomatic support as a bastion of Western imperialism in the region. There can be little doubt that Israel would not have come to exist in Palestine without the tacit and actual support of the British mandate administration which allowed and facilitated Jewish immigration, settlement, organisation, economic development and the building of a Jewish security structure. Arab responses to the Israeli state have been fairly ideologically consistent – in practical terms, however, the states of the Red Sea have determined their own national priorities in their dealings with Israel. One might have looked to Nasser's post-1962 socialism as a source of reconciliation with corporatist labourism of Ben Gurion's state. However, the colonial characteristics of Israel, and its implications for Egypt's Arab (Palestinian) brethren made such an option unthinkable. Equally, however, at the pragmatic level, the spawning of

Palestinian revolutionary movements in refugee-ridden Gaza, then as now, posed a direct threat to Egypt's own security. Not only was Nasser fearful of the overspill into Egyptian domestic politics, he was also profoundly aware of Israel's policy of disproportionate retaliation for Palestinian incursions onto Israeli soil from Egyptian territory. Like Abdullah of Transjordan before him, and numerous Arab leaders who followed him, Nasser's policies towards Israel were to be defined by pragmatic concerns for his own nation-state rather than idealistic concerns for the Arab nation. Zionism has not been a passive partner in the equation either. As right-wing variations have been in the ascendant since the mid-1970s, it has provided the ideological impetus for Israeli territorial expansion and colonisation of occupied lands. Nor has it been without its own contradictions, for the consolidation of the Israeli identity has distinguished the sabra from the diaspora Jew even as Oriental Sephardi and Mizrahi Jews have believed themselves to be the victims of discrimination in an Ashkenazim-dominated Israeli socioeconomy. The existence of a sizeable Arab minority living within Israel's borders, possessing citizenship but being denied political and socio-economic equality, has added further dimensions to the ethnic map of the state.

Like Israel, post-independence Ethiopia was composed of a variety of ethnic groups and nationalities. Large sections of the population had ancestries relating back to Semitic immigrants from Arabia or the Nilotic peoples of southern Sudan, and they were divided between the Ethiopian Orthodox Christian religion (35 per cent in 1985), Islam (45 per cent) and smaller groups of followers of Judaism or animistic religions.[10] Despite the sensitivities of the Muslim population and the regional perception of Israel as being a colonial outpost of the West, the Ethiopians developed a close military and diplomatic alliance with Israel in the 1950s. The alliance was based on Haille Selassie's belief that Ethiopia was, like Israel, surrounded by hostile Muslim states, a belief reinforced by wider Muslim support for the Eritrean Liberation Front. The pro-American stance of both countries reinforced their common interests and Israel was to assist the Ethiopian monarchy in resisting insurgency and threats to the regime on a number of occasions. In return, Ethiopia provided Israel with friendly port facilities at the entrance to the Red Sea and access to the African hinterland. The relationship survived despite the formal ending of diplomatic relations in 1973 and the new relationship between Mengistu and the Soviet Union after 1977. The implications for regional politics extended beyond the Horn of Africa itself, with the security of the Red Sea being critical to both Arab and Israeli thinking in their relations with Ethiopia and the Eritreans.

The ethnic mosaic, nationalism and the post-colonial state

The ethnic complexities of the Horn of Africa have been reflected in other 'national' struggles and conflicts. Indeed, cross-border ethnic seepage resulting from arbitrary colonial cartography has been at the heart of much of the tension between southern Red Sea states. It has equally provided convenient justification for states to play out their geo-strategic interests through interference in the ethnic struggles of their neighbours. In particular, the ethnic mosaic of the Horn of Africa has been a fertile ground for the political manoeuvrings of Red Sea states as they have sought to increase their own, or decrease each other's, influence over the waterway.

Ethiopia's efforts to maintain its territorial integrity, and even its imperial ambitions, provide the classic example. After the restoration of the throne in 1941, Haille Selassie laid claim to Eritrea, managing through federation in 1950 to add it to the already ethnically diverse Ethiopian entity. Eritreans themselves had great difficulty initially in establishing a national resistance to Ethiopian rule since they were divided into two main religions and nine linguistic groupings. Their society, while collectively hostile to either Italian or Ethiopian imperial rule, had not progressed beyond clan-based affiliations. Thus, the early Eritrean Liberation Front was little more than a conservative clan-based, Muslim rebellion in the coastal lowlands,[11] inspired by exiled Eritreans living in Cairo, Saudi Arabia and other Arab countries.[12] By the time the movement had spread more widely and across confessional divides, it was facing new challenges from those elements that wished to pursue a socialist agenda. In 1969/1970, this latter group had split to form the Eritrean People's Liberation Front, and a civil war ensued between the two groups which was to last until the mid-1970s and which significantly reduced their collective ability to challenge Ethiopian rule. The Eritrean Liberation Front initially found support from Nasser, who provided military training facilities for its fighters and allowed the headquarters to be located in Cairo. While Nasser sought to neutralise the Ethiopian alliance with the United States, Ethiopia was equally concerned over Egyptian claims to the Nile waters.

The Ethiopian empire was also under attack from three other ethno-national groupings. In the south, west and east of Ethiopia, the Oromo peoples (at the time making up around half the population of the country) found their language and identity under attack by the dominant Amharic traditions. An underground movement was formed in the 1960s after the Mecha-Tulema organisation was banned. Following the 1974 'revolution', which promised land reform in their favour, the Oromo leadership began making more substantial political demands, including the right to elect their own representatives freely. When the Dergue predictably refused most of their demands, the Oromo Liberation Front (OLF) emerged from the earlier Oromo movement and began a campaign aiming at national self-determination. The OLF had to take on not just the Ethiopian government, but also the Western Somalia Liberation Front, and the Somali government, which claimed parts of Oromo territory as their own, only finally recognising the OLF as a legitimate national front in 1978/1979.

The predominantly Christian Tigray peoples of Northern Ethiopia had also resisted Amhara rule since the nineteenth century. Periodic rebellions led to the disarming of the Tigray by Haille Selassie's imperial government and the establishment of an underground Tigray National Organisation in the early 1970s. When the 1974 revolution was hi-jacked by the military, and with no prospects for recognition of Tigrayan rights, a Tigray People's Liberation Front (TPLF) was established in 1975 which began armed struggle against the Dergue's regime. By 1978, the TPLF was able to unite with the Eritrean EPLF to score a number of victories against the Ethiopian government, demonstrating that ethno-national movements could find common cause against the regime.

A final challenge to Ethiopian integrity was to come from Somalia, with a war being waged over the Ogaden province in the southeast, also known as Western Somalia. Although divided along clan lines, the Somalis share a history, language and culture, with Islam playing a strong role in their national identity. They have a long history of resistance, first, to colonial rule and then to what they perceived to be the illegitimate carve-up of their territory into independent states. Ogaden was just one loss of several and in 1977 the Somalis launched an attack on Ethiopia determined to retrieve it. Although they had been beaten back by 1979, the Ogaden war succeeded in drawing in both superpowers, Cuba, a number of the Arab states, the UN and the OAU in efforts either to support one side or mediate between the two.

In all these national struggles, which found little use for the borders left by the colonial powers, regional neighbours served to muddy the waters in their own interests, at times engaging in bizarre alliances or indeed changing sides as soon as it was opportune to do so. Here we illustrate the point.

In the early years of his regime, Nasser had supported Somali claims to land held by Ethiopia, supplying arms to Somali fighters. By the mid-1960s, however, his desire to play a role in the newly-formed Organisation of African Unity (OAU) led him to moderate his position on Ethiopia, downgrading his support for both the Eritreans and Somalis. Saudi Arabia played an aggressive role in the Horn of Africa, as it sought, in league with the United States, to undermine or expel what it saw as communist influences from the Red Sea Lake. Thus, for example, they offered Somalia $300 million to break its military alliance with the Soviet Union and return to the Islamic fold.[13] While the Saudis have generally emphasised the Muslim character of their alliances, in this case, they identified more closely with the monarchy in Ethiopia. Conservative Arab states had no desire to see a socialist or revolutionary Eritrea or Somalia, and even socialist states were wary of ideological competitors that challenged the sanctity of borders. Nasser's virtual desertion of the Eritrean and Somali causes, despite their ideological affinity, reflected African concerns over the potentially disastrous implications of an ethnically-based redrawing of political lines in that sub-continent. Meanwhile, Saudi Arabia was later to alter its position to provide military and financial support for both the Eritreans and Somalis when Ethiopia fell under Marxist rule. In the end, as Lefebvre[14] has pointed out, Red Sea states took a pragmatic rather than ideological position when it came to interference in each other's affairs. Ideology complicated their entanglements but it did not rule them.

The transplanting of the Arab–Israeli conflict onto the Eritrean struggle became similarly bizarrely confused:

> Although the assertion that an independent Eritrea would add significantly to Arab military capabilities in the southern Red Sea region was questionable, Israel took this threat seriously. Thus, in the late 1960s and early 1970s the war in Eritrea was viewed by Israel as well as the Arabs as a southerly extension of the Arab–Israeli conflict.[15]

The strategic manoeuvring did not always result in natural alliances. Israel, for example, continued its close military relationship with Ethiopia despite the ending of diplomatic relations in 1973 and the installation of a radically leftist government in 1974. Saudi nervousness over the radical nature of the Eritrean liberation forces, especially when Christian elements became dominant in the late 1970s, did not prevent it from supporting (albeit reluctantly) the Eritrean opposition to Ethiopia in the 1980s.

The ultimate result of this interaction between the cross-border dimensions of the ethnic mosaic of the sub-region, and most notably of the Horn of Africa, and the strategic interests of Red Sea states, has been threefold. First, lack of ethnic homogeneity has left regimes weak or unstable; second, it has opened the door to intervention in each other's domestic affairs on the basis of religious or ethnic solidarity; and, finally, it has allowed strategic interests of stronger states to be played out by proxy in the domestic arenas of weaker neighbours. One might add that these combined phenomena have contributed to the fragmented and para-military nature of opposition groups which have been susceptible to the strategic whims of external funders and military supporters.

Islamic dimensions of nationalism

The Ethiopian example highlights another angle to the discussion of nationalism: the relationship between Islam, national liberation struggles and associated political ideologies. Islam as a political ideology has an appeal and a logic which transcend borders. Moreover, Islamist movements like the Muslim Brotherhood played a substantial role in articulating and mobilising resistance to colonial rule around the region. However, the existence of non-Muslim populations, most notably in Sudan, Ethiopia, and Egypt, has made their convergence with Arabism problematic, to say the least. Conversely, while the preoccupation with secular paths to modernisation in many of the post-independence states of the region precluded the possibility of overtly Islamic state structures, even secular-leaning leaders like Nasser recognised that Islam represented an authentic value system and one which was common to all the region's Arab states. The states of the Red Sea dealt with the dilemmas in different ways. In Egypt, Nasser's socialism did not preclude but rather incorporated Islamic ideals; 'a society without injustice, which meant freedom from hunger, want and exploitation, which in turn implied common ownership of the means of production and a planned society'.[16] As Dekmejian was to say:

> The Nasirites soon discovered that the retention of a slightly reinterpreted form of Sunni Islam coupled with a peculiar form of Arab unity nationalism would prove beneficial to their cause. As the officers were exposed to socialist influences on the one hand, and began to manifest Pan-Arab tendencies on the other, the crucial ingredients for the new ideology came into sharp focus: selected portions of a revived and reinterpreted Egyptian-Arab past had to be merged with certain elements of Islamic thought which in turn had to be fitted into the modern Nasirite conception of socialism.[17]

However, Nasser excluded the possibility of religious influence on the institutions of power. The routinised inclusion of token Copts in his cabinet while abolishing their own religious courts, on the one hand, and the suppression of the Muslim Brotherhood after 1954, on the other (with the regime turning on the Ikhwan's membership, arresting and torturing thousands, and staging public show trials and executions), demonstrated clearly that only the state could determine the role and status of either religion as a political force. President Anwar al-Sadat initially appeared more accommodationist to the Brethren. His links with the organisation went back to pre-revolutionary times, and he made a point of emphasising both his own faith and piety and Nasser's unacceptable materialism. He allowed the Muslim Brothers more political space, aiming to unleash them against old-guard Nasserists, Marxists and 'the adventurous left'[18] in a classic divide and rule strategy. Unfortunately for him, Islamic radicalism was enjoying its own revival and his inability to direct the Ikhwan's political activities led first to accommodation, then to renewed repression and finally to his own assassination in 1981. The struggle to establish the legitimacy of a moderate and controlled form of state Islam even as Islamic militancy has become the principal challenge to the regime, has ever since shaped both the domestic and foreign policies of his successor, President Hosni Mubarak. Mubrarak's efforts in this regard have brought him at times into direct confrontation with the regime on his southern borders.

As the Cold War was coming to an end in 1989, Sudan was entering a period of uncertain rule as a military-Islamist alliance wrested power away from the incumbemt President Numeiri. The Ikhwan in Sudan emerged as a political party in the 1960s, but was driven underground when Gaffer Numeiri staged a socialist coup in 1969. As Numeiri's ideological bias swung away from socialism in the 1970s, he initiated efforts at reconciliation which led in 1977 to an agreement with the Islamists, then led by Hassan al-Turabi. The next few years were spent building a range of mass-based Islamist organisations alongside the state, including an extensive Islamic banking operation and culminating, in 1983, in the introduction of Sharia law. In 1985, Numeiri grew nervous of the growing authority of the Islamists, turning against them once again, only to be ousted himself by a military-democratic alliance. A short period of parliamentary rule did nothing to staunch the tide of Islamic militancy and the coup in 1989 by a section of the army and with the authority of Turabi himself, led to a radically Islamist state being born, which fiercely prosecuted a war against the SPLA-led Afro-Christian south, instigated the Darfour crisis in the west of the country, provided shelter to Islamist groups originating from elsewhere in the Middle East, and began harbouring Egyptian oppositionists who had been accused of both terrorist attacks in Egypt and the attempted assassination of Mubarak, which took place on the Egyptian president's trip to Ethiopia in June 1995.

Christian–Muslim conflict has also played a part in Sudan's relations with its southern neighbour, Ethiopia. Ever since its independence, the government in Khartoum has been charged by Ethiopia with supporting the Eritreans in their liberation struggle on the basis of shared Arab and Islamic identities. In the

1950s, Sudan levied the counter-charge of Ethiopian support for the revolt of the Anya Nya, an organisation whose leaders had been educated in Christian missionary schools. More recently, Ethiopia was charged by Khartoum with providing sustenance and material support for the SPLA, a charge also ironically levied at Eritrea since its independence in 1993, the ruling group of which is drawn from the Christian-led EPLF. Eritrea has in turn been supported in its dispute with the post-1989 military Islamic leadership in Sudan by Israel, Saudi Arabia and Egypt. All three sought to counter Iranian influence exercised through growing close Iranian-Sudanese ties. Israel sent arms and military assistance to both the Sudanese anti-government SPLA and Eritrea in an effort to assist those forces which oppose the Islamisation of the Horn. Not unrelated, it was subsequently unsurprising that the Eritrean seizure of the Yemeni-held Hanish Islands in the Red Sea was attributed by many to Israeli efforts to improve their own strategic access to the sea.

Egypt took a more diplomatic line since its fears of the Islamist government in Khartoum were balanced by concern that any southern secession would endanger Nile water arrangements. Saudi Arabia has been more equivocal still. While it has sought to reduce Iranian influence in Sudan, it has simultaneously been supporting other Islamist groups in order to enhance its own regional standing.

For Jordan, political Islam has been accommodated within the political system in recent years. After 1948, secular Palestinian nationalism represented the greatest internal threat to the integrity and authority of the state and, in particular, to the Hashemite monarchy. Indeed, some Islamist groups such as the Muslim Brotherhood, were perceived as essentially prepared to play the political game, although others (such as the Islamic Liberation Movement, or Hizb al-Tahrir, which has its roots in the Palestinian West Bank) have always opposed the monarchy itself.[19] By 1984, when elections were allowed, militant Islam had appropriated some of the garb of Palestinian rights in the name of the umma (Muslim community). Moreover, it was at the forefront of popular dissent against the harsh economic regime of structural adjustment. In the 1989 elections, Islamists standing as independents but frequently allied to the Muslim Brotherhood, were able to win enough seats to form a government. They proved unable to tackle the country's economic ills any more efficiently than their secular predecessors, and in 1993, despite being allowed to enter the elections as a political party for the first time, they lost their grip on the parliament. The electoral system had been reformed in such a way as to reinforce traditional lines of patronage at the expense of Islamic ideological voting. The subsequent strains put on the Jordanian political system by insurrections in Palestine, war in Iraq, economic crises and the peace process with Israel, have led the Joranians to tighten up on political activities, leading the Islamists to boycott recent elections. Being excluded from power-sharing has not, however, eradicated the influence of the Islamists. Their opposition to the peace process with Israel, to the American military presence in the Persian Gulf, and to the secularism of neighbouring Egypt, have all served to sour Jordan's relations with some of its Red Sea neighbours.

The Islamist challenge to Israel has not come solely from Jordan, of course. The Palestinian organisations Hamas and Islamic Jihad are perhaps the best-known Islamic opposition groups based in the West Bank and Gaza. Hamas, or Harakat al-Moqawmah al-Islamiyya, grew out of the Gazan branch of the Muslim Brotherhood as a response to the Palestinian uprising, the Intifada, in 1987. Islamic Jihad, however, was a pre-Intifada reaction to the Muslim Brotherhood's failure to adequately 'resist' Israeli occupation and unite religion and national-ism.[20] It was in effect a Muslim counterpart to the secular Palestine Liberation Organisation. Indeed, there was little escaping from the fact that the traditionalist Muslim Brotherhood had actually been courted by the Israelis to fulfil exactly this function. Both Hamas and the Islamic Jihad have utilised armed struggle in their efforts to both attack Israel and undermine the PLO peace process with Israel. Israel in turn has made extravagant and not entirely unsubstantiated claims of an Islamist conspiracy with funds being transferred to Hamas and Islamic Jihad by Muslim groups and governments around the Middle East. The Red Sea states of Sudan and Saudi Arabia have both been considered 'guilty' parties , as indeed has Iran, while Egypt and to some extent Jordan are considered allies in terms of campaigning to combat terrorism.

Ironically, for the Jewish state, and not unlike its Arab neighbours, Jacob Landau has also pointed to an Islamist challenge emerging within Israel itself. He argues that young Israeli Muslims, frustrated by the institutional and social dis-crimination which they face, and radicalised by the Intifada of the late 1980s, have increasingly turned to a form of militant Islam which unites their Islamic and Arab identities and aspires to replace the Jewish state with an Islamic alterna-tive: 'Let us reach true union, in which Islam would be its spirit, original Arabism its blood, noble nationalism its body, peace and just equality its objective, broth-erhood its relation and mutual assistance its custom.'[21]

The second Intifada of 2000, though purportedly instigated by the late Yasser Arafat, helped to reinforce the link emphasised by Landau, leading Hamas to secure a major electoral success in Palestinian elections in 2007 and its subse-quent monopoly of authority in Gaza.

The relationship between Islam and nationalism, however, is still a matter of controversy. Some Muslim scholars rejected nationalism as a colonial devise which served to divide the umma. For them, pan-Islamism provides a political response to foreign imposition and subjugation. In the modern era, pan-Islamism has played a role in the international relations of the Red Sea. For example, King Faisal of Saudi Arabia (reigned 1964–75) utilised the language of pan-Islamism as a rallying cry to draw Muslim states to his side in his Yemeni war with secular Egypt:

> In his speeches, he appealed for a wholehearted return to Islam, based on co-operation, which would eventually lead to the union enjoined by the Prophet Muhammad. Further, he emphasised that there was no contradic-tion between his Muslim solidarity and Arab unity, both of which, accord-ing to his perceptions, faced the same foes – imperialism, Zionism and Communism.[22]

Clearly, nationalism, Arab nationalism and Islamism have all acted as ideologies that both unite and divide populations within nation-states, and equally unite and divide those states themselves. These ideological dynamics, many of which can be traced directly or indirectly to the struggle for liberation from colonial rule, have all served to shape the international relations of the Red Sea. Constantly eroding the process of national construction and institutionalisation has been the legacy of imperial borders which divided ethnic, religious and tribal groupings, or placed one such group above another. Identities frequently failed to conform to the national constructs of the new states and efforts at forced homogenisation were as likely to fail as attempts to ignore the demands for alternative political formations. The fragility of the nation-state, and the overlapping of sectarian, ethnic, confessional and national identities, mean that the consequent struggles for power have rarely been discreet and confined to territorial borders.

Building the nation-state: consolidation, coups and crises

However, ideology has not been the sole building-block of the state-building process. Efforts to consolidate or replace political structures in the aftermath of independence, and the need to mobilise and organise resources within new nation-states, reflected greater realities than ideology alone, serving to draw states together through common interest, or thrust them apart through mutual aversion. As each nation-state constructed its own political institutions and criteria for legitimacy, it was similarly forced to address the question of its relative position in the region and to devise foreign policies that would reinforce its own stature and stability. The point was made earlier that differences in regime types (i.e., socialist, conservative) created fissures in the relations between states despite common pan-Arabist ideological position. These very differences, which emerged from the conjuncture of historical, colonial and socio-economic specificities within the various states, also reflected the fragility of the new nation-states and their vulnerability to external influences and manipulation.

When Britain withdrew from its colonial territories, it generally left behind weak parliamentary structures dominated by previously co-opted traditional elites. Such structures immediately came under assault from those social forces which sought dramatic change in the post-independence era in favour of social justice, wealth redistribution, truly representative government and a break with the collaborationist politics of the past. Even those territories which had avoided colonial intrusion found that their new status as nation-states demanded the creation or formalisation of political structures which could satisfy the requirements of organisation and government. The monarchies of Jordan and Saudi Arabia have survived the challenge, in the first case, through the delicate balancing of traditional interests with progressive change; in the second, through the distribution of rent and the maintenance of strong but relatively informal patriarchal political structures. Elsewhere, monarchies were swept away by progressive forces supported by disgruntled military leaders. Egypt, Sudan, Ethiopia and South Yemen were all to adopt more populist corporatist political systems that married imported ideological blueprints with the same perceived need to centralise and consolidate the state in the interests of development, modernisation and wealth redistribution. The state itself became the critical player in the new era. Where monarchies could mould the state such that it became all but indivisible from themselves, they were able to survive. Where they found themselves at odds with the goals and ambitions of the state, they fell before it.

Yet for most Red Sea states, the state has grown to be a fierce, rather than a strong, phenomenon.[23] Both traditional and populist state forms denied the relevance of opposition in the process of their political, social and economic development. Political choice was viewed as divisive, a distraction from the national task and open to manipulation by foreign powers. Thus the determination of regimes to forestall any challenges to the set paths towards modernisation led them to assert the coercive powers of the state in their favour, whether they were traditional or populist in orientation. The absence of political choice, or the freedoms which would have made it possible, have ironically legitimised the very challenges they sought to pre-empt. As the economic strategies of states foundered on the inadequacies of import-substitution industrialisation (ISI), on excessive borrowing, on over-dependence on hydrocarbon exports, on corruption, excessive consumerism and a lack of accountability, and as the Arab nationalist dream of retrieving Palestine for the Arabs slipped further from their grasp, the regimes of Jordan, Saudi Arabia, Egypt, Sudan and Yemen have all faced additional crises of legitimacy. The regimes of Ethiopia and Sudan have had additional pressures resulting from drought and famine (in part the consequence of poor resource management and corruption) and from their own internal wars. Only in Israel, which has had the benefit of diaspora revenues, enormous foreign assistance, a highly-educated and motivated labour force, early technology transfers, a highly-developed military-industrial complex, preferential access to foreign markets, and largely democratic political structures, has the state been able to assert itself over its own people without the need to curtail their freedoms or the assistance of the military. Even there, however, the state has succumbed until recently to an inflated bureaucracy, corporatist visions of popular entitlement, economic mismanagement (even corruption) and consumption beyond its own productive capacity. Until 1977, successive parliaments were ruled by a Labour-led coalition which was closely integrated into the fabric of the state and which acted much like the single parties of neighbouring states.

Without doubt, the festering Arab–Israeli conflict and the struggles between states for ideological hegemony and strategic dominance within the region facilitated the creation of enlarged military apparatuses, which were then courted and spoiled by regimes dependent upon them for their continued rule. In turn, the military, or military personnel, often moved into power, either through direct coups (Egypt, Sudan, Ethiopia, South Yemen), or more subtly through the electoral process in Israel. The prominence of the military in the political structures of Red Sea states, and indeed the role the military must inevitably play in a region which harbours such a running sore as the Arab–Israeli problem, not to mention numerous border disputes and cross-border resource and ethnic spillages, have all contributed to the regional preoccupation with security and territorial integrity, and the propensity for regimes to interfere in the domestic politics of neighbouring states.

This chapter has identified a number of features common to most, if not all, Red Sea states which leave them interested in, and vulnerable to, the affairs of one another. Unsurprisingly, the Red Sea states, like most of their developing world contemporaries, have been shaped in large part by the struggle for independence and the subsequent requirements of the state-building process, the only exception to this being Saudi Arabia which was never actually subject to colonial rule. Even there, however, the capacity for establishing a modern nation-state which can successfully and peacefully interact with its neighbours has been determined as much by post-colonial Arab world conditions as by domestic forces. In this process, ideological considerations have been interwoven with efforts to construct, reconstruct and deconstruct identities that can support the political structures of a nation-state. Political systems have been established which ultimately suffer from the contradictions between the social environment and the territorial integrity of states whose borders have been derived from a colonial rather than an evolutionary history. The continuing Arab–Israeli dispute and the determination of post-colonial regimes to resist domestic instability which threatens national goals have enhanced the role of the military and subverted aspirations for democracy or genuine popular participation within stable civilian political structures. Instead, *coups d'état*, civil wars and authoritarian modes of rule have been the norm. While Israel has of course been more successful in creating a stable democracy (at least for its Jewish majority), it too has witnessed a military establishment with unusual political influence. Moreover, the existence and policies of Israel have had an inestimable effect on both the domestic and foreign politics of its Red Sea neighbours. Finally, the drive for economic development and modernisation has impacted upon political ideology, structure and policy, reinforcing the role of the state in ways which have often ultimately weakened the legitimacy of the state even as they have enhanced its authority.

For the most part, the key states of the sub-region are the following: Saudi Arabia, Egypt, and Israel, since they are the most able to project their strategic interests. Correspondingly, the states of the Horn of Africa are the weakest and most subject to the intervention of others. As Jeffrey Lefebvre has argued:

> Middle East intervention in the Horn is not simply a post-Cold War phenomenon, but part of the long-term and enduring political landscape of the region. For many years their interventionist policies were over-shadowed by the Cold War. This is no longer the case ... Because the Horn is located just south of across the sea from these Middle Eastern states, what happens in the Horn may affect the entire Red Sea region. Since they cannot move out of the neighbourhood, these states have attempted to influence the ideological or foreign policy orientation of local actors through arms, aid or subversion.[24]

Lefebvre argues that the intervention has been essentially one-way, with the conflicts of the Middle East being played out in the Horn of Africa but the Horn's own struggles having little impact upon the Middle Eastern states themselves. While this is by and large true (precisely because of the concentration of resources and capacities in the Middle Eastern states), there have also been occasions, especially during and as a result of Cold War politics, when states in the Horn have acted in ways that affect their more powerful neighbours. The inclusion of Somalia and Djibouti in the American security arrangements for the Middle East in the 1980s, for example, or more recently the support by Sudan of extremist (including Saudi) Islamic dissidents are appropriate examples.

This chapter has attempted to illustrate the sub-regional effects of these state-level factors. Any analysis would, however, be faulty if it were not to refer to the wider regional and international contexts within which the Red Sea states were operating at any given point in time. The following two chapters will attempt to locate the Red Sea states within such a context by broadening and multiplying the levels of analysis.

2 International politics of the Red Sea in the Cold War era

Introduction

In analysing the immediate post-war period, it is not hard to see that both super-powers would inevitably find themselves embroiled in the Middle East. An indication of their deep involvement came in 1948, when both the USA and the USSR condoned the birth of Israel. Unity over this post-war settlement, however, was already overshadowed by more serious tensions between Moscow and Washington over their respective strategies in the Middle East. Dating back to 1946, the Azerbaijan crisis in north-east Iran was arguably the opening chapter of the Cold War which was to shape the destiny and determine the course of the international system in the next 50 years.[1] Even at the beginning, the Cold War was a serious threat to international security. As Louise Fawcett indicates, as early as March 1946, Britain and the United States had talked 'of the possibility of war with the USSR over Iran'.[2] It was during these early days of the post-war era that President Truman sharpened America's sensitivities about Soviet intentions. The fear of a Soviet strategy which would include a pincer movement to take control of the Mediterranean and the Near East was being widely expressed in Washington at the time. US policy towards the region in general, and Iran and Turkey in particular (Moscow's only direct southern neighbours in West Asia), was, at this time, already being shaped by wider calculations about the emerging post-war international system and American and Soviet influence within it. So it was then that the forces shaping the nascent post-war international system were to set the mould for the MENA sub-system as well, even though, as Halliday notes, the overall impact of the Cold War (in terms of actually shaping the destiny of MENA) may have been a 'mild' one.[3]

The international sphere was transmitted to the regional in two ways. First, the rivalry between Moscow and Washington, the new great powers of the century, soon divided the world, particularly Europe and Asia, into opposing armed camps. The Middle East, being an integral part of both continents, could not escape superpower attention. Its territory was now firmly on the great powers' chessboards.

Second, as we saw in Chapter 1, the slowly gathering nationalist winds, which had gained pace after the victory of India's independence struggle in 1947, inevitably reached the shores of the Middle East. Here, the birth of Israel in 1948 had already provided the logic and the impetus for Arab peoples to seek independence from their European colonial masters. The end of the British and French mandates in the Levant were soon followed by independence struggles of other Arabs. The struggle for independence enjoyed wide support, of course. The movement, however, was radicalised by the rise of left-leaning forces in the Arab world, most notably Arab nationalist revolutionaries who surfaced in Egypt in 1952 to take charge of the country, and the Syrian and Iraqi Ba'athists who were to have their moment in the next decade. In non-Arab Iran, moreover, the communist and nationalist forces had already made significant advances against Iran's pro-Western monarch.

We can say, with the benefit of hindsight, though, that both superpowers might have misread the radicalising shift in the Middle East in the immediate aftermath of the Second World War, which was epitomised by Mossadegh's rise to power in Iran in 1951 and the Free Officers in Egypt soon after. For the United States, both events were synonymous with the rise of Soviet power in the Middle East, with encroaching communist influence. The Soviet Union, on the other hand, interpreted the actions of Mossadegh and Nasser (their nationalisation of British assets in their respective countries) more as signs of their anti-imperialist credentials and less as expression of their countries' nationalist aspirations that they truly were representing. Both superpowers, in other words, misread the nature of change in the area as well as each other's policies.

There can be little doubt, however, that the withdrawal of colonial power left the Middle East and North Africa with severe political and economic problems still to resolve. In Chapter 1 we outlined the complexities of regional relations which resulted from ill-defined and unstable borders, the challenges of leadership, regime legitimacy and ideology, and economic vulnerability. The regional states were not to be left alone, however, to resolve their problems in splendid isolation. The demise of the pre-Second World War great powers was accompanied, via the dynamics of the war itself, with the rise to power of two new superstars, the United States of America and the Soviet Union. Their subsequent struggle for military and ideological supremacy was to be played out around the globe, introducing new catalysts for change and interaction in regional relations among, not least, the MENA states.

Domestic instability in the Middle East, moreover, also attracted superpower intervention and anticipated the ensuing rivalry between the great powers. As has been said of the 1948 Arab–Israeli war, for example, 'what seemed at first a regional confrontation became increasingly in the 1950s a superpower issue, as the Soviet Union gained footholds in the Arab world'.[4]

Thus, the Cold War era, defined here as the period between 1946 and 1990, represented a period of critical change for the states around the Red Sea. Their relations with one another were profoundly altered by three clusters of factors, the end result being that they were increasingly propelled towards sub-regional activities and identities. The three clusters of factors were the combined products of colonial legacies and new, specifically Cold War related, factors. First, domestic instabilities which had implications for regional behaviour and intervention by other regional states. Regime weaknesses and other problematic domestic political structures, began to make stability deteriorate in a number of states, the implications being felt at a wider sub-regional level and propelling new levels of inter-state activity and intervention. Concurrently, the breakdown of nation-state structures introduced or magnified existing sub-state and trans-state identities, reinforcing sub-regional identities and, at the same time, threatening other state-centred identities within the sub-region.

Second, regional inter-state instabilities, including wars, left a profound mark on the area as a whole. Inter-state conflict in the region demanded responses from the states of the regional system. Two arenas of war were particularly critical for the Red Sea states: the Horn of Africa, where Ethiopia and Somalia were engaged in a bloody conflict, and the running sore of the Arab–Israeli conflict.

Both sets of factors outlined above contributed to the rise of the third: the involvement of the superpowers in the wider region and their pursuit of the core Red Sea states. Engaged in their own struggle for influence, the superpowers willingly pushed themselves into the region, but they were also pulled into it for two other reasons. First, in pursuit of their perceived interests in the MENA region; and, second, in response to the actions of the sub-system's major states. The net result of superpower involvement was the internationalisation of sub-regional politics and a drive for alliances on the part of the sub-regional players. The classic Red Sea syndrome in the Cold War era that we discuss at length in this chapter is encapsulated by Legum and Lee, who state in relation to super-power involvement in the Horn in the 1970s: 'Either both super-powers become engaged, thus converting essentially local conflicts into international confrontations; or if one of the super-powers opts out, the field is left open for the other.'[5]

Regional politics and the evolution of superpower involvement

Commensurate with the demise of British and French influence in the Middle East in the decade after the end of the Second World War was the steady rise in superpower interest in the area. The Egyptian revolution and the Suez Crisis marked the turning points in the superpowers' involvement. The former provided the conditions for the Soviet Union to enter the heartland of the Middle East and develop a relationship with the Arab world's most significant power. The Suez Crisis, on the other hand, was the opportunity for the United States to establish itself as the premier Western power in the Middle East. In the course of the crisis, it drew closer to the Arab world while maintaining its influence over its two European allies. By 1957, American interests in the area were such that a new security doctrine, the Eisenhower Doctrine, had been devised for the sub-system. For a while, American interests extended to an embrace of the largely pro-Western Khalil government in the Sudan as well. The USA was, by the end of the 1950s, therefore, firmly entrenched in the region, much as the Soviet Union had become.

Table 2.1 American and Soviet arms transfers to the Middle East, 1950–73 ($million, 1973 prices)

Country	Year				
	1950–54	*1955–59*	*1960–64*	*1965–69*	*1969–73*
USA	33.5	242.5	199.0	1,087.0	2,041.0
USSR	—	542.5	732.0	1,587.0	2,838.5
Total	253.0	1322.0	1,309.5	3,375.0	5,903.5

Source: *SIPRI*.

As will be shown below, the Free Officers Movement and the Suez Crisis in 1956 left a definite mark on the Red Sea area. It started with the Soviet-Egyptian arms deal in 1955, the first of its kind for both countries, which paved the way for Soviet presence in the MENA sub-system and the Red Sea sub-region, and continued with the slide towards the second war between Israel and Egypt. Within the consolidating MENA sub-system itself, the Suez Crisis provided the catalyst for Nasser to launch Egypt on the pan-Arabist trajectory that was to dominate inter-Arab relations until the 1967 War. More broadly, the Suez war was the watershed for superpower involvement in the Red Sea as well, just as it had marked the decline of the Mandate powers in the Mashreq.

Several historians of the Cold War period have noted the way in which the Cold War stalemate encouraged militarisation of key regions in the international system.[6] Certainly it was evident by the 1950s that the Middle East region was no exception to this rule; indeed, the sub-system experienced militarisation on a vast scale. Both Cold War sides used the supply of arms to curry favour with local actors, and, in the Soviet Union's case, arms transfers were used as a major policy instrument in the 1950s and 1960s (Table 2.1). The Soviet tactic of cementing friendships through military ties continued to pay dividends, particularly, 'so long as the West played the Cold War in the Middle East in terms of bases and pacts'.[7]

This indeed is one of the core issues in our view. Soon after the end of the Second World War, the Middle East became the playground of the superpowers. By the late 1950s, the superpowers' tactic of recruiting regional alliances through military and security pacts was plainly affecting the balance of power in the Red Sea zone, where the area's key protagonists (Egypt and Israel) found themselves in a 'relationship', if not an alliance, with the competing superpowers. These two powers' rivalry, thus, soon acquired an international dimension.

Superpower interest in the strategic Red Sea waterway sharpened further with the end of the Condominium in the Sudan in 1956, on the one hand, and the realisation that Egypt was now able to extend its influence on both shores of the sea, on the other. The $56.5 million loan secured by the Suez Canal Authority with the help of the US government from the World Bank in 1959 for the development of the Canal zone was another indication of America's continuing interest in Nasser's Egypt and its surroundings. In the same year, Emperor Haille Selassie, a close American ally and one referred to as a tool of American imperialism by

Pravda, paid an official visit to the Soviet Union to secure a loan of 400 million rubles promised to him by the Soviet leader himself, Khrushchev.[8] By then the United States had already secured its place in the southern Red Sea through a lease agreement with Addis Ababa for exclusive use of the Kagnew communications station near Asmara.[9] The Kagnew station was to play an important role in US evolving global military communications and command network in the 1950s and 1960s.[10]

It was not long before Egypt's strategic rival, Israel, also began taking an active interest in developments in southern Red Sea countries. First, it established diplomatic relations with Ethiopia in 1956, shortly after the Suez War. Then it seized its opportunity in Sudan in the 1960s in support of the southern Sudanese forces. But at the same time Israel also managed to establish a presence in Khartoum, which often gave it direct access to circles close to President Numeiri. From such solid bases, Israel's relations with the Sudanese government warmed markedly after the end of the southern rebellion in 1972 and flourished until Numeiri's downfall in 1985.[11]

Red Sea dynamics and the superpowers after the Suez Crisis

Thus, it is clear that, soon after the Suez Crisis, superpower interest in the Red Sea area was being supplemented by the competitive activities of the Red Sea states themselves. By the late 1950s, the northern Red Sea states were keen to establish their own zones of influence in this vital waterway, and through it in the rest of Africa. This was a new and significant factor for the superpowers to take into consideration.

Soon after the rise of the superpower Cold War, therefore, a regional cold war was born, but this one out of the tense relationship between Egypt and Israel. The Egyptian-Israeli cold war was now rivalling that of the great powers in the Afro-Arab realms. As has been noted by Bernard Reich and others, Israel's activities in Africa after the Suez Crisis were sufficient to steer Egypt into action and 'direct the anti-Israel offensive in Africa'.[12] Egypt's interests in Ethiopia and Somalia, in political, military and cultural terms, from the late 1950s onwards could be viewed in the same light.[13] President Nasser set about countering the US-Ethiopian alliance, for example, soon after the USA established its presence in Ethiopia in 1953. So Egypt allowed the Eritrean Liberation Front (ELF) to establish its headquarters in Cairo in 1961, and provided military training and camp facilities for the ELF fighters.[14] At the same time Egypt aided Somalia in its confrontation with Ethiopia.

As already stated, the growing interest of the northern Red Sea states in the waterway was being matched by that of the superpowers themselves. From the superpowers' perspective, developments in the northern Red Sea zone after the 1956 Suez Crisis were also making the position of another Red Sea country central to their strategic calculations. The country in question was Saudi Arabia, huge territorially, and at the heart of the Mashreq geographically. Its emergence in the course of the 1960s and 1970s as the region's most well-endowed state financially was to make Saudi Arabia's international policies another important calculation for the superpowers.[15] Indeed, with support from the West, by the mid-1960s, Saudi Arabia had already emerged as one of the sub-region's most influential players.

At the other end of the Red Sea, around the Horn of Africa, it was Somalia which provided the incentive for the Soviet superpower to actively intervene in the Horn, in Mogadishu's defence against a Western-armed and Western-protected Ethiopia. As was said in 1977, 'now the Somalis are themselves the victims of Moscow's opportunistic policies ... it is Saudi Arabia, Egypt and the Sudan which have recently been pressing for Western military aid to be sent to Somalia'.[16]

1960s: superpower rivalries spread

Regional developments in the 1950s and the deepening of the Cold War between NATO and the Warsaw Pact countries ensured that the 1960s would be a period of intense superpower rivalry in the sub-system. At the core of the sub-system lay the Arab–Israeli conflict, which, even before the June 1967 War, was shaping the great powers' policies towards the region. President Kennedy's decision in 1962 to directly supply arms to Israel was the first concrete indication of America's growing security involvement in the northern Red Sea zone. At the same time, the US administration was keen to keep Egypt on-side as well, which it tried to do through the offer of economic assistance and friendly relations with Egypt. At the other end of the sub-region, a new state was being born, that of Somalia (in July 1960), and the Soviet Union was already calculating what strategic advantages it could accumulate through its support for the Yemeni republican movement.

Indeed, it was events in Yemen in the early 1960s which were to redraw the geopolitical map of the Red Sea. By the autumn of 1962, the establishment of a left-leaning republican regime in the Imamate of Yemen was threatening to suck in the superpowers into the southern tip of the Arabian Peninsula, where Egypt and Saudi Arabia had already lined up behind opposing camps in what was to become a bloody campaign for control of the country. The superpowers' initial diplomatic manoeuvres and their rush to adopt diametrically opposed positions merely exacerbated the tense situation on the ground.[17]

The crisis in Yemen, where Egypt found itself at war with Saudi Arabia and local Yemeni forces, not only complicated Egypt's pan-Arabist plans, but also served to worsen Nasser's relations with the United States, where it increased American suspicions of Egypt's role in assisting the Soviet Union's presence on the oil-rich Arabian Peninsula and adjacent to the Bab el-Mandeb choke point. This interpretation of Nasser's plans was reinforced by Saudi fears that 'the presence of Egyptian forces in Yemen meant the expansion of Egyptian power and influence to the Arabian Peninsula, and, with it, Soviet and communist influence'.[18] The Saudis, having few options of their own to counter Nasser's intervention in Yemen, turned to the United States, whose declared position on the Yemen conflict was one of 'nonintervention'.[19] It was not until the more hawkish Johnson administration took office in 1964 that America's position on the Yemen conflict began to harden. President Johnson's decision in 1965 to offer to modernise and develop the Saudi armed forces was another sign of a more active US involvement across the sub-region.

The Soviet Union, for its part, did not fully understand the Yemeni forces it was increasingly supporting, and remained concerned that it might be getting involved in a conflict it could not resolve to its own advantage. Moscow's fears proved to be short-lived, however, as the gathering winds of war in the northern Red Sea zone in May and June of 1967 eventually forced Nasser's hand in Yemen and compelled him to abandon his campaign there and leave the field free for the political field for Soviet Union to cultivate. By then, as Gerges has noted, the Yemen conflict had become another landmark in the growing set of conditions which were increasingly linking regional and international politics, the 'internal and external politics' of the sub-system.[20] By the 1960s, the Red Sea sub-region was at the centre of these regional and international cross-currents.

The June 1967 War, itself a largely local-based conflict, was another decisive event of the 1960s which left a more or less permanent mark on the geopolitics of the Red Sea sub-region. The war, though short in duration, disrupted normal inter-state relations in the MENA sub-system for at least a generation and is still proving to be as durable as the Cold War that lasted for 50 years. While the war affected the region as a whole, it left a very lasting mark on three northern Red Sea states: Egypt, Israel and Jordan.

Not surprisingly, the tensions which led to war also directly affected the superpowers' policies towards the Red Sea sub-region, within which some of the warfare was bound to take place, as Nasser's plan (unveiled in a speech on 22 May) to close the Gulf of Aqaba to Israeli shipping clearly demonstrated. The United States, as usual, better informed than the Soviet Union, had already braced itself for a military confrontation, even before Foreign Minister Abba Eban had begun his meeting with American officials in Washington on 25 May. By the time that the Egyptian 4th Armoured Division had begun arriving in Sinai, and the Egyptian Minister of War, Shamseddin Bedran, had met his Soviet counterpart in Moscow (25 May), it should have been clear to both superpowers that neither had managed to moderate the position of its ally. War was imminent and the superpowers had little choice but to line up behind their respective allies. Another regional dispute, coming just as the Yemen conflict was waning, was again forcing the superpowers to line up on opposite sides.

The outcome of the June 1967 War, a devastating defeat for the Arabs, was to determine the superpowers' strategies towards the sub-system in general and the Red Sea in particular for a considerable length of time. By the end of the 1960s, the Red Sea sub-region had entered a new phase in its life. Nasser's dream of Arab unity was in tatters, the Yemen was carved up between two competing camps, Arab divisions were greater than ever, and the United States had emerged as the emphatic and powerful champion of three northern Red Sea states closest to Egypt (Israel, Jordan and Saudi Arabia), which was still to all intents and purposes a Soviet ally, and much Arab territory in the northern Red Sea area was occupied by Israel.[21]

The American position in the region, while never overtly hostile to Egypt in the 1960s, was reinforced by extensive military ties with its anti-Nasser regional partners. At the other end of the Red Sea, Somalia's new military government, which was born out of a coup carried out in 1969, was increasingly seeking military support from the Soviet Union. The Soviet Union had been Somalia's sole supplier of weapons systems since 1963. Soviet aid to Somalia until its departure from the country in the 1970s was consistent with what the USA had provided Ethiopia at the height of its alliance with Addis Ababa.[22]

Among the Arab states, the 1967 crisis, which resulted in the closure of the Suez Canal, increased their interest in the Bab el-Mandeb. In strategic terms, concerns over Ethiopia's position vis-à-vis this choke point and its close politic-military relationship with Israel encouraged several Arab countries to try and unsettle the Haille Selassie regime there. For Ethiopia's neighbour across the strait, South Yemen, the Selassie regime was nothing more than a Zionist collaborator, a view that was being echoed in several Arab capitals.[23] After the Six Day War, it is worth noting, radical Arab regimes were increasingly 'interested in the Red Sea within the context of the Arab–Israeli conflict, as a theater of operations for advancing anti-Israeli and anti-American strategies'.[24] Thus, by the end of the decade, South Yemeni and PLO support was very evident for the Eritrean guerrillas, which was being translated into significant battle victories in their campaign against the Ethiopian armed forces.

One could see Israel's behaviour in the Horn through the same Arab–Israeli prism. The target of their affections of course was Ethiopia, which had agreed to the establishment of a close military relationship with Israel. The military relationship after the June war included the establishment of a joint naval base in Assab port, Israeli access to Ethiopian air bases and its air space, and the creation for Ethiopia of a new mechanised brigade. Israeli Foreign Minister, Abba Eban, who visited Addis Ababa in June 1969, had arrived to develop their bilateral relationship, and this he did by responding to a long-standing Ethiopian grievance over the presence of the Ethiopian Church in Jerusalem. He had gone to Ethiopia to agree to transfer the control of the Deir al-Sultan in the Old City in Jerusalem from Egyptian Copts, who had taken control of the monastery in 1838, to the Ethiopian Church.[25]

With regard to the Horn of Africa, then, throughout the 1960s, Arab meddling in support of the Eritrean movements in Ethiopia merely served to reinforce the Ethiopian-Israeli relationship. Only after Nasser's death in 1970 did the opportunities for a new beginning present themselves.

1970s: superpower rivalries intensify

The superpower–client relationship in the Red Sea sub-region changed again from the start of the 1970s, and the pattern of alliance-building already witnessed was to be applied more systematically in the Red Sea sub-region by both superpowers in the 1970s and 1980s. By the end of the 1970s, moreover, conflict in the Horn of Africa had become such that it would not only qualify as a 'hot spot' in the international system, but also an internationalised one, in which the interests of third parties tend to converge with the development of a particular regional conflict.[26]

This decade was to mark the rise of new alliances and the development of superpower intervention around two competing axis: a Soviet/Cuban one and an American/Arab one.[27] First came the forced departure of the Soviet Union from Egypt in 1971, which seriously weakened Moscow's position in the area. This was the prelude to the October 1973 Arab–Israeli war which acted as a catalyst for improved relations between Egypt and the United States and eventually between Cairo and Tel Aviv. Israeli-Egyptian détente in 1977 further exposed Moscow's already weak hand in the Middle East. By the late 1970s, not only had not the linchpin of its Middle East policy changed sides in the Cold War, but its position was increasingly vulnerable in the People's Democratic Republic of Yemen (PDRY) as much as it was becoming precarious in some of the countries on the west bank of the waterway, Sudan and Somalia, in particular.[28]

The emergence of pro-US Saudi Arabia as a powerful regional player in the 1970s also helped to put extra pressure on Moscow and on its regional allies. With ever closer links between Cairo and Riyadh after the October 1973 war, Soviet fears that Saudi money could now be used to counter Soviet influence in the Arab world had entered the realm of reality. Compared with its remarkable gains in earlier post-war decades, the 1970s had become a period of major set-backs for the Soviet Union's strategic position in the Middle East sub-system as a whole and the Red Sea sub-region in particular. This was despite a radicalisation of Third World politics in Asia and Africa.

In the Red Sea sub-region, Moscow's position had been weakened by the growing strength of Washington's old allies (Israel and Saudi Arabia), Egypt's defection to the Western camp, the PDRY's vulnerable position, better relations between Ethiopia and the regional Arab states between 1970 and 1974, and Somalia's civil strife. The fact that Sudan was also moving closer to the Arab allies of the United States further damaged Moscow's position in this strategic waterway. The Soviets were arguably losing their strategic footing to their American rival, and in doing so as they lost control of the domestic politics of their client states.

Nevertheless, the creation of the Rapid Deployment Force by the United States at the end of the decade was a sign that Washington remained sufficiently nervous of Soviet intentions in this area, and was concerned enough about Middle East regional developments to spawn a significant military structure to project its power in defence of its interests. Despite the success of the Camp David Accords in bringing the two Red Sea adversaries together under the US regional umbrella, Washington was still concerned about developments further afield in the sub-system, namely the Soviet military presence in Afghanistan and the Iranian revolutionary movement.

Unquestionably, the 1970s were a period of intense political activity in the Red Sea area, during which the waterway entered centre stage as one of the flashpoints of the Cold War, with at least one 'hot spot'. The 1970s were also characterised by several changes at the state level; it started with further radicalisation of the South

Yemeni regime and its slide into the Soviet orbit (which was confirmed by the victory of Abd al-Fattah Ismail's staunchly pro-Soviet Marxist wing of the ruling party in 1978), followed by the Omani civil war in 1974, in which Aden was implicated, and the Ethiopian revolution in the same year. These domestic developments left their mark on the character of the Red Sea, all the while that new regimes were undermining the stability of the area.

Beyond the domestic changes, two wars in the 1970s added to the Red Sea sub-region's tensions. First came the October 1973 Arab–Israeli war, which had a huge impact on the entire Middle East region. By its end, Egypt had been able to recover from the débâcle of 1967 (during which it had lost much of its military assets as well as control of the Sinai peninsula). The October war also acted as the catalyst for the oil revolution of 1974, when oil prices quadrupled to over $11 per barrel. The October war may have brought the superpowers very close to an exchange of blows, but its most dramatic impact was in the way in which it changed the dynamics of inter-state relations in the sub-system and how it paved the way for dialogue between Cairo and Tel Aviv.

The second conflict, the 1977–78 Ethiopian–Somali war in the southern Red Sea area, was an altogether different affair. This war was aggravated by the direct intervention of the Soviet superpower. Moscow's shifting of its support from Somalia to Ethiopia in 1976 merely added to the tensions between Addis Ababa and Mogadishu. By the time war broke out in 1977, the Soviet Union was in place to extend considerable military assistance to the Marxist regime in Ethiopia. The Soviet airlift of military supplies to Ethiopia began shortly after the Somali Socialist Revolutionary Party had decided to sever all its military ties with Moscow in November 1977. Ironically, Ethiopia was just beginning to reap the benefits of friendship with the United States, which had already agreed to transfer two squadrons of its advanced F-5E fighters to Ethiopia, the first squadron of which had arrived in April 1976, in addition to a promise by Secretary of State Kissinger of a further $100 million in military equipment.[29]

Somalia's military intervention in the Ogaden region of Ethiopia, spearheaded by 12 mechanised brigades and 250 main battle tanks and air support, set the mould for Soviet participation, and invited Arab involvement, and inevitably American interest. As Somalia was now an Arab League country (having joined the League in 1974), and as its enemy was being aided by the Soviet Union, regional states (first, Saudi Arabia, followed by Egypt and Sudan) saw fit to adopt pro-Somali positions. Their diplomatic support was augmented by financial assistance from Saudi Arabia and some military advice from the others. In 1978 alone, Saudi Arabia provided some $300 million in aid in support of Somalia's war effort. Both Egypt and Sudan had another worry of course: that Addis Ababa might be emboldened to threaten the two Arab countries' national security by disrupting of the flow of the Blue Nile. President Sadat of Egypt had spoken in strong terms in 1978 about the steps his country was prepared to take if Ethiopia attempted to interfere with the river's flow.[30]

Also, with Riyadh's encouragement, the United States adopted an increasingly pro-Somali position in the war, though never getting militarily involved. So, in a relatively short space of time Red Sea alliances had shifted. While Ethiopia was to emerge as one of the Soviet Union's key Third World allies, by 1980, the USA was looking upon Somalia as a regional partner, whose territory (air fields and facilities of the port of Berbera in particular) was central to US naval operations in the area. It was with no hint of irony that the USA 'adopted' the very Somali port which had been developed and expanded with Soviet assistance.

In sharp contrast to the position of the three named Arab states, another Red Sea Arab state, South Yemen, came out in support of Ethiopia – a country that Aden had condemned as a 'Zionist conspirator' until 1974. During the war, the Soviet Union had used South Yemeni bases to transfer much of its substantial military aid to Ethiopia, which of course translated into battle victories for the Ethiopians.[31] Several hundred Yemeni military advisers were also seen in the country, aiding the Ethiopian war effort.[32]

South Yemen's position during this crisis highlights the impact that competing patterns of inter-Arab relations were having on the Red Sea region's international politics in the 1970s. As noted earlier in this study, Saudi Arabia was active in Arab efforts at this time to turn the Red Sea into an 'Arab lake', trying in this endeavour to create a regional pact of Red Sea Arab states (Egypt, Sudan, the Yemens, Somalia and itself). Yet, despite its stated interest in Arab action, South Yemen's policies ran counter to this, practically undermining the co-ordinated pan-Arab policy towards Red Sea security issues which Saudi Arabia and Egypt were seeking.[33] Riyadh's pan-Arab strategy, furthermore, hinged on ensuring that no outside power, and certainly not one which was such a powerful adversary (i.e., the Soviet Union), should have a foothold in the area.

For non-Arab Israel also, the principle of 'containing' the Soviet presence stood. But the strategic implications of the tensions in the Horn generated an altogether different response from Israel, forcing it to make some calculated risks. On the one hand, Israel was anxious not to see the complete 'Arabisation' of the Red Sea and the territories on the Horn. Its concern being that such a development might compromise its freedom of shipping and passage through the Bab el-Mandeb. On the other hand, Israel was concerned that American aid to Somalia and Washington's close co-ordination of its policy with Saudi Arabia, and its opposition to Soviet presence around the Horn, might lead it to embrace the Arab plan for the Red Sea, its 'Arabisation'.

With these concerns in mind, it set about responding to the security and strategic challenges posed by the conflict in the Horn. Its policies, however, provide an excellent example of the degree of confusion that Cold War superpower interventions in the Red Sea had created for the regional powers and the serious problems that superpower behaviour had created for the local powers in their responses to sub-regional challenges. Naturally, Israel's instinctive response was to aid non-Arab Ethiopia (with which, as we have seen, it had had close security relations until the 1974 revolution) against the country supported by the pro-US Arab states and the USA itself. In practice, the outcome of Israel's policy was not to be limited only to that of aiding pro-Moscow Ethiopia against the interests and policies of its own American ally;[34] the Israeli policies had required it, albeit unintentionally, to jump into bed with such Arab adversaries as Libya and South Yemen, the latter being the only Red Sea Arab country allied to the Soviet Union. Furthermore, with the strategy of supporting Ethiopia in the war, Israel was allowing itself to be lined up against America's regional allies, all referred to as 'Arab reactionary regimes' by Addis Ababa and Moscow, and also the only Arab country which was to become Israel's friend in the Arab world for many years to come, namely, Egypt.

The Soviet superpower, however, was already compensating for the loss of Egypt and Somalia by expanding its presence in South Yemen (a country on the tip of the Arabian Peninsula and a neighbour of Saudi Arabia), as well as in non-Arab Ethiopia. Thus, the lasting impression which one carries of this period in the Red Sea is that all the time that regional players were busy with their efforts to carve zones of influence and alliances, the Soviet Union, in its relentless pursuit of strategic advantage over the United States, was continuously disrupting these inter-Arab flows, and in so doing was adding to regional tensions. These regional tensions in turn aggravated superpower rivalries, which reached their zenith in the Horn of Africa in the 1980s.

The American role and presence in the sub-region in the 1970s were not insignificant either. This is best illustrated by its military ties, which is put in perspective by the significance the US superpower attached to its Red Sea Middle East allies. Between 1976–80, for example, just four Red Sea countries (Israel, Saudi Arabia, Jordan and Egypt), had taken some 30 per cent of America's total major weapons exports to the Third World.[35]

Nowhere is the superpower confrontation of the 1970s for influence in this waterway more apparent than in the Horn of Africa. By looking at the superpowers' military relations, Table 2.2 chronicles the evolution of US and Soviet policies towards Ethiopia, Somalia and Sudan. It is noticeable that in each case most arms were imported between 1975 and 1979, to the tune of $2.7 billion, at the height of military tensions there.

The 1970s ended with swift changes in the Horn of Africa, and, as we have seen, in the northern zone of the Red Sea. In the Horn, the most significant changes were associated with Ethiopia, which became one of 16 African states to break off relations with Israel (which it reluctantly did on October 24, 1973), as the regime of Emperor Haille Selassie, Israel's and America's close ally, had been overthrown (in September 1974); Moscow emerged as the key Ethiopian ally (1977) and aided it in a major military campaign against Somalia. Eritrea was, albeit uncomfortably, adopted as an Arab issue but the control of the Eritrean movement steadily shifted from the ELF to the more radical and Christian-dominated Eritrean Peoples Liberation Front (EPLF) which had split from the ELF in 1970; flushed with petro-dollars, Saudi Arabia launched its own campaign to reverse the advance of socialist and Soviet-aided forces and regimes in the Horn; under the protection of the Soviet Union, PDRY and Ethiopia, the 'guardians' of the strait, developed a close military and political relationship, despite the fact that many other radical Arab forces (bar Libya which had also switched its allegiance to the Ethiopian government) remained loyal to the Eritrean cause;

Table 2.2 Sources of arms imports to selected Horn countries, 1961–79 ($million, selected years)

Country	USA	USSR	Total arms import	Years
Ethiopia	104	0	126	1961–70
	90	1500	1830	1975–79
Somalia	1	47	58	1961–70
	0	210	450	1975–79
Sudan	2	63	136	1961–70
	120	10	415	1975–79

Source: Compiled from Henze (1982).

and, finally, Sudan emerged as a new chest-space for Red Sea powers engaged in 'Horn politics'.

1980s: Soviet–American rivalries in the twilight of the Cold War

Despite earlier setbacks, by the end of the 1970s, the Soviet Union had managed to establish itself as the dominant external power in the Horn of Africa, being militarily present, as it was, in South Yemen and Ethiopia simultaneously, the two 'gatekeepers' of the Bab el-Mandeb pass. In the words of Bruce Porter:

> With leftist regimes in Addis Ababa and Aden both heavily dependent on Soviet support, the Kremlin was in a promising strategic position on the strait of Bab el-Mandeb ... From Ethiopia, the USSR could potentially exert strong pressures on Egypt, Saudi Arabia, Sudan, Kenya and Somalia.[36]

The Soviet Union, furthermore, had taken the lead in the 1970s and the 1980s to radically change the military balance in the Horn of Africa and the neighbouring regions.[37] Over this period it had developed into the main supplier of weapons systems to the two Yemens, as well as to both Somalia and Ethiopia. In the latter case, by 1982, the Soviet Union had transferred several types of high performance weapons systems, including, 65 MiG-21 and 20 MiG-23 combat aircraft, 700 T-54 main battle tanks, 20 transport aircraft, and 24 Mi-24 helicopters.[38]

The American response to the Soviet advances took time to develop, but when it did come, in the course of the 1980s, it was vigorous and decisive. By the start of the 1980s, then, the political landscape of the Red Sea had again changed. The American alliance with Egypt, Israel and Saudi Arabia, now set in stone with the development of the RDF and its successor, the Central Command, was matched by a chain of Soviet alliances.[39] The Reagan administration took it upon itself to retip the balance in the West's favour.

The main security concerns of the West in the Red Sea area in what was to become the last decade of the Cold War were regional problems associated with the Numeiri regime's collapse in Sudan; the dangers associated with Ethiopia imploding as a result of severe national degradation caused by years of civil war and national mismanagement; and the aggressive intent of the pro-Soviet regime in Aden against the Gulf Arab allies of the United States. Cordesman, writing with a focus on the Persian Gulf sub-region, summarised the Red Sea's security problems in the 1980s as follows:

> These tensions and conflicts in the Red Sea area will have an impact on Somalia and Egypt, but it is unclear how they will affect the Gulf states. They would only be dangerous if the PDRY could take over YAR, if the more radical Red Sea states could agree on effective action, or if a charismatic leader could successfully unite one of the radical Red Sea states. None of these conditions seems likely in the near future.[40]

While Cordesman and American policy-makers did not seem unduly worried about a spill-over effect, others in the West were more concerned about South Yemen's diplomacy towards the West's regional allies. Aden after all had just signed a Friendship and Co-operation Treaty (in October 1979) with the Soviet Union, and had agreed to host several thousand Soviet and Cuban military advisers in the country, and had joined forces with other radical Arab regimes in the Arab rejectionist front. More worrying still, as far as other Red Sea powers were concerned, was the fact that the friendship treaty had been signed only months after the South Yemeni forces had carried out military operations against the North (in February 1979).

Another cause of tension was associated with the Reagan administration's revamping of his country's Middle East policy, and the White House's declared policy of developing closer military relations with Israel. The Reagan administration elevated the Jewish state's status to that of a 'strategic ally' of the United States, which not only raised Israel's regional position , but also tied more closely America's regional profile to that of Israel.

This American strategy completely disrupted the already shaky Middle East balance of power and heralded in another round of superpower rivalries and alliance building. From the US–Israel strategic alliance flowed increased military assistance to Israel and the transfer of even more advanced military hardware to the country. The new relationship between Israel and the United States was developing in conjunction with America's growing military commitments to Egypt, which, in the context of the Camp David Accords, facilitated the transfer of advanced American military hardware to Egypt as well. Thus, significant militarisation in the northern Red Sea area in the 1980s directly followed the new Middle East policies of the United States, in which the security of Israel, the blunting of Soviet influence, and the protection of America's interests in the Persian Gulf were seen as America's core interests. In strategic terms also, more systematic US military assistance to a string of Red Sea countries in the early 1980s left a deep imprint on the region:

> On the list [of countries receiving US aid in 1982] are Oman, Somalia, and Kenya – the three key countries letting the US use facilities on their territory. The list also includes Egypt, Israel, Sudan and Turkey. Egypt is making

available to the US facilities at Ras Banas on the Red Sea. It also allows the US use of Cairo West airfield, well out in the desert outside the Egyptian capital. Voices have been raised in Israel and among Israel's supporters in the US in favour of persuading Washington to develop, instead of Ras Banas, the Israeli-held airbases at Etzion and Eitam in Sinai ... A further argument for Ras Banas is the proximity of the oil refinery at Yanbu which the Saudis are building opposite Ras Banas. This would make fuel for US equipment at Ras Banas easily available.[41]

The US presence in the Red Sea and its strategic significance in regional terms were tested in 1984 when the waterway was mined by mysterious forces, possibly the Islamic Jihad organisation.[42] The 200 mines laid around the Red Sea's two choke points in protest to the Israeli and US involvement in Lebanon were the first time that this waterway had been caught up in a dispute beyond its immediate area. Several Red Sea states, notably Egypt and Saudi Arabia, openly asked for American assistance to clear the mines. While the mine crisis passed without serious consequences, it did concentrate the mind not only on how significant the US military role had become, but also on how vulnerable the waterway was to attack from outside. The event also brought home the reality of the importance of the sub-region to regional and international stability.

Added to the US new military alliance structures was the Reagan administration's obsession with countering the Soviet presence in the Horn of Africa. By 1982, the point of another Ethiopian–Somali border clash, the United States had already committed itself to aiding Somalia militarily. Thus, US military assistance to Somalia rose from $20.4 million in 1981 to $51.6 million in 1983.[43] The Pentagon also undertook the expansion and modernisation of the Berbera port's facilities. As Schraeder has noted, the primary US focus in the Horn

> was military access to Somalia's northern city of Berbera, although it was only in the aftermath of the 1982 Ethiopian–Somali border conflict that US military aid to Somalia significantly increased ... this conflict was the crucial element that attracted the attention of the Reagan White House.[44]

The 'new Cold War' of the 1980s also ensured that Somalia pocketed almost $800 million in US economic and military aid between 1980 and 1991.

By the end of the decade, the international system as we knew it had entered a new phase of dramatic change, stemming from the close of the superpower Cold War and the Soviet policy of co-operation with the West in regional conflict resolution. This new chapter in US–Soviet relations had direct implications for strategic regions of the world. Soviet readiness to abandon some of its Third World outposts and its stated desire to remove regional competition from its overall relations meant that it was no longer prepared to compete with the West in the Red Sea. The direct result of the new Soviet policy was the abandonment of its strategic advantages in the countries of the Red Sea. It has been observed that:

When the Cold War came to an end ... so did the perceived global strategic value of the Horn. By the end of 1989, Moscow was disengaging militarily from Mengistu Haille Mariam's regime in Ethiopia, Washington had suspended military assistance to President Mohammed Siad Barre's regime in Somalia in the Autumn of 1988, and terminated all aid to General 'Umar Bashir's regime following the June 1989 military coup in the Sudan.[45]

Looking back, it is clearer than ever that 1989 and 1990 were new watersheds for the Red Sea sub-region, as they were for the MENA sub-system as a whole.

3 Red Sea sub-regional developments in the post-Cold War era

Introduction

The Cold War may not have been entirely responsible for shaping inter-state relations in the Middle East, but in parts of the MENA sub-system where the superpowers did display an overt interest, they were at times decisive in shaping the sub-region. The Persian Gulf sub-region, for example, is one such location. As we showed in Chapter 2, the Red Sea is another part of the MENA sub-system where the superpowers played a decisive role. As we have argued, here, the behaviour of the Red Sea states themselves as well as the relations between them was largely determined by the strategies of the superpowers and their allies. The lifting of superpower pressure led to the emergence of new conditions in the sub-region. Our aim in this chapter and the next, therefore, is to try and account for the ways in which the sub-regional states have reacted and have been responding to the realities of a world without superpower presence on their soil or on their doorstep.

In the Red Sea sub-region, the backdrop to the post-Cold War situation, in which the superpowers did not compete for supremacy, was the intensification of a series of conflicts which had flared up in the 1980s. It is true that the 1980s produced the Soviet doctrine of 'balance of interests' with the West, but it is also the case that the decade was marked by serious security challenges for virtually every Red Sea country. Somalia, Ethiopia and Sudan were experiencing devastation on a grand scale; Saudi Arabia, Jordan and Egypt were distracted by the Iran–Iraq War, on the one hand, and the emergence of the strategic partnership between their neighbour Israel and their global ally, the United States, on the other; and Israel was embroiled in a bloody military campaign in Lebanon and increasingly at odds with the Palestinian population of the West Bank and Gaza who, by 1987, had embarked on a strategy of confrontation with Israel. The region, therefore, was already in flux when the Cold War ended.

The passing of the Cold War in the Red Sea resulted in a consolidation rather than the deconstruction of the sub-regional dynamics, whose origins can be traced to the Cold War itself and the course of superpower actions and rivalries in the area. Within the Red Sea sub-region, as elsewhere in the international system, the end of the Cold War caused a slow but definite diffusion of power among the regional players. That process itself enabled the larger littoral countries to seek to consolidate their positions in their respective regional systems. In the Red Sea sub-region, the uncertainties arising from its inherent instabilities provided extra incentives for the key Red Sea powers to develop their own role in the area.

Under the new circumstances, where no single patron was any longer in charge, one of the ways in which regional powers sought to strengthen their position was to establish new alliances, drawn largely from the wider MENA hinterland. As Lefebvre notes, with the superpowers taking a backseat, 'support provided by Middle East governments to local actors in the [Red Sea] region has become in the 1990s more critical to the survival of these regimes and opposition movements'.[1] Since 1990, therefore, an indelible mark has been left on the Red Sea political scene less by the actions of outside actors than by the behaviour of the dominant Red Sea actors themselves based on their strategic calculations.

Looking at the sub-region more closely, it is undeniable that the end of the Cold War created new inter-state relations, but what it did not do was terminate the many, largely civil, conflicts which had come to plague the area. Thus, the most serious of the Red Sea sub-region's civil conflicts, largely along the sea's western shores, in Sudan, Somalia, Ethiopia, and Djibouti, remained unresolved. Furthermore, tensions have not been absent from the east side of the sea either: while the Palestinian national struggle against the Israeli state has continued, albeit in somewhat of a different form since 1991, and particularly after the signing of the Oslo I and II Accords between the Palestinian Authority (PA) and Israel in the 1990s. The unification of Yemen in 1990 moreover merely acted as a prelude to other bloody confrontations, first, between North and South Yemenis in 1994, which ended in a decisive victory for the northerners, and more emphatically this century along confessional and tribal lines.

An explanation of the catalogue of political changes that the sub-region has experienced since 1990 is therefore badly needed if we are to be able to complete our mapping of the sub-region since the end of the Cold War. Looking back at the first decade of the post-Cold War era in the Red Sea area, we can say that the 1990s were a period of rapid political change, brought about largely, but not exclusively, by local actors and forces. While the catalyst for change was the end of superpower rivalry in the sub-region, the main instigator of change has undoubtedly been the Red Sea states themselves.

Red Sea political dynamics since the end of the Cold War

The first shock to the sub-region came with the political changes in Sudan in 1989. The political changes in that country were marked by the emergence of a radical military-Islamist regime in Khartoum, which unnerved all of Sudan's neighbours, and the deepening of the civil war in the south, with the consequent result of the weakening of central government control over vast tracts of territory in the south and east of the country. The deepening of the civil war in a post-Cold War setting, during which no superpower discipline on client states could check their regional ambitions, meant that other regional powers could – and did – intervene in that country's internal affairs. Apart from Egypt, which in any case has a special relationship with Sudan, every other East African and Horn country found itself embroiled in the civil war as well.

Khartoum's own behaviour, it has to be said, did not help matters either. Its support for Islamist groups from Egypt and elsewhere in Africa and other Red Sea countries meant that the government in Khartoum was increasingly seen as part of the problem in regional security terms, rather than a satisfactory outcome of the ending of superpower rivalry in the Red Sea. As the 1990s wore on, this certainly became the view of Washington and its core Red Sea military allies, Egypt and Israel. Thus, the Sudanese civil war, which intensified as a consequence of the Islamist victory in Khartoum, threatened to suck in several of the neighbouring countries, more often than not in support of the anti-Khartoum opposition forces. The policies of Sudan's neighbours, partly shaped by the adversarial behaviour of the ruling Islamist regime in Khartoum, complicated Sudan's relations with virtually all of its neighbours.

The regional problems associated with the Sudanese civil war have been particularly acute, and not solely because of the Islamist challenge to regional stability. With Sudan bordering nine African and Arab, Muslim and non-Muslim majority countries, inevitably its internal disputes reached a much wider circle of states. But inter-state tensions relating to Sudan's civil conflict have been most problematic for its southern and eastern neighbours (Uganda, Eritrea, Ethiopia), the very countries which have been prepared to provide shelter and protection for Sudanese opposition forces. Several times in the 1990s these tensions came close to open hostilities between Khartoum and its neighbours, causing a breach in diplomatic relations between Sudan and Eritrea in December 1994 and stretching Khartoum's ties with Addis Ababa after the June 1995 assassination attempt on President Mubarak's life while visiting Ethiopia. Until 1999, when a new chapter was opened in Eritrea–Sudanese relations, Eritrea continued to accuse Khartoum of attempts to destabilise the country by sponsoring two rebel groups, the Eritrean Islamic Jihad and the Eritrean Liberation Front.

Sudan's relations with its most important neighbour, Egypt, have also been a victim of domestic problems in both countries. On Egypt's side, the government of Hosni Mubarak was particularly concerned that Khartoum might be aiding its vibrant (and armed) Islamist opposition. Accusations that Khartoum is the safe haven for the Islamic Armed Group (GIA), and that it provides the training for its members, are often heard in Cairo. Egypt is also worried that Khartoum has been facilitating Iranian access to Egypt's violent Islamist forces. Such access, Egypt fears, could give another regional rival, Islamist Iran, considerable political and diplomatic leverage over Cairo, and also bring another regional power into the Red Sea. But more covertly, Egypt and others have feared that Khartoum would be giving Tehran the much vaunted access to the heartland of the Arab (and Sunni Muslim) world which it is said to have been pursuing for the best part of the past twenty years.[2] The third dimension of Cairo's interests in the Sudan is of course the Nile, on which both countries are almost completely dependent. It has never sat comfortably with Egypt, the more populous of the two states, that Sudan is the country lying upstream from it. Domestic Sudanese politics, therefore, are a part of Egypt's national concerns.[3]

Khartoum, on the other hand, has never disguised its suspicion that Cairo was the chief co-ordinator of the opposition to its leadership, which was the Arab world's only ruling radical Islamist regime. Sudanese Islamists argue that Egypt's policies stem from its age-old hegemonic ambition of bringing Sudan under its own tutelage. Sudan's worries about Egypt's policies have amplified over the years as the USA has also been seen to be drawing closer to Egypt's position. These tensions manifested themselves in direct political confrontations, rigidity over their border dispute, and confrontation in Arab and other regional fora. In one celebrated incident, Turabi himself accused Egypt of manipulating the Halayeb triangle dispute with Sudan, going as far as suggesting that Egyptians were jealous of the Sudanese and that they mocked the Sudanese people.[4]

Egypt's decision in 1998 to host the conference of the Sudanese opposition coalition, the National Democratic Alliance (NDA), was the clearest signal yet that Egypt was more actively involved in weakening the Khartoum regime, particularly as this move came only a few months after Cairo and Khartoum had signed a security co-operation agreement designed to control the activities of Sudan-based Egyptian Islamist groups. News of Egypt's involvement with the NDA was received with some dismay in Khartoum, partly because it indicated Egypt's more active involvement with an organisation that had managed to mount military operations as far north as the strategic city of Port Sudan and the Kassala area,[5] but more so because the NDA had already secured the support of Sudan's neighbours to the south, Ethiopia, Eritrea and Uganda, in its military campaign against Khartoum.[6] Sudan, thus, has been a constant source of instability in the Red Sea since the end of the Cold War.

The next post-Cold War development with major ramifications for the Red Sea states was the unification of Yemen in 1990, under a joint leadership dominated by the Sana'a political establishment. There was hope expressed at the time that the peaceful unification of Yemen would provide a new model of co-operation in Third World conflicts. Significantly, the unification scheme enjoyed the blessing of both the USA and the USSR, as well as Yemen's main regional rival, Saudi Arabia. The new Yemen was, geopolitically and strategically-speaking, an even more significant Red Sea country.

The unification mechanism, based on a shared leadership structure, moved quickly to start the task of 'standardising' the economic and political structures of what had evolved into very different societies and value systems.[7] The organisationally successful legislative elections of April 1993 provided more cement for the unity of Yemen, now the largest country in terms of population on the Arabian Peninsula. While the elections gave the majority of the seats to the northern-based General People's Congress (GPC), in another remarkable move after the election, the Yemen Socialist Party (YSP) of the south agreed to merge with its northern counterpart to create a single ruling party in Yemen.[8]

Peace in Yemen, however, proved to be short-lived as before too long pressures from within the two halves of the country surfaced to shatter the relative harmony which had prevailed since 1990. A new north–south Yemeni war in May–June 1994 led to a political divorce between the two political parties championing the unification drive, and finally allowed the GPC to emerge as the dominant party in the country. From then on, General Saleh had a free hand to bring all of the new country under his own control, which he set about doing with active support of the northern-based tribal and Islamist forces.

Domestic tensions notwithstanding, Sana'a moved quickly to develop Yemen's relations with the outside world, focusing on bettering relations with neighbouring and Red Sea Arab states (Oman, Egypt and Saudi Arabia in particular), European powers, China, Russia, and the United States. The country's closest to Yemen, however, were still those (largely Red Sea) Arab states which had found themselves on the 'wrong' side of the Iraq–Kuwait conflict, namely Jordan, Sudan and the Palestinians. More broadly, the priority for Yemen in the aftermath of the Kuwait crisis and its worsening economic situation (which was not helped by Saudi Arabia's decision to expel some one million Yemenis from the Kingdom, the cutting back of economic aid to Sana'a, and hampering Yemen's drive for oil in or near their disputed borderlands), was to recruit Western support for its slow-growing hydrocarbons industry.[9] It was not until after 1994 then that Yemen really emerged to act as a unitary player in the sub-region, by which time it had also developed a strategic vision of its role in the sub-region. A sense of its national economic needs and the potential role of hydrocarbons in helping it fulfil its national and regional aspirations had also begun to surface. The links between unification and Yemen's national economic development could not be more apparent: Yemen's oil output, though small by the standards of the chief Arab producers, increased substantially after unification, from 197,000 barrels per day (bpd) in 1991 to 350,000 bpd in 1995 to 390,000 bpd in 1997, to provide a real boost for a failing economy.[10] As Nonneman shows, higher oil output was one of the bright spots of an increasingly cloudy economic picture in Yemen, where the trade and current account deficits had reached $850 million and $1.3 billion respectively in 1994. The regional dimensions of Yemen's economic needs were to make their mark soon after. First, there was the steady escalation of the ongoing disputed territory with Saudi Arabia, then there was the rather rapid resolution of the Yemeni–Omani territorial dispute in 1992, and finally the eruption of a new territorial (island) dispute with the nascent republic of Eritrea a few years later.[11]

The solitary post-Cold War lesson that the southern Red Sea states have had to learn with regard to Yemen has been that a united Yemen, while it may be weak economically, is a much greater regional force to contend with than a half-Yemen with close links with a superpower (namely South Yemen and the USSR). The Yemenis, increasingly self-aware, are increasingly of the view that in today's unstable Red Sea sub-regional setting they hold one of the golden keys to stability. The leadership seems willing to share the key with its Red Sea friends, but more importantly, also to share its assets and geography with the remaining superpower (the United States) with a direct presence in the Persian Gulf sub-region as well as the wider regional system. United Yemen, itself a by-product of the end of the Cold War, has been able to demonstrate since the mid-1990s its potential to influence regional relations along both sides of the Red Sea, sometimes in quite unexpected ways. An example of Yemen's influence in the subregion since unification was its rather intimate ties with Arab Islamist groups. Several prominent Islamists and a number of such groups developed rather close relations with Yemeni tribal and Islamist political organisations in the course of the 1990s and found safe haven in Yemen throughout the period after the 1994 civil war. It was only in 1998 and 1999, after the murder in December 1998 of several Western tourists by a non-Yemenis armed Islamist group in Yemen, that the full extent of Yemen's involvement with Islamists from across the region came to light.[12] This was still before the events of 9/11 of course and the rise of al-Qaeda as a regional menace to haunt Yemen and its stability. By the late 1990s, pressures on Yemen from Britain, the USA and also Egypt to put its house in order and to curtail the activities of such groups as the Islamic Jihad and the Aden-Abyan Islamic Army had already been mounting. The Islamist connection has since threatened to damage Yemen's relations with two powerful Arab Red Sea countries, namely, Egypt and Saudi Arabia. Cairo has traced several of its radical Islamist opponents to Yemen and the Yemeni government has had little choice but to oblige Egypt and agree to the extradition of the known activists to Egypt.[13] In the case of Saudi Arabia, central government weakness in Yemen has been seen as a serious issue, which in Saudi eyes has not only encouraged al-Qaeda's presence there, but has also led the Shi'a communities (such as the Houthis) to develop into dangerous autonomous actors.

Within two years of the unification of Yemen, another of the Red Sea's taboos was also broken. 1993 came to mark a new beginning for war-torn Ethiopia, which for many years during the Cold War had come to be regarded as the strategic prize of the region. Free of superpower pressures and unable to sustain a military campaign against the Eritrean forces unaided, by the beginning of the 1990s Addis Ababa's resolve to pursue its long conflict with its Eritrean opponents had been broken. This was so even before the fall of the Marxist regime in Addis Ababa. Indeed, as Paul Henze suggests, in purely military terms, the equation had begun to change as early as 1990, well before the fall of the Dergue. As he argues, the capture of the strategic port of Massawa by the Eritrean People's Liberation Front (EPLF) in February 1990, enormously weakened the grip of the Ethiopian government on the Eritrean highlands – without access to which Addis Ababa could not hope to defeat the EPLF.[14] Assab was now the only port still under government control. The establishment of the State of Eritrea on 25 May 1993 opened the way for the creation of a new Red Sea republic, the first such development since the establishment of the People's Democratic Republic of Yemen.[15] For Eritrea to be born, Ethiopia had to forego much of its territory, including its entire Red Sea coastline, as well as swallow its attachment to territories which a large proportion of the Ethiopian people still regarded as their sovereign territory. The nature of Eritrea's birth, through a referendum and peaceful transfer of territory and power to a new political entity, did raise the prospect of peaceful co-existence between the two warring nations. In addition, the fact that both leaderships were products of liberation struggles with strong democratic aspirations engendered the hope that the formal divorce of the two peoples might lead to the establishment of new and mutually supportive partnerships between the two. Thus, the first government of Eritrea, headed by Isaias Afewerki of the socialist-oriented EPLF, took control of the destiny of the new state. It did so, however, by a process of exclusion, which left out of the new political establishment the largely Muslim Eritrean Liberation Front (ELF) which had traditionally enjoyed the support of the Red Sea Arab states. This act, as we shall see later, did leave the door open to tensions arising in Eritrea's relations with some of its Muslim neighbours.

The peaceful way in which the state of Eritrea was founded may have been a model of behaviour for the so-called 'New World Order', and one that the West was so anxious to encourage across the regional systems. But within five short years the two countries were at war, providing a major new inter-state flashpoint in the Red Sea. In 1999, with thousands killed on both sides, this new and dangerous inter-state conflict acquired the honour of being one of the bloodiest wars in the Third World. As we will show below, the post-1993 Eritrean–Ethiopian conflict has contributed to new tensions creeping into the region, but more worryingly, this war has also encouraged the other Red Sea states, as well as the larger African countries, to renew their efforts to get involved.

More immediately, the emergence of independent Eritrea and Ethiopia with friendly relations encouraged the rise of a new, Western-looking, East African grouping, championed and headed by Uganda. From 1993 until the rupture in Ethiopian–Eritrean relations, the three countries provided a united, co-ordinated and sustained front against Sudan's Islamist regime, for example. This trilateral relationship provided very direct and tangible benefits for the Sudanese opposition groups, in terms of shelter, arms, training, resources and access to the outside world, but also benefits for the partners to boot. In 1996, for instance, the United States chose to reward this 'containment belt' of countries around southern Sudan by providing them with $20 million for what were said to be 'defensive purposes'.[16]

The break-up of Ethiopia after the Cold War then changed the political geography of the Red Sea, as it created the conditions for new, regionally-focused, alliances to emerge. Ultimately also such changes provided the ingredients, in terms of diverging interests and lingering animosities, for new conflicts to surface. So, while after years of labour pains the birth of Eritrea proved to be a peaceful affair, this new state was leaving a definite mark on the sub-region. Its presence was soon felt by two of its Arab neighbours, Sudan and Yemen; in the former, through support for its armed opponents and, in the latter, in the course of a short naval battle over the control of the Hanish Islands. But it was not until 1998 that the separation of Eritrea and Ethiopia came to disrupt again the slowly emerging post-Cold War balance of power in the southern Red Sea.

Changing focus somewhat now, the southern end of the Red Sea was not the only zone to respond to the realities of a post-Cold War world. At the other end of the sea, the longest conflict, and said to be the most intractable of all, was, by the end of 1990, entering a new and dynamic phase as well. On the back of the

Kuwait crisis a new momentum was generated in the area to seek a peaceful resolution of one of the great and open wounds of the MENA sub-system. Ironically, it was the Kuwait crisis that provided the impetus for tackling once and for all the Arab–Israeli conflict. The Kuwait crisis highlighted the continuing dangers that ongoing Arab–Israeli tensions posed for the post-Cold War international order.

Thus, the Arab–Israeli conflict, the main strategic feature of the sub-system for more than a generation, entered a new phase. Under the supervision of the United States, the October 1991 peace talks in Madrid provided the momentum for open contact between the Arab states and Israel. The Madrid Conference provided the forum for 'first contact' between several adversaries. At this early stage, the other northern Red Sea states either enthusiastically endorsed the Madrid process (Egypt and Jordan) or participated in it with some reservations (the PLO and Saudi Arabia). The PLO, which was forced to be part of a joint Jordanian-Palestinian delegation at the Madrid talks, soon began looking for a more independent voice in the negotiations with Israeli delegates. Saudi Arabia, on the other hand, was more cautious and remained concerned about the possible damage to its reputation regionally and its legitimacy domestically if it displayed too much overt support for the process. In addition, the Saudis were constrained by the Islamic dimension of the conflict and the question of Jerusalem and Muslim rights and also access to this holy city. Riyadh did, however, support the lifting of secondary sanctions on Israel after the Palestinian–Israeli Declaration of Principles (DoP) were signed, which were quickly translated into a boon for the Israeli economy during Rabin's premiership.

After nearly 50 years of conflict, in two short years after the start of the Madrid talks, the breakthrough came. In 1993, and despite many outstanding and unresolved problems, the process changed gear and entered a new, unexpected and rapid phase of reconciliation between some of the Arab parties and Israel. So, in September of that year in Washington, after months of secret diplomacy in Oslo and elsewhere, the PLO established relations with Israel. Within a year of the Palestinian–Israeli agreement which, for the first time since 1948, gave a purely Palestinian political authority access to, and control of, some parts of Palestinian territory, Jordan was to follow suit and establish diplomatic relations with Israel. Within three years of the ending of the Cold War then, not only had Israel and some of its Arab neighbours managed to improve their relations, but they had apparently also managed to move the agenda forward from a confrontational zero-sum game towards a win–win scenario based on economic co-operation.

In the meantime, the Israeli government took full advantage of the new atmosphere to develop relations with the rest of the international community and also with several Arab states further afield, most notably, Kuwait, Qatar, Oman, Morocco and Tunisia. Few Arab states actually maintained an openly adversarial posture towards Israel any longer. Ironically, of those Arab countries still retaining an ambivalent position on the peace process, several were located in the Red Sea sub-region: Sudan, Saudi Arabia and Yemen in particular.[17]

Red Sea inter-state conflicts in the new era

For all the talk of a New World Order prevailing in the MENA sub-system after the restoration of Kuwait's sovereignty in 1991, inter-state conflict grew to become one of the features of the Red Sea sub-region in the first post-Cold War decade. Between 1989 and 2000, virtually every southern Red Sea country was in conflict with one or more of its neighbours. Generally speaking, the most important (and visible) of Red Sea conflicts in the 1990s tended to occur on the eastern shores of the Sea, largely originating from earlier conflicts and tensions. Thus, the main conflicts which caused general tensions in the sub-region invariably included Sudan, Ethiopia, Eritrea and their neighbours. Elsewhere, inter-state conflict focused on the Red Sea states of Saudi Arabia and Yemen and their long-standing border dispute.[18]

For our purposes, we have identified five Red Sea conflict situations in the first decade of the post-Cold War era which need further examination. These being: the conflict between Sudan and its neighbours; the Ethiopian–Eritrean conflict; Saudi–Yemen border clashes; the Yemen–Eritrea conflict; and the Ethiopia–Somalia tensions.

Sudan and its neighbours

Sudan has been an Arab pariah state since 1989, for the policies of its Islamist government in the 1990s and for the war in its Darfur region in the 2000s. Among the Red Sea countries too, its Islamist government has been a cause for concern. Egypt, Eritrea, Ethiopia, in particular have become increasingly embroiled in the Sudanese civil war. Part of the impetus for seeking to influence events in Sudan was a direct response to the regional and international activities of the Islamist regime itself. As Khartoum became more involved in Arab Islamist politics in the 1990s – support for Hamas in the Occupied Territories, for Egypt's radical Islamist groups, for Osama Bin Laden, for the FIS in Algeria and the Tunisian Nahda Party, the alleged assassination attempt on President Mubarak, support for Islamic groups in Ethiopia and Eritrea, to name but a few – so those Red Sea states likely to be directly affected by Sudan's new policies took a keen interest in that country's foreign relations.

Sudan's geography and the government's inability to police its entire territory have meant that what might have been its domestic affairs has easily found a regional dimension. In the south, where the civil war was at its most intense, Ethiopia was already heavily involved even under the Dergue. Addis Ababa was providing a wide range of facilities for the SPLA: direct military support (planes, helicopters trucks for transportation, for instance), help in military operations, training camps, logistical centres, and a radio station.[19] Since then, as already mentioned, both Ethiopia and Eritrea have been militarily active against Khartoum. For Khartoum, both these countries' anti-Sudan policies reflected a wider agenda: their desire to draw closer to Sudan's main ideological adversary, the United States. Since the mid-1990s, tensions between Sudan and its southern neighbours have threatened to escalate into open warfare. Indeed, until Eritrea's own problems with Ethiopia erupted in 1998, Asmara had made the overthrow of Sudan's Islamist government one of its main foreign policy objectives. President Afeworki had declared as far back as October 1995 that 'we are out to see that [the Sudanese] government is not there any more ... We will give weapons to anyone committed to overthrowing it'.[20] Sudan-Ethiopian relations were not much better. Despite attempts by both parties to maintain cordiality after the fall of the Dergue in Ethiopia, by the mid-1990s, relations had deteriorated to a dangerous level. By then, Khartoum was regularly referring to the Ethiopian president as an American agent, and Addis Ababa would increasingly be found aiding the Sudanese opposition forces.[21]

The Ethiopian–Eritrean conflict

To the south of Sudan, the cause of stability in the Horn of Africa was dealt a serious blow in the second half of the 1990s with the escalation of violence between Ethiopia and Eritrea, two countries with close and deepening relations with the United States. With ample evidence to the contrary, virtually every Red Sea country was adamant that it would not like to get involved on either side in this conflict.

After five years of peaceful co-existence and cordial relations underpinned by the close association between PM Meles Zenawi and President Isaias Afeworki,[22] during which period virtually all of Ethiopia's trade with the outside world was conducted through the Eritrean Red Sea ports of Assab and Massawa, fighting exploded along their long joint border in May 1998. The 400 sq km Badme region, which both countries claimed, was the partial cause of the first round of fighting between the two countries, as relations had begun to turn sour in 1997, when Eritrea chose to separate its economic path from Ethiopia's by introducing its own currency and slowly changing labour migration patterns between the two countries.[23] Ethiopia's response was to require all future payments from Eritrea to be made in hard currency, a very scarce commodity in the new republic, and refusing to accept the proposal that the Eritrean Nakfa and the Ethiopian Birr be legal tender in both countries.[24] Ethiopia's decision to transfer its trade away from the Red Sea port of Assab virtually closed the port down, ironically making thousands of Ethiopian port workers unemployed in the process.[25] But the biggest blow was to the war-oriented Eritrean economy.

By the end of June it was clear that Eritrean forces, who had initiated the hostilities, had taken control of the disputed Badme region. Ethiopia, looking for a solution to the conflict, chose to accept international mediation and bowed to an OAU cease-fire plan presented in November, which the victorious party failed to accept. Ethiopia's decision, however, was preceded by a mass deportation of several thousand Eritreans living and working in the country.[26] Thus, although the fighting did die down, tensions remained high between November and February, by which time Ethiopia, having regrouped militarily, felt obliged to return to the battlefield.[27] By this time both parties had devoted substantial financial assets to military procurement, which in turn strengthened the role of external and regional powers in the conflict. Advanced Russian weaponry found its way into the armouries of both countries: Su-27 fighter-bombers in case of Ethiopia and MiG-29 fighters in the case of Eritrea.[28] Italy provided Asmara with attack helicopters, China has been engaged in selling large quantities of ammunition to Ethiopia, while Bulgaria was supplying both sides (BM21 multi-barrelled rocket-launchers to Eritrea and over 100 T-55 tanks to Ethiopia).[29] The most powerful Red Sea actor, Israel, which already had a contract with Ethiopia for upgrading and refurbishing 50 of its mothballed MiG-21 and MiG-23 fighters, was also being linked to the Eritrean military build-up. It has been estimated that by the end of 1998, Ethiopia had taken delivery of eight Su-27s and Eritrea as many as 10 MiG-29s, both countries joining a small group of Sub-Saharan African countries with such high-tech military hardware (see Chapter 4 for a closer look at the military aspects of the conflict).[30]

As already mentioned, Ethiopia added an economic dimension to the war by denying Eritrea the benefits of trans-shipment fees and also hurting Asmara by denying it access to its much larger economy, on whose market 67 per cent of Eritrea's exports depended. For the Eritreans, the military aspect of targeting the Assab area was the perceived Ethiopian plan to create a territorial corridor to the Red Sea and also to take control of parts or all of the port.[31]

On the diplomatic front too, there was much activity to observe, dating back to the first round of fighting in May 1998. In 1998 and 1999, Asmara turned to Yemen, with which it had fought in 1995, and Egypt to use their good offices and mediate between the two sides.[32] For its part, Ethiopia was less keen to see Egypt or Yemen directly involved. With Egypt, Ethiopia still had major differences of opinion and approach with regard to Somalia. As far as Yemen was concerned, Addis Ababa was already concerned that Sana'a was not only emerging as an important ally of Asmara, but was actively engaged in helping the Eritreans and the Somalis to arm and train the ethnic Ethiopian Oromos against the Tigrayan-dominated government in Addis Ababa.[33] Furthermore, reports reaching Addis Ababa that Yemeni groups and individuals, albeit perhaps loosely associated with the government, were smuggling weapons across the Red Sea to the Eritrean forces ensured that Sana'a would not get a fair hearing in Ethiopia.[34]

Nonetheless, Yemen, Egypt and several other Red Sea countries had already expressed deep concern about the fighting. For Egypt, as many of its officials were at pains to show, stability in the Horn of Africa was the most important goal. As its officials put it, while Egypt was not going to ignore 'any military conflict in the region', it was 'not going to get into the game of taking sides' in this conflict either, being content to let the US–Rwanda peace initiative to take its course. One unnamed Egypt official, however, did express the worry that the fighting between Ethiopia and Eritrea could allow regional actors, notably Israel, to play out their grievances against each other in the Horn, an area of vital importance to Egypt. Israel's close relations with the two countries, the official said, 'while perfectly legitimate ... could well turn out to be harmful to Egyptian interests, if Israel decided that Egypt was obstructing the development of its relations with

Arab countries and sought to hit back'.[35] Egypt was also concerned with the growing role of Yemen in the Horn, a country that Cairo has regarded as a potential rival in relation to the Arabian Peninsula and one that has been known to have provided shelter for Egypt's Islamist opponents. Israel, in the meanwhile, viewed 'with grave concern the fighting between Ethiopia and Eritrea', two countries, it reminded the world, with which it maintained 'friendly relations'.[36] In strategic terms, however, both Israel and Egypt were to find themselves leaning towards Eritrea. The former, keen on having a strong non-Arab riparian state in the strategic Horn zone had little option but to assist Asmara, while Egypt, still worried about Ethiopia's position in relation to the Nile, was also interested in seeing a weak Ethiopia, hoping that a weak Ethiopia would not be able to resist Egypt's policies with relation to the Upper Nile and the Horn.

Regionally, both Sudan and Yemen took advantage of the war to improve their relative position. In Sudan's case, it seized the moment and capitalised on the tensions between Ethiopia and Eritrea, both active backers of Khartoum's opponents, by unleashing a new offensive against the SPLA and its allies in the south. The battles in February and March produced many casualties on the opposition side. The war also allowed Khartoum to try and strengthen its bargaining position and also to stiffen its resolve in its negotiations with the opposition groups. In Yemen's case, the start of Ethiopia's February 1999 offensive coincided with the start of a new round of bilateral border talks between Sana'a and Asmara regarding their maritime boundary.[37] With its back against the wall, Asmara was much more susceptible to Sana'a's overtures (which Yemen carefully underlined by helping Eritrea militarily) on the dispute and agreed to direct talks on the establishment of the maritime boundary between the two countries.[38] Assessing the information coming out of Sana'a and Asmara, direct contact between the two sides must have started about the same time as the Ethiopian offensive. The talks, according to Yemeni sources, were conducted in a friendly and 'very cordial atmosphere'.[39] So much so that the parties agreed to side-step the established channels of arbitration and the court. Curiously, Yemen's improving relations with Eritrea were underwritten by Libya, which had been busy bankrolling Eritrea's war effort and Asmara's assistance to Ethiopia's opposition movements.

The new Ethiopian offensive, launched on 6 February 1999, yielded quick results and the return of Badme to Ethiopian control, at least for a time. But during this phase of the conflict the border war spread to other disputed parts of the border, notably the Zalambessa. Within days of the Ethiopian offensive, fighting had spread to three fronts along their long joint border, encompassing a 1,000-km front.

Despite thousands of casualties in its battles, Addis Ababa pronounced the February–March 1999 offensive a great success.[40] Ethiopian statements in late March spoke of some 45,000 Eritreans having been killed, wounded or captured since 23 February, 77 Eritrean tanks destroyed, 19 captured, and two MiG-29s downed.[41] Eritrea, on the other hand, maintained that Addis Ababa was paying a heavy price for its offensive, with many thousands killed or wounded, and 'two [Ethiopian] brigades were completely routed and another two brigades severely battered'.[42] More ominous still, Eritrea claimed that its close ally during the war of liberation, the Tigray People's Liberation Front, was actively engaged in the campaign, and was enlisting what it termed 'foreign mercenaries' to fly the helicopter gunships and fighter aircraft that Ethiopia had deployed.[43] Deployment of air power was itself a violation of the moratorium on air strikes.

Asmara, despite its initial military successes in fighting during February, was nonetheless feeling the pressure sufficiently to agree to talk, and readily accepted the original OAU peace plan on 27 February. This gesture, however, the Ethiopians rejected as 'insincere'. Eritrea backed its new position with a promise that it conditionally withdraw from parts of the disputed territories. The intense fighting, which did not cease with Ethiopia's battlefield victories in February 1999, merely strengthened the resolve of the parties to gain the upper hand.[44]

The tense Ethiopian–Eritrean relations were not helped by the residual memory of the bitter years of warfare between Eritreans and other groups in Ethiopia, the Tigrayans' decision (who had spearheaded the creation of the EPLF and in whose territory the border conflict was now brewing) to remain in Ethiopia, and the deep-rooted ethnic tensions between the Tigrayans, who largely found themselves at the head of the Ethiopian government after the fall of the Dergue and the Amhara, from whose ethnic group Ethiopia's ruling elite traditionally hailed, and who have not fully reconciled themselves to the separation of Eritrea from their country.[45] In this part of the sub-region, it seems, despite many common features among neighbouring countries (the fact that the governments of Ethiopia and Eritrea hail from the Tigrayan ethnic group, for example), which ought to provide the gel for closer co-operation, once unleashed, tensions tend to spiral, particularly as the ever-present complex ethnic and politico-historical webs tend to tighten the knots in the fabric that still holds these two countries together. The pursuit of the 'national interest', infused with memories of past battles and grievances, provided the logic for a highly intense conflict situation that has seemed hard to comprehend by Western observers, many of whom were convinced that after the traumas of Cold War-related regional politics a new peaceful order was returning to the war-torn Horn. Conflict, never fully absent from the area, returned to the east side of the Red Sea with a vengeance. This has been so, partly because of the lingering legacy of past misdeeds, partly a result of a new scramble for territory and resources, and partly due to the fact that no mechanisms have been developed as a means of containing tensions. On top of all this is the unresolved problem of ethnico-politics in the Horn. As Ali has noted, the ethnically-based expansionist and hegemonic ambitions of groups and actors in the area have not ceased; indeed, the lifting of Cold War curtain could be said to have worsened this problem.[46]

Other potential problems which could be in store for the two countries themselves, as well as for relations between them, relate to the political make-up of Eritrean and Ethiopian governments. In the former, the exclusion of the non-Tigrayans, who also happen to be largely Muslims, from the government machinery is slowly eroding the powerbase of the government, storing problems for the future. Also, as the non-Tigrayan Eritreans begin to mobilise, and in some instances seek support from neighbouring Muslim and Arab countries, so they will establish closer and closer links with outside forces. In so doing, they will, in due course, open up access to the country to other regional actors, and in their attempts to redress what they regard to be a political imbalance in their country, will create the conditions for new regional conflicts and, ultimately, further destablisation of the Horn.

In Ethiopia, the political problem is associated with the fact that the Tigrayans, who make up less than 10 per cent of the country's population, have taken charge of the country. The location of the Ethiopian rulers' Tigray region, which is a poor border zone in the north of the country and geographically and ethnically very far from the rest of the country, raised the suspicion of other ethnic groups in the country that theirs is a sectarian regime with little interest in the development of the rest of the country. In such a charged atmosphere, in the first few years that it took power the Ethiopian government had to show that it was fully committed to the preservation of Ethiopia and its national integrity and, where necessary, to fight for it. The war with Eritrea, despite the fact that the Asmara regime is also dominated by Tigrayans, is one of the macabre examples of the ways in which ethnico-politics are still shaping politics of the Horn zone. As is clear from the Eritrean and Ethiopian examples, apart from creating the conditions for change, the end of the Cold War had very little impact on inter-state and inter-ethnic relations in this part of the world. To underline this point, we can also refer to the three-day war in 2008 between Djibouti and Eritrea, which itself was a result of rising tensions between the two countries dating back to the 1990s. This brief war did not resolve any of the border and related access issues between Djibouti and Eritrea and only aggravated Asmara's relations with another of its neighbours and raised the security temperature around an already overheated Horn region. Having occurred nearly 10 years after (in April 1996), the two countries almost went to war over sovereign control of some territories on their joint border, the neighbours (most notably Ethiopia) have understandably become very sensitive to any instability in Djibouti, for the stakes have also grown immeasurably. For both countries the transit route has become a true lifeline, providing Ethiopia with reliable access to the global economy; and Djibouti with desperately needed employment and business opportunities. Thus, in the period between 1996 and 2007, cargo traffic to Ethiopia increased five-fold: from around 3 million tonnes to 14.2 million tonnes, now accounting for almost all of Ethiopia's overland trade.[47]

Saudi–Yemen border clashes

Inter-state tensions are also evident on the eastern side of the Red Sea. Border clashes between Yemeni and Saudi forces, for example, were not a new development, but the fact that they continued, more or less unchecked after the unification of Yemen in 1990, made this a cause for concern. For much of the 1990s, both countries remained highly suspicious of each other and failed to find a satisfactory solution to their border dispute. One reason for this was that the wider political and geopolitical factors continuously hampered better relations. Saudi fears of a strong Yemen to challenge its position on the Peninsula were matched by Yemeni concerns that their richer neighbour was bent on weakening a united Yemen through all kinds of economic, military and political pressures.

The border clashes, though brief, did little to instil confidence in Riyadh and Sana'a. In January 1995, for instance, when Saudi and Yemeni forces clashed on several places along their long border, it took direct pressure from the United States to bring the two sides to the negotiating table.[48] In July 1998, their forces clashed again, this time in an attempt to gain control of the Red Sea island of al-Duaima.[49] These clashes have proved much less dramatic and intensive than other inter-state conflicts in the Red Sea since the end of the Cold War. Having settled their border and territorial disputes in 2000, relations between the two countries improved immeasurably, bringing Saudi military and financial support for the Yemeni forces in their domestic conflicts with the Shi'a al-Houthi tribe and also al-Qaeda in the 2000s.

The Yemen–Eritrea conflict

The armed clashes between Yemeni and Eritrean forces over the Hanish Islands in 1995 were a warning to all neighbouring countries that relations in the southern Red Sea zone as a whole were far from stable. The war started suddenly and at the initiative of Eritrea, which was laying claim to these strategically placed islands. Having used these islands as military bases during their long war of liberation, the Eritreans resorted to the use of force in an attempt to warn off Yemen from attempting to develop the islands and their surrounding waters.[50] The brief military campaign of 15–18 December 1995 resulted in Eritrean occupation of Hanish al-Kabir island in this chain of islands near the Bab el-Mandeb choke point.Within 24 hours, the attacking force of 2,000 troops and 45 gunboats had taken the island, and 160 members of the 500-strong Yemeni garrison on the island were held captive. The imbalance of forces (Eritrea had inherited a reasonable naval force from Ethiopia but had no air force, while Yemen had a reasonable air force and no navy), however, and lack of adequate hardware to conduct an intensive off-shore military campaign did mean that the conflict would not easily escalate. But this brief conflict caused much anxiety among other Red Sea powers. Some Arab states, already suspicious of the Eritrean–Israeli relationship, feared that Israel, for its own strategic calculations, had been an active partner of Eritrea in its assault on Hanish al-Kabir. This perception, which had become Arab conventional wisdom by early 1996, was reinforced by President Afeworki's 4-hour visit to Israel in February to meet with Israeli leaders. Israel itself poured more fuel on the fire by admitting that for strategic reasons it regarded Eritrea as an important Red Sea friend. Good relations with Asmara were said to be 'of great importance because of the country's geo-strategic position on Israel's maritime and air routes to Africa and the Far East'.[51]

On the Arab side, both Egypt and Saudi Arabia adopted a fairly pro-Sana'a attitude, at times even blaming Israel more than Eritrea for the invasion. Yemen itself had already accused Israel of supplying Eritrea with military hardware as well as advice and personnel for the attack.[52] To many, the occupation was nothing more than Israel's drive for a presence at the southern end of the Red Sea.[53] But at another level both countries could find some strategic gains in Yemen's troubles. For the Saudis, Yemen's new dispute with Eritrea merely helped them in their border troubles with the united Yemen. Yemen, it was thought, could not sustain a campaign on more than one front. Another thought was that such a conflict, if prolonged, could bring Yemen to seek assistance from its Arab neighbour, thus helping to weaken its resolve in its negotiations with the Saudis.[54]

By early January 1999, when Eritrea was required by the international tribunal to accept Yemeni sovereignty over the islands, this border conflict had been reduced to a set of friendly discussions over technicalities rather than diplomatic pasturing for the sake of gaining geopolitical advantage.[55] Nonetheless, the conflict did highlight several potential problems in this volatile region. First, the ease with which simmering tensions can escalate into flashpoints. Second, the ease with which the Red Sea powers act in the sub-region in search of strategic gain. Third, it is clear that in addition to inter-Arab problems, there are continuing tensions between the Red Sea's Arab and non-Arab members, particularly in terms of the deep suspicions that the Arab side still has of Israel and its motives. Fourth, one can not help but be struck by the fluidity of alliances between Red Sea states. Our evidence suggests that since the end of the Cold War, these have been compounded by a deep sense of distrust of the neighbouring states' motives.

The Ethiopia–Somalia tensions

Finally, let us turn to one of the oldest inter-state Cold War wounds in the Horn, which unfortunately has continued to bleed. The sporadic clashes between Ethiopian troops and Somali rebels and 'warlords' did not cease with the end of the Cold War and the withdrawal of superpower involvement. Part of the problem has undoubtedly been the lawlessness in Somalia that has prevailed there since 1991.[56] The absence of any central authority in Somalia since the withdrawal of the US marines in 1993 has tended to exacerbate tribal and ethnic factionalism in that country, and has encouraged the rise of powerful, regionally-based 'warlords'.[57]

One of the results of factional divisions in Somalia has been the deepening of animosities between the pro- and anti-Ethiopian groups in the country. Addis Ababa, which has been worried about the activities of anti-Ethiopian ethnic and political groups residing in the Ethiopian–Somali borderlands (in particular among the Oromos, who are ethnic Somalis, and the militant al-Ittihad al-Islam group), has maintained substantial military forces in and around the Ogaden region in readiness throughout the post-Cold War period. Ethiopia also tried to build a close relationship with the self-proclaimed Somaliland republic under Mohammed Ibrahim Egal.[58]

Nonetheless, news reports emerging from these remote border regions often speak of continuing conflict between Ethiopian troops and Somalis.[59] 1998 in particular was a bad year for Ethiopian–Somali relations. During that year, undoubtedly encouraged by the political anarchy in Somalia, Ethiopian troops made repeated incursions into Somalia. In Spring 1999, at the height of their border tensions with Eritrea, a motorised battalion of Ethiopian troops, aboard tanks and armoured personnel carriers, were again in action in Somalia, in pursuit of rebel forces and also in search of military hardware. A Somali faction, the Somali National Front, has alleged that Ethiopian troops engaged in looting military stores during their two-day incursion in March 1999.[60] They entered the eastern regional town of Balanbale and over two days had cleared it of valuable military and civilian equipment.

Despite the continuing warfare between Ethiopia and its Somali-based enemies, it is clear that no end will be in sight so long as central authority is not restored in Somalia. The anarchy in Somalia continues to fuel Ethiopia's anxieties and will keep this part of the Horn a highly militarised and unstable region for years to come. This rather tense situation was not helped, of course, by reports that anti-Ethiopian forces were being armed by Eritrea through the good offices of the infamous Aideed family, whose forces controlled the Somali capital and the nearby airport.[61] Additionally, Addis Ababa was increasingly sensitive about reports that substantial aid was heading to the al-Ittihad from Sudan and Libya. Sudan, already in a regional partnership with Libya,[62] was seeking to counter Ethiopian support for its rebels by developing a front against Ethiopia on its southern borders. Ironically, another of Khartoum's opponents, Eritrea, is also pursuing the same game with the assistance of Yemen. As one Somali faction leader has explained, 'Eritrea wants to arm Ethiopian opposition groups through Aideed to create tensions in the Somali-dominated eastern Ethiopian region of Ogaden'.[63] Thus, Somalia, in anarchy and without government for much of the period since the end of the Cold War, has emerged as the battleground of competing Red Sea states. In this deadly game, Ethiopia stands to lose a great deal if the forces ranged against it do manage to destabilise its eastern and southern borderlands.

Other problems can also surface to destabilise the Horn and its hinterland. Eritrea's border quarrels with Saudi Arabia and Djibouti, for instance, which Asmara raised in the midst of the Hanish Islands dispute with Yemen, could easily escalate into open conflict.[64] As indeed could again localised fighting around the tiny Horn state of Djibouti.

Inter-state relations into the twenty-first century

Above all, it will be the nature, type and tempo of inter-state relations, combined with the role and strategic concerns of the United States, as the remaining superpower and the one with substantial military presence in the sub-system, which will determine the dynamics of the Red Sea sub-region into the twenty-first century. The new millennium began with many of the sub-region's deep strategic problems remaining unresolved. The Arab–Israeli peace process ground to a halt after the Clinton presidency and only began showing signs of life in 2010 when President Obama made the resolution of the Palestinian–Israeli problem a top diplomatic priority. But the fate of the process is far from clear and the domestic tensions in both Israel and Palestine will mean that lasting peace remains a distant dream still. Absence of peace will continue to affect Israel's relations with its Red Sea neighbours and will not help establishment of diplomatic relations between Tel Aviv and Riyadh.

Sudan remains in a state of crisis. While the largely Christian southern regions of the country stumble towards formal independence from Khartoum, in the west, problems in Darfur leave the central government stretched and exposed to international pressure and sanctions. In the 2000s the conflict in Darfur has done much to fracture the country even more profoundly and also to isolate it internationally; yet the peace agreement with the SPLM-led (Sudan People's Liberation Movement) forces in the south in 2005 did provide a glimmer of hope for a peaceful transfer of power from Khartoum to the regions. The rub, however, will come in the aftermath of the 2011 referendum in the south and the population's support for formal separation from the rest of the country. The undoing of another Red Sea state in less than 20 years since the end of the Cold War (the other being Ethiopia in the early 1990s) will have many implications for the politics, economics and security dynamics of the sub-region. Our previous example of national disaggregation, though conducted peacefully at the outset, shows that in a relatively short period of time bilateral hostilities can become a precursor for more violence and protracted conflict to engulf the sub-region. Given the troubled history of relations between north and south of Sudan, concerns about the medium-term consequences of Sudan's break-up, given its greater geographical reach and its much more complex relationship with its neighbours, are real and growing. Lack of confidence in the south's ability to produce a stable post-referendum government, moreover, has generated a different set of issues for the sub-region: will the new government be democratic or proletarian?, will the new state cause rapid disruption by scrambling to seize as much of Sudan's natural resources as possible?, will it act as a safe haven for anti-Arab/Islamic forces in the region?, will it cultivate a close relationship with the United States (to the detriment of Arab interests in Palestine and East Africa, and with regard to Egypt's interests over the Nile)?, and, finally, will it adopt a hostile or co-operative posture towards Khartoum? Emerging answers to such questions will likely provide the essence of the 'post-Sudan' sub-regional geopolitical environment.

Sudan's status as a fragile entity has not improved, placing it in the same category as Yemen on the tip of the Arabian Peninsula. Indeed, fragilities in Yemen in the 2000s have become so pronounced that it has arguably been drifting towards a failed state status. Alarmed by the prospect of state collapse, under pressure from tribal divisions and a resurgent al-Qaeda, Saudi Arabia and the United States have become more directly involved in efforts to stabilise and also counter its domestic radical forces. The USA now provides millions of dollars in annual aid and security assistance to Yemen, and Saudi Arabia in 2009 deployed its far superior military power in order to bring under control the Shi'a-led Houthi rebellion on the Yemeni-side of its border. More than 150 Saudi soldiers may have been killed in these operations, marking the Kingdom's largest military losses since 1991. Despite the growing external security support for the Yemeni government, evidence of domestic stabilisation is weak and the peninsula branch of al-Qaeda remains active and menacing. If this was not enough, at the same time, Saudi Arabia's construction of a security barrier, which has been pursued since 2004, on the border of the two countries has again caused some tensions between them, enraging the Yemeni side since work on it accelerated in 2008. According to military sources in Yemen, 'Yemeni border guards tried to stop Saudis from building the new wall. In response, the Saudis mobilized their military and threatened force if they were unable to start construction of the barriers'.[65] This is hardly a promising development in an already problematic relationship between weakened Yemen and a dominant Saudi Arabia, as work on the barrier was preceded by mass deportation of more than 60,000 Yemeni nationals from the Kingdom in 2007. Many of the deportees were former residents of the adjacent Harad district. More generally though, the barrier will store more trouble for Yemen as:

> of the untold numbers of Somali and Ethiopian refugees that arrive on the shores of Yemen daily, those who make their way to Saudi Arabia usually travel through the Harad district. Those still in Yemen hear from the odd ones who make it to Saudi Arabia and believe that the trip is possible for them too. Since Yemen itself offers few job prospects for the migrants, most head to Saudi Arabia or other Gulf states, where the need for menial labor is much greater.[66]

To make matters worse, the conflict with the al-Houthi rebels in 2009 prompted the Saudi military to put in place a much more extensive border fence to cover the entire 1,600-km border, as an immediate measure to contain the Shi'a from crossing into the Kingdom. The Saudi Army has also reinforced its presence along the Yemeni border: M1A2 main battle tanks, Bradley infantry fighting vehicles, Piranha LAV-25 armoured vehicles, and AH-64D Apache Longbow attack helicopters now regularly patrol the long and rugged border. Reinforcing Saudi nervousness about the fragility of Yemen, it emerged that its navy had imposed a blockade of Yemen's northern Red Sea coast to Bab el-Mandeb to prevent the flow of weapons to the rebels. In terms of the wider geopolitical picture, the announcement that in military operations in late November 2009 that as many as 75 Ethiopians and 70 Somalis had been captured along the Yemeni border, underlined the growing security links now present across the sub-region. This reality was further reinforced by other reports that in late 2009 Jordan also had reportedly deployed several hundred troops from its special operations forces to help the Saudi military: 'Western intelligence sources report that Jordanian King Abdullah was acting on a request from his Saudi counterpart. The sources add that the need for additional troops came when Saudi units dominated by Shiites refused to fight the al-Houthi rebels.'[67] The reality that Red Sea states now had a series of common problems which needed collective action was very clear to the parties. The awareness that Red Sea states had little option but to address the growing role of non-state actors threatening the sub-region's security collectively also emerged in the course of the 2000s, after many years of inaction.

But Saudi unilateral action, in terms of limiting transit access through Yemen to Saudi Arabia and the other GCC countries will ultimately mean that the bulk of such migrants stay in an already overstretched Yemen and thus put further pressure on its meagre resources, to the detriment of its stability and that of its Arabian Peninsula neighbours.

On the eastern coast of the Red Sea, Eritrea, Ethiopia and Somalia each pose unique problems of their own and their bilateral interactions continue to challenge the sub-region's security around the Horn of Africa. Take Eritrea, referred to as the 'siege state' by the International Crisis Group in 2010.[68] Developments in Eritrea provide an overview of the eastern Red Sea's problems since the end of the Eritrea-Ethiopia war in 2000. It is said that militarism and authoritarianism define the political culture of Eritrea and its culture of militarism is reinforced by years of conflict and the siege mentality dominating the country's worldview. Its militarism 'profoundly impacts its politics, society and economy, [and] causes the fragility which characterises national life and affects foreign policy and the stability of the surrounding region'.[69] The view that Ethiopia remains the enemy at the gates feeds the state's 'permanent war' mentality and the elite's view that the international community is at best neglectful of the country and its precarious situation and at worst hostile to Eritrea's interests. To be fair, the Ethiopia-hosted Eritrean Democratic Alliance (a coalition of 13 opposition groups), since 2008 Eritrea's so-called 'government in exile', will have helped fuel Asmara's suspicions and fears of direct intervention in its internal affairs by its bigger neighbour.

Under these conditions, Eritreans have felt compelled to reinforce their military establishment, as their first line of defence in this hostile regional environment. The social pressures from such a militarised state are such that hundreds of young Eritreans flee the country every month, constituting a massive brain and skills drain for an already vulnerable economy. The loss of access to its main markets in Ethiopia since the late 1990s, moreover, has made the country more dependent on other equally weak neighbours. So, many of its exports now go to Sudan and its main imports come from Saudi Arabia and the United Arab Emirates. Eritrea thus has gotten into a structurally dependent relationship with two of its other Red Sea neighbours at the cost of losing its profitable trade links with its bigger neighbour in Ethiopia. The irony of this situation is that soon after the Darfur rebellion broke out in 2003 in Sudan, Eritrea was the first to offer support to the rebels, supply them with arms and other resources and also offer them sanctuary on its own soil.

By 2006, Eritrea was effectively holding Sudan hostage and seeking energy and related security support from Khartoum. From a broadly anti-Arab posture in the 1990s, by 2010, Asmara was directly dependent on its Arab hinterland for support. And yet it has also been courting non-Arab and anti-Israel Iran since the late 2000s, giving Iran the option of access to the strategic port of Assab. With regard to Somalia, Asmara was bent on supporting anti-Ethiopian forces there in an effort to weaken Addis Ababa's drive to contain the anarchy of Somalia. Thus, it lent support to the Islamist and hard-line Union of Islamic Courts which entered the capital in 2006 and confronted the Transitional Federal Government in Mogadishu which was supported by Ethiopia and the wider regional and international communities. Ethiopia's subsequent military intervention in Somalia in late 2006, which lasted until 2009, not only added to the agony of Somalia but further destabilised relations between the neighbouring countries. Asmara's support for a new post-2006 coalition – the Alliance for the Re-Liberation of Somalia – has acted as another thorn in the side of Ethiopia.

As already noted, Eritrea's short war with its much smaller neighbour, Djibouti, in 2008 destabilised their bilateral relations and has brought additional tension to the Horn area. Eritrea's actions against Djibouti have influenced Ethiopia's behaviour towards Somalia, brought it even closer to Djibouti, and has also prompted Yemeni intervention, albeit on the diplomatic front. Eritrea's actions towards its East African neighbours since the early 1990s and its links with countries further afield, then, have made the greatest contribution to the shaping of the southern Red Sea's geopolitics, effectively 'securitising' it.

But the most problematic geopolitical entity by far is Somalia, which continues to burst its borders as its polity repeatedly convulses and fragments. If it is not piracy, then there is the growing tendency to broaden intra-Somali communal tensions to engulf Djibouti, the Ogaden region of Ethiopia and even Kenya and Uganda. In the meanwhile, it continues to tear itself apart from the inside as Somalilanders and Puntlanders lay claim to the remains of what was once a viable and potentially prosperous country. Despite its many complexities, Somalia is in some ways a mirror image of what could happen in the sub-region's other fragile and potentially failing states. Civil strife can easily spill over to other countries, and a political vacuum in a given state will suck in intervention by others. Moreover, while the southern states of the sub-region have found it impossible to move beyond conflict and continue to suffer the consequences of intermittent warfare, off-shore Somalian piracy has grown to inflict major harm on Red Sea shipping and the lifeline of the sub-region. As a consequence, international navies have become regular visitors, and indeed residents, of the waterway, rekindling global interest in the Red Sea sub-region and its geopolitical significance. This growing interest, however, has not resulted in stabilisation of the sub-region.

Somalia could be the mirror for others and the failure to accept the end of that country, and also the consequences and realities of a post-state geographical space take a heavy toll on the region. In Trumbull's words, 'There exists no coherent concept of what a nation might or should look like in Somalia, and assertions of state control in Somalia seem to precipitate violence'.[70] This seems to be the ultimate legacy of the Cold War and its aftermath in the Red Sea sub-region. Despite the many efforts of such regional bodies as the seven-member InterGovernmental Authority on Development (IGAD) to contain East African crises and insecurity around the Horn, there is still no organisational framework in place which could be capable of meeting the security challenges of the Red Sea sub-region. With its advanced institutional structures, IGAD's focus on development and regional integration can be usefully utilised in the interest of regional security. Its support for integrated transport networks between Ethiopia and its two neighbours of Djibouti and Somalia is a case in point, as indeed is IGAD's drive towards settlement of conflicts in Sudan and Somalia, and confidence building between Djibouti and Eritrea.[71] But more co-ordination between regional bodies and Red Sea states will be needed before the sub-region can address the problems associated with the fragility of its states and the many cross-border disputes feeding inter-state tensions between them.

Peace remains elusive on the Red Sea's northern shores and the southern part of the sub-region remains fragile, unstable and prone to domestic and inter-state conflict. Meddling in the neighbours' affairs has also increased as state fragility has been exposed. In this environment of uncertainty and fluidity the potential for conflict remains high and as such the strategic signature of the Red Sea sub-region on global security remains ominously present. At both ends of the Red Sea, conflict has remained a major impediment to integration; yet conflict (and indeed piracy!) have also helped the bordering states to focus more on the Red Sea as a shared zone of conflict, and also one of opportunity.

4 Security, militarisation and arms flows

Middle East conflict zones and Red Sea security

The brief naval combat between Eritrea and Yemen over the Hanish Islands in late 1995 and the conflict situation between Eritrea and Ethiopia since 1998 have highlighted the ease with which Red Sea states can engage each other militarily. These military encounters also showed that even the weakest of Red Sea countries now have the potential to directly threaten each other's strategic interests, in terms of facilities, urban centres, national networks, etc. The military exchanges between Yemen and Eritrea was made all the more striking due to the destruction which has befallen the East African naval base of Massawa and the newly formed Eritrean navy's ability to deploy elements of the naval power the country had inherited from Ethiopia. In the battles Eritrea deployed the two Petya II-class frigates which it had inherited from the Ethiopian navy, and effectively used a host of other naval vessels and weapons systems which Ethiopia had imported from the Soviet Union in the course of the 1980s.

The conflict between Ethiopia and Eritrea, on the other hand, has highlighted Asmara's ability to plan and execute aerial attacks on targets far away, and its effective use of its military assets, including several MiG-29 fighters which are said to have been flown by Russian and Ukrainian pilots.

The Eritrean–Yemeni and Eritrean–Ethiopian encounters serve to demonstrate how easily a conflict, albeit a skirmish, can help create a long-term headache for the security calculations of the neighbouring countries. In these cases, localised battles have given birth to a new line of tensions between Asmara, on the one hand, and Sana'a and Addis Ababa, on the other, and the three countries' respective backers.

But more generally, it is easy to see how conflict, normally in the form of major inter-state war, has become one of the defining features of the security parameters of virtually every Middle Eastern state. Several wars in the Levant and the Persian Gulf theatres, for instance, have been instrumental in shaping the military profile and security strategies of a number of the parties to these conflicts.

Few countries, however, have found their security envelopes formed by the convergence of several regional conflicts as much as have the Red Sea littorals. Here, a number of regional conflict faultlines meet. At one end is the Arab–Israeli conflict, which has been instrumental in shaping the security strategies of Egypt, Jordan and Israel for the best part of 60 years. This conflict has also left a significant mark on the security outlook of such other neighbouring countries as Saudi Arabia and Sudan.

Then there are the instabilities associated with the Persian Gulf sub-region – two wars in ten years, regime change in Iraq in 2003, revolutionary turmoil, predatory politics, external power presence, tense borders – that have become the modern characteristics of this MENA sub-region. Persian Gulf instabilities since the early 1970s, for instance, have been the primary motive for Saudi Arabia's military build-up and its security alliances. A close look at Riyadh's arms procurement strategy since 1973 will show how this has mirrored its broader calculations about its own security in the context of regional tensions. It will show how these have changed in the aftermath of the British withdrawal from territories 'east of Suez' and in the context of American security calculations from the Nixon Doctrine of early 1970s onwards.

In the 1980s, it was the Iran–Iraq War, and the danger of it spilling over, which played a big part in the Kingdom's security concerns. Also, the type of war that this was, in terms of threatening international shipping and the security of the Persian Gulf emirates, focused Saudi minds on its security requirements. The tense Iraq–Kuwait stand-off, the continuing feud with Iraq, and Iran's rearmament drive after 1989 continued to act as pressures on Saudi Arabia to keep its guard up, which in practical terms meant importing more modern and sophisticated weapons systems.

Thus, not unlike the Arab–Israeli theatre, the net result of this prolonged period of crisis in the Persian Gulf has been massive armaments drives by the littoral states and militarisation of the entire sub-region. As we have implied, the pattern of militarisation is nowhere more clearly evident than in the case of Saudi Arabia.

In addition to these two general conflict theatres meeting in the Red Sea sub-region, there are other significant cross- border clashes which have helped to fuel its militarisation. The war between Ethiopia and Somalia in the 1970s is a good example of this problem, where both countries enjoyed considerable military support from regional and international actors. More recently, we can point to the clashes (in the mid-1990s) between Yemen and Eritrea, which again have fed into the military calculations of the littoral states. Such inter-state clashes, whether short in duration or prolonged, cause considerable militarisation of the parties. So, for example, the Hanish dispute has, to a degree, coloured the military needs of Eritrea and its Yemeni neighbour and has also fed their appetite for more types of weapons. A classic case of a new military escalation could be said to be in the making.

Barely three years later, Eritrea's military experience with Yemen served the state well in another regional conflict situation, when its armed forces found themselves embroiled in a tense border dispute with Ethiopia. The rapid degeneration of their quarrel into open and intensive war and the speed of Eritrea's aerial attacks on strategic Ethiopian targets, as well as their rapid armour placements in the disputed Badme region, speak volumes about the steep learning curve that the Eritrean armed forces have been on since independence, and the emergence of the Eritrean armed forces as an increasingly experienced and competent military force in the Horn of Africa. For the Ethiopians, the bloody conflict marked what was called a 'bitter divorce' between the two former partners, and also pressured the government to seek rearmament and mobilisation of its superior force in manpower terms.

Another security vector which feeds into the military situation in the Red Sea sub-region is that of the security of the fixed assets of the littoral states. We have already shown in earlier chapters the significance of the Red Sea to the economic well-being of its littorals, and to international traders. Now, looking at the same question in a slightly different way, it can be seen that most Red Sea countries' industrial and urban assets are quite exposed and vulnerable to attack. Second, as these economic assets have become more important over time, so the protection of each country's fixed Red Sea assets has become a considerable security concern. The Red Sea since the 1970s has been criss-crossed with significant transportation routes; its ports and coastal industries have grown; the flow of hydrocarbons through the Suez Canal as well as through the territory of several of its littoral states has increased. In view of the growing importance of the fixed assets which facilitated the littoral states' economic development, several Red Sea countries have become more attuned to devising ways of defending their primary national assets. The simplest solution to the complex problem of ensuring national security has routinely included expansion of military power and the deployment of what are deemed to be suitable weaponry.

Rapid and sustained military procurement can quite often be a by-product of domestic civil tensions of course. The history of the Red Sea states attests to the fact that the cycle of violence between competing groups within a given territory not only forces the ruling regime to militarise, but also encourages the rejectionist/sessionist forces to develop their own military machine to match, or at least compete, with the ruling regime's military deployments. As we have seen, such civil strife affects the security calculations of the neighbouring countries as well, in terms of their military purchases, deployment and doctrine. Developments in Yemen are a good example of this trend, where we witness since the mid-2000s such a dramatic deterioration in state–tribal relations in that country that by 2009 armed conflict broke out between Yemen's Shi'a Houthi fighters and the state, even involving a border confrontation with Saudi Arabia which succeeded in sucking in the Kingdom's armed forces on the side of the Yemeni government forces. The longer such kinds of strife continue, the more likely also that they will emerge as core issues for neighbouring countries as well.

Civil wars often fuel military tensions in other ways too, particularly as they sometimes cause the convergence of significant firepower on a small – often border – area. This pattern of militarisation has been evident in the case of Sudan since the mid-1980s, for example. In the 1990s and 2000s, the impact of the Sudanese civil war became even more complex with the addition of an overt religious dimension to the conflict.

It took much of the 1990s for the Middle Eastern states to digest the security challenges of their regional environment in the post-Cold War international system, which were no longer being shaped by the overwhelming pressures of the Cold War and the intense pressure of superpower rivalries. The process of adjustment by the MENA states, however, was disrupted, in fact, coloured, by the Iraqi invasion of Kuwait at the beginning of that decade. The Iraqi invasion occurred so soon after the fall of the Berlin Wall that the MENA countries were only able to develop their grander strategies towards a unipolar – US-dominated – international system with an eye on the immediate security challenges posed by Iraq, and the overwhelming Western military response which followed it. Despite vociferous assurances by the West that such military adventures as Iraq's invasion of its neighbour would not come to pass in the New World Order, Persian Gulf states as well as Israel, Syria, Egypt, Turkey – and even the Maghreb countries – set about trying to find an effective antidote to an Iraqi-style aggression. Some even attempted to plot a solution to the problem of an indefinite US military presence in the Middle East.

Thus, while much of the rest of the world had begun the 1990s looking forward to reaping the benefits of a 'peace dividend' from the palpable reduction in international tensions, the MENA sub-system as a whole continued to experience high military expenditures, and indeed expansion of military outlays among several of its members. The biggest spender then was Saudi Arabia, which allocated some $35 billion to its defence sector in 1991. Since then, regional military expenditures as a whole have fluctuated between around $45 billion and $50 billion a year in the 1990s, somewhat lower than the 1980s, but rising to well over $75 billion a year in the 2005–10 period. Also, defence outlay has remained considerably higher in per capita terms there than in other regions of the world.

Curiously, the peace dividend issue took an unexpected form in the Middle East. In the Arab–Israeli theatre, for example, it included discussions of strengthening further Israel's defences, which of course resulted in bigger Israeli arms transfer agreements. In the case of Egypt too, the 1990s proved to be as bountiful as the Cold War years; for the end of the Cold War facilitated the transfer of several types of advanced weapons from NATO's theatre to Egypt. For other MENA countries, several of which happen to be Red Sea states as well, the first post-Cold War decade became the period in which they set about strengthening their defensive postures, in some cases, making defence the country's most important foreign policy priority. As a consequence, per capita military expenditures did not drop substantially in the MENA region following the Cold War, even though overall military expenditure may have been adjusted downwards. The countries which continued to pursue the defence expansion route included familiar names: Saudi Arabia and other GCC countries, Israel, Egypt, Syria, Iran, and, to a lesser degree, Jordan.

Perhaps the most striking feature of this period with regard to the leading Red Sea military powers was their increased reliance on the United States for military support. It is clear that, for somewhat different reasons and through different mechanisms, virtually every important Red Sea power ended up in a closer military relationship with the USA. In an indirect way, therefore, the American superpower has continued to permeate the Red Sea sub-region. This is clearly visible

Table 4.1 US military deliveries to the MENA region, 1980–95 ($ million, selected years)

	1980	1985	1989	1990	1991	1992	1993	1994	1995
World Total									
	5,973	6,742	8,946	7,575	8,805	8,674	11,262	9,539	11,835
Middle East and North Africa									
Total	4,324	4,465	3,198	2,999	4,862	5,270	6,791	4,062	6,899
Red Sea Countries									
Total	3,979	4,115	2,930	2,519	4,159	4,621	5,689	3,671	5,929
Egypt	209	669	574	654	644	1,112	1,263	1,034	1,788
Israel	853	717	1,229	564	384	710	787	452	332
Jordan	277	151	83	56	24	21	25	32	47
Saudi Arabia	2,640	2,578	1,044	1,245	3,107	2,778	3,614	2,153	3,762
Other Middle East countries									
Kuwait	79	48	62	56	113	256	882	221	487
Morocco	69	55	41	44	32	42	19	17	22
Oman	8	5	2	8	45	8	8	9	6
Tunisia	11	161	26	33	28	21	17	28	27
Sub-Saharan Africa									
Total	53	83	93	58	50	32	14	18	15
Latin America									
Total	139	493	378	504	413	363	199	179	167
Asia									
Total	1,329	1,464	4,385	3,447	3,239	2,796	1,813	2,379	2,932
Europe									
Total	128	237	892	567	241	213	2,273	2,693	1,647

Source: Calculated from the CIA (1996).

in the pattern of US arms sales to the region in the critical period of conflicts and also in the immediate post-Cold War period (see Table 4.1).

Red Sea states' security concerns

Regionally, a number of potential security problems rotate around the economic interests of the Red Sea countries. The critical concern of virtually every Red Sea country in this regard is the security of its territory and population centres, physical (industrial and infrastructural) assets, natural (mineral and agricultural resources as well as touristic) resources, and key urban centres.

In several cases, aggression against these countries' Red Sea assets can compromise the security of the entire state. The countries most vulnerable to attack are: Saudi Arabia, Jordan, Israel, Egypt, Sudan, and Eritrea. Let us briefly survey their most important security vulnerabilities in terms of their fixed national assets.

For Saudi Arabia, the security of the city of Jeddah must be the paramount preoccupation. Jeddah is the heart of an increasingly vast network of new industrial and economic zones and cities mushrooming along the country's Red Sea coast, which will be driving the Kingdom's development in the twenty-first century. So, Jeddah has become the Kingdom's most populated urban centre, forming the largest single settlement along the shores of the Red Sea, to be augmented with at least another 600,000 inhabitants by 2030 when the other new cities and industrial zones are complete. Second, it is the most important commercial port of the country, and one of its most important naval bases. The new military city at Jizan, which includes a large naval base, underlines the security significance of the Red Sea to the Kingdom. Furthermore, its airport handles the largest volume of cargo, which had already reached 78 million kilograms in 1981 – nearly twice that of Riyadh airport.[1] Third, Jeddah is the point of arrival for most Muslim pilgrims visiting Mecca. As many as 10 million people travel through Jeddah's King Abdul Aziz airport annually, making security and safety a prime concern of Saudi authorities. Fourth, Jeddah forms one of the main links in the country's national network of oil refineries which feed the ever expanding domestic market. Saudi Arabia's economic reliance on its Red Sea coast is illustrated by the rapid expansion of industrial activity around the city of Jeddah and the purpose-built industrial city of Yanbu. Saudis themselves view the significance of their industrial city in international terms:

> with the location of [Yanbu], and its modern port facilities on the Red Sea and with the Suez Canal nearby, an investor ... has easy access to markets in Europe, the United States, Canada and South America. In the other direction the investor has access to the markets of Asia, Australia and the Far East. Directly across the Red Sea lies the markets of Egypt, Sudan and other countries of North and East Africa.[2]

Saudi Arabia is reliant on its Red Sea coast for another reason as well, and in this its interests are shared by its oil customers; the impact of tensions in the Persian Gulf on oil exporters and on price can be circumvented through storage of oil off the Saudi Red Sea coast, and its transportation from the Red Sea to international markets. In the 1980s, for example, in order to minimise the impact of the Iran–Iraq War on its oil exports, Saudi Arabia had begun storing in off-shore storage tanks as much as 70 million barrels of oil in the Red Sea.[3] This strategy was also considered during the Kuwait crisis. Today, Saudi Arabia exports as much as five million barrels of its oil every day through the Red Sea. This makes access through the Red Sea of vital importance to Saudi Arabia.

For Jordan, the Red Sea is the only open route to the rest of the world, and as such the security of the Gulf of Aqaba and that of the port of Aqaba are critical. Virtually all of Jordan's trade is conducted through Aqaba. Keeping this port free of interference is a Jordanian priority therefore. Jordan's Red Sea port of Aqaba not only serves as the Hashemite Kingdom's only outlet and transport route to the outside world, but for nearly ten years acted as Iraq's only lifeline as well, its only outlet to international markets – bringing in grain for its people and taking its oil to countries as far away as Brazil. In 1989, over 6 million tons of goods headed for Iraq through Aqaba. The port has become a vital factor in regional politics since Jordan managed to expand its coastline by swapping some desert land with seven and half miles of Saudi Arabia's Red Sea coast in the 1960s. Furthermore, if visions of a 'Red–Dead' canal were ever realised, then Jordan's port would be the primary site for the development of any new joint Israeli–Jordanian facilities. Aqaba's importance to the Hashemite Kingdom and its immediate neighbours, Israel, the Palestinian Authority and Iraq, cannot be exaggerated.

In the case of Israel, it is Eilat as a major tourist centre which is important. As such, Eilat is a substantial currency earner for the country. But in military terms too, Eilat plays an important role. It is one of Israel's military (naval) bases, and is responsible for the safety of Israel's southern borders. Israel's dependence on its Red Sea port of Eilat has also been amply demonstrated since its independence. In the second half of the 1970s though, with tensions receding between Israel and Egypt, Israel began investing in the port as a major touristic and commercial centre. One feature of these developments was the agreement reached with Iran in the 1970s for the delivery of oil to Eilat and its transfer to the Mediterranean port of Ashkelon via a jointly owned pipeline. The development of this new transportation link was a strategic decision by Israel, and was based on two factors: first, the security of its Red Sea port, which has been well-founded; and second, the relationship with Iran (which proved short-lived). It is also of historical significance that in an effort to weaken Israel, its three Red Sea neighbours (Egypt, Jordan and Saudi Arabia) had been busy trying to court non-Arab Iran in the early 1970s to loosen its links with Israel in the interest of forming a (US-sponsored) triangular alliance with Riyadh and Cairo.

Two lessons relating to the security of the Red Sea can be drawn from the eventful 1970s. First, that the Red Sea balance of power was increasingly being shaped by non-Arab regional actors (in this case, Iran and Israel); and second, that Middle East regional powers exercised overwhelming influence in the Red Sea area. The latter reality was again demonstrated by the role the Shah of Iran played in aiding Egypt to widen the Suez Canal and redevelop Port Said. Just as he had been responsible for creating the Eilat–Ashkelon pipeline link for Israel, so it was he again who would loan Egypt the finance to lay down a new pipeline from Suez to Alexandria.[4]

Egypt too has much at stake in the Red Sea. Egypt's desire to ensure the security of Suez and Port Said is obvious, but the safety of tourists (one of Egypt's main foreign currency earners) visiting Egypt's interior and its expanding Red Sea resorts is a growing problem. In addition, Egypt's efforts to exploit the on-shore and off-shore hydrocarbons deposits of the Sinai Peninsula have made security of the seas around the peninsula more vital to the Egyptian economy.

Not unlike Jordan, Sudan's lifeline is also tied to the Red Sea. Port Sudan is the country's only major Red Sea settlement and the country's only commercial port. Virtually all of Sudan's trade is conducted through this port, which provides the only independent access that Sudan has to the outside world. Port Sudan is vulnerable to attack from both north and south, and has been threatened by the Sudanese armed opposition throughout the recent decades.

To the south, Eritrea, the post-Cold War country carved out of Ethiopia, is almost entirely dependent on the Red Sea. Most of its economic activities take place along its Red Sea coast. In addition, not too dissimilar to the case of Iraq and Jordan, Eritrea acts as the gatekeeper for (landlocked) Ethiopia, which until the late 1990s was channelling its trade and contact with the outside world. Between 1993 and 1998, Massawa was the main port which served both countries. Eritrea's long coastline, stretching 1,000 kilometres from the Bab el-Mandeb to the Sudan, is of immense economic and strategic importance to the Horn countries. Indeed, since the break-up of Ethiopia into two countries, all East African countries have developed a keener awareness of the importance of the Red Sea to their national security. For a while, it seemed that this recognition was a sufficient enough reason for the two countries to reinforce their bilateral co-operation. The prospect of Addis Ababa and Asmara adopting identical positions on Red Sea issues in international fora was also beginning to happen, which raised the spectre of a new pro-US alliance emerging between these strategically placed Red Sea-dependent neighbours. In the mid-1990s this alliance was keenly watched by Yemen and Sudan, the two Arab states which have had some political problems with both Eritrea and Ethiopia. The big three Red Sea countries (Egypt, Israel and Saudi Arabia) of course were already fully engaged in the rivalries between the four southern Red Sea countries.

As for Yemen, perhaps the key country as far as the Bab el-Mandeb is concerned, the Red Sea represents an important lifeline, particularly as oil has begun to feature more prominently in the country's overall economic profile. The Ras Eissa oil refinery in Hudaidah on the Red Sea, whose construction began in 1996, symbolises the trend in which Yemen is moving; this is the main export terminal for the Hunt Oil Company-operated Ras Safer oil fields in the Ma'arib governorate.[5] But Yemen is also conscious of the destabilising effects of its internal strife on relations with Saudi Arabia and the wider Horn of Africa.[6]

The Red Sea military balance and regional security

Naturally, carrying out sophisticated military operations in the Red Sea is an easier task for some states, and practically impossible for others. While Eritrea may have fared well against Yemen's poorly trained troops in the mid-1990s, in a conventional exchange, its armed forces are unlikely to make much of an impression on the larger equipped military powers of the Red Sea sub-region (Egypt, Israel and Saudi Arabia). Weaker still in military terms is the strategically placed Western-supported state of Djibouti, which sits at one side of the entrance to the Red Sea.

At the other end of the Red Sea, Jordan may possess a fairly well-developed military machine, but remains quite vulnerable to its stronger neighbours. Other Arab countries, however, like Yemen and Sudan, do have a latent military capability, but this potential is unlikely to be realised without substantial external assistance. Table 4.2 shows the Red Sea states' military expenditures in selected years. In the case of Yemen, US military support is following the increases in al-Qaeda activities in Yemen and from Yemen, providing access to American

Table 4.2 Red Sea countries' military expenditures, 1985, 1997 and 1998

	Defence expenditure ($mn)			% of GDP			Per capita ($)		
	1985	1997	1998	1985	1997	1998	1985	1997	1998
Northern Red Sea									
Egypt	3,679	2,743	2,776	7.2	4.3	4.1	76	45	45
Israel	7,196	11,143	11,040	21.2	11.5	11.6	1,700	1,917	1,844
Jordan	857	496	537	15.9	7.0	7.4	245	105	110
Saudi Arabia	25,585	18,151	20,476	19.6	12.4	15.7	2,217	1,071	1,173
Southern Red Sea									
Djibouti	46	20	21	7.9	5.0	5.1	106	30	30
Eritrea	–	196	286	–	25.2	35.8	–	52	74
Ethiopia	636	139	372	17.9	2.1	6.0	15	3	7
Somalia	66	40	39	6.2	4.8	4.7	12	7	7
Sudan	152	413	377	3.2	5.5	4.8	7	14	12
Yemen	696	403	388	9.9	7.0	6.6	69	25	22

Source: IISS, *The Military Balance* (various years).

military know-how. Sudan's military relations by contrast clearly illustrate that without Iranian and Chinese assistance Khartoum would most likely have been unable to expand its deployment of the types of weapons its armed forces needed in the war with the armed opposition groups in the south of the country. Between 1994 (when the flow of arms accelerated) and 1997 (by which time Iran's military assistance had been reduced), Sudan imported from China six new fighter aircraft, 50 Z-6 helicopters, and 100 (82mm and 120mm) mortars. The most direct Iranian support may have reached Sudan as early as 1991, coming in the form of military training for the Sudanese army and the militia, some small arms supplies, munitions, RPGs, and as many as 60 main battle tanks.[7] Such assistance enabled the government forces to put up a spirited defence against the well-armed opposition groups operating in the southern half of the country, and also to rout the Darfur rebels in the 2000s. In this context, Russian delivery of 10 MiG-29 fighters to Khartoum in 2004 boosted the government forces' ability to attack rebel targets at will and deep into their strongholds.

At the other end of the Red Sea, the growing threats from the expansion and modernisation of Saudi and Egyptian navies (as well as that of Syria) since the 1970s have compelled Israel to seek suitable responses.

> One sphere in which the Israel Navy experienced a pronounced decline in capability [in the late 1980s] was the Red Sea theatre. The direct reason for this was the IDF's withdrawal from Sinai, resulting in the loss of the naval base at Sharm al-Sheikh. This reduction in Israel Navy in the south would render it more difficult to open the Strait of Tiran, should it be blocked, and to engage in long-range missions both in the Red Sea and the Gulf of Suez.[8]

Basically, what is being said here is that despite peace with Egypt and Jordan, there still exists a serious security threat to Israel in the Red Sea sub-region. Theoretically, a hostile force can squeeze Israel hard if it were to manage to deny its shipping access to the Suez Canal or to block access to its Red Sea coast. The growing sophistication of two Red Sea Arab navies in particular (Egypt and Saudi Arabia) since the 1970s has been occurring just as Israel has been reducing its own military presence in the Sinai area. The combination of these developments does pose an indirect but significant challenge to Israel's security planners, as might do Iran's naval presence in Sudan and its broader ties with Palestinian groups (particularly with regard to Hamas and its smuggling networks through Egypian territory and the Sinai Peninsula). It is interesting that having seen its shipping to and from the Red Sea (at Suez and at Bab el-Mandeb) disrupted by the Egyptian navy during the 1967 War, in the 1980s and 1990s Israel invested less in the security of its Red Sea coast, focusing instead on its Mediterranean assets. Thus, as Israeli military analysts note, strategically speaking, Israel is vulnerable in the Red Sea theatre, a situation which is magnified by geography, whereas the sea lanes to Israel in the Red Sea are 1,000 nautical miles, the distance from Arab states in the sub-region to Israel's coastline are much shorter, below 120 nautical miles.[9] Its only effective responses seems to be to strengthen its already formidable air power, and, on the diplomatic front, its relations with two of its Red Sea Arab neighbours, Egypt and Jordan.

The overall military edge, however, has remained with Israel and it is unlikely ever to be matched by more than two or three Arab armies (Table 4.3). But while Israel's traditional advantages in land and aerial combat remain intact, its navy started to lag behind the two largest Red Sea Arab navies (Egypt and Saudi Arabia), and it was only in the early 2000s that Israel improved its naval strength. But worth noting that even in the maritime realm of warfare, as recently as 1988, only the Saudi navy (among all Arab navies) could match Israel's shipborne helicopter capability. It is in the Red Sea sub-region, however, that the naval balance is tilting very much in Saudi Arabia's favour. But, in view of the growing importance of the Red Sea to Saudi Arabia's economy, its naval expansion there can be seen as a direct result of its broader national security concerns – and not because of Arab–Israeli rivalries.

In the Horn of Africa in the meantime, several local conflicts continue to undermine attempts at security building. As has been shown, inter-state tensions – between Yemen and Eritrea, between Somali warlords and Ethiopia, and between Ethiopia and Eritrea – have been augmented since the end of the Cold War by a series of local disputes and civil wars in Sudan, Somalia, Yemen and Djibouti. The net result of these conflicts and disputes among the Red Sea sub-region's poorer and weaker economies has been further domestic instability and meddling by the more powerful regional players. But what is particularly disturbing, and which the aggregate military data do not show, is the continuing militarisation of the Horn region since the end of the Cold War (Table 4.4). The Horn's armed forces may be poorly equipped in comparison with their northern Red Sea counterparts, and their military expenditures may have dropped in real terms, but they can still inflict serious damage on each other, as the Ethiopian–Eritrean war has

Table 4.3 The northern Red Sea military balance, 1987 and 1998

	Egypt		Israel		Jordan		Saudi Arabia	
	1987	*1998*	*1987*	*1998*	*1987*	*1998*	*1987*	*1998*
MBTs	2,250	3,655	3,660	3,800	790	1,217	300	1,055
Combat aircraft	443	585	629	474	119	93	216	432
Submarines	12	4	3	3	no	no	no	no
Frigates/ destroyers	9	9	no	no	no	no	4	8
SSMs	yes	yes	yes	yes	no	no	no	yes
Total armed forces (000)	445	450	149	175	72	104	68	105

Source: IISS, *The Military Balance* (various years).

graphically demonstrated, and also on others. While the southern Red Sea states may never be able to acquire the knock-out punch that a country like Israel can pack, they will nonetheless always be able to deploy the type of weapon (say, surface-to-surface missiles, or particular types of munitions) which can provide them with a decisive military advantage in relation to the other Horn countries. The larger Horn states, and those at war, have been shopping around since 1996–97 in search of this military comparative advantage. In most cases, they have been able to purchase most of the weapons on their shopping lists.

Also, it is worth noting that despite political chaos in several Horn countries, indeed in spite of it, the military has remained a powerful national force. We also see from the military data that political instability has only served to fuel the militarisation of this strategic area. Note Sudan's military allocations for instance: its armed forces have doubled in number in a decade (from 56,000 soldiers to over 90,000 in the early 2000s), and had grown further to nearly 110,000 active personnel by 2010. Its military budget today is much larger than what it was in the mid-1990s and likely exceeded $2 billion in 2010.

Second, the end of the Cold War has not reduced local tensions sufficiently to reverse the militarisation trend in the Horn. Despite some variations in the national data, there are still around 200,000 men under arms in the Horn of Africa. Although these figures register a drop in absolute terms from the highs of the Cold War situation in the mid-1980s, if we were to add Sudan's numbers to the total (an addition of some 110,000 soldiers), then it would leave the southern Red Sea region still a heavily militarised area, with over a quarter of a million people under arms. The figures speak for themselves; at least 200,000 Eritreans are now directly under arms, some 140,000 in the case of Ethiopia, and 67,000 in Yemen. In the cases of Yemen, Sudan, Somalia and Eritrea, with a combined population of over 70 million, these figures represent a net increase in the size of their militaries since the end of the Cold War.

Table 4.4 The military balance in the Horn of Africa and surrounding area, 1987 and 1998

	Djibouti		Eritrea		Ethiopia		Sudan		Somalia		Yemen	
	1987	1998	1987	1998	1987	1998	1987	1998	1987	1998	1987	1998
MBTs	no	no	n.a.	n.k.	1,000	500	140	280	201	n.k.	570	1,320
Combat aircraft	no	no	n.a.	12	145	85	35	60	63	n.k.	208	65
Submarines	no	no	n.a.	no	no	no	no	no	no	no	no	no
Frigates/ destroyers	no	no	n.a.	1	2	n.a.	no	no	no	no	no	no
SSMs	no	no	n.a.	no	no	no	no	no	no	n.k.	no	no
Total armed forces (000)	5	10	n.a.	200	227	325	57	95	43	225	64	66

Source: IISS, *The Military Balance* (various years).

On the Arabian Peninsula, the tensions between Saudi Arabia and Yemen remained a constant feature of its geopolitical reality in the 1990s. As if Yemeni unification, which made Yemen the most populous country on the peninsula, were not enough of a concern for the Saudis, their fears of Yemen's regional strategy were momentarily heightened by Sana'a's tacit support for Iraq in the 1990–91 Kuwait crisis. But while the direct tensions emanating from the Kuwait crisis may have passed, differences over access to natural resources along their joint border, and labour migration issues continue to complicate relations between Yemen and Saudi Arabia. The two sides remain suspicious of long-term developments next door and although Yemen has little to fear from Saudi Arabia's massive armament programme, Riyadh's involvement in Yemeni politics has been a constant worry for the Yemeni people. This issue of course became an important factor in their relations when in 2009 Yemen had to rely on Saudi military support and aerial and naval bombardment of al-Houthi Shi'a Yemeni rebels active near their joint border since 2004.

Military and security developments in the Red Sea in the 1990s

We have argued that the Arab–Israeli conflict and Persian Gulf tensions have been the two main factors driving the high levels of arms imports in the Mashreq for several decades now. We will now consider how the pattern of military build-up may have changed in these conflict zones since the end of superpower competition in the Middle East. We will complete the picture through an assessment of the impact that the relative calm in both of these theatres since 1990 has had on regional military patterns. In this endeavour, we are particularly interested in exploring how fear of an all-out military confrontation in the Levant and the Persian Gulf has had an impact on military developments in the Red Sea sub-region. This objective we aim to accomplish, through a detailed survey of the arms procurements and defence strategies of the Red Sea countries since the end of the Cold War. To conduct the survey, we have divided the Red Sea sub-region into two zones of countries: the northern (Egypt, Jordan, Israel and Saudi Arabia), and southern (Djibouti, Eritrea, Ethiopia, Somalia, Sudan, and Yemen) zones.

Northern Red Sea countries

All four northern Red Sea countries have been engaged in a programme of defence modernisation since 1990, which has involved the transfer of a substantial amount of new or more modern types of weapons systems. We look at each country's military profile in turn.

Israel

First, Israel, which started the 1990s with serious concerns about its security and defence capabilities. The main sources of the challenge was neither Syria, the traditional enemy, nor the three-year-old Palestinian Intifadah. In fact, the most serious military challenge to Israel's security emanated not from any of the 'front-line' countries, but from a country with which Israel did not share a border. The attacks on Israeli territory came in the form of missile bombardments in 1991 against which Israel had no effective defence. In a total of 17 attacks the Gulf state of Iraq launched some 40 SSMs on Israeli territory.[10] Israel's inability to counter these attacks formed the basis of the IDF's military assessment of Israel's vulnerabilities. The main fear for the Israeli defence establishment was that its formidable deterrence capability had been punctured by Iraq's Scud attacks. A fact that perhaps appeared more real than it actually was due to Israel finding it impossible (under American pressure) to exercise its offensive option against Iraqi targets. A real fear by the IDF, however, was that in the battlefields of tomorrow, as the Kuwait crisis had shown, scenarios in which missile attacks could be launched from distant countries with which Israel did not share a border could become a reality. Some of these enemies might prove to be beyond the reach of the Israeli air force, and might not indeed be vulnerable to Israeli counter-measures. In the Red Sea sub-region, both these concerns have tended to feed into Israeli military plans. Although the missile threat is something that all Middle Eastern states will have to cope with, in Israel's case the 2006 war with Hezbollah showed such a threat (relatively cheap, with a mobile option, and an increasingly accurate form of offence) has increased the burden on its air force and its air defence planners to develop an effective response. Finding an effective response has proved to be expensive, which means high military budgets and purchase of greater numbers of the more advanced types of fighters and air defence systems.

An immediate Israeli response to the SSM threat was the development of an effective anti-SSM missile defence system. Israel's short-term defence against SSM attack was the deployment of the US Patriot system, but in the medium term Israel will be able to deploy the dedicated anti-SSM Arrow (Hertz) system which it has developed with the United States. In view of the simmering SSM threat in the sub-region, the pace of the Arrow project was accelerated so much in the second half of the 1990s that it was expected to come into service ahead of schedule.[11]

In addition to the Arrow defence umbrella, Israel is also debating how to make its deterrence capability more transparent. One school maintains that the country should consider making its nuclear deterrence capability more explicit. This would entail telling the world of Israel's advanced nuclear weapons capability, and also use it as a way of making a saving on its general defence outlay by not doing some of the things it now has to do. Opponents of this line ask, rather rhetorically, that Israel's 'known' nuclear capability did not deter Iraqi missile attacks in 1991, so how might its explicit declaration do so? Also the proponents of the conventional deterrence school express their grave concern about the political and diplomatic ramifications of such a declaration by Israel, and feel that Israel may not be able to contain the pressures from the Western countries (largely European ones) and the regional powers to abandon its nuclear monopoly once it declares its nuclear capability. Such a declaration, then, according to this line of argument, would actually work against Israel's security interests and foreign policy objectives in the Middle East.

Others fear that making Israel's nuclear deterrence explicit would damage its standing with the United States, particularly with the main base of its support, the US Congress. Shai Feldman, a leading Israeli strategic thinker, has observed, for instance, that 'if Israel detonated [a nuclear device] or changed its nuclear policy, that would require the automatic imposition of the Glenn Amendment, and that stipulates the end of all economic and military assistance [from the US]'. Even though the nuclear arms race has begun in earnest on the MENA sub-system's periphery, in the Asian subcontinent, Feldman still insists that:

> by following Pakistan's example [of detonating nuclear devices, Israel] may be making [its] nuclear deterrence slightly more sharper and articulated, but [it] would pay dearly. We are much more in bed with the United States on [active and passive defence] issues than are India and Pakistan.[12]

Therefore, for those not wishing to declare Israel's nuclear capability, the only sure deterrence profile for the country remains its readiness to strike first at hostile forces and countries, anywhere in the sub-system. This means developing and maintaining Israel's first strike capability, and not being afraid to use it. Before the 2006 Lebanon débâcle, it was argued that the only way that the ghost of the 1991 missile attacks could be put to rest was for Israel to show its regional competitors that it will strike at their targets at the first hint of anti-Israeli military activities. Given Hezbollah's effective and robust military confrontation with Israel and its repeated attacks on Israeli territory throughout the 34-day campaign, the country should publicise the power of its armed forces, such as the strike capability of the advanced F-15I combat aircraft and its long reach, and its long-range Jericho II SSM and Shavit space launcher (with its ICBM potential), it is argued. The development and modernisation of the Israeli air force and development of its strategic SSM force, therefore, must be Israel's top priority, along with its development of an effective air defence system.

In more general terms, one can see that the core principles of Israel's defence doctrine did not change with the passing of the Cold War. As Brigadier General Levran has put it:

> Given that the Arabs have, and will always have, overall physical superior-
> ity, it is essential not to weaken any of Israel's three pillars of military
> might: manpower, weaponry and territory. Substantial erosion of any of
> these will severely weaken Israel's side of the delicate strategic balance
> between her and the Arabs. The idea that one of these components can be
> traded off for another, strengthening one while weakening another, lacks
> foundation and is highly irresponsible.[13]

The other dimension of making an Israeli deterrent work, some Israelis have argued, is ensuring that the American and Israeli perceptions of the threat are identical. In the Kuwait crisis, while both parties saw Iraq as the source of threat, because of the prevailing political conditions, Washington had to pressure Israel not to retaliate against Iraqi targets. Next time, some Israeli planners, maintain, Israel must be alongside the USA if its strike capability is not to be checked and for its deterrence to be taken seriously. This line of thinking has clearly been feeding into Israeli policy towards the Persian Gulf's other state threatening Israel, Iran. In the case of Iran, Israel has been ensuring all along that its views of the Iranian threat are not only identical to that of the United States, but is actually helping to shape American thinking about this country – a task which perhaps was made more manageable by successive US administrations' inherent distrust of Iran and its growing regional role, and of course America's deep commitment to Israel. Here, the Israeli priority was not to help the USA build a coalition against Iran, but rather to ensure that it and the United States assessed the level of the threat jointly and together planned to counter it. As a former chief foreign policy adviser to PM Netanyahu put it back in 1997: 'If we fail to convince our friends in the face of [the Iranian] non-conventional threat, Israel would have to have an effective deterrent.'[14]

Over the course of the 1990s Israel developed all areas of its military capabilities. In the first half of the decade, thus, the IDF ordered two types of military aircraft from the United States (F-16s and F-15s), expanded its force of the locally built Merkava main battle tank, and purchased more corvettes and coastal defence vessels armed with advanced surface-to-air and surface-to-surface missile systems. In the second half of the 1990s, it intensified its space research and facilities. Israel also prepared to take delivery of two German-built submarines, more modern missiles, MLRS, new APCs and other sophisticated hardware (Table 4.5).[15] Reports in 1998 suggested that Israel's new submarines could be armed with nuclear cruise missiles (sea-launched version of the long-range Jericho missile).[16] In 1999, it announced that it was in the process of purchasing 50 additional highly versatile and effective F-16 fighters from the United States, all for the purpose of maintaining Israel's air superiority.[17]

These military advances are in addition to steps taken in recent years to develop its sophisticated nuclear arsenal, which is said to include intercontinental-range

Table 4.5 Major weapons systems purchased or ordered by Israel in the 1990s

Type of weapon	Supplier	Year	Number
AH-64 attack helicopter	USA	1991	19
Dolphin submarine	German	1991	3
Merkava MBT	Indigenous	1992	140
F-15 Eagle	USA	1992	15
F-16 Falcon	USA	1992	40
F-15I	USA	1994	25
Merkava MBT	Indigenous	1993	70
AH-64 attack helicopter	USA	1994	24
F-16 Falcon	USA	1995	50
F-16I Falcon	USA	1999	50

Sources: IISS, SIPRI, national sources.

fractional-orbit-delivered thermonuclear weapons and two-stage, solid-fuel, intermmediate-tange ballistic missiles with a range of about 3,000 kilometres.[18]

Egypt

As already mentioned, Israel's neighbour, Egypt, became one of the main military beneficiaries of the force reductions agreements in post-Cold War Europe. It started the 1990s with new purchases of 40 F-16Cs (assembled in Turkey), worth $1.6 billion, and 80 advanced M-1 Abrams MBTs from the USA, in addition to several types of tactical missile systems. Its purchase of surplus US weapons in the first half of the 1990s included 1,500 M-113 APCs, over 800 M-60-A3 MBTs, C-130 and KC-135 transport and tankers aircraft. More advanced hardware followed in the second half of the 1990s: 36 Apache attack helicopters, 76 122mm SP artillery systems, 384 Patriot missiles with 48 launchers, and 4 improved US-made Romeo-class submarines. In March 1999, the US Secretary of Defense Cohen announced the transfer of the last big arms transfer package to Egypt in the twentieth century. The US–Egyptian deal focused on the transfer of yet more high-technology military hardware to Egypt. As part of a $3.2 billion military package, the new agreement anticipated providing Egypt with 24 F-16 fighters (costing $1.2 billion), 200 M1-A1 MBTs (costing $680 million) to be assembled in Egypt, and eight-unit Patriot missile battery.[19] With these transfers, in addition to the transfer of five American-supplied naval vessels (3 Perry-class and two Knox-class), the military establishment will have gone a long way towards fulfilling its modernisation plan of the Egyptian armed forces. By the end of the 1990s Egyptian armed forces were not only one of the largest in the Middle East, but also one of the best equipped.

But Egypt's rearmament drive pales into insignificance when compared with another of its Arab neighbours, Saudi Arabia's – the third northern Red Sea country to which we now turn.

Table 4.6 Major weapons systems purchased or ordered by Saudi Arabia in the 1990s

Type of weapon	Supplier	Year	Number
M-60A3 MBT	USA	1990	150
M1A3 MBT	USA	1990	235
M2 Bradley	USA	1990	400
M-113 APC	USA	1990	207
AH-64 attack helicopter	USA	1990	12
MLRS	USA	1990	9
Partriot air defence unit	USA	1990	6
KC-130H tanker aircraft	USA	1990	7
C-130H/C130H-30 transport	USA	1990	8
F-15S	USA	1992	72
Tornado IDS	UK	1993	48
Lafayette-class frigate	Fr	1994	3
M113 APC	USA	1996	56
AS-532 helicopter	Fr	1996	12

Saudi Arabia

Saudi Arabia's arms market in the early 1990s was said to be a 'bonanza' for Western arms manufacturers. In its own way, Saudi Arabia's new defence strategy, in terms of its military alliances and its military build-up, was a reflection of the strategic approach it had adopted in the turbulent 1980s. Then it was the fear of Iranian aggression that had propelled the Saudis into action. In the 1990s, it was the realisation of the country's inability to deter either one of its northern neighbours, and the recognition that it needed supreme power in order to be able to defend the Peninsula by itself. Its security calculations were pushing the Kingdom towards larger arms deals and closer alliances with Western powers. Thus, between 1991 and 1997, Saudi Arabia devoted in excess of $120 billion to its defence budget, around half of which has been spent on importing big item (and expensive) advanced weapons (Table 4.6). To this end, its 1999 military expenditure was 19 per cent over budget, according to the IISS, standing at $18.7 billion for that year, dwarfing other regional states' military commitments. Perhaps as much as $60 billion has been spent on arms imports from the USA, Britain and France alone.

For a fuller picture of Saudi Arabia's impressive arms build-up projects in the 1990s, one must set these purchases against the Kingdom's equally active military-related programmes in the 1980s, during which time Saudi Arabia practically transformed its armed forces from a weak military machine to one of the most well-armed and sophisticated in the MENA sub-system. In the 1980s, with a total military outlay of some $185 billion,[20] Saudi Arabia imported some of the most advanced weapons systems and military equipment available on the open market, and set about creating the large and modern military infrastructure (different types of bases, air strips, workshops, communications systems, etc.) needed for the Kingdom's defence.[21] Its large item purchases included several firsts for the country: five E-3A advanced airborne early warning systems (AWACS), 60

F-15C/D fighters (which had been ordered in the late 1970s), 72 Tornado fighters, 315 M1A2 MBTs, a wide range of air-to-air and air-to-surface infrared, radar- and laser-guided missiles for its fighters, four guided-missile equipped frigates, approximately 25 long-range CSS-2 SSMs (secretly purchased from China), plus additional purchases of military hardware already in its armoury.

Saudi Arabia thus created a whole new military machine in a relatively short period of time. The Kingdom's airforce, in particular, multiplied in the last quarter of the twentieth century, from just 97 fighters in 1975 to 274 top of the range combat aircraft twenty years later. The Kingdom's military plans provided for the country to have operational some 348 fighter aircraft by the year 2000.[22] By the year 2000, Saudi Arabia was operating more F-15s than Israel, deploying the advanced F-15S aircraft based on the USAF F-15E airframe. But, as Cordesman notes, the Saudi F-15S has been configured in such a way as not to pose a military challenge to Israel. The superior F-15S, while capable of neutralising non-US weapons systems deployed by Saudi Arabia's neighbours, precludes 'effective penetration of Israel's air space because Israeli fighters, surface-to-air defenses, and electronic warfare assets all use US or Israeli designated systems, and none of the electronic warfare assets on the F-15S will be tuned to counter such systems'.[23]

Many of the Kingdom's military purchases in the 1990s have tended to complement the considerable military resources already amassed by the country, but in some areas of defence the Iraq–Kuwait war of 1991 forced the Saudis to make additional provisions. Iraq's launch of around 45 SSMs against Saudi targets, for instance, prompted the Kingdom to develop further its air defence and aerial attack detection capabilities. Also, its short military skirmishes with the Iraqi army encouraged it to strengthen the army's heavy weaponry force, which today includes new American tanks, armoured fighting machines, and armoured personnel carriers. It transpired in the course of the crisis that Iraqi armour outnumbered Saudi Arabian forces by a large margin: 10:1 in MBT holdings and by 4:1 in combat aircraft.[24] At that time, Saudi Arabia possessed no attack helicopters either, nor many multiple rocket launchers. Many of these gaps in Saudi military holdings were rectified in the course of the 1990s.

Jordan

Jordan has the smallest military force of any northern Red Sea state. But even small Jordan had to modify its defence strategy considerably to suit the markedly different environment of the post-Soviet era. This was prompted by the military defeat in 1991 of its main Arab partner, Iraq, and Baghdad's subsequent political isolation in the region. The close ties between President Hussein and King Hussein which had emerged during the 1980s had increasingly acquired a military edge in the years prior to the Kuwait crisis. Also, the Middle East peace process, which reintegrated Jordan into the American-sponsored Egypt–Israel peace camp, provided further incentives for military modernisation.

The termination of Jordan's military relationship with Iraq following Operations Desert Shield and Desert Storm, which had included the transfer of heavy weapons to Jordan from the Iraqi armoury between 1988 and 1990, the planned formation of joint military units of all three services (which was intended to be implemented in 1990), and a joint air force training squad, placed considerable pressure on the country's defence structures. Despite its sympathies with the Iraqis, Jordan's military establishment showed tremendous keenness after 1990 to substitute military aid from Iraq with assistance from the West.

Jordan's rapid reorientation towards its pro-Western neighbours in the 1990s, therefore, facilitated the smooth transfer of badly needed modern military assets from the West. The most important contributor to the Hashemite Kingdom's defence modernisation exercise has been the United States, which has been trans-ferring reasonably large quantities of modern military hardware to Jordan under its Foreign Military Assistance programme. American military aid has included several big ticket items. In 1995 and 1996, for example, Jordan was allowed to acquire 22 transport helicopters (four UH-60L and 18 UH-1H) from the USA, in addition to 16 F-16 fighters (12 F-16As and four F-16Bs) for the Kingdom's air force, 60 M-60A3 main battle tanks, and two C-130 transporters.[25] This squadron of F-16s has become the most modern aircraft in Jordan's air force. This purchase also marked Jordan's only acquisition of modern fighters since the 1980s. Upon receiving the first four of the Falcons in December 1997, King Hussein stated that 'no country can afford to slip back on having the minimum requirement to be able to defend itself and the future of its peoples'.[26]

Another country involved in Jordan's military modernisation programme is Britain. In March 1999, Britain agreed to transfer a total of 288 advanced Challenger 1 main battle tanks to Jordan as part of Jordan's heavy armour devel-opment. The Challengers (designated Al Hussein locally) eventually replaced Jordan's ageing Centurion MBTs (locally known as the Tariq), of which the Jordanian armed forces possessed 293, and complement its fleet of Khalid (274 Chieftains which were destined for Iran when the Iranian revolution took place) MBTs armed with a 120mm rifled gun.[27]

Southern Red Sea countries

In the southern Red Sea area, Sudan has been one of the key countries seeking to expand and modernise its armed forces (Table 4.7). Another, Eritrea, embarked on a policy of equipping its newly created air force by purchasing six Aermacchi MB-339C light fighters/training aircraft, which it begun integrating into its forces in the second half of the 1990s.[28] The Eritrean air force used this aircraft to great effect in its clashes with Ethiopia in June 1998. Soon after, Eritrea was able to purchase six MiG-29 fighters for $120 million, which it made extensive use of in its war with Ethiopia.[29] Both countries turned to their respective expatriate com-munities for assistance to finance the war, and have continued to cultivate these relationships. Eritrea, which has a diaspora four times the population of the coun-try itself, was able to raise some $400 million in 1999 to finance the war.[30] Ethiopia, which has a much larger population but perhaps fewer external resources was not shy of splashing out on weapons imports either; in just one

Table 4.7 Weapons systems purchased by the southern Red Sea states in the 1990s

Country	Type of weapon	Supplier	Year	Number
Eritrea				
	Armoured combat vehicle	Qatar	1995	30
	Mi-24 attack helicopter	Russia	1995	4
	Y-11 transport	PRC	1995	4
	MB-339 training/fighter	Italy	1996	6
	IAI-1125 transport	Israel	1997	1
	MiG-29 fighter	Russia	1998	6
	MiG-21 fighter	Moldova	1999	6
	Su-25 fighter	Georgia	1999	8
	SA-18 surface-to-air missiles	Russia	1999	200
Ethiopia				
	C-130B transport	USA	1995	4
	MiG-21 fighter	Romania	1998	10
	T-55 MBT	Bulgaria	1998	140
	Mi-24 attack helicopter	Russia	1998	4
	Su-27 fighter-bomber	Russia	1998	8
Sudan				
	Type-59 MBT	PRC	1990	10
	J-6 fighter	PRC	1990	9
	Mi-24 attack helicopter	Kyrgyzstan	1995	1
	F-7 fighter	PRC	1995	6
	Z-6 helicopter	PRC	1995	50
	helicopter	Yemen	1995	12
	T-55 MBT	Belarus	1995	9
	Mi-24 attack helicopter	Belarus	1995	6
	T-54/55 MBT	Yemen	1999	20
Yemen				
	Huangfen patrol craft	PRC	1991	3
	Mi-24/35 attack helicopter	Russia	1991	8
	Su-22 fighter	Ukraine	1995	4
	Balkan-class fast attack craft	France	1996	6
	Su-27 fighter-bomber	Russia	1999	14
	T-54/55 MBT	Czech	1999	unknown

instance, it spent $150 million on advanced, but second-hand, weapons from Russia in late 1998/early 1999, which was half-again as much as the country's entire 1995 defence budget.[31] In the course of the conflict, Ethiopia pressed to mobilise some 200,000 soldiers to fight at the front, costing it much of its development budget for years to come. Ethiopia, in the meanwhile has reportedly entered discussions with Israel's Israel Aircraft Industries for an upgrade of its dozens of ageing MiG-21 fighters imported from the Soviet Union.[32]

Yemen emerged from its intense civil war with the desire to unify its military structures, consolidate its force structures, and expand its military base. In its military restructuring in the 1990s Yemen was responding to domestic realities, as well as to the changing strategic situation in the Red Sea area. At home, President Ali

Abdullah Saleh's priority since 1994 has been to try and consolidate his regime's grip on the armed forces, while also managing a scaling down of the country's military budget. He has, thus, been taking measures to merge some active units in the armed forces, and has sweetened this bitter pill by instituting 30–50 per cent pay rises for the remaining personnel. As part of his military-related reforms, President Saleh has also brought into play tribal and political groups loyal to him personally.

The president has also tried to respond to the country's military weaknesses by attempting to purchase from the former Soviet republic of Moldova some 30 MiG-29 fighters.[33] This $300 million contract remained unfulfilled largely because of Yemen's financial difficulties. By the autumn of 1997, however, this deal had fallen through, with the United States stepping in and purchasing the aircraft on offer. Though, as we show below, Yemen did finally manage to acquire the MiG-29 fighter at a later date and in much greater numbers than above.

Yemen also devoted considerable resources to bolstering its naval forces. For a short period in the 1990s, for instance, its navy doubled in personnel – from around 1,500 men to 3,000.[34] It also took delivery of two Tarantul-I class corvettes, one Natya class off-shore minesweeper, and two inshore Yevgenya-class minesweepers.[35] These purchases were designed to strengthen Yemen's naval presence in and around the Horn and also along its long Indian Ocean coastline. Yemen has also been busy buying heavy armour from the CIS and former Warsaw Pact countries. Its purchases of T-54/55 MBTs from Poland and the Czech Republic in 1999 were indicative of its intentions to bolster its ground forces as rapidly (and economically) as possible.[36] But a more disturbing aspect of Yemen's arms imports has been the way in which the country emerged as a second-hand arms proliferator in the Red Sea. Yemen's transfer of 20 Polish-supplied MBTs to Sudan in 1999 provided a good example of this trend, as did Yemen's readiness to help arm Eritrea in its war against its more powerful neighbour, Ethiopia.

In the other Horn countries, until the Eritrean–Ethiopian war, few centralised military purchases had surfaced in the post-Cold War period, as both money and effective central authority had proved to be scare commodities in the Horn states. But nonetheless, as we have shown, Ethiopia, Eritrea, Sudan and Yemen were already becoming engaged in a significant arms build-up, which suspiciously resembled a politically driven arms race between them.

Military and security developments in the Red Sea since 2000

The new century began with the promise of peace in the Arab–Israeli conflict, due to President Clinton's efforts in the dying days of his second term in office in 2000. But the breakdown in the talks, followed by a new Palestinian Intifadah, set the cast for new tensions in this part of the region, and further military confrontations between Israel and the Palestinian groups in Gaza and the West Bank. For Israel, however, relative peace on its borders between 2000 and 2006 (i.e., the war with Hezbollah in Lebanon) shifted the emphasis in its military planning southwards, with more emphasis on low intensity counter-insurgency warfare, on the one hand,

and missile defence in anticipation of Iranian SSM build-up, on the other. Over the decade the politico-security crisis in Gaza grew in military importance, adding substantially to Israel's defence burden and also forcing the IDF to refocus its efforts towards the militant groups operating in the Strip. Under financial constrains, the defence budget shrank by nearly $1 billion between 2001 and 2006. In the aftermath of the 34-Day War with Hezbollah, Israel's defence budget began to increase quite dramatically, to nearly $10 billion at the end of the decade. This was in part a response to the 2006 war and in part due to the costs of the IDF's Operation Cast Lead in Gaza in 2008, as well as of course the improvements in Israel's economic outlook. Israel also made a concerted effort to recover its naval prowess, adding more *Dolphin*-class submarines to its fleet, and at least seven fast patrol craft.

In Sudan, Yemen, and Somalia the security situation continued to deteriorate, and although Eritrea and Ethiopia showed no appetite for more warfare, relations between them has remained frosty ever since the mid-1990s. Apart from this, al-Qaeda's attack on *USS Cole* in 2000, offshore from Yemen, provided the first indication of the growing impact of Islamist terrorism on the greater Middle East, and the Red Sea sub-region in particular. As a consequence of this act and the growing level of Islamist and tribal violence in that country, as exemplified in a number of terrorist acts during Yemen's 2001 presidential race, from the early 2000s onwards, a new military relationship began to appear, in which the United States directly begun subsidising the Yemeni purchases of advanced Russian-made hardware.

For Saudi Arabia, the fall-out from regime change in Iraq in 2003 and the consolidation of Iranian power and influence in the Persian Gulf and the Levant, provided the backdrop to its security assessments, challenged as these were by a weakening grip of central government in neighbouring Yemen and al-Qaeda's growing presence in that country from 2004 onwards. Combined, these geopolitical developments provided concerted new security dilemmas for the Arab world's premier geo-economic power. Fortuitously for the Kingdom, rapid increases in oil prices post-2003 provided it with the financial resource base to substantially increase is defence outlay in response. With a budget surplus of nearly $60 billion by 2005, its defence spending mid-decade had increased by a quarter compared with early 2000s, standing at a staggering $25.3 billion in 2005 (Table 4.8).

The 1990s was marked by conflict in the lower Red Sea area and stalemate in the northern part of the sub-region, which in essence led to the rapid militarisation of the lower Red Sea states, with Yemen, Sudan, Ethiopia and particularly Eritrea investing rather heavily in their military and security sectors (Table 4.9). As we saw, the militarisation was partly fuelled by internal conflict and insurgencies, and partly due to inter-state conflict. What we see happening in the lower Red Sea in the twenty-first century is a consolidation of the force structures established in the 1990s, with Yemen and Sudan very much focused on internal security. In the case of Sudan in particular, we have seen a substantial increase in heavy military hardware in the 2000s.

In the northern Red Sea area, Israel and Saudi Arabia have, for largely different reasons, been leading the field in substantial increases in their military expenditures and purchases. But Egypt and Jordan too have devoted considerable

Table 4.8 Red Sea countries' military expenditures, 2002, 2005 and 2009

	Defence expenditure ($ mn)			% of GDP		
	2002	2005	2009	2002	2005	2009
Northern Red Sea						
Egypt	3,300	3,834	4,560	4.0	4.1	3.0
Israel	9,677	10,745	12,960	9.3	8.3	8.0
Jordan	776	973	2,310	8.1	8.0	11.0
Saudi Arabia	18,502	25,372	41,200	9.8	8.1	9.5
Southern Red Sea						
Djibouti	25	12	13	4.3	1.8	1.5
Eritrea	253	65	n.a..	40.5	6.3	n.a.
Ethiopia	350	300	317	5.8	2.7	1.3
Somalia	n.a.	n.a.	n.a.	n.a.	n.a.	n.a.
Sudan	388	1,169	n.a.	2.8	4.4	n.a.
Yemen	731	584	1,550	7.1	3.7	6.5

Source: IISS, *The Military Balance* (various years).

Table 4.9 The northern Red Sea military balance, 2005 and 2009

	Egypt		Israel		Jordan		Saudi Arabia	
	2005	2009	2005	2009	2005	2009	2005	2009
MBTs	3,855	3,723	3,657	3,501	1,139	1,182	1,055	910
Combat aircraft	572	461	402	461	100	102	291	280
Submarines	4	4	3	3	0	0	0	0
Frigates/destroyers	11	10	3	3	0	0	7	7
SSMs	18	18	107	107	0	0	50	50
Total armed forces (000)	468	468	168	176	100	100	199	235

Source: IISS, *The Military Balance* (various years).

resources to military modernisations early this century, with each making purchases of major platforms.

In the case of Israel, its acquisition of over 200 advanced fighters from the USA reinforced its position as the region's premier air force. Its purchase of submarines from Germany also extended its ability to enter and exit the Red Sea's waters. This comes on top of Israel's sophisticated ballistic missile defence capability and its advanced drone fighting force, which is already the most advanced in the region. Israel, then, has established a strong deterrence force, as the region's only nuclear power, alongside a powerful offensive capability which enables Israel to extend its reach to the far corners of the sub-region (Table 4.10).

Indeed, as Arab military power in the Red Sea has grown, so too has Israel's capability with regard to military power projection. Of particular concern to Israel was Saudi Arabia's growing military might, alongside Egypt's military modernisation

Table 4.10 Major weapons systems purchased or ordered by Israel since 2000

Type of weapon	Supplier	Year	Number
S-70 Black Hawk helicopter	USA	2001	24
WAH-64 Apache helicopter	USA	2001	3
F-16I	USA	2001	102
Merkava MBT	Indigenous	2001	400
F-15	USA	2004	110
AH-64 Apache helicopter	USA	2004	12
Dolphin-class submarine	Germany	2006	2

Sources: IISS, SIPRI, national sources.

Table 4.11 Major weapons systems purchased or ordered by Saudi Arabia since 2000

Type of weapon	Supplier	Year	Number
Eurofighter	Britain	2005	72
M1-A1 MBT	USA	2008	373
UH-60L helicopter	USA	2008	22
F-15S	USA	2010	84
UH-60 helicopter	USA	2010	72
AH-64D Apache helicopter	USA	2010	60

Sources: IISS, SIPRI, national sources.

efforts since 2001. From the Kingdom's point of view, however, its military purchases are consistent with its growing economic and industrial power, and the new security challenges presented in Yemen, Somalia, and of course in the Persian Gulf sub-region. Its arms purchases after 2005 thus show the return of Saudi Arabia as the region's biggest arms purchaser, which inevitably also underline the re-emergence of the close military partnership between Saudi Arabia and the United States. Saudi Arabia was to make history in 2010 with its biggest single military agreement to date with the United States. Coming on the back of the $20 billion US arms sales in 2007, in the new $60 billion deal, the United States agreed to supply to the Kingdom a major upgrade of existing US-supplied equipment and vast array of new and highly advanced military hardware. Some 84 F-15S combat aircraft, 60 AH-64D Apache attack helicopters, 72 UH-60 helicopters, a mix of naval vessels and patrol crafts with advanced weapons, upgrade of Patriot PAC 2 air defence missile systems form the backbone of this new contract, which is designed to meet the challenge of Iran, but of course will also enhance the Kingdom's military capabilities in relation to the Red Sea theatre (Table 4.11). As presented to the Congress, the package looked like this:

- Eighty-four new Boeing F-15 combat aircraft to replace aging F-15C and F-15D air defense variants purchased between 1978 and 1992.
- Upgrades for seventy F-15S strike variants, potentially including advanced long-range munitions for the aircraft.

- Seventy-two United Technologies Corporation UH-60 helicopters, to add to the twenty-two helicopters of the same type now held by the Saudis.
- Sixty Boeing AH-64D Longbow Apaches and upgrades to Saudi's twelve current AH-64A Apaches may also be included.
- Up to $5 billion in advanced, helicopter-carrying offshore patrol vessels.
- Upgrades to Saudi Arabia's ninety-six US-supplied Raytheon Patriot Advanced Capability 2 missiles.[37]

Saudi Arabia, with these purchases, will be the premier Arab military power and the dominant force along the shores of the Red Sea.

As we saw above, Egypt's steady rearmament continued unabated into the new century (Table 4.12), having already purchased 21 F-16 fighters in 1996. It followed its purchases with 200 M1-A1 main battle tanks, and 24 F-16 fighters from the United States in 1999. Its most recent efforts in strengthening its air defences is significant in the Red Sea context, as indeed is its purchase of over 100 M1-A1 MBTs to augment the force it had begun to built up in the late 1990s.

The biggest spender around the Horn has been Yemen, which over the 2000s multiplied its stores of heavy tanks and fast attack aircraft and fighters from Russia (Table 4.13). Yemen's fleet of over 100 advance fighters, augmenting its existing fleet of some 75 Russian-supplied fighters, provides the country with a strong platform for undertaking air operations well beyond its borders.

As we have tried to show, in the post-Cold War era, all Red Sea states have placed a high premium on the maintenance of a well-equipped military machine (Table 4.14). Thus, virtually every Red Sea state has devoted fairly substantial

Table 4.12 Major weapons systems purchased or ordered by Egypt since 2000

Type of weapon	Supplier	Year	Number
AH-64A Apache helicopter	US	2000	35
Hercules air transport	US	2004	21
M1-A1 MBT	US	2007	125
F-16C	US	2009	20

Sources: IISS, SIPRI, national sources.

Table 4.13 Weapons systems purchased by the southern Red Sea states since 2000

Country	Type of weapon	Supplier	Year	Number
Yemen				
	MiG-29	Russia	2001	15
	T-72 and T-80 MBT	Russia	2009	Unknown
	MiG-29	Russia	2006	32
	MiG-29	Russia	2006/7	66
Eritrea				
	Mi-8T helicopter	Libya	2001	2

Sources: IISS, SIPRI, national sources.

Table 4.14 The military balance in the Horn of Africa and surrounding area, 2005 and 2009

	Djibouti		Eritrea		Ethiopia		Sudan		Somalia		Yemen	
	2005	2009	2005	2009	2005	2009	2005	2009	2005	2009	2005	2009
MBTs	0	0	150	270	250	246	200	360	–	–	790	790
Combat aircraft	0	0	17	31	48	42	34	79	–	–	75	79
Submarines	0	0	0	0	–	–	0	0	–	–	0	0
Frigates/Destroyers	0	0	0	0	–	–	0	0	–	–	0	0
SSMs	0	0	0	0	0	0	0	0	–	–	28	28
Total armed forces (000)	00.9	01.0	200	200	182	138	105	110	–	–	0.67	0.67

Source: IISS, *The Military Balance* (various years).

resource to the defence sector, a pattern of behaviour that inter-state conflict, terrorism, and piracy have encouraged. In addition to the problems associated with insecurity in the Red Sea, several of the larger Red Sea states also have more to protect nationally than they did 20 or 30 years ago, which has also sustained high defence expenditures. Although there exists a definite north–south divide in the quality and size of the armed forces of Red Sea states, there is no doubt that all Red Sea countries entered the twenty-first century with their eyes very much on the wider applications of force, and their military power projectability. Insecurity breeds militarisation in the absence of a regional approach to security and co-operation, and in this context we have the makings of sub-regionalisation on the basis of mutual fear and a shared sense of insecurity permeating the sub-region.

5   Land boundaries, maritime borders and territorial issues

Introduction

The relations between Red Sea states are of course predicated on their mutual recognition of one another as legitimate and sovereign entities. Relations therefore become complicated by the inevitable disputes between them over land border delimitation and demarcation, maritime boundaries and ownership of cross-border resources that are the legacy of colonial territorial division, the subsequent emergence of independent states, conflicts between national, tribal, religious and ethnic groups to gain self-determination within, or by challenging, the resulting regional systems, and the new discovery of cross-border resources. All the Red Sea states have been at odds, at some time or other, with their neighbours over exact delimitation of territory or maritime resources. In some cases, territorial disputes between two states have drawn in third parties. In most, it has been obvious that there are implications for at least some of the other Red Sea riparian states. During the Cold War, border disputes between Red Sea states were either held in abeyance by the larger interests of the superpowers, or themselves became subject to that larger international scenario. Thus the disputes between Israel and her neighbours were never truly bilateral. The GCC states subordinated border disputes to a greater collective security requirement, and the Horn of Africa was a playing field for American and Soviet balance of power politics. Regional states were not free to pursue their own local interests without regard for a wider frame of reference. Yet boundary disputes resulting from the arbitrary drawing of colonial borders, from incompetent or incomplete early efforts at delimitation and demarcation, and from the emergence of independent states, lingered on. The discovery of hydrocarbons, a growing reliance on scarce water resources, and the increasing desire by states to exploit natural resources found on or under the land or sea bed, combined to add urgency to the desire by states to establish incontestable sovereignty over lands and waters which they considered their own. At times, inter-state crises, wars and external interventions provided opportunities for some to extend their aspirations and physical control over territories at the expense of others, adding to the lists of grievances and disputes which the maturing states became increasingly eager to resolve. Equally, as they sought to find allies for their claims, Red Sea states looked beyond their own neighbourhood, to Africa, the Arab world and elsewhere, obstructing the emergence of any collective political, economic or security arrangements.

In the 1990s, however, there were a number of serious efforts, some of which have been successful, to delimit and demarcate controversial boundaries by states around the Red Sea. This chapter seeks to survey these efforts, as well as the histories and variables which have prompted them. From this examination a number of patterns emerge. First, one can see that there are developing political, economic and security dynamics which lead some states to address boundary disputes with a new degree of vigour. This has been particularly true in the Arabian Peninsula and in Israel's relations with its neighbours. Second, the very importance of these dynamics can itself hinder resolution of boundary disputes as other broader interests take precedence over specific boundary negotiations. Third, the states of the Red Sea are increasingly aware of the importance of their own relations with one another. Efforts by regional powers such as Egypt, Saudi Arabia and Israel, to assert themselves in place of retreating superpowers, have heightened the stakes in these relationships, just as they have collectively come to realise the economic and strategic value of their access to the sea itself. Thus, boundary disputes between Red Sea states have implications beyond the immediate actors and we can observe new efforts at intervention, manipulation and even co-operation by third party Red Sea states in many of the disputes and negotiations. Finally, one can see a growing concern as the lower end of the Red Sea seems to be becoming increasingly unstable. The combination of a general superpower retreat, Islamic resurgence, piracy, lawlessness, and the emergence of a newly-independent Eritrea, has profoundly altered the balance of power in the Horn of Africa, with implications for all regional actors. On the other side, a weak but more assertive Yemen has at critical times found itself at odds with its larger neighbour Saudi Arabia, which itself seeks to establish its regional dominance over the Red Sea. The resulting tensions have raised international concern, even as the Arab–Israeli conflict at the northern end of the sea has appeared to be diminishing in intensity to the point of virtual normalisation in many areas.

Resource development meets politics: Egypt and Sudan

A good example of the coincidence of resource and political interests in a border dispute can be found in the ongoing dispute between Egypt and Sudan over the Halaib Triangle at the eastern end of their mutual border. With the exception of a small salient at Wadi Halfa, the Egyptian–Sudanese border follows the 22nd parallel of latitude. This was the line chosen in the 1899 Condominium Agreement between the British government and the Khedive of Egypt relevant to the future Administration of the Sudan after their joint forces had defeated the rebellious Mahdist state.[1] When Sudan's independence was finally recognised by Egypt in 1956, this line was treated as the international boundary, although a dispute arose as early as 1958 over the Wadi Halfa salient itself. After Sudanese efforts to hold elections in the area north of the parallel, Egypt claimed that this salient actually fell under its own sovereignty, a position it has continued to hold although without having taken any unilateral steps to enforce its claim. The claim is based on a preamble to the 1899 Agreement, an *arrêté* in 1902 and a subsequent Decree, all of which identified administrative as opposed to international borders which, for the purposes of convenience, had allocated administrative control of some areas north of the parallel to Sudan and some south of the parallel to Egypt. The Wadi Halfa was one such area, as were tribal grazing lands that crossed the parallel. Egypt argued that administrative borders were not international borders and that Sudanese sovereignty ended at the 22nd parallel. Either way, neither border has been formally demarcated.

The dispute was to arise again in 1992 when Sudan began to sign agreements with international oil companies allowing them to explore for oil in Red Sea waters north of the parallel, again claiming that the administrative borders could legitimately be considered as international borders for such purposes. Egypt had itself intended to issue exploration licences for a large block running south to the 1899 'political' boundary, overlapping with the northern end of the block offered by Sudan in the Halaib area.[2] This is a triangular block of land, amounting to 10,304 square kilometres and extending into the Red Sea and potentially a rich source of hydrocarbon deposits.

A brief attack by Egyptian military vehicles on a Sudanese police station was acknowledged by Egypt to have been a regrettable incident and the two sides subsequently agreed to a joint committee to try to resolve the border dispute. Tensions continued to build, with Sudan accusing Egypt of denying Suez Canal access to oil tankers on their way to Sudan and of building up a sizeable troop presence on the border. Egypt, for its part, pointed to what it saw as a Sudanese effort to amass troops and 'illegal structures' in the disputed area. The dispute rumbled on, with periodic bouts of Moroccan and OAU mediation being interrupted by accusations and counter-accusations until, in June 1995, they were exacerbated by political tensions over Egyptian accusations of a Sudanese collaboration in an assassination attempt on President Mubarak. Armed skirmishes turned into a larger-scale Egyptian attack, following which Egypt threatened to end the joint-policing efforts along the disputed border. Sudan retaliated by threatening to cut Nile water flows to Egypt. Relations rapidly deteriorated into threats of war, Egyptian calls for the overthrow of the Sudanese Islamist government and Sudanese claims that Egypt's actions were part of a grand strategy to exert pressure on Sudan to withdraw all its official presence from the Halaib area which included cutting off water supplies to Sudanese inhabitants, driving out civilians and depriving them of food and medical supplies. In March 1996, the dispute escalated once again as Egyptian troops shelled Sudanese forces in the area. Once again, the border dispute was intensifying as a result of more deep-seated political grievances – in this case, including the smuggling of weapons from Sudan to Islamist rebels in Egypt itself.[3] The long dispute has intensified further with the discovery of oil. In October 2009, the Electoral Commission that prepared a comprehensive plan for Sudan's general elections in April 2010 declared that Halaib was one of its electoral districts and that its people should exercise their constitutional rights and register in order to participate in the general elections. Typically, voter registration did not take place in the Halaib Triangle area because the team from the Sudanese election commission was refused entry by Egyptian authorities. The problem continues to fester and complicate bilateral relations between Khartoum and Cairo.

How oil fuels a dispute: Saudi Arabia and Yemen

The discovery of oil resources that straddle borders has a particular propensity to fuel disputes when the border itself has never previously been recognised. This has been an acute problem for the states of the Arabian Peninsula, and nowhere more so than on the Yemeni-Saudi Arabian boundary.

In the case of the Saudi Arabian border with Yemen, only the western section from the Red Sea to the Oasis of Najran was delimited and demarcated after the 1934 Treaty of Taif (also known as the Treaty of Islamic Friendship and Brotherhood) marked the end of a brief war between Ibn Saud and the Imam of Yemen. The remaining 800 miles (1500 km) of border remained subject to British and Saudi counter-claims dating back to the so-called violet-line,[4] a boundary between Ottoman and British spheres of influence agreed in 1914. Saudi Arabia rejected British claims that this, and its own proposals for delimitation, should determine international boundaries, claiming instead the so-called Hamza Line, which was based on alleged tribal allegiances and which stretched significantly more southwards. What was to become North Yemen itself claimed a different boundary based on its own interpretations of tribal allegiances and those of the British explorer, H. Philby in the 1930s. In subsequent years, both Yemens were to find themselves at odds with Saudi Arabia over the delimitation and demarcation of boundaries and it was only in the 1990s that the matter was to be resolved following a number of brief but intense crises. Prior to that, and despite commitments to periodic reviews of the Taif Accord which had only been implemented in the 1950s, little had been done to address the issue of undemarcated borders other than to ultimately agree to present their respective cases at some point to the International Court of Justice. For the most part Yemen was allowed by Saudi Arabia to establish some limited structural assets in the disputed territory and the larger country would respond only when Yemen transgressed across the Ottoman-British lines.

However, Saudi Arabia became alarmed by the Yemeni unification in 1990, fearing the strengthening of the reunified entity on its southern flank and the new state's apparent preference for a democratic mode of government. Whereas the Cold War era had seen a general American sympathy for Saudi support of North Yemen against the South, the unification and moderation of a single Yemeni regime led to a shift in the American position to one which was somewhat more equitably balanced between Saudi Arabia and the new Yemen. Thus, Saudi Arabia increasingly felt the pressure to itself take responsibility for preserving traditional forms of rule in the Gulf at the expense of what it perceived to be threatening modernisations on its southern flank.

Saudi fears were heightened by a series of high level delegations visiting Sana'a from Tehran, indicating the possibility of an Iranian–Yemeni axis that would dominate both the Straits of Hormuz on one side of the Peninsula and the Bab el-Mandeb on the other. Furthermore, some elements in Yemen began reasserting a claim to the territories of Asir and Najran, allegedly 'lost' to Saudi Arabia in 1934 and representing part of the 'Greater Yemen' which had dominated the southern Peninsula in the seventeenth century.

The Saudi response was to make unspecified claims on territory which North Yemen and now the new unified state considered to be its own. In spite of calls by the new Yemeni President, Ali Abdullah Saleh, for a new initiative to settle border issues with both Oman and Saudi Arabia in 1991, the dispute came to a head in 1992 when Yemen granted oil concessions to foreign companies for exploration in areas claimed by Saudi Arabia, notably in the Hadhramaut, al-Mahra, Marib and offshore in Red Sea waters. Saudi Arabia in return sent letters to the oil companies concerned (BP, Elf Aquitaine, Total and Petro Canada),[5] informing them that any attempts to implement the concessions would amount to trespass, given that Saudi Arabia disputed Yemeni claims to sovereignty over the territories in which they were working. The Saudi position was triggered not least by its own fears that Yemeni-Omani border negotiations appeared to have resulted in an agreement in principle to define their own borders north from the coast to a latitude of 19 degrees, stretching into desert territory claimed by Saudi Arabia. Added to this were the unresolved tensions which had evolved out of Yemeni support for the Iraqi position in the 1990/91 Kuwait war, the subsequent forced repatriation of nearly one million Yemeni workers from Saudi Arabia, and Saudi intervention in Yemeni domestic affairs through its own influence among certain northern tribes. The discovery of oil along the boundaries in question had provided the final incentive for both sides to start asserting their claims. Despite efforts by some elements of the Yemeni press to incite their own country to take up arms in defence of their claim, both governments expressed themselves willing to negotiate the borders and the United States was drawn into a mediation effort. They were unable to make significant progress, however, and the dispute rumbled on with reported troop build-ups and minor skirmishes along the border throughout the mid-1990s. Saudi Arabia took the opportunity of a civil war in Yemen in 1994 to attempt to sponsor groups aiming to undermine the unity of the state, further antagonising the regime and delaying prospects of substantive negotiations over borders. It was also accused of moving troops and armour to the border and of encroaching upon Yemeni territory by 'erecting monitoring posts and building a number of roads deep inside Yemeni territory'.[6]

In February 1995, the parties signed a Memorandum of Understanding confirming the binding nature of the Taif Accord, providing for the demarcation of the Taif line, and establishing joint committees to negotiate and demarcate the remaining boundaries (including a sea border). The Memorandum was in effect a defeat for Yemen, confirming as it did Saudi sovereignty over the Tihama Plain and the lost provinces of Asir and Najran, but by now the fledgling state was in urgent need of both international oil company investment (and accompanying oil revenues) and Saudi investment. The Saudi action had led a number of companies to freeze or withdraw from operations in Yemen and the economy was rapidly stumbling into a full-scale crisis. Thus Yemen was forced to make the concession in order to jump-start substantive negotiations on the remaining majority portion of the border. A Joint Committee was established and began working on the demarcation of border posts, despite further minor border clashes, while another committee began work on demarcating a maritime border. Relations seemed to have significantly improved when a security co-operation agreement was signed in July 1996 to deal with drug trafficking and smuggling across the border but took a turn for the worse when Yemen began to alter the administrative organisation of territories claimed by Saudi Arabia, which was rumoured to have plans for an oil pipeline to cross the areas to the Indian Ocean.[7] 1997 saw renewed border clashes, and in May 1998 Saudi Arabia effectively invaded the Yemeni island of Huraym in the Red Sea as well as smaller islands in the archipelago. In July, the Saudi navy also attacked and occupied al-Duwaima island, although Yemen claimed to have recaptured the island shortly afterwards. For Saudi Arabia, which has no direct access to the Indian Ocean, improving its strategic influence in the Red Sea is vital. With negotiations with Yemen going nowhere, and with Yemen still seeking to establish its rights over oil reserves below the waters, the larger state was clearly inclined to assert its interests forcibly. Simultaneous clashes in the al-Jawf and Ma'rib provinces have seen Saudi-sponsored tribes attacking Yemeni oil pipelines. In sum, unresolved border issues which were relatively unimportant prior to Yemeni unification and the discovery of oil in disputed territories and waters, now moved much higher up the national agendas of the two states, to the point where they were prepared to take military action to defend their interests. This is not least a result of the fact that both states can and must take new responsibility for defending their interests in the region themselves since there are no superpowers willing or able to either comprehensively restrain their ambitions or advance them on their behalf. In June 2000, the two parties finally signed another agreement reiterating the 1934 Taif agreement, which has formed the basis for better relations since then.

It is worth noting that Saudi Arabia has had disputes over borders with pretty well all its neighbours at some time or other. Agreement with the UAE was reached in August 1974 (although there are suggestions that a minor amendment was agreed in 1977) after a full 40 years of negotiations and three years after the British withdrawal from the Gulf when the UAE was formed by the federation of seven emirates. The boundary is as yet largely unrecognised in international legal terms but has *de facto* status with both parties. Agreement with Oman over their 676-km border was only reached in March 1990 and the actual border demarcated in 1992–95. An agreement with Kuwait was reached in 1969 over their shared land border, but controversy remained over the offshore boundaries, including over the islands of Qanah and Umm el-Maradim. The land boundary had initially been settled in a 1922 agreement between Kuwait (then under British control) and the sultanate of Nejd. It included a so-called 'neutral zone' on the southern borders, resolution of the sovereignty over which was left for a later date. The discovery of oil in that area in 1938 led to an agreement in 1965, to take effect in 1969, to divide the neutral zone equally into two parts, one to be taken by each state. While this resolved the land border, demarcation of the off-shore boundaries and the islands of Qanuh and Umm el-Maradim was not agreed upon until 1996.

The boundary agreement with Qatar was reached in 1993, in an agreement ratified by Egypt, although its details were kept secret and the text remained unpublished. Previously, and as with the Yemeni border, Ibn Saud had refused to accept the validity of borders agreed between the Ottoman and British governments. Once again, it was the need to establish rights over oil deposits that forced the two states to address the issue of demarcating borders, with an agreement officially being reached in 1965. The British challenged the agreement on behalf of Abu Dhabi, which lost part of its own territory under the terms of the agreement. When the Saudi government attempted to formally delimit its borders with the UAE in the 1970s, the Qataris became nervous at what were seen as expansionist Saudi aspirations. In 1992, for example, there was an alleged Saudi attack on a Qatari border post at Khafus which the Saudis claimed fell within its own territory. Subsequent negotiations and the secretive agreement of 1993 did not fully resolve the problem. A map, which was agreed but not published, purportedly maintained Qatari sovereignty over Khafus but gave territorial concessions to Saudi Arabia elsewhere along the border including over a corridor of land previously held by the UAE which linked Saudi Arabia to the southern Gulf. However, it seems that the technical process of demarcating the border was poorly done and there have since been a number of armed skirmishes between Saudi and Qatari troops (the Saudis deny military involvement, placing the blame on tribal elements acting independently). In 1996, international companies were employed to professionally demarcate the boundary to prevent further problems but in the meantime both parties have spoken of the disputes as threatening the unity of the GCC itself. For Saudi Arabia, resolving border disputes is about a combination of securing sovereignty over sub-soil resources, reinforcing regional dominance and establishing guaranteed access to the waters that surround the Peninsula: the Persian Gulf, the Indian Ocean and the Red Sea.

It is unclear exactly why the 1990s saw this spurt of GCC activity towards resolving boundary disputes and establishing mutually acknowledged demarcation. Certainly the Iraqi invasion of Kuwait, and the claims made against the sovereignty and independence of the smaller state, indicated the dangers of leaving such matters ill-defined. Struggles within the GCC also account for the activity as Saudi Arabia seeks to assert its dominance and the smaller states to restrict it. Finally, the question of cross-border hydrocarbons has become more important as prices and national incomes have come under pressure. Either way, notions of informal inter-state or inter-regime relationships based on common forms of government or traditional links, have become less salient in an era when national interest has been shown to be so closely tied to the territorial integrity of states.

The strategic angle: Yemen and Eritrea

The strategic importance of Red Sea boundaries was clearly illustrated by the dispute between Yemen and Eritrea over the Hanish islands in the 1990s. At first glance, there is little to recommend the Hanish Islands to either Yemen or Eritrea. Like most of the numerous islands and coral formations at the southern end of the Red Sea, they are barren and uninhabitable, traditionally used only by local fishermen. However, they lie 60–70 nautical miles north of the strategic waters of the Bab el-Mandeb. These straits link the Red Sea (and by extension the Suez Canal and the Mediterranean) with the Gulf of Aden and the Indian Ocean. Eritrea, Yemen and Djibouti all have direct coastal interests at stake, but as the example of the Saudi–Yemeni dispute showed, the strategic importance of the waters is felt much more widely by all the states bordering the Red Sea itself (especially those with major port facilities to serve the transit trade) and the international powers which consider themselves to have a stake in the security of navigation. Other islands of importance in the area include Kamaran, the Dahlak Archipelago, islands in the bay of Assab and, most importantly of all, Perim, which divides the straits themselves into two waterways. Most traffic passing through the Bab el-Mandeb uses the western channel which is just nine and a quarter miles across and which reaches depths of up to 1000 feet.[8]

The value of the Hanish islands for Eritrea and Yemen is enhanced by the fact that the mainland coastlines have few indentations and are edged with shallow reefs, 'leaving only a relatively narrow but deep channel free for navigation'.[9] Shipping has little choice but to pass by them. The islands lie almost centrally between Eritrea (22 nm or 40 km distant at its nearest point) and Yemen (16 nm or 30 km) and both have much to gain from recognition of their own sovereignty over them. As well as their strategic importance, they offer significant fishing, hydrocarbon and even tourism potential.

The strategic value of the islands was evident when they were briefly occupied by Egypt in the 1970s in order to enforce a blockade against Israeli shipping, according to some, with Aden's unofficial blessing. Israel has subsequently remained deeply concerned with the question of freedom of navigation and control over the islands which can ensure this. Not surprisingly then Israel has featured prominently in the subsequent conflicts over sovereignty of the islands, with its interests tied closely to those of Eritrea rather than either Yemen. Indeed, in 1977, Yemen deployed its own troops to some of the islands, considering them to be under threat from Israel. During the 1980s, both Yemens and Ethiopia took their dispute over ownership to the United Nations as they fought to win recognition for their claims when signing the UN Law of the Sea Convention. Despite their concerted efforts, no legal ruling was made and sovereignty remained in dispute until tensions erupted into direct confrontation in 1995. The argument, which had focused in the early 1990s on rights to the lucrative fish resources in the coastal waters and the impounding by Eritrea of Yemeni fishermen and their boats, was to escalate dramatically in September and October of 1995 as the islands themselves became the focus of attention. Eritrea signed an agreement with the American firm, Anadarko Petroleum Corporation, for exploration in its 'Zula Block' (worth a reported $28.5 million),[10] which extends into the Hanish area,[11] while Yemen was busy allowing a German firm to establish tourist-oriented diving operations on Greater Hanish. Yemen had itself earlier issued three offshore concessions, including Block 24 which cuts through Greater Hanish, while Eritrea had been disappointed that a German company had decided not to build a tourist diving facility on islands closer to its own shores. Clearly both states were racing to compete for revenues which could be derived from the islands and their maritime surroundings.

Both states declared their determination to establish their own sovereignty, and the dispute over fishing rights gained a new momentum, but – according to Yemen – Eritrea was to pre-empt any diplomatic solutions by landing naval forces on three islands (Greater Hanish, Lesser Hanish and Zukar) on 15 November. According to Yemeni sources, the Eritrean forces removed Yemeni military and fishing personnel from the islands, claiming that they lay in Eritrean waters. Eritrea denied having invaded the islands thus, arguing that Yemen had itself been beefing up its own military presence there since March 1995.[12] Both sides asserted their own willingness to take the matter to the International Court of Justice (although Yemen preferred in the first instance to attempt bilateral negotiations)[13] and the reluctance of the other side to do so. In the meantime, even as the Yemeni president, Abdullah Saleh, was reported to have solicited intervention from the United States, Yemen announced that it was launching its own combing naval operation to remove Eritrean troops from the islands and reinforcing its own military presence. Throughout November, the sides engaged in talks trying to resolve the dispute, aided – or in some cases impeded – by a flurry of willing diplomatic initiatives.

Egypt and Jordan, while generally falling on Yemen's side, were keen to see stability restored to the Red Sea. They therefore urged both sides to resolve the dispute peacefully and, as the crisis developed in December, both offered to act as mediators. The Arab League was more ardently pro-Yemen. On 18 December, the League confirmed Yemen's right to and sovereignty over the three Red Sea islands and its right to defend its territory, insist on its national borders and regional waters, and protect them against any encroachment. Not surprisingly Eritrea condemned what it saw as Arab intervention, arguing that this was a matter for Yemen and Eritrea only and that the Arab League had no moral or legal obligations to intervene. The Arab interest became complicated, however, as military confrontations began in December with reports of an Israeli involvement emerging from some quarters.

While Eritrea claimed that its positions on the islands (and in particular its own units on Lesser Hanish) were attacked by Yemeni forces on 15 December, on the 17 December, Yemen claimed that Eritrean gunboats had attacked Greater Hanish and its manned garrison. Following skirmishes with Yemeni units, they withdrew two days later, taking 180 Yemeni prisoners with them and leaving a small number dead on both sides. Yemeni Republic Radio station claimed that the Eritrean troops had used Israeli-made gunboats and civilian ferries to carry out their 'treacherous aggression'[14] and that Israel was assisting the Eritreans by providing advanced military equipment.

The claims were repeated by the Arab media around the Middle East, despite denials from both Eritrea and Israel, and one newspaper went so far as to state that Yemeni units intercepted 'communications conducted in Hebrew among the attacking Eritrean forces – which prompts one to believe that they are using Israeli gunboats and Israel guides'.[15] It was further suggested that the military aid was in return for Eritrean promises to allow Israel to establish a military base of its own on the island.[16] Even the Eritrean opposition leader, Idris Abdullah Mohammed of the mainly Muslim Eritrean Liberation Front (ELF), accused the Eritrean government of using the island dispute to distract attention from domestic troubles and of assisting external colonial powers headed by Israel. He said that there was already an Israeli land base in the mountains near the border with Sudan and another in the Dahlak Archipelago.[17]

Yemen attempted to portray the Eritrean action as hostile to the interests of all Arab states, not least since many of them had given Eritrean forces strong support in their struggle for independence from Ethiopia. Indeed, the Yemeni president went on to say that Yemen had allowed Eritrean guerrilla forces periodic use of the islands themselves as a military base during their war of independence. Eritrea, for its part, counter-argued that the islands were at risk of being used by extremist groups, supported by Sudan, as a base for launching operations against his own government. The Sudanese response was manifest in a statement by the Sudan Foreign Ministry about the 'dubious and planned role being performed by the Eritrean regime to destabilise the security and stability of the Horn of Africa and the Red Sea region'.[18] Other more radical Arab states such as Libya and Iraq, as well as Iran, also made strong statements asserting their solidarity with Yemen in the face of what they saw as efforts to impose foreign, Zionist, hegemony over the Red Sea. More moderate Egypt, Qatar, Algeria (whose national energy company, Sonatrach, holds a stake in Andarko Petroleum Corporation), and Ethiopia (which had a joint defence agreement with Eritrea but which did not wish to see its own relations with Arab states deteriorate) saw opportunities to enhance their own regional positions by offering their mediation services. A similar offer from the United Nations was matched by competing bids from the OAU and the OIC. The intensity of international concern to play a part in the resolution of the conflict reflected not just the strategic value of a peaceful Bab el-Mandeb for all concerned, but equally their desires to see an outcome which enhanced their respective interests.

Amidst a confusion of claims and counter-claims of Eritrean and Yemeni military activity around the islands, a cease-fire was announced, as well as the decision to form a committee to supervise the cease-fire that would include two US diplomats. America, like most international actors, was profoundly concerned by the dispute, falling as it did so close to the international navigation line in the Red Sea. Fears were quickly given more tangible foundations when a Russian cargo ship was hit by Eritrean forces as it crossed the navigation channel. Both Yemen and Eritrea now expressed their willingness to resolve the dispute peacefully, although it was not until May 1996 that the two countries formally agreed to settle the issue peacefully by arbitration according to an Accord of Principles mediated by the French. They entered the mediation efforts, previously dominated by Egypt, Ethiopia and the United States, in January. The proximity of the French garrison and naval base in Djibouti and their own multi-million dollar gas project in Yemen had given them direct interests in resolution of the conflict. The Accord agreed to the establishment of a five-judge arbitration court in London, to start work by April 1997. Eritrea and Yemen each appointed two judges, none of whom were to be from their own nations. A president for the panel was jointly chosen, in this case, Sir Robert Jennings, the former president of the International Court of Justice. As the panel was being formed, France sent observers to monitor activity on the islands themselves, while American, French, United Nations and Ethiopian pressure was successfully brought to bear on Eritrea to withdraw its military presence from them and to release Yemeni citizens whom it had seized from the islands.

At the end of the first phase of arbitration, which saw hearings in January and February of 1998 and a judgement in October, the sovereignty of the islands was determined. Eritrea was awarded the Mohabbakah islands, Haycock Islands and the South West Rocks. Yemen was meantime awarded the Zuqar-Hanish Islands, the island of Jabal al-Tayr, and the islands and rocks of the Zubayr group. Both countries could enjoy traditional fishing rights within the waters of islands awarded to Yemen. A second phase which would delineate a maritime boundary between the two countries began in 1999.[19]

Although there were clear economic reasons for both parties to lay claim to the islands, the aggravation of the dispute into a military confrontation left a number of unanswered questions. Many commentators considered it odd that Eritrea should seek so overtly to offend Yemen, which had been an ally during its own war for independence. For Arab states in particular, the answer lay somewhere in Israel's self-declared 'special relationship' with Eritrea, in Israel's interest in substituting Red Sea fish stocks for the depleted Mediterranean stocks that had previously sustained its fishing fleets,[20] and in joint Israeli-Eritrean fears over pro-Sudanese Islamist operations which might have utilised bases on either the islands or Yemen itself. Eritrea's importance as a key ally against Islamist Sudan found resonance in Egypt, which took a neutral stance in the dispute despite its Arab League membership and Arab links with Yemen. Saudi Arabia too, was possibly happy to see another state applying pressure on Yemeni control over the southern waters of the Red Sea,[21] even as it was itself engaging its fishing fleets in the disputed waters with Eritrean approval. Thus, the three 'regional powers' bordering the Red Sea, found an odd coincidence of interest in Eritrea's activities which was based strictly on their strategic view of the division of Red Sea waters as a variable in a regional balance of power and their own economic aspirations for the resources of the sea. Concern over the strategic aspects of the dispute reached further afield, however, demonstrating that the wider Africa,

Arab and Islamic worlds all considered the Red Sea to be of direct importance to their own interests.

Concern leads to collaboration: Saudi Arabia and Sudan

Rivalries over the Red Sea need not always lead to confrontation, however. One illustration of co-operation in exploiting underwater resources can be found in the Saudi Arabian–Sudanese agreement to jointly exploit metaflous muds and effectively share sovereignty in waters that fall between them.

The arrangement finds its roots in the peculiarities of the Red Sea; in the abnormal variations in temperature and salinity and in the existence of 'deeps' created by the rift valley running through the centre of the sea. Some of the deeps are consequently full of warm brine, at the bottom of which lie mineral and metal-rich sediments. The existence of these so-called metalliferous hot brines was confirmed in 1966 and three principal deposits were confirmed in the Atlantis II, Discovery and Chain Deeps. All three deeps lie within 'a small area of less than ten by ten nautical miles, between Saudi Arabia, west of Jeddah, and the Sudan'.[22] A number of smaller possible deposits were also identified, in a line stretching for three hundred miles up the Red Sea. The brines, or 'oozes', contained what were generally considered to be commercially exploitable quantities of sodium, calcium, manganese, magnesium, copper, zinc and iron, as well as other minerals. Thus, when an American firm applied to the United Nations for an exploration lease to a 38.5 square mile section of the Red Sea bed, on the basis that no nation had as yet asserted contrary rights to the sea bed, Saudi Arabia was quick to consider the implications. The United Nations argued that it did not have the competence to grant the lease for a number of legal reasons which amounted to an assertion that the width of the Red Sea placed any sea bed and subsoil resources within the sovereign rights of states bordering the sea. The onus was now on those states to claim their sovereign rights and Saudi Arabia promptly did so with its 1968 Law relating to the Acquisition of the Red Sea Resources. The claim was made over the continental shelf of Saudi Arabia, as well as an area extending beyond the shelf and related to the concept of the 200-mile exclusive economic zone. It was made clear that the limited size of the Red Sea did not allow all states to establish a similar sized exclusive zone, and Saudi Arabia was forced to take the initiative in order to preserve its own interests. However, and in an effort to pre-empt disputes with neighbours (including states on the other side of the Red Sea), it was made equally clear that Saudi Arabia was open to joint exploration projects with those neighbours who might have similar rights in areas which the Saudi government could consider as jointly shared, or in areas where neighbours might claim similar overlapping rights with those of Saudi Arabia. The priority for Saudi Arabia might have been the assertion of its own rights, but it was equally keen to preserve the unity of the Red Sea states in the face of external claims on their collective resources. The two issues were closely related in terms of protecting Saudi Arabia's regional position and the principle of its rights to resources of the wider region. Thus, in July 1972, the Saudi government invited its neighbours to attend the first Conference of States bordering the Red Sea, the purpose of which was to establish the rights of Red Sea states over deep mineral resources in and under the sea itself and to agree on how those rights should be exercised and regulated. Egypt, Ethiopia and the Yemen Arab Republic attended, but more importantly for Saudi Arabia, so too did Sudan.

Since the primary deposits were virtually equidistant between Saudi Arabia and Sudan, it had been immediately clear that an arrangement needed to be made between these two states. In fact, the deposits of the Atlantis II, Discovery and Chain deeps fell on the Sudanese side of the median line of the Red Sea and it might have been argued that they therefore fell under Sudanese sovereignty. In the event, an agreement was reached in May 1974 whereby each state recognised the sovereignty of the other over sea bed extending from their respective coastlines towards one another to a depth of 1,000 metres. The area between these two lines was considered to come under equally shared sovereignty and all rights therein fell exclusively to them. The mineral-rich deeps fell within this common zone and a joint commission was established under the agreement to supervise the surveying, delimiting, exploration and exploitation of the resources. Inevitably, Saudi Arabia was to provide the initial funding for this commission, although it could later recoup its costs from future income generated by the resources. The agreement conformed to international law and set 'a valuable precedent for the delimitation of other offshore boundaries in the Red Sea'.[23] It was also important in establishing a nascent Red Sea identity which recognised common economic interests as well as a collective interest in preventing unrestrained international activity in the Red Sea. For Saudi Arabia, the cost of underwriting the joint commission and of forfeiting some of the rights its had claimed for itself under the 1968 law in its agreement with Sudan, were offset by the leading role which it was now playing in determining the status of Red Sea resources and co-ordinating joint efforts to claim and exploit them.

Such an imaginative and constructive approach to the establishment of boundaries does have precedents in the region. In 1965, the Treaty of Amman modified the border between Saudi Arabia and Jordan (originally largely established in the 1925 Hadda Agreement) in such a way as to give Jordan a longer coastline on the Gulf of Aqaba in return for Saudi Arabia acquiring a chunk of inland desert. Efforts like these, where Red Sea states have recognised one another's interests and compromised their own accordingly to the mutual benefit, indicate that a balance of power may already be emerging among Red Sea states that allows for negotiated balancing of interests rather than direct dispute and confrontation.

Introducing independent states: Israel and its neighbours

Unfortunately, not all the Red Sea states have found it so simple to find solutions to their border disputes. The northern end of the sea has been as equally beset by border disputes as the south, and again the origins of the disputes can be traced to the fragility of understandings regarding boundaries which were left in the wake of colonial withdrawal. Not surprisingly, Israel found itself in the midst of disputes with Egypt, Jordan and – in more recent times – with the Palestinian Authority with regard to its Red Sea borders and Syria and Lebanon over its northern borders.

In the case of Israel's border with Egypt, the present boundary is a reflection of a combination of factors including the struggle for control over the Sinai between the Ottoman Empire and Britain, the series of four wars between Israel and Egypt, and two world wars which introduced other external players into the game.[24] In the first instance, efforts to establish a border between British-controlled Egypt and Ottoman-held Palestine were obstructed by British determination to preserve its own control over the Suez Canal and the sea route to India, and Ottoman-German efforts to maintain the security of the Hejaz railway which enabled them to transfer troops from Damascus to the Indian Ocean (freeing themselves of the need to make use of the Canal). For both parties, the desolate Sinai desert represented a useful potential buffer zone to deter aggression by the others' forces. In 1906, the British attempted to enforce their own preferred border, along a line from Rafah to Aqaba, allocating the entire Sinai to Egyptian sovereignty. British gunboat diplomacy forced the Ottoman Sultan to accept the proposed border as an 'administrative separating line'. When the line was finally demarcated, however, and in the face of Turkish determination not to give access to the Wadi Araba, it ended at Ras Taba, 10 kilometres west of Aqaba, rather than at a point 3 miles west of Aqaba as originally envisaged by the British. This was ultimately to become a major sticking point in Egyptian-Israeli border negotiations in the 1980s. Although the Ottoman authorities did not accept the line as an international boundary, the British enforced it as such once they came to control Mandate Palestine as well as Egypt after the First World War. When Egypt and the new Israeli state came to blows in 1948, an initial Israeli occupation of part of Sinai brought threats from Britain which led ultimately to an Israeli withdrawal and an armistice line which coincided almost exactly with the 1906 boundary, only the Gaza Strip presenting a deviation. From that point in 1949, until its demarcation under the terms of the 1979 Israeli-Egyptian Camp David peace treaty, the border remained insecure. In 1956, Israeli troops swept across it towards the Suez Canal as part of a British-French-Israeli plan to recapture the Canal from Nasser's nationalisation for the former colonial powers and the Sinai for Israel. Israel was motivated not least by Egypt's use of its military positions in Suez and Sinai to close the Canal and the Gulf of Aqaba to Israeli shipping. Having been forced by international pressure to withdraw, Israel was nonetheless able to break the blockade of her ships through the Gulf of Aqaba (but not through Suez) and to gain a UN presence in the Sinai which temporarily served to secure the border from guerrilla infiltration. By the mid-1960s, tensions between Egypt and Israel were resurfacing. In 1967, Egypt demanded the withdrawal of the UN forces from the border zone and again closed the Gulf of Aqaba and the Straits of Tiran to Israeli shipping. The result was an Israeli attack, the so-called Six Day War in June 1967, during which Israel occupied the Sinai as well as other Arab territories. The war, in a revised attrition-based format, moved to the Suez area but by 1973 Egypt was ready to embark on a full-scale military adventure to recapture its Sinai territories. An unclear outcome, as well as domestic and international political circumstances, encouraged both states to seek a formal peace. As part of the ensuing negotiations and staged agreements, Israel gradually withdrew from the Sinai, with the ultimately agreed international border being demarcated in 1981 essentially along the same 1906 Agreement line. The only significant point of controversy (out of 15 initial points of dispute) concerned the termination of the land border at Taba. When the British had originally demarcated the border with poles and then masonry pillars, they had placed the last-but-one post (number 90) north of Taba itself. A final post, number 91 (otherwise known as the Parker Stone) had not actually been placed on the coastal shore since the particular shore was susceptible to winter floods which might unroot it. Instead it was placed on a nearby hill. Thus, when Egypt and Israel came to the question as to where exactly on the coast the boundary ended, they made counter-claims as to where post 91 should actually have been. The total shoreline under dispute did not amount to much, but Israel naturally was concerned to extend its very limited access to the Red Sea as far as possible, while Egypt was equally concerned to stick to what it believed to have been the original line that lay in its favour. International arbitration in 1986 ultimately came down in Egypt's favour on the basis that Egypt's claims were based on 1906 maps that had been accepted by Israel since 1948 and which should not now be subject to new challenges. While Taba was thus not divided between Egyptian and Israeli sovereignty, Rafah – at the northern end of the boundary – was divided between Egypt and the Gazan section of Israeli-occupied territory. The areas adjacent to the boundary in-between were subject to demilitarisation commitments on the part of Egypt and, to a lesser extent, Israel. These arrangements were subject to international supervision which would also ensure free navigation through the Straits of Tiran and up the Gulf of Aqaba.

In the event, the border has held and been respected by both parties since it was agreed upon. This has been in spite of the fact that the peace has never evolved into the warm relationship aspired to by Israel but has rather been constantly victim to Egyptian disappointments over what is sees as aggressive Israeli foreign policy throughout the Middle East and the Zionist state's failure to satisfactorily resolve the Palestinian question. If one is to draw a lesson from this border dispute, one can argue that resolution and demarcation can result from common interests in stable peaceful borders but that those interests and the establishment of a mutually agreed international border do not necessarily make friends of neighbouring states. Wider political and strategic interests predominate in international relations. One can also point to the importance of external players, in this case the superpowers, and latterly the United States alone, in imposing their own interests upon the parties to the dispute. The pursuit of stability in the Middle East has been a key goal in American policy-making since the Second World War, as has the preservation of Israeli security. The two aims combined neatly in the Camp David Accords – and in their inadequacies.

Israel has also signed a peace agreement with Jordan which includes an agreement (Annex 1 of the Treaty of Peace Between The Hashemite Kingdom of Jordan and The State of Israel of 1994) on their mutual borders. In this instance, there was no relevant border to speak of until the British decided to separate Transjordan from Palestine in 1922 one year after the Cairo Conference. They did so in only a vaguely delimited way with the main part of the border lying along the 'line of lowest points' in the Wadi Araba. Other parts of the border, including that along the Dead Sea (which was supposedly equidistant from the eastern and western shores), and that which followed the Jordan river northwards, were badly marked on maps and made redundant by shifts in the water level of the sea and the directional flow of the river.[25] Like Egypt, Jordan was to wage war on Israel in 1948–49, although secret negotiations with Israel[26] ensured a final armistice line which, while generally based on the British line, also placed the hilly chunk of territory west of the River Jordan which has since become known as the West Bank under Jordanian administration, as well as the eastern half of Jerusalem. The line separating these territories from the new Israeli state became known as the 'Green line'. Israel was to conquer these territories in 1967, ultimately annexing East Jerusalem and placing the West Bank under first military and then a pseudo-civilian administration. The dispute over sovereignty of these areas was confused by further claims by the emerging Palestinian nationalist movement that they should form part of a future Palestinian state, and by right-wing and religious Zionist claims that they were irrevocably part of a Greater Israel. Meanwhile, the cease-fire line between Israel and Jordan was supposed to follow the lowest point of the river bed but was never marked on the ground. It consequently shifted when the wadi changed course after flooding and silting, notably in 1983 when a hard winter led to a large flow of water sweeping land from the West Bank of the river to the east, adding several dozen dunums of land to Jordan at Israel's expense.

In August 1988 and in support of the Palestinian Uprising (Intifada), King Hussein of Jordan relinquished Jordanian claims to the occupied territories, but political tensions between Jordan and Israel over Palestinian national rights, Israeli military activities in and occupation of parts of Lebanon and continued Israeli rejection of the claims of Palestinian refugees to return to their homelands, continued to prevent any meaningful moves towards a peace agreement between the two states which might include any formal delimitation and demarcation of an international boundary. Jordan was unable to advance in that direction, given its position that Israel was not eligible to establish a border between Jordan and land which Israel illegally occupied. Moreover, the King's freedom to manoeuvre in his dealings with Israel was always limited by the need to balance Jordanian national interests with those of the substantial Palestinian majority who lived either as Jordanian citizens or as refugees within Jordan. The absence of a formal agreement did not stop informal border arrangements from largely holding sway during the 1948–94 era. Jordan and Israel continued to manage a steady flow of cross-border trade (usually via the West Bank) and peoples, and discreet co-operation between the two leaderships became routine. In this context, and in as much as it was able to control radical and extremist Palestinian incursions across the border, Jordan tried to maintain both its border with Israel and with the occupied West Bank much as it would have a recognised international border. Indeed, in the 1960s and 1970s, when Palestinian raids were common, King Hussein apparently agreed with Golda Meir on a site for a permanent security fence. However, matters were complicated when Israeli villagers along the border unilaterally annexed odd kilometres of land to enable them to sink bore holes for water.[27]

It was only when the Palestine Liberation Organisation reached agreement with Israel on initial steps towards resolving the Palestinian–Israeli conflict with a Declaration of Principles in September 1993, that Jordan was really politically free to begin its own direct negotiations on a peace agreement between itself and Israel. An agreement was finally signed on the 16th of October 1994 and it included within it a principle of boundary settlement (Article 3) and an annex devoted to the delimitation and demarcation of the international boundary.

The boundary was to have four parts; the Jordan and Yarmouk Rivers, the Dead Sea, The Wadi Araba and the Gulf of Aqaba. In the first part, the border followed the middle of the main courses of the rivers, following natural changes as they occurred unless otherwise agreed. A Joint Boundary Commission would be established to monitor and respond to such changes. In the second part, a boundary line was established through the Dead Sea and the surrounding salt plains. The third part, that of Wadi Araba proved more complex.[28] Since 1967, Jordan had claimed that Israel was occupying and had illegally settled around 400 square kilometres of Jordanian land in the Wadi. Under the agreement this land was ultimately returned to Jordan, although in a number of areas Israelis would retain private land ownership and usership rights for an initial period of at least 25 years. For the final section of the boundary, the maritime boundary in the Gulf of Aqaba, the Joint Boundary Commission (comprising of three members from each country) was to work further on establishing the exact co-ordinates. A Maritime Boundary Agreement was eventually signed in January 1996 with the equidistant line between the coasts of the two states in the Gulf of Aqaba forming the greater part of the boundary. There was a small kink in the line, however, as it approached the northernmost end of the Gulf and a final straight stretch of 2.84 kilometres which finally meets the shore at Boundary Pillar 0 (the co-ordinates of which were not actually established in the agreement. A Joint Team of Experts was established to determine this.) The outstanding problem for Israel and Jordan remains the stretch of boundary between Jordan and the West Bank itself, which includes the northern end of the Dead Sea and the adjacent section of the Jordan River. Until Israel and the Palestinian Authority have reached agreement on sovereignty over the lands which lie along the western side of these waters, Jordan will have no-one to negotiate with and the boundary must remain only provisionally defined.

The negotiations between Jordan and Israel over their borders have been subject to much less direct external involvement than those between Israel and Egypt. Whether that has proved to be a good or a bad thing in terms of the balance of interests achieved in the agreements is open to question. There can be little doubt, however, that while the United States is still prepared to be a facilitator in Arab–Israeli talks, it considers its own role today to have been fundamentally changed by the Oslo Accord of 1993 between Israel and the PLO. It needs no longer aspire to be an honest broker (if it ever did in reality) and can safely leave Israel to argue its own corner against the fragmented and weakened Arab alliance. Meanwhile its place as principal interlocutor is nonetheless preserved in the absence of an effective Russian alternative and with the European Union subordinated to the role of banker to the peace process.

While Jordan has been able to extract a comprehensive peace agreement from the new environment, the Palestinians have so far been less fortunate. The 1993

Declaration of Principles (the Oslo Accord), and the subsequent 1994 Cairo agreement, 1995 Interim Agreement (Oslo II), the 1997 Hebron Accord and finally the 1998 Wye Plantation Agreement, ultimately resulted in only temporary arrangements in terms of establishing the sovereignty over the lands in dispute between the Jewish state and the Palestinian people. With America unwilling to apply serious pressure on Israel during a particularly obstructive period of Likud Party rule in Israel (1996–99), the peace process ground to a halt in 1996. President Clinton's efforts to resuscitate it in 1998 at the Wye Plantation produced an agreement that effectively renegotiated agreements already reached but which Israeli Prime Minister Netanyahu nonetheless proceeded to ignore. Only in September 1999, following the election of a new Labour Party Israeli prime minister, Ehud Barak, did even that Accord take on some symptoms of life. But these so-called Camp David talks in 2000 failed to deliver, and subsequent to the failure of these intensive talks relations between Israel and the Palestinians have only deteriorated. By 2010, the parties were only able to agree to meet for the purposes of 'talking about talks'. This was a far cry from the heyday of the 1990s and the return of the PLO to the occupied territories as the nascent Palestinian Authority. The reality is that the stilted peace process between Israel and the Palestinians has become a distorted process of Palestinian capitulation to Israeli security considerations. Throughout the period since 1993, despite the commitments made in Oslo not to take actions that preempt a final settlement, and as it has done effectively since 1967, Israel has been busy attempting to establish its own frontier over disputed lands through policies of land expropriation, closure, and settlement, and by pursuing economic and military policies which drive the Palestinian population from those lands which Israel seeks to annexe as part of any final settlement. Not surprisingly, the strategically vital Jordan Valley, has been a particular target:

> Between 1967 and 1993, Israel confiscated 100,000 dunums of the Jordan Valley as 'closed security zones', making the land off-limits to Palestinian farmers. It also set up some 20 Jewish settlements (with fewer than 3,000 settlers) on prime farming land.[29]

Since the 1990s and post-2000 Intifadah, the restrictions and expropriations have intensified. Moreover, new travel restrictions and the seizure of traditional bedouin pasturing lands have forced a wave of Palestinian migration into areas which Israel has proved more willing to relinquish.[30]

The agreements of the 1990s themselves resulted in the division of the West Bank into three types of territory, categorised as A, B or C. The main towns were placed under Palestinian self-rule at least as far as their administration and internal security were concerned (category A). Smaller towns and villages are placed under Israeli security control and Palestinian civilian self-rule (category B). The remaining areas were under complete Israeli security control and administration. The picture which emerged suggested that the territorial division of the occupied territories did not allow for any continuity of Palestinian self-rule between Palestinian-populated areas. The retention of the vast majority of the Jordan valley under Israeli administration further limited the viability of Palestine. Moreover, there was no commitment on the part of Israel that Palestinian areas should ever see anything more than the Palestinian administrative or internal security control than they experienced under Oslo, and Israel retained for itself the right to send its own troops into Palestinian-designated areas when it considered it necessary to do so. The full implementation of the Oslo II Accord and the Wye Agreement would ultimately render 40 per cent of the West Bank land and 96 per cent of the Palestinian population under Palestinian control (whatever that finally looks like) but any final settlement with the Palestinians, whether it leads to a Palestinian state or merely some form of autonomy, was more likely to look like a patchwork quilt of Palestinian living areas in the midst of an expanded Israeli state, than a real bi-national division of territory. Even before the separation of Gaza from the West Bank, such a prospect was being likened by many to the creation of bantustans in South Africa which offered little chance of realistic sovereignty for the Palestinians. Without either a superpower sponsor, or engaged Arab allies batting on its behalf, the Palestinians have proved too weak to negotiate for the state to which they aspired. Thus the territorial entity they are likely to get, and the nature of the boundaries which separate it from (or incorporate it within) the Israeli state, have become victims to the combination of their own collective weaknesses and the new regional environment in which they find themselves. The likelihood is therefore that ultimately the Jordanians will still be negotiating, at least in part, with Israel when it comes to determining the final demarcation of the remaining boundaries between the east and west banks of the Jordan River.

Israel may have largely resolved its border disputes with its Red Sea neighbours, but it remains at odds with its northern neighbours. As with Egypt and Jordan, the boundary issue is part of a far larger political issue – the continuing absence of formal peace agreements. The additional and complicating factors, at least as far as Lebanon is concerned, are first that no realistic agreement can be reached until Israel has resolved its outstanding disputes with Syria, and, second, that Israel has continued to occupy a strip of southern Lebanon since it invaded that country in 1978. Despite its pullout from much of Lebanon in early 2000s, Lebanon and Israel still quarrel over a narrow strip of land still occupied by Israel. Since ceasing its support for an anti-government militia, the South Lebanon Army, which enabled Israel to pursue 'an aggressive policy of intervention and pre-emptive raids into south Lebanon'[31] in response to guerrilla attacks on settlements in northern Israel by radical Palestinian or Islamic armed groups, it is now the IDF itself which has to engage with its arch-rival in Lebanon – the Hezbollah. The summer 2006 war with Hezbollah marked the first of direct and fierce confrontations of the IDF with this enemy and since then all that Hezbollah has done is to consolidate its political and social power base within the Lebanese state while also arming itself with much more advanced Iranian and Syrian-supplied military equipment and missiles.

Notwithstanding the ongoing permeability of the border, the irony lies in the fact that there is actually little real dispute over the location of the boundary itself.

The line was agreed by the British and French governments in 1920 and demarcated over the next three years. To the chagrin of the Zionists in Palestine, it left the entire Litani River – considered to be vital water resources for the future Jewish state – in French-held Lebanon. For the Arabs, however, it was all but meaningless and they happily ignored it where possible. Although the Zionists reached the Litani in the 1948–49 war, they withdrew to the British-French line under the terms of the armistice. Despite their periodic invasions and the occupation of southern Lebanon, they have nonetheless seemed to accept the general principle of the line, bar a few very minor territorial adjustments. It is yet to be seen whether proper negotiations over the establishment of a formal international boundary will cause them to deviate from this position.

The boundary with Syria is more problematic. Syria was effectively created by the 1920 Treaty of Sèvres, when Britain and France divided up the Levant into mandates, largely on the basis of the 1916 Sykes–Picot Agreement. In 1923, however, the Golan Heights were added to the new Syrian entity. The 1948–49 Arab–Israeli war resulted in an armistice agreement between Syria and the new Israeli state which, while it fell back to pre-war borders, included a number of controversial demilitarised zones being allocated as Israeli territory. During the 1950s, Israeli efforts to settle these areas and utilise their resources, in particular a project to divert waters from the Jordan River, led to continual disputes over sovereignty over, and rights within, the demilitarised zones. The continued Israeli expropriation of Jordan waters, and Arab counter-measures, were to develop into one of the prime causes of the 1967 War during which Israel occupied the entire Golan Heights. Israel thereafter rejected United Nations calls on it to withdraw to and recognise the 1949 armistice line, arguing instead that any demarcated boundaries would have to become part of a formal and final peace agreement between the two states. In the meantime, however, Israel moved to expel Arab populations living on the strategically important heights, to expropriate and settle the land, and to establish an extensive monitoring network backed by a military presence. During the subsequent 1973 War, Israel occupied a further stretch of Syrian land, although it later withdrew from this under the terms of a disengagement agreement.[32] Today Syria continues to demand complete Israeli withdrawal to the pre-1967 lines before a comprehensive peace with Israel can be considered, while Israel insists that any withdrawal must be negotiated, subject to Israeli security requirements, and part and parcel of such a peace. Following the Oslo Accords between Israel and the PLO, intensive new negotiations were initiated and the two sides were reported to be close to an agreement in 1995/96, but some 15 years later there is still no light at the end of this particular tunnel. The election of a right-wing government in Israel in 1995 seemed to scupper the talks but the Barak Labour-led government elected in 1999 committed itself to reaching a speedy agreement with Syria and Lebanon, something that the Likud-led Netanyahu government has found almost impossible to deliver upon taking power in 2009.

Israel's boundary problems with its neighbours are therefore far from over. Domestically it must reconcile those who prioritise peaceful relations with their neighbours, albeit at the expense of territorial acquisition, and those who believe ardently in a Greater Israel which reaches into the territory which its neighbours consider to be their own. Equally it must balance direct security preferences with compromises that will win its neighbours over to comprehensive peace agreements. The Arab states, in terms of the Arab Peace Plan, and even the Palestinians, have already come a long way in accepting that such peace agreements will ultimately have to be reached, thereby recognising the rights and sovereignty of an Israeli state. For the moment, however, the colonial legacy lives on both in the political obstructions to peace and in the detail of border delimitations, even as the various states adjust themselves to a new international order with repercussions on the regional balance of power.

A final dispute worth mentioning in the context of the Gulf of Aqaba is that over the islands of Tiran and Sanafir. These islands lie in the Strait of Tiran and maritime traffic must navigate its way past them up its way in and out of the Gulf. The islands were uninhabited until 1949 when Egypt, in order to enforce a blockade against Israeli shipping, occupied the islands. Significantly, in statements on the occupation, Egypt asserted its rights, but not its sovereignty, and acknowledged ill-defined Saudi Arabian rights. The move had been made, according to Egypt, 'in full accord with the Kingdom of Saudi Arabia'.[33] Indeed, it seemed that the two Arab states had agreed to defer any competing claims that they might have over the islands in order to prioritise preventing the new Jewish state from either establishing a claim to, or a presence on, the islands. Egypt has since claimed the islands as historically Egyptian territory, while Saudi Arabia made a formal claim to the islands in 1957. Israel, despite having occupied the islands during the 1956 war, has not claimed the islands. In the 1979 peace treaty with Egypt, it did, however, agree to Egyptian civilian policing control over the islands in conjunction with a United Nations presence and an Egyptian commitment to maintaining freedom of navigation and overflight. In other words, it accepted Egypt's claim on condition that its own interests were not compromised. Saudi Arabia has since repeated its own claims (notably in a 1990 Plan for Protected Areas) but been unwilling to force the issue. Thus, Egypt is left essentially in control of the islands, while the issue of sovereignty is left unresolved, despite the fact that Saudi Arabia's claims – at least from a geographic point of view – appear somewhat the stronger. The complexities of the competing claims, including Israel's claim to a right of navigation,[34] might account in part for the reluctance of Egypt and Saudi Arabia to assert themselves more forcefully, but it is more likely that their mutual interests have been better served by the current arrangement. Until the recent, if limited, thawing in relations between Israel and its Arab neighbours, it was in both Egypt and Saudi Arabia's strategic and political interests to ensure that the islands were first and foremost in Arab hands and that they should not prove themselves to be divided over the issue of sovereignty. As maritime trade has developed, especially that carrying Saudi oil exports, the principles of free navigation have also become more important to both states, confirming a common interest with Israel and Jordan at the higher end of the Gulf. Thus, today, a protracted and acrimonious dispute over sovereignty would not serve the interests of any of the riparian states of the Gulf of Aqaba and the present status quo is thus perhaps the most acceptable alternative for all concerned.

The Horn of Africa: Eritrea's impact

The southern end of the Red Sea has also witnessed the arrival of a new state on its shores, this time, the more recent creation of an independent Eritrea in 1993. Within five years, Eritrea appeared to be engaged in violent disputes with Sudan, Djibouti and Ethiopia, although with varying degrees of intensity.

The most serious dispute has undoubtedly been that between Eritrea and Ethiopia, with a full-scale ground war erupting on three fronts of their 625-mile-long border in 1998. At the time of Eritrea's independence it seemed that not much attention had paid much attention to the need to establish Eritrea's territorial boundaries. One region where proprietorship remained vague was Badme, the centre of tensions between the two parties. Although Badme was marked to be within Eritrea, it continued to be administered by Ethiopia. But in 1997, Ethiopia produced its own maps showing Badme to be on its territory. Soon after, it sent its border police into the area to enforce the new boundary with Eritrea.[35] The situation exploded on 6 May, when a handful of Eritrean troops were killed in the disputed territory. Two days later, the Eritrean army moved tanks in and the relatively intensive aerial bombardment of each other's urban centres that followed the first border clashes has demonstrated the depth of hostility that now separates the two sides.[36] The Ethiopian government sources have put Eritrean casualties (killed or wounded) in the first month of the campaign at 11,000, while Eritrea found it prudent to deploy cluster bombs against Ethiopian targets.[37] Over a year later, the two sides were still slugging it out, with the war taking an ever heavier toll in terms of lives and resources. For the Eritreans, the struggle with Ethiopia, their former masters now ruled by Tigryans (many of whom serve as maids and cleaners in Asmara) had turned into an existential one. As an Eritrean minister put it in response to a question about the war with Ethiopia: 'Do you think we fought 30 years in the bush, with the whole world against us, to have our territory carved up by anyone who comes along? This is an insult to the Eritrean people.'[38] While for the Ethiopians, it is said to be the 'sanctity of Ethiopia [which] is at stake ... [where] nationalist fervor is the engine of Ethiopian politics'.[39]

The war had a number of broader international dimensions. For the Red Sea states, and indeed for all those states whose maritime fleets utilise the Red Sea, it was worrying evidence of a deepening process of destabilisation in the Horn of Africa. Civil war in Sudan, tensions between Eritrea and Sudan over the former's support for anti-Khartoum Muslim forces (which frequently erupt in pitched battles), the breakdown of central government in Somalia and now this mutually devastating war, all pointed towards a post-Cold War propensity for ethnic, tribal, national and religious confrontation in states which were already resource-poor. The withdrawal of a substantive Soviet (or post-Soviet) presence in the Horn has left it open to American interests. However, the US preoccupation with containing

Sudanese-style Islamism and its unwillingness to commit itself to military adventures after its disastrous foray into Somalia, had left it unable to create a balance of power that could stabilise the Horn. Regional players such as Egypt, Saudi Arabia and Israel did try to fill the vacuum but the incompatibility of their own interests only fuelled the instability. In such a politically volatile environment, borders become permeable victims to the ambitions of regimes, opposition movements, terrorists, smugglers[40] and identities.

One consequence of this has been the virtual manufacturing of boundary disputes out of thin air. Djibouti's claim in 1996 that Eritrea was making aggressive moves on their mutual border was a case in point. In 1996, Djibouti claimed that the Eritrean government had produced, and presented to Djibouti, a map which, according to the Djiboutian government, claimed that over 490 square kilometres of Djibouti actually belonged to Eritrea. The area, known as Dar Elwa to the Eritreans, reportedly became the scene of an Eritrean military incursion in April of that year, with the Djiboutian foreign minister, Mohammed Mussa Chehem, asserting that 600 Eritrean soldiers had entered his country and fired shots on Djiboutian soldiers. The accusation of a military incursion was later retracted but Djibouti continued to complain that Eritrea was laying claim to its northern region.[41] Eritrea itself has always denied the incident ever occurred. But the fact that problems were not addressed in the 1990s led to open conflict between the two neighbours in June 2008. Having broken off diplomatic relations between 1998 and 2001, it was their dispute over their border which led to three days of war and over 70 deaths and injuries.[42] Interestingly, Yemen stepped in well before war finally broke out as a mediator, and landlocked Ethiopia made it known that it would do whatever was necessary to secure its trade and transport routes through Djibouti.

Confusion over the boundary arises not least from the complex processes through which it first came to be drawn. In this instance, France originally established its colonial rule over the Territory of the Afars and Issas (now Djibouti) in the 1860s, while Italy was to colonise and establish its own rule over Eritrea in the 1890s. In the period 1900–01 a series of protocols and treaties between Ethiopia, France and Italy delimited many of their mutual borders, although the agreements did not always produce boundaries which met one another or provided final resolutions to issues such as ownership of offshore islands. The Italian invasion of Ethiopia in 1936 led to the incorporation into Eritrea of three Ethiopian provinces. The subsequent British military administration after Italian capitulation in 1941 and the federation of Ethiopia and Eritrea in 1952 complicated efforts to establish post-war borders in the Horn and consequently – despite boundary agreements reached between Ethiopia and France in 1953–55 – there remains room for contestation over the exact and legal demarcation between Djibouti and the newly-independent Eritrea. Thus, although both states have endorsed the Organisation of National Unity Charter which enshrines the principle of the inviolability of borders inherited from colonisation, and while it remains unclear exactly what happened in this instance or why, there remains the serious possibility that another incident, this time involving direct military confrontation, could occur. Ultimately, the fragility of this boundary is a potential victim to the instabilities of the Horn itself in the absence of any power or powers strong enough to impose some form of order. Regional powers may be exercising their muscles in this regard, but so far they have served more to muddy the waters than secure stability.

In previous decades, boundaries between Red Sea states were fragile and uncertain. What borders did exist on paper were usually drawn up by external powers with little regard for the demographic or physical features of the territories concerned. The independent states which inherited these borders were ill-equipped to either enforce or challenge the borders. The need to do so has become increasingly clear, however, as a number of dynamics have asserted themselves over the past few decades.

First, the constant drive for development has necessitated a resources grab in a region where deposits of natural resources (be they hydrocarbons, agricultural, water, minerals or even manpower) have shown little regard for *de facto* boundaries. Second, the state itself is an entity under threat. Ethnic, religious, national and tribal identities have resurfaced, forcing regimes to clearly define and assert themselves over the territories they claim. Since these identities are themselves trans-border, it has become increasingly important to gain recognition of territorial claims by neighbouring regimes that might, or do, attempt to intervene in domestic politics. Third, the end of the Cold War has in effect removed what was in many ways a stabilising influence over the Red Sea, and one which made regimes more dependent upon external alliances than legal recognition for the defence of their interests. Today, as regional powers seek to replace the superpowers as brokers of, and players in, a regional balance of power, they themselves must clarify the extent of their influence. Equally, smaller regimes must defend their own corner by gaining recognition of their rights and territories from others who might seek to intervene. The combination of these processes can serve to both exacerbate or diffuse tensions between states arising over border disputes. Young states like the united Yemen or Eritrea seek to flex their muscles and discover their potential, while regional powers like Saudi Arabia and Egypt seek to contain political and social forces around the Red Sea that threaten their own interests. Boundary disputes become tools in the hands of those with broader political, economic or strategic interests, or may themselves be the source of angst between regimes and peoples. Thus, the impetus for confrontation meets the momentum for resolution and the outcome will depend on the relative strength of both. Thus, as the Gulf of Aqaba and the Arabian Peninsula have seen the predominance of the momentum for resolution, the Horn of Africa and the lower end of the Red Sea have seen a greater impetus for confrontation.

Finally, the momentum for resolution of border disputes, where it has predominated, has brought with it a growing recognition of a common interest among Red Sea states in establishing internationally recognised borders that necessarily reduce the potential for arbitrary external intervention. Nowhere has this been more true than in the demarcation of maritime boundaries, where foreign companies have been increasingly frustrated in their efforts to take advantage of weak claims to sovereignty by regional states as those states resolve their disputes. That dynamic for some kind of recognition of a common Red Sea interest has been mirrored in the interest (and even intervention) by Red Sea states in each other's border disputes as they utilise such disputes to advance their own interests.

6　The economics of the Red Sea

Trade, migration and capital flows

The Red Sea waterway has been a major trading route between Asia, Africa and Europe for thousands of years. The littoral territories have been both the origin and the transit routes for the movement of resources, goods and peoples. More recently, finance has crossed the sea in the form of development aid and investment capital. The modern states have consequently been shaped in part by their economic relations with their Red Sea neighbours, even as they are collectively more or less dependent upon the sea and its role in international exchange for their economic provision. This chapter seeks to examine the nature of economic linkages between the Red Sea states, and to determine the extent to which they service each other's needs. Furthermore, as all the Red Sea states are linked to a greater or lesser extent to the wider international economy, the relative importance of their neighbourhood is a further subject of this discussion, as we seek to understand if and how they act and interact together.

Rich and poor

Perhaps the most obvious feature of the economies surrounding the Red Sea, making comparison a problematic exercise, is the enormous disparity between their size and relative wealth (Table 6.1). While the western coast includes some of the poorest nations in the world, the northern and eastern coasts harbour Israel (which has developed nation status), and Saudi Arabia which is perhaps the most resource-wealthy state on earth. Similarly there is enormous disparity in populations, with the city-state of Djibouti barely meriting comparison with Egypt, one of the most populous MENA states. Thanks to sustained high oil prices after 2002, Saudi Arabia's GDP rocketed to over $450 billion in the new century, nearly doubling in less than ten years. Ethiopia, in the meantime, emerged as the Red Sea's most populous country, dwarfing its neighbours. Egypt's economic policies saw its GDP/capita double between 2004 and 2009 from just over $1,000.

A closer examination shows the great variations in the economic bases of these states. Although agriculture is generally a declining sector, it still provides a third of national product in Sudan while it contributes far less to the economies of

Table 6.1 Basic economic indicators of Red Sea states, 2008

Country	Population (million)	GDP ($million)	GDP per capita ($)
Djibouti	0.72	1,000	1,473
Egypt	78.9	157,00	2,035
Eritrea	5.7	1,750	285
Ethiopia	85.2	29,800	362
Israel	7.2	199,000	28,042
Jordan	6.3	20,000	3,261
Saudi Arabia	28.7	468,000	16,647
Sudan	41.1	52,700	1,311
Yemen	22.9	23,500	1,058

Source: Compiled from figures in the International Institute for Strategic Studies (2010), and the World Bank database.

Djibouti and Israel. The nature of agricultural production ranges from nomadic pastoralism and subsistence farming in the Horn to the sophisticated agrobusinesses in Saudi Arabia and Israel. Collectively, and not simply due to a regional problem of limited water supplies, the Red Sea states have historically neglected their agricultural sectors and become reliant on food imports, even Sudan which during the 1970s was expected to become the breadbasket of the Arab world. Djibouti is particularly vulnerable, as have been Sudan and Eritrea during times of civil war, drought and famine. While the Saudi policy of investing in cereal, poultry and dairy production was intended to somewhat offset its own food import bill, the end result has been vastly over-priced supplies of goods for export, due to the cost of water inputs.[1]

Manufacturing output around the Red Sea ranges from the advanced electrical equipment, weapons and cut diamonds produced in Israel to the heavy industry focused on petrochemicals encouraged by the Saudi government, to textiles and food processing which dominate Egypt's industrial production (Tables 6.2 and 6.3). Eritrea and Djibouti focus on cottage and light industries such as tanning, ceramics, glassware, footwear manufacture, furniture, canning and bottling and light electromechanical works. Sudanese industry is reliant on domestically grown agricultural inputs, leading to cotton, flour milling, sugar refining, textiles and footwear. Jordan meanwhile focuses on oil refining, cement production and chemicals. It also produces tobacco, food and beverages for export to its neighbours. Yemen also has small and medium-sized firms producing light consumer goods, food products and construction materials although in this case mostly for domestic consumption.

Interestingly, in a country like Sudan, agriculture continues to provide employment for 80 per cent of the country's workforce and accounts for nearly a third of the country's gross domestic product, and in Ethiopia too 80 per cent of the workforce is in the agricultural sector and it accounts nearly half of the country's GDP. In Eritrea, as many as 80 per cent of the population finds itself in the agricultural sector – farming and herding largely – and yet it accounts for around a quarter of the GDP.

Table 6.2 Sectoral contributions in Red Sea states, 1993 and 1999 (as % of GDP)

	Agriculture		Industry		Services	
	1993	*1999*	*1993*	*1999*	*1993*	*1999*
Djibouti	3	3	17	15	81	82
Egypt	17	17	28	31	51	52
Eritrea	20	25	20	23	62	52
Ethiopia	57	60	10	13	33	36
Israel	2	2	17	18	81	80
Jordan	5	2	29	26	67	72
Saudi Arabia	6	6	42	47	45	47
Sudan	39	45	11	16	51	39
Yemen	20	17	32	42	48	41

Sources: Statistics compiled from Arab Banking Corporation, (1994), World Bank indicators, and Economist Intelligence Unit database, http://www.odci.gov/cia/publications/factbook/er.html.

Table 6.3 Sectoral contributions in Red Sea states, 2004 and 2008 (as % of GDP)

	Agriculture		Industry		Services	
	2004	*2008*	*2004*	*2008*	*2004*	*2008*
Djibouti	4	4	17	17	80	80
Egypt	15	13	36	38	48	53
Eritrea	29	17	26	23	57	60
Ethiopia	47	44	13	14	42	39
Israel	2	3	21	32	75	65
Jordan	3	3	29	34	69	63
Saudi Arabia	3	3	54	60	34	38
Sudan	32	27	26	36	39	37
Yemen	14	10	40	39	45	51

Sources: World Bank indicators, Economist Intelligence Unit database, http://www.odci.gov/cia/publications/factbook/er.html.

Hydrocarbon, mineral and water resources

The issue of resources is central to economic development and planning. Apart from agricultural land, the three most important are undoubtedly water, hydrocarbons and minerals although in varying orders of priority for the different states (Table 6.4).

Saudi Arabia is the most generously endowed of Red Sea states in terms of hydrocarbon deposits, having the largest proven reserves of oil in the world and contributing over 30 per cent of OPEC's annual output. It is also the world's largest exporter of oil, since it absorbs relatively little of its own production compared to other major producers. In the mid-1990s, oil, refined products and plastics comprised 96 per cent of exports while crude oil and gas accounted for up to 30

Table 6.4 Hydrocarbon resources and exports of Red Sea states (proven reserves), 2009

Country	Oil thousand million barrels	% of world total	Natural gas trillion cubic metres
Djibouti	(some reserves, quantity as yet unknown)		
Egypt	4.4	0.3	2.19
Eritrea	(undersea petroleum and gas reserves, quantity as yet unknown)		
Israel	–	–	–
Jordan	–	–	0.53
Saudi Arabia	264.6	20.0	7.92
Sudan	6.7	0.5	–
Yemen	2.7	0.2	0.49

Source: *BP Statistical Review of World Energy 2010.*

per cent of GDP. Greater efforts have been made in recent years to develop refin-ing capacity, not just in Saudi Arabia itself but also in key consuming countries which then become locked in to Saudi oil exports. Gas has also become increas-ingly important, with Saudi Arabia contributing nearly 3 per cent of world output by the end of 2010. Liquefied natural gas and petroleum gas are also exported, although domestic supply is now beginning to run short.

For Egypt, crude oil and oil products accounted for 45 per cent of exports in the mid-1990s, and by 2010 its proven reserves were standing at 3.7 billion barrels. Thus, its daily oil output in 2009 averaged 685,000 b/d. While oil finds are largely located round and in the Gulf of Suez, the Western Desert has also produced quan-tities of both oil and natural gas. Gas has also been found in the Suez Canal area, the Nile Delta and off Alexandria, and Egypt is set to rival Algeria and Libya as a major Mediterranean producer. In Africa, Egypt has emerged as the continent's third largest gas state with an estimated 58.5 trillion cubic feet of reserves in 2010. Indeed, by the end of the first decade of the twenty-first century, Egypt was accounting for 2.1 per cent of global gas ouput, outstripping Libya's 0.5 per cent as it approached Algeria's 2.7 per cent. Furthermore, Egypt has emerged as the largest producer of refined products in Africa after South Africa, with eight refin-eries processing 570,000 b/d in the early 2000s. Much greater future capacity has emerged over the decade as private sector refineries have been given permission to begin operations, so increasing refined products output to 975,000 b/d in 2010.

To the south, Sudan is a newcomer to the oil production and export business, oil having only been discovered in Bentiu and Melut in the early 1980s. The civil war with the south obstructed exploitation of the fields until the mid-1990s, after which international companies such as the French Total Oil began to move in to exploration and field development, and it achieved self-sufficiency at the end of the 1990s. In fact, its proven reserves have increased from 0.3 billion barrels in the 1990s to 6.7 billion barrels in 2009, overtaking Egypt and Yemen in a decade. Sudan thus has emerged as an African and Arab oil player in its own right, over-coming Egypt in terms of proven reserves and prospects. According to industry sources, Sudan's proven oil reserves have gone from an estimated 563 million barrels in 2006 to over 5 billion barrels in 2010, making it Africa's fifth largest oil state.[2] The country's dependence on oil income has increased significantly since the 1990s, making the country very vulnerable to global energy conditions and trends. Be that as it may, Sudan has successfully secured a long-term energy partnership with China, which by 2009 was taking 55 per cent of Sudan's oil exports. Sudan also has increased its refining capacity in the 2000s, to reach 121,000 b/d by 2010. Oil production has saved the country an annual $450 million in oil imports, and allowed it to export the surplus for hard currency.

Yemen is the other relatively large hydrocarbon producer, with hydrocarbons and related activities making up some 20 per cent of GDP. Domestic consumption of oil accounts for around a fifth of the 390,000 b/d produced, while liquefied natural gas reserves (LNG) are being developed primarily for export. A major project is being advanced with the French company, Total Oil, for the extraction and transport of LNG to a Red Sea terminal, which came onstream early in the 2000s. By the end of the 2000s, Saudi Arabia's oil output of nearly 10 million b/d was accounting for 12 per cent of global production of oil, and Sudan had managed to increase its out put from just 63,000 b/d in 1999 to 490,000 b/d in 2009. Yemen meanwhile saw its production decline from 405,000 b/d at the end of the 1990s to 298,000 b/d in 2009, despite its national dependence on oil income growing over the previous 10 years.

Israel has only small petroleum and natural gas reserves, relying for the most part on imports. During the era of the Arab boycott, and when the Suez Canal and Straits of Tiran were actually or potentially closed to Israeli shipping, fuel import costs posed a considerable burden on the economy. In recent years, however, Israel has been keen to develop links with fuel suppliers in its own region. A much talked-about gas supply from Qatar collapsed along with the peace process in the late 1990s. More recently, Egyptian gas exports to Israel have come on the agenda, with the possibility that supplies will be piped via Izmir in Turkey to avoid domestic Egyptian political constraints. The Israeli government also remains nervous of the deal and of increasing its reliance on Egypt as a supplier – it already imports 20 per cent of its petroleum supplies from Egypt.[3] The Palestinian Authority has no such qualms and in October 1998 signed a deal to import piped Egyptian gas, reducing its own costly dependence on fuel imports from Israel. Jordan has also been considering taking new gas supplies from Egypt. For the most part, the Kingdom is dependent on oil imports for its energy needs, its own domestic production from limited shale oil deposits in the south being minimal. Until 2003, the majority of imports still came by road from Iraq, although Saudi Arabia has also contributed around 14 per cent and in emergencies Syrian and Yemeni suppliers have been utilised. In 1987, natural gas deposits were discovered and by 1990 they were fuelling 15 per cent of electricity requirements. Production has since risen sharply.

Djibouti and Eritrea, despite both having proven if unknown quantities of hydrocarbon deposits, which in the case of Eritrea include offshore fields, do not have the investment resources to exploit them and so far international interests have considered them to be commercially unviable. Thus they both import their hydrocarbon requirements. In Djibouti's case, imported fuels account for 90 per cent of its energy requirements, the rest being made up of geothermal energy which may in the long-distance future be sufficient for export to neighbouring countries. There is a clear line of supply around the Red Sea from surplus oil and gas producers to energy-deficit countries which is unsurprising given the relatively short distances and low costs of transporting the hydrocarbons. For the most part (with Israel currently but not indefinitely being the exception) Saudi Arabia and Egypt supply their Red Sea neighbours, Egypt becoming an increasingly important international gas supplier.

The Red Sea states, as part of the larger MENA region, are also vitally important for the international hydrocarbons markets. With around two-thirds of the world's proved crude oil reserves lying in Arab territories, with the Middle East being known for relatively low production costs, and with some cash-strapped MENA governments slowly introducing FDI-friendly legislation, the MENA states are likely to remain the primary source of energy for major international companies in the next few decades, and this is despite the investments being made in the Caspian basin and in the territories of West Africa.

The region is also rich in mineral deposits, with Jordan and Israel both benefiting particularly from phosphate exports (Table 6.5). Jordan is the more dependent on its mineral reserves than Israel, with phosphates, potash and chemicals being by far its largest exports. Indeed, Jordan is the fifth largest phosphate producer and third largest exporter in the world. Sudan is able to export both gold (some of which is extracted from the Red Sea itself by French companies), chromium and a small quantity of gypsum, but its other mineral resources remain largely untapped, as do Eritrea's deposits, due to war and an absence of investment. Saudi mineral extraction focuses on the components of cement and other building materials, gold and more recently coal. Local limestone is also utilised in Yemen for cement, while high-quality Yemeni salt is almost entirely exported to the former USSR, North Korea, and Bangladesh.

Unlike hydrocarbons and some minerals, water is generally in short supply in the region. For some countries, such as Eritrea, recurrent drought is a serious problem while for others, like Jordan, Israel, Egypt and Sudan, the problem lies as much in water-sharing arrangements.

There are two major river systems affecting Red Sea states: the Nile and the Jordan. The Nile, which essentially derives its water from rainfall on the Ethiopian highlands and the Equatorial Lakes, flows through ten African states, including Egypt, Sudan and Eritrea. Although some rainfall in Sudan contributes to the flow, virtually nothing is added in Egypt, which is 95 per cent dependent on water originating beyond its borders. Both countries rely on the Nile for most of their agriculture,[4] for hydro-power generation,[5] and, in Egypt's case, for some tourism as well. Yet neither can control the flow which they receive. Even the Aswan High Dam, while regulating flows within Egypt, can still provide no protection from prolonged periods of low flow such as was the case in the 1980s. Numerous efforts have been made by the riparian states to regulate, manage and share the water, leading to the only legal water-sharing arrangement, the 1959 Egyptian–Sudanese Agreement for the Full Utilization of the Nile Waters. Thereafter relations between Egypt and Sudan improved significantly, with Sudan allowing

Table 6.5 Mineral resources of Red Sea states

Country	Resource
Djibouti	Geothermal areas, salt, limestone, gypsum and materials for making cement
Egypt	Iron ore, phosphates, manganese, limestone, gypsum, talc, asbestos, lead, zinc
Eritrea	Gold, potash, zinc, copper, salt, magnesium, iron ore, marble
Israel	Copper, phosphates, bromide, potash, clay, sand, sulphur, asphalt, manganese
Jordan	Phosphates, potash, shale oil
Saudi Arabia	Iron ore, gold, copper, limestone, gypsum, marble, clay, salt, bauxite, magnesite, zinc, silver, uranium, coal
Sudan	Iron ore, copper, chromium ore, zinc, tungsten, mica, silver, gold
Yemen	Rock salt, marble, coal, gold, lead, nickel, copper, limestone, zinc, iron sulphur, silver, uranium

Sources: http://www.odci.gov/cia/publications/factbook/html; Europa (1998a, 1998b).

Egypt to proceed with the Jonglei Canal project in 1976 to augment the waters of Lake Nasser.[6] However, the upstream states have ultimately proved reluctant to enter into agreements with Egypt and Sudan, given their own financially and technically weaker positions[7] and their not wishing to have downstream states limiting their own freedom of action. In any case, they are generally less dependent on the Nile, having heavier rainfall patterns. The issue of water management exacerbated political difficulties between Ethiopia, Sudan and Egypt during the 1970s and 1980s, but the fall of the Mengistu regime in 1991 enabled Ethiopia to mend fences with, first, Sudan and then Egypt. This is just as well given the fact that, while a total of nearly 300 million people currently share the waters of the Nile Basin,[8] by the year 2050, this figure will have risen to 1 billion. New efforts are being made to raise international funds to assist in collective management and sharing arrangements but any substantial agreement is still a long way off.[9] In the meantime, governments continue to act alone, devising their own unilateral initiatives such as the 1999 Ethiopian Master Plan for the Nile.[10] Meanwhile, Egypt has embarked on its own 'New Valley Project' to pump 6.5 billion cubic metres a year from Lake Nasser to the Western Desert while Sudan is planning new dams on the Nile to improve its own access to, and usage of, river waters. To this end it has repeatedly called for revisions to the 1959 Agreement to enhance its share of the flow. Egypt is almost aggressive in its refusals, but recent Ethiopian efforts to mobilise international capital for its own water master-plan, and its construction of 10 small dams in the Nile catchment area, threaten the water security of both Egypt and Sudan and imaginative responses may soon have to be found.

The waters of the Jordan River have also been a source of tension, not least since it is a tiny river by world standards yet vital to the economic interests of both Israel and Jordan. The origins of the river lie in Syria, Lebanon and Jordan, with the river starting at the confluence of the Dan, the Banian and the Hasbani rivers.[11] The largest tributary is the Yarmuk, which flows into the river below the Sea of Galilee (Lake Tiberias) and which draws mostly from rainwater-fed rivers in Syria. After 1948, the state of war between the countries in the Yarmuk basin extended to the issue of water access. In the 1950s, the Israelis embarked on the construction of a National Water Carrier which diverted Jordan waters from the Sea of Galilee through Israel and on to the Negev Desert while Jordan constructed the East Ghor project diverting Yarmuk waters into the King Abdullah Canal. As a result, the flow of the Jordan River has diminished dramatically. Other efforts by Jordan and Syria to reduce the Yarmuk flow into the river have been thwarted by threats of, and actual, Israeli military action. The implications of this deadlock were compounded by disagreements over the acquifers lying beneath the West Bank and Gaza Strip. When Israel occupied these areas in 1967, it began exploiting the underground water resources, simultaneously restricting access to them by the indigenous Palestinian population. Around a quarter of Israel's annual supply now comes from West Bank sources, while Israeli settler populations consume additional water. For many years Israel's consumption has exceeded the annual recharge, the net deficit leading to a lowering of the water table and in some cases a creeping salination of the waters. Meanwhile the pressure laid on Gazan acquifer resources by population density has much the same effect. The results have been environmental degradation, agricultural loss, significant health and dental problems and an enormous sense of bitterness on the part of the Palestinians.[12] From Israel's perspective, it has little choice but to secure all the water resources it can for a population which has been swelled by immigration and which consumes higher levels of water per capita than in neighbouring countries. Not surprisingly water featured highly in peace negotiations, first, at Madrid in 1991, then in Oslo and later between Israel and Jordan. Article 6 and Annex II of the Jordanian–Israeli peace treaty are devoted to water-sharing arrangements. Agreement was reached on the distribution of waters from the Yarmuk and Jordan rivers, although in 1999 Israel failed to deliver the quantities promised to Jordan, claiming a generally low annual supply. The text of the treaty also reflected their common concerns over the need to find additional sources of water, to build joint storage facilities on both rivers, to monitor and protect water quality and to share access to wells in Wadi Araba, which was returned to Jordan by Israel. A joint water committee would oversee all of these measures. In theory, the treaty significantly addressed some of Jordan's water concerns. In 1993, Jordan required 4.3 billion cubic metres of water just to escape from the category of water-poor, yet its actual rate of extraction was just 975 million cubic metres (MCM). The additional waters received under the treaty amounted to 215 MCM annually, representing a significant but still inadequate improvement.[13]

Between Israel and the Palestinians, water rights have been defined as a final status issue, indicating the serious problems which will arise when Israel is forced to confront its own water deficit, although some aspects of water management have been passed to the Palestinian Authority and a Joint Water Committee has been established to co-ordinate matters of water management and wastage. Negotiations with Syria over the waters of Golan have stalled, although a number of proposals for regional water sharing which would compensate Syria with additional water from the Euphrates have been mooted. Israeli access to the Hisbani waters is also likely to be a feature of any agreement with Lebanon.

Acquifers are found elsewhere around the Red Sea. Jordan and Saudi Arabia share the Qa Disi acquifer fossil waters which are soon likely to find their way to Amman via pipeline and which already provide irrigation for Saudi agriculture. There are significant problems, with Jordan accusing Saudi Arabia of over-pumping and lowering the water table, and with the cost of extraction on the Jordanian side being possibly too high for them to manage. Jordan also shares the Azraq acquifer with Syria. In Sudan too there are also indications that as yet untapped groundwater will be a potential source for the future for the western areas. It is known that Egypt, Sudan and Libya straddle the extensive Nubian Sandstone acquifer which is being exploited by Libya for its Great Man-made River project. The exact implications of this for Sudan and Egypt are as yet unknown. Saudi Arabia has also exploited ground reserves in its Eastern province, but again these straddle borders with Qatar and Bahrain, and Saudi usage has made the water level in those countries fall. Not surprisingly accusations that Saudi Arabia is developing uneconomical agriculture at the expense of its neighbours' water potential abound.

In general, the Red Sea states are located in an arid zone, where rainfall is neither plentiful nor regular.[14] While Yemen experiences flash-flooding in the Hadramut area, and Sudan sees periodic flooding of the Nile basin, for the most part, Red Sea states are susceptible to drought and, as populations grow, so too they are continually constrained in their policy-making, not least in regards to relations with their neighbours, by the need to exploit existing or seek out new water resources. In some cases, this has given impetus to efforts at bi-national, multinational or regional co-operation. Following the signing of the Oslo Accords, and the end of the Arab secondary boycott against Israel, talks resulted in a number of regional initiatives such as the development of desalination technology in Oman. Equally as often, disputes over water have threatened to degenerate into conflict and the Middle East is frequently cited as being due for a major water war. Thus water is one of the arenas in which basin-wide or multi-riparian arrangements have to be found for the security of all and are indeed long overdue. In the meantime, desalinisation, or the conversion of sea water to fresh water, remains an excessively expensive option which presents no solution to agricultural irrigation and barely deals with the requirement for drinking water. Other ambitious proposals mooted in recent years, such as the so-called 'Red-Dead' or 'Med-Dead' canals remain both economically prohibitive and potentially ecologically disastrous.[15]

Economic policy and the role of the state

Another aspect of comparability lies in the economic development policies pursued by governments in the past 50 years. All the Red Sea countries have seen the state take a major role in investment, production, and distribution decisions. This has been, as with other states which achieved independence only in the second half of the century, largely a result of the perceived urgency for catch-up development, as well as the prevailing economic orthodoxy which emerged in the post-Second World War period.

In Djibouti's case, it was perhaps all the more inevitable given the neglect of the economy under French rule (till 1977), the reliance on just three assets (the port, the airport and the railway), and the need for massive foreign assistance. Industry, farming and banking remained essentially private sector activities, with the state focusing on infrastructure provision and maintenance. While the first two are relatively minor economic activities due to the absence of resources, and while banking services enjoyed an all too brief boom in the days of Ethiopian and Somali Marxism, the infrastructure has dominated the economy in terms of employment and income. Furthermore, the state has managed the external assistance, first, predominantly from France but in later years from more diverse sources. These functions, combined with the instabilities which spilled over from neighbouring conflicts, as well as domestic ethnic struggles for political power, led to a concentration of economic power within the public sector, a feature which overseas lenders have been pressuring the government to reverse.

Egypt turned to centralisation, nationalisation and eventually a local version of socialism after the 1952 Free Officers' 'revolution'. Industrialisation, a national priority, came almost entirely under the remit of the state, while only some parts of the agricultural and urban real estate sectors still provided livings, albeit tightly controlled, for the private sector. Despite an early boost in growth rates, by the end of the 1960s, the Egyptian economy was mired in inefficiency, excessive bureaucratisation, import shortages due to an inability to generate export revenues, a diminishing agricultural base, an inflated defence burden, rising unemployment and general economic stagnation. Thus, in 1974, President Sadat initiated an about-turn with his *Infitah* or Open Door Policy, which encouraged private investment as a way of generating growth and employment. The policy only partially succeeded, with the inflated public sector and bureaucracy deterring private investment in most sectors and with speculative activity predominating over sustainable development. The country grew increasingly dependent on migrant labour remittances, oil exports, tourism and Suez Canal dues, although these did not alleviate a growing problem of debt. Consequently, in 1990, the government initiated structural reforms, supported by the IMF and the World Bank after 1991.

Eritrea only achieved formal independence from Ethiopia in 1993. The 30-year struggle left the country with neglected and devastated infrastructure. Consequently its primary economic goals have been to rebuild and improve energy and transportation provision, to develop a broad market-based private sector, to attract foreign investment, to construct appropriate health, education and social welfare systems, to provide jobs for a labour force, a large part of which is being reintegrated after military life, to establish food security and to develop mutually beneficial economic ties with its neighbours. The starting point for these efforts is still low, however. Large parts of the population currently live in extreme poverty. Eighty per cent live in rural areas, where they have traditionally been dependent on livestock grazing and subsistence agriculture. War and drought have devastated both, with livestock stocks being depleted by as much as 70 per cent even before the most recent conflict with Ethiopia began.[16] Agricultural production is low, utilises old-fashioned techniques, and has been weakened by recurrent drought, deforestation, and erosion. Consequently up to 70 per cent of the population is dependent on food aid for part of all of its supply. The government is utilising foreign assistance to try to improve food production and even exports, providing targeted help, identifying potentially irrigateable river basin lands, expanding small-scale irrigation schemes, and improving general agricultural services and infrastructure. In the past, up to 25,000 hectares of modern commercial farms produced fruits, vegetables and agricultural products for export and the government hopes to encourage private farmers to recreate and eventually better this output. Eritrea also once had a thriving industrial sector,[17] which was all but destroyed by the rule of the Dergue. A liberal new investment code was introduced in 1991, together with plans to return nationalised property to the original owners but, while market economics is a mainstay of policy, supported by external assistance agencies, the reality is that the very planning, management and distribution of assistance in the meantime reinforce the current economic functions of the state.

Israel undoubtedly has the most developed economy of all the Red Sea states. In its early years the imperatives of immigrant absorption and Hebrew exclusivism led to a highly centralised economy, with a dominant public sector and an enlarged *Histadrut* or trade union federation empire. The former employed as much as 20 per cent of the labour force by 1980 and contributed 25 per cent of GDP by the mid-1980s. The latter accounted for a quarter of all industrial enterprises in Israel and itself employed a further 15.4 per cent of the labour force by 1990. Together they owned almost all land, water, energy sources, communication networks, mines, defence industries, air transportation systems, and a large proportion of the industrial, agricultural and service sector enterprises including banks, hotels, etc. The private sector, by contrast, was comprised of mainly small-scale enterprises which were able to counter the lobbying power of the public sector by making use of government protection and subsidies.[18] By the mid-1980s, excessive consumption, inefficient production and commitments to full employment had created a wage–price spiral, a balance of trade crisis and a severe debt burden. An economic stabilisation plan introduced in 1985 was followed by efforts to significantly liberalise the economy. By the early 1990s Israel seemed well on the way to its target of regional 'tiger' status. Foreign investment was encouraged not only by the impressive growth rates and technological superiority of the economy, but also by the post-Oslo promises of regional economic integration and the lifting of the Arab (and Islamic) boycott. In particular, Israel's strategy of linking in to the markets, technology and investments of the Far East and South East Asia seemed set to consolidate the achievement of developed nation status.

Jordan, meanwhile, has always been nominally committed to a market economy, with the state stepping in to provide strategic infrastructure and mitigate against the worst effects of the poor resource base. In practice, the high defence burden (an average of 9 per cent of GDP in the 2000s), the reluctance of domestic investment capital to commit to the country's productive base, the importance of transit trade to the economy, and the foreign assistance and subsidisation needed to counter poverty and low labour participation, have all given the state a larger role than it might have chosen for itself, with all the attendant problems of borrowing, inefficiency, bureaucracy and poor management. Not surprisingly a debt repayment crisis in 1989 led to a series of rescheduling accords and an IMF-supported structural adjustment package.

Saudi Arabia is the rentier oil-state *par excellence.* Since the 1960s, oil and related hydrocarbon exports have provided the finances for a massive development drive. Given the scale of the financial resources at its disposal, especially after the price hike in 1973, the government embarked on ambitious programmes to simultaneously develop infrastructure, industry and agriculture. The economy has subsequently been characterised by the high contribution of consumption, especially government consumption, to GDP. The government has laid great emphasis on developing a diversified and modern industrial sector which can absorb the growing labour force and reduce dependence on oil revenues. Strategy has focused on developing heavy industry and the production of chemicals, petro-chemicals, fertilisers, metals, plastics and industrial goods. The sector is dominated by one largely government owned company and is closely tied to the oil industry. Lower oil prices in the mid-1980s, and a small tax base, meant that revenues dropped dramatically and the government had to resort to domestic borrowing to cover budget requirements. The resulting strains, accompanied by harsh criticism from the IMF, led the Kingdom to introduce an adjustment programme which includes various privatisations, domestic price rises, encouragement of the private sector, Saudisation of the labour force where possible and improving economic efficiency.

For Sudan, poor investment decisions, over-concentration on large-scale public sector projects which necessitated heavy capital and intermediate goods imports, neglect of traditional agriculture, as well as the effects of an ongoing civil war in the south led to government borrowing and heavy external debts by the late 1970s. Despite an IMF-funded structural reorientation in the early 1980s, severe droughts and floods contributed to still growing debt arrears, the suspension of international credit, and a reliance on donor aid. A more profound restructuring programme was interrupted by a military coup in 1989, although the new regime subsequently begun to implement many of the measures required by international lenders. Even so, the IMF announced a policy of non-co-operation with Sudan in 1990 and in 1993 withdrew the country's voting rights. Only in 1997 did the IMF and Sudan reach an agreement which involved monthly repayments by Sudan and promises to introduce management reforms. By 1999, the IMF was able to express satisfaction with a growth rate of 6 per cent, a fall in inflation to 17 per cent (from 133 per cent in 1996) and a balance of payments deficit of half the 1998 figure.[19]

Yemen's economy has undoubtedly suffered from the political complications of, first, division into a Marxist state, on the one hand, and a tribal monarchy, on the other, in the 1960s, and then an opportunistic reunification in 1990. While the former was a result of civil war, the latter was to lead to renewed civil strife in 1994. The end result is a country in which central administrative control is weak, tribal social formations predominate in rural areas, yet the economy remains shaped by former attempts at central planning. Oddly enough, and despite their ideological rhetoric, the former two Yemens had both seen public sector predominance in development planning and investment, as neither the domestic private sector nor foreign investment were excluded. However, the traditional subsistence farming sector remained the dominant form of production. Unification brought a new industrial strategy, the centrepiece of which is a free industrial and commercial zone in Aden which will bring with it enlargement of harbour, airport and power generation facilities. The zone will ultimately be wholly privatised, with the public sector taking a reduced role in industrial development.

In sum, we can see that the state has in past years been the dominant economic actor for these Red Sea states but that all of them are now eager to increase the role of the private sector in investment and production, especially for export. Undoubtedly, the hand of the IMF has been forceful in advancing this trend, highlighting another common feature of almost all these states – a previous over-reliance on international borrowing and/or domestic consumption to fuel economic growth.

Current performance

The most successful of Red Sea economies today are undoubtedly Israel, Egypt and Saudi Arabia. While the first two have managed a successful turnaround to export orientation and product diversity, Saudi Arabia continues to base its development on its fortuitous resource base.

The Israeli economy has undoubtedly benefited in recent years from the combination of liberalisation measures coming to fruition and the advances in the Arab–Israeli peace process of the mid-1990s. Growth between 1992 and 1996 averaged 7 per cent per annum, thus helping push up per capita incomes on a par with OECD countries such as Ireland and New Zealand. GDP per person was higher than in some other high-growth economies such as Argentina, Brazil, Chile, India, Taiwan and Turkey. Unemployment and inflation, although still higher than desirable, were brought down to 6.9 per cent and 8 per cent respectively, and the debt servicing ratio down from 25 per cent of export revenues in 1986 to just 16 per cent in 1993 (although absolute debt continued to grow). Moreover, the peace process allowed Israel to take vital steps towards its goal of export-led growth by encouraging the interest of multinationals and itself becoming virtually fully integrated into a global economy. The election of the right-wing government in 1996 led to a faltering in and finally the collapse of the peace process. As dreams of regional co-operation and integration faded, so too did the boom in Israeli economic growth. As well as deterring foreign investors who had begun to believe that Middle East peace would provide Israel with enormous opportunities, Netanyahu's policies were beset by budgetary problems which arose from his desire to keep political parties which were sustained by specific interest groups behind his coalition. The religious right-wing and the Russian immigrant parties were particularly greedy for financial concessions in return for their political support. Not only does Israel suffer from a rapidly falling labour participation rate due to increases in the non-working Haredi population,[20] but it must also subsidise this population with welfare payments which threaten to bankrupt the entire welfare system if allowed to grow at current rates. Meanwhile, investment has not reached anticipated levels. In the 1990s, investment was hit as much by the East Asian financial crisis as by lack of confidence in the peace process, with foreign investment in 1998 plummeting by 55 per cent on the previous year and the Tel Aviv stock exchange falling by 6.6 per cent.[21] Thus growth has stagnated from over 6 per cent a year in the mid-1990s to between 2 per cent and 4 per cent in the 2000s. Inflation, at 9 per cent in 1998, and unemployment at 8 per cent, also crept up, adding to Netanyahu's woes. From 9 per cent in the early 2000s, unemployment declined slightly to 6.4 per cent of the working population by the end of the decade. The other success story has been on consumer prices, which dropped from the highs of the 1990s to average 2 per cent in the first half of the 2000s and never getting above an average of 2.5 per cent for the decade as a whole. Indeed, in 2010, consumer prices had risen by no more than 2.5 per cent. Thus, despite lingering problems, the Israeli economy has remained soundly diversified, with a high-technology base, relatively liberalised trade, a highly educated labour force, and a well-developed infrastructure. External debt, however, remains a real problem: standing at $18.7 billion in 1997, it has since ballooned to reach nearly $90 billion in 2010, having exceeded $70 billion in 2005. Interest payments on this huge external debt have cost Israel an average of $8.5 billion a year in the 2000s in debt servicing, reaching a staggering $11.8 billion in 2008.

Today, after painful years of IMF-led reform, Egypt's macroeconomic indicators are also good – sustained growth of around 5 per cent a year, inflation below 4 per cent, a budget deficit of just 1 per cent of GDP and foreign reserves covering over a year of imports. Nearly 80 per cent of the economy is now in private hands, exchange controls have been abolished and the IMF view Egypt as a star pupil. On the downside, bureaucracy still obstructs activity, the state continues to employ nearly a third of the workforce, education and social provision are disaster zones, there has been a sharp increase in poverty and gradualism is the keyword for privatisation and deregulation.[22] In recent years Egypt has benefited enormously from the forgiveness of debts to the Gulf Arab states (around $7 billion) and small amounts owed to the West, the reward for supporting the Allied Coalition in the 1990/91 Kuwait crisis and considerably reducing the repayments required. Budgets have been brought under control through, first, austerity and later prudent expenditure and Canal dues have benefited from turbulence in the Persian Gulf, (although labour remittances were reduced as many workers were forced out of the Gulf Arab states). In sum, and despite continuing problems with the slow pace of reforms, especially privatisation of the remaining 60 or so public companies, Egypt's medium-term outlook is reasonably good. The prospects of an Association Agreement with Europe offer both opportunities and challenges for the economy, and there is still a long way to go in reducing bureaucratic obstacles to investment, production and distribution. However, foreign investors have been increasingly interested in what is perceived to be a new emerging regional market, reaching $11.2 billion in 2008 as the economy opened up from 2001 onwards.

Despite government policies to encourage the private sector to engage in product diversification, the Saudi economy remains essentially dependent on oil revenues which accounts for 37 per cent of GDP, almost 75 per cent of government revenue, and a little less than 90 per cent of export receipts. Since the late 1980s, efforts have been made to diversify production and exports, to reduce the economy's dependence on government expenditure, to Saudiaise the labour force, and to encourage the private sector to take up a larger part of the development burden. In the 1990s the programme met with only limited success, although higher-than-expected oil prices in 1996/97 allowed the budget deficit to be cut to 3.3 per cent of GDP in 1996 and 1.1 per cent in 1997.[23] In the 2000s, oil prices of over $80 per barrel for much of the decade enabled the Kingdom to significantly lower its budget deficit.

The stock of domestic debt remains high, however, despite the rise in oil prices reducing the pressure on the government to hold back its spending, especially in the defence realm, which have mounted since the early 2000s. Foreign investments in the Kingdom, both direct and through the stock market, are increasing and inevitably revolve around the oil extraction and processing industries, as well as retailing. Nonetheless, the Saudi economy has some impressive assets. Official foreign assets remain high, despite the impact of two wars in just over 10 years, and the existence of a stable investment environment and a promising stock market facilitate inward flows, as well as a long-term source of substantial revenues. Growth remained sluggish during the 1990s, with the 3 per cent growth in GDP in 1997 being due to a temporary buoyancy in the oil market rather than any sustainable non-oil growth. In the next decade, growth rate has been consistently above 5 per cent. Thus, future prospects depend not only on trends in oil prices, but on the success of the structural changes which are now being introduced under the influence of King Abdullah; an increasing role for the private sector, restraint in public spending, control of national consumption and the expansion of non-oil exports and overseas-based industrial production.

Jordan has been described as the world's only non-oil-producing oil economy, a reflection of the importance of Gulf labour and export markets, on the one hand, and credit and development assistance, on the other. With regard to the first of these, Jordan has been hard hit by the loss of the Iraqi market, and by Gulf suspicions following Jordan's siding with Iraq in 1991. Exports declined just as large numbers of migrant labourers were forced to return, placing additional pressures on an already struggling economy. In 1989, Jordan had been forced to resort to IMF stand-by credit in return for adopting a restructuring package. On the heels of the additional hardships caused by the Kuwait crisis, a new package was negotiated for the 1992–98 period. It was hoped that the signing of the Jordanian–Israeli peace accord of 1994 and Jordanian–PLO economic agreement in 1993 would bring new markets and trading opportunities, but hopes were quickly dashed when it was realised that Israel was hardly interested in Jordanian products, sent tourists who spent little or no money in Jordan, and was preventing the Palestinian and Jordanian economies from freely engaging with one another. Some co-operation has been managed in areas such as transport and phosphate industry development, but despite an agreement on water-sharing arrangements, Israel has proved unwilling to keep to its side of the bargain and, as the peace process has ground to a halt, so too have the economic aspirations of Jordanian peace-makers. The country remains $6.8 billion in debt, with unemployment at 25 per cent, poor foreign direct investment interest,[24] and a budget deficit of nearly 10 per cent of GDP.[25] While tourism and financial services are growing areas of activity, Jordan remains dependent on aid, assistance and loans from outside the country.

Yemen is another country which, despite having made significant gains from its close proximity to other Gulf Arab states, has also found itself increasingly vulnerable to them. Historically the majority of Yemenis (around 60 per cent of the labour force) were engaged in cultivation of crops such as sorghum, wheat, millet and barley,[26] although cash crops like cotton and coffee have also played a role. Some Yemenis were engaged in fishing, but industry played only a small part in the economy, employing just 5 per cent of the workforce. The political division of the country was to be reflected in industrial structure: in the North, activity centred on textiles, handicrafts, construction and food processing with light engineering, household chemicals and plastics and mechanical services being sponsored by the government in the 1980s. In the South, the state dominated industrial production although the Aden petroleum refinery was the only large industrial complex. The discovery of commercial quantities of oil and gas in the 1980s offered a new lucrative sector, although the South was quick to realise that the foreign investment which would allow its development was unwilling to come to a Marxist state. North and South thus embarked on a process of reunification which had, at its heart, the desire to create a new investment-friendly environment. Oil and gas have since come to account for about 20 per cent of GDP (including related products), and some 70 per cent of the source of government expenditure. In the meantime, however, large tracts of cultivated land have been diverted to production of the mildly stimulating *qat* evergreen plant leaves, responding to local demand, reducing food production (including coffee for export) and creating a growing need for food imports. The potentially lucrative fishing sector is hampered by low technological input and a poor ability to market and transport to wider markets. Thus despite the advent of hydrocarbon revenues, total Yemeni national production and earnings are not nearly enough to cover needs. In order to fulfil demands upon its own resources, the government of North Yemen had previously turned to Saudi Arabia for substantial budget subsidies every year, subsidies which could amount to a large portion of all state income. As with the South, aid from other oil-rich Arab countries, as well as China, the USSR and international organisations also supported development work, military expenditure and budget equilibrium. Much of the aid unfortunately disappeared into the hands of corrupt officials, tribal sheikhs and the military. In the years following unification, the Yemen was still beset by the dilemmas of a growing budget deficit that runs at between 20–30 per cent of GDP a year. Matters were made worse by the return of many migrant labourers from the neighbouring Gulf states after the 1990/91 Gulf War[27] and a sizeable national debt with the ultimate result that Yemen was forced to engage, with World Bank and IMF help, in a frequently unpopular[28] aid and restructuring programme to liberalise the economy and improve investment opportunities.[29]

Sudan and Eritrea continue to suffer from the economic ills associated with war. Sudan's economic activity is concentrated in the agricultural sector, with the country remaining exceptionally vulnerable to the vagaries of drought and flood. The population is predominantly rural (70 per cent), with 65 per cent of the workforce being employed in agriculture, in production of crops such as cotton, groundnuts, gum arabic, sesame, sorghum and sugar cane. While most of these provide basic export crops, sugar production only just exceeds local consumption. The manufacturing sector is meanwhile hampered by a lack of investment capital and poor national infrastructure, a shortage of foreign exchange to buy necessary inputs, and shortages of both water and electricity. Foreign investment is deterred by the combination of continuing civil war and a militant Islamic regime, which together with Sudan's support of Iraq in the Kuwait War also made Gulf Arab and Western regimes reluctant to contribute aid, although the UNWFP and the Islamic Development Bank and African Development Fund remained actively engaged in providing assistance. Persistent budget deficits have also been due to the narrow tax base, inefficient collection systems and the political concerns which have been raised when public demonstrations and strikes have resulted from spending cuts and subsidy reduction. Living standards have suffered from high rates of inflation (although the late 1990s saw this brought down to 46.6 per cent annual change from an annual average of 88.3 per cent during the 1993–97 period)[30] and a simultaneous decline in real wages, leading unsurprisingly to a national brain drain and a growing reliance on remittances.

Given the military's continued demands for financial resources to pursue internal wars (in the south and the west respectively), it is hardly surprising that Sudan has been mired in indebtedness and is hard pushed to sustain even existing economic life. All is not bleak, however. Since the early 1990s, the combination of gradual (if limited) reforms and improvements in agricultural production have led to GDP growth rates of over 4 per cent per annum, and as much as 5.5 per cent in 1997. Some Arab aid has been forthcoming in assisting the country with some of its development projects and the recent development of hydrocarbon resources helped to ease the current growing trade deficit given that Sudan has been realising its own oil exports for around a decade now.

Eritrea's economy is still too young to have achieved any startling recovery from the war for independence and already it is thrust once more into an expensive combat with Ethiopia. Until now it has been drawing on the international donor community, led by the United States, which is keen to support Eritrean efforts at establishing a liberal market economy and democratic political institutions. The government has been careful to ensure a sufficient geographic spread of development initiatives so that the poorer, and predominantly Muslim, lowlands do not fall behind the urban areas. In general, however, Eritrea's potential lies mostly in its coastal areas which can benefit from the development of marine and fishing resources.[31] More importantly perhaps, the war-damaged ports of Massawa and Assab were being repaired and enlarged to fully service Ethiopia's and the rest of the Horn of Africa's trading needs.[32]

The relationship with Ethiopia is critical for both states' economic health and, as tensions rose in the late 1990s, so the economic ties became the subject of claim and counter-claim. By 1998, Ethiopia was claiming that Eritrea had been economically bleeding Ethiopia, charging higher port fees than those charged to Djibouti, closing the port at Assab to Ethiopian cargo, re-exporting Ethiopian coffee (the latter's largest agricultural export), insisting on payment for port services in dollars after Eritrea abandoned the Ethiopian currency, the Bir, in favour of its own new Nacfa, over-charging Ethiopia for refined oil products and utilising cheap Ethiopian labour for its own industrial growth.[33] Eritrea in turn has asserted that Ethiopia was implementing a unilateral boycott of Eritrean ports in favour of Djibouti with deliberate intent to harm the Eritrean economy, and that it has unilaterally decided itself not to touch the Eritrean currency, creating havoc in their economic exchanges. With hostilities transforming into outright war between the two sides, Assab and Massawa were not only boycotted by Ethiopia, but Assab also became the target for renewed shelling. By Spring 1999, it had all but closed down, while Massawa was also suffering from the redirecting of Ethiopian trade to Djibouti. Ultimately, however, both parties show an interest in reviving the co-operation agreements that they signed after mutual recognition. The integration and interdependence of the two economies which existed during the period of Ethiopian rule cannot be undone in a matter of a decade and since there is much to be gained from larger sub-regional markets, free movement of labour and rationalisation of production and exchange, the relationship between these neighbours has remained close. Given that Ethiopia itself has, since 1991, embarked on a reorientation towards a market economy and integration with world markets, its access to Red Sea port facilities can only increase. The war has in the meantime proved to be too expensive to both, costing Eritrea up to 20 per cent of its national income[34] and almost all the foreign investment which had previously shown an interest.

Djibouti remains in some ways the most fragile of the Red Sea economies, almost totally dependent as it is on transit trade through the Red Sea, on external assistance, and on local demand from the 15,000-strong French ex-patriot community which revolves around the remaining garrison of French soldiers. The majority of working Djiboutis are employed in providing goods and services to the French community, and the country is almost entirely dependent on imported foodstuffs and energy. Unemployment is estimated at anything up to 50 per cent, made worse by recent recession, neighbouring wars, a population growth rate made high by immigration and refugees, stiffer competition for Red Sea port trade, and an overall decline in per capita consumption of 35 per cent since 1992. The country was successful, however, in increasing Arab and US assistance in the period following the Kuwait crisis. The government even went as far as introducing anti-alcohol measures to woo Saudi and Kuwaiti development aid, while the USA was keenly aware of Djibouti's strategic value, not least when it has served as a service centre for the international community's efforts to contain the fall-out from the implosion of Somalia. As the overall economic picture deteriorated, however, in the mid-1990s, Djibouti was forced to turn to the IMF for help. The

IMF in turn insisted first on a series of reductions in government expenditure and the rescheduling of debts to France. Public sector salaries were reduced but further reforms led to a general strike and were ultimately rescinded. A stand-by agreement with the IMF was finally reached in April 1996, ultimately extended to March 1998. Concessionary funding and EU assistance followed thereafter, but French suggestions that it might withdraw its forces from Djibouti stirred alarm at the potential economic implications for Djibouti, even as the port has been able to benefit from Ethiopian traffic diverted from Eritrea's ports. In sum, the conclusion reached by the *Middle East Review* in 1981 may still be said to hold true: 'If the region prospers, then Djibouti will prosper too; but if trade and commerce in the Horn of Africa and the Red Sea stagnate, then Djibouti's future will be bleak.'[35]

Trade around the Red Sea

One way of measuring the extent of the economic relationship which exists between Red States collectively, on the one hand, and between Red Sea states and the wider world, on the other, is to examine trading relations. As Table 6.6 shows, Red Sea states not surprisingly traded more with the rest of the world than with one another in the 1990s, with so many of their economies still taking shape and in the case of Eritrea and Yemen not quite there yet as sovereign states with an unified economy. While they were variably engaged in trade with each other, in general, they did not feature among one another's main trading partners.

This was less true for the smaller, poorer countries, which have little to export beyond agricultural commodities, hides, and low-grade manufactures, machinery and transport equipment (although Yemen and to a much lesser extent Sudan do of course have developing hydrocarbons exports). Since they have little access to developed-country markets, with the exception of Djibouti's privileged access to the French market, they are inevitably drawn into greater trade with their regional

Table 6.6 Intra-Red Sea trade in 1992 ($000 and % of total)

Country	General imports (c.i.f.)		General exports (f.o.b.)	
	1992	*(%)*	*1992*	*(%)*
Djibouti*	30,600	13.9	2,796	17.6
Egypt*	116,117	1.4	543,092	17.8
Ethiopia	180,579	27.5	62,130	35.1
Israel*	NA	NA		
Jordan	114,663	3.5	175,621	15.0
Saudi Arabia	409,194	1.3	386,110	0.9
Yemen	273,634	10.6	39,236	11.9

Source: Compiled by the authors from *World Trade Statistics 1998*.

Notes: Figures for Sudan were not included in this resource. 1992 was the only year for which data was available for all countries, although it does therefore exclude Eritrea as an independent state.

* Figures relate to special imports and exports.

neighbours. Djibouti counts Saudi Arabia, Yemen and Ethiopia/Eritrea among its largest trading partners while Eritrea's include Djibouti, Ethiopia, Saudi Arabia, Sudan and Yemen.

In the decade following the 1990s, things begin to change, however, and the trade between the big actors increased rather significantly, in part due to the growing sub-regionalisation of the Red Sea. Thus, trade between Saudi Arabia and Egypt multiplied over this decade, from $670 million in 1996 to $1.7 billion 10 years later. By the end of the decade, bilateral trade had stabilised, hovering at over $4.3 billion, with each exporting over $1.5 billion to the other's market. Saudi trade with Sudan equally grew rapidly in the period following the end of the Cold War, from $220 million to $710 million ten years later. On the eve of the second decade of the 2000s, bilateral trade had reached $1 billion. Egypt also has emerged as a major trading partner of Sudan, increasing its exports to its southern neighbour by multiples of ten into the 2000s. To put this in context, let's note that bilateral trade in 1996 had stood at no more than $40 million, which by 2006 had grown to $500 million. In 2009, Egypt's exports to Sudan were over $600 million, and Saudi Arabia's some $583 million.

To underline the growing importance of Saudi Arabia as a Red Sea sub-regional hub, one need not look any further than at the growing trade and broader economic links between the Kingdom and Yemen and Ethiopia. With regard to the former, bilateral trade has grown from $160 million in 1996 to $680 million in 2006, with the Kingdom's exports standing at $540 million in 2009.

However, the larger and richer states specifically target developed markets for their products. Israeli and Egyptian manufactures and Saudi hydrocarbon products go principally to America, Europe, Japan, the Republic of Korea, Singapore and Hong Kong. Equally, the United States is their largest source of imports, followed by Europe, Japan and the Far East.

The continuing Arab preference not to trade with Israel, and its own preference for modern consumer imports and high-tech exports have meant that Israeli trade with Red Sea neighbours is insignificant, although it did receive up to 5 per cent of Egyptian exports in the mid-1990s.[36] Egypt also sends around 4 per cent of its exports to Saudi Arabia, including vegetables, fruit, lentils, peas, beans, tea and coriander seeds. With these two exceptions, however, intra-Red Sea trade is relatively unimportant for Egypt's economy. Saudi Arabia, while importing and exporting relatively little to and from its Red Sea neighbours in terms of its own trade balance, is more important to the trading profiles of Djibouti, Eritrea, Jordan, Yemen and Sudan, from whom it imports livestock, flowers, vegetables, fruits, coffee and cardamoms. In total, in the early 1990s, Saudi Arabia accounted for 10 per cent of Djibouti's exports, 7 per cent of Yemen's, 25.5 per cent of Ethiopia's and 9.4 per cent of Jordan's. In terms of exports, Saudi goods accounted for 4 per cent of Djibouti's imports, 7.4 per cent of Yemen's, 17.2 per cent of Ethiopia's and just 2 per cent of Jordan's (not including oil). Eritrea has maintained the trading links developed by Ethiopia with Saudi Arabia, receiving 16.5 per cent of its imports from that country in 1994 and sending 12.7 per cent of its exports. Just three countries were taking over nearly 81 per cent of

Djibouti's exports at the end of the 1990s, which had grown to 87 per cent less than a decade later in 2006.

Clearly intra-Red Sea trade is more important for the smaller states and less for those with exports that appeal to the developed world. This may yet change, however, as the stronger economies attempt to maximise their mutual interests. It was reported in June 1999, for example, that Egypt and Saudi Arabia had agreed to set up a joint free trade zone in Egypt, the purpose of which is to support Saudi investments in Egypt (currently 38 per cent of total Arab investment in Egypt).[37]

Another way in which this is visible, although one which is virtually impossible to quantify, is through smuggling. Yemen has complained for decades about smuggling from Saudi Arabia, and reports in 1994 that Saudi agents were smuggling subsidised food and oil into Yemen, where it is bought at high prices even as food supplies in Yemen are set on fire, led to accusations by the Yemeni government that Saudi Arabia was deliberately trying to sabotage the Yemeni economy.[38] Less political illegal trading is also known to cross the Egyptian–Sudanese border, the Jordanian–Saudi border, and the Red Sea itself.

In general, however, trade around the Red Sea has been less significant for the collective of countries than has been their trade with the international economy. Despite efforts at developing regional trade, such as the Arab Trade Enhancement Agreement of 1981 and the establishment of an Arab Free Trade Area (AFTA)[39] in the late 1990s, inter-Arab trade accounts still for only a small proportion of Arab international trade overall (the level fluctuating between 5.6 and 8.5 per cent over the 1973–90 period).[40] Indeed, Rodney Wilson has noted of the MENA region that:

> In some respects the area has displayed more the characteristics of a common market than a free trade area, as the mobility of factors of production such as labour and capital has been much more economically significant than the movement of traded goods.[41]

Thus, we must turn now to the movement of people and money around the Red Sea if we are to complete the picture of the exchange of assets.

Migration and refugees

The movement of peoples across the Red Sea can be traced back to ancient times. MacMichael has traced the ancient movement of migrants from southern Arabia to Ethiopia, Sudan, Nubia and even Egypt[42] and there have been many attempts to follow the migration of Jewish tribes into Africa. A further wave of migrants crossed the sea with the Islamic conquerors, while slavery provided the reciprocity in transference of population. In modern times, the movement of peoples has resulted from two phenomena: labour migration and the creation of refugee populations out of regional crises (Table 6.7).

The Horn of Africa has witnessed more than 20 years of armed conflict and it is hardly surprising that there were subsequently an estimated 1.3 million refugees from Djibouti, Eritrea, Ethiopia, Somalia and Sudan, many of whom have travelled

Table 6.7 Refugee and internally displaced populations in Red Sea states, 1997 and 2009

By country of asylum/residence	1997	2009
Djibouti	23,600	13,032
Egypt	6,400	108,000
Eritrea	2,600	4,893
Ethiopia	323,100	124,360
Jordan	700*	415,360**
Saudi Arabia	5,800	71,000
Sudan	374,400	1,426,412
Yemen	38,500	422,222

Source: UNHCR, *Annual Statistical Overview* (various annual editions).

Notes: * Figure for Jordan does not include Palestinian refugees, whose welfare comes under the United Nations Relief and Works Agency. ** Figure for Jordan includes post-2003 Iraqi refugees.

out of the Horn itself to Yemen, Sudan, Egypt,[43] Uganda and Kenya. The problems created by war have been exacerbated by environmental and economic factors. Floods, droughts and conflicts have destroyed livelihoods and undermined traditional rural survival strategies. Moreover, for many of the refugees, who come from nomadic or pastoralist roots, international boundaries have little meaning and movement in times of crisis is the norm. Ethiopia, thus, acts as home for 140,000 refugees from the surrounding area, with nearly 70,000 of them from Somalia and 60,000 from Eritrea. According to UNHCR, in 2010, around 2,300 Somalis a month were arriving into Ethiopia and a further 1,300 from Eritrea, putting extreme pressure on Ethiopia's already stretched infrastructure and food supplies.

An estimated 900,000 Eritreans left that country between 1967 and 1990. Although many returned after independence in 1993, the post-independence conflict with Ethiopia created new population movements and displacement. Some 52,000 Eritreans were forcibly deported from Ethiopia into Eritrea, for example. Some 349,000 Eritreans still live in Sudan. While co-operative efforts to repatriate them have been hindered by the mutual accusations that subversive elements are being sponsored in each other's territory, Eritrea claims that some 127,000 have returned voluntarily. In 2008, just 1,200 Eritrean were repatriated to their place of birth from Egypt, while Eritrea itself harbours 2,800 Somali refugees and 144 Sudanese. Internal repression in Eritrea since the war has not abated migration and many hundreds have continued to leave the country on a monthly basis between 2000 and 2010, according to the UNHCR, often heading to Ethiopia.

Sudan is home to over 400,000 refugees. As well as those from Eritrea, there are 51,000 Ethiopians, 4,400 Chadians and 10,000 from other countries. Meanwhile, an estimated 210,000 Sudanese have fled to Uganda, 110,000 to Zaire, 78,000 to Ethiopia, 28,000 to Kenya and 27,000 to the Central African Republic. In total, before the Darfur crisis, some 4 million Sudanese had been either internally or internationally displaced. Djibouti is home to Ethiopian and Somali refugees, although there is little agreement on the numbers. In 1994, Djibouti claimed it was home to 150,000 refugees, while the UNHCR put the number nearer to 45,000.[44] Following UNHCR repatriation programmes, the US Committee for Refugees stated that by 1996 the figure was down to 25,000, of whom only 5,000 were Ethiopian, but by then some 10,000 Djiboutians had sought refuge from internal conflict between the government and the Afar-dominated *Front pour la restauration de l'unité et de la démocratie*, with a further 50,000 being internally displaced.

Yemen has become a particular haven for refugees from conflict in the Horn (as well as Muslim warriors of the Afghan war). Their residency is usually illegal in as much as the Yemeni administration cannot make provision for many of them and, if it finds them, is happy to expel them. For a country with an unemployment rate of at least 36 per cent, the presence of over 130,000 refugees is hardly welcomed and barely tolerated. Much has been made of the dangers for small boats of the crossing from the Horn in efforts to discourage more refugees from making the trip, and yet Yemen remains home to thousands of Somali 'boat people' crossing the Horn to the Peninsula. Saudi Arabia, next door, has seen the refugee/asylum population grow from 5,800 people in 1997 to 311,000 in 2005! The vast majority of this population come from just five, Red Sea-related, places: Eritrea, Ethiopia, Palestine, Somalia and Sudan. The Kingdom, conscious of the growing numbers, began deporting individuals from Somalia in late 2000s, allegedly deporting over 2,000 back to lawless Somalia in 2009/10. Somalia's internally displaced populations, according to the UNHCR, had reached 1.55 million in 2009.

Egypt is also home to refugees from Sudan and the Horn of Africa. The UNHCR recognises some 6,000 refugees, mostly from Somalia but also from Sudan, Yemen, Rwanda, Ethiopia, Libya and Burundi. A further 3–5 million Sudanese have moved to Egypt over the past 30 years, but until recently only a few had applied for refugee status and only a very small number have been granted it. Also, the Darfur crisis has created a further 2.6 million internal Sudanese refugees, with some 250,000 seeking refuge in neighbouring Chad.

Meanwhile some 600,000 Ethiopians, 500,000 Eritreans and 143,000 Chadian refugees escaping drought problems in the east and west are believed to have crossed into Sudan. Saudi Arabia has some Iraqi refugees left from the aftermath of the Kuwait crisis and the 2003 invasion of the country, although resettlement and voluntary return have drastically reduced numbers. Jordan is also home to over one million Iraqis, as well as smaller numbers from Bosnia and Russia. Its main concern before the Iraqi influx was with the 3.2 million Palestinian refugees dispersed between Jordan, Syria, Lebanon, the West Bank and Gaza Strip. This is the longest-standing sizeable refugee problem of the region and one which places considerable pressures on all those states hosting such numerous refugee populations. Israel, on the other hand, has refugees and/or asylum seekers from Sudan and Eritrea, 6,000 and 8,500 respectively, according to the UNHCR (Table 6.8).

Indeed, the financial burden of housing refugee communities is considerable for many Red Sea states. The UNHCR does not recognise as refugees all those who claim such status, and regional governments are therefore forced to assume the economic costs of provision and support. For countries like Jordan, where 1 in 4 of the population are refugees, or Djibouti where 1 in 6 can claim that status,[45]

Table 6.8 Indicative number of refugees around the Red Sea by country of asylum and origin, late 1990s

Country of asylum	Country of origin	Total refugee population
Djibouti	Ethiopia	2,000
Egypt	Sudan	1,600
Egypt	Yemen	600
Eritrea	Sudan	100
Ethiopia	Djibouti	8,000
Ethiopia	Sudan	56,900
Sudan	Eritrea	315,000
Sudan	Ethiopia	44,300
Yemen	Ethiopia	900

Source: United Nations High Commission for Refugees website, http://www.unhcr.ch/refworld/refbib/refstat/1998/98tab03.htm.

the burden – even with international assistance – can be enormous in both economic and political terms.

It is not only conflict which inspires large-scale population movement. Inevitably, given the disparities of wealth and poverty among Red Sea countries, labour migration – either external or internal – has become a common feature of daily life for their populations. The shared use of the Arabic language has assisted this, as have the diversity of resources and income levels.

Wilson highlights three directions of MENA labour migration: (1) out of the region to Europe; (2) to the oil-rich states of Arabian Peninsula and Libya; and (3) from the Palestinian Occupied Territories to Israel.[46] Labour migration from and between Red Sea states has principally fallen into the latter two categories, with the poorer populations of Yemen, Egypt, Sudan, Eritrea, Djibuoti and Jordan (as well as the Palestinians) inevitably being the seekers of work, with the richer countries, Saudi Arabia and Israel, being principal destinations. While migrant labour generates labour remittances and eases domestic unemployment statistics, it is not, however, without its own problems.

Many of Yemen's economic ills originate from the fact that Yemeni labour has historically sought more remunerative employment abroad, especially since the oil boom of the 1970s, during which decade migrant earnings represented 40 per cent of GDP. By the early 1980s, over half a million Yemenis worked in Saudi Arabia alone. Indeed, a common joke in Yemen is that when Americans landed on the moon, they found Yemenis already working there. While labour migration brought rewards in terms of educational opportunities and greater demands for responsive government, it also pushed up the money supply, forcing a spiral of inflation, consumption of foodstuffs and durable goods, and imports. Moreover, it pushed up land prices (land being the favoured form of investment by returning migrants in the absence of alternatives) beyond the means of those peasant farmers who might have still cultivated it. Instead, land became a commodity, the value of which was underexploited as housing took the place of farming. Ironically, a shortage of rural labour led to inwards migration from across the Red Sea and further afield. At the same time, the growing consumer demand created a lively retailing sector which focused on facilitating imports. Yet, while dependence on labour migrants for remittance income carries its own perils, Yemen has been equally hard pressed to deal with the decline in demand for that labour which accompanied the 1990/91 Kuwait War and Saudisation efforts. By example, as a result of Yemen's pro-Iraqi stand, and the resulting expulsion of Yemeni labour from neighbouring GCC states, the UN's Economic and Social Commission for West Asia estimated that Yemen lost at least $1.7 billion in remittance income by the end of 1992.

Egypt has also seen a significant part of its workforce seek employment overseas. According to the 1996 census, 2.18 million Egyptians live abroad as temporary migrants, although this is less than the 2.25 million recorded in 1986, reflecting the economic downturn in Arab oil-producing countries as well as the fact that Egypt's head-start (in terms of the educational standard of the labour force) which was created by Nasserist policies in the 1960s, has been eroded by faster educational development elsewhere in the region and by the increased pressure on Egypt's own system. Egypt is also the destination for labour migrants from poorer African states, including Sudan, Ethiopia and Eritrea, although political sensitivities inevitably impede the free movement of labour between these states. Ironically, the flow again was once from Egypt to these states as teachers and agricultural technicians used to carry the Nasserist message out to Egypt's poorer neighbours.

Sudan is another principal source of Red Sea migrant labour. Upwards of 200,000 Sudanese were working abroad in the 1980s, mainly in the Gulf, but many returned following the onset of the Gulf crisis in 1990. They brought back with them new fundamentalist interpretations of Islam which have in some cases altered entire village and regional identities in Sudan, introducing new 'traditions' and social norms (such as regulations in female modesty), as well as consumerist tendencies that go along with remitted wages. As Victoria Bernal has explained:

> The social relations of kin and community that once structured many aspects of villagers' lives have been increasingly subordinated to or supplanted by relations to global markets and the state. The social map in which villagers locate themselves and others now includes not only Khartoum and other Sudanese towns where some of the village live and work, but Saudi Arabia, Abu Dhabi, Yemen and other destinations as well.[47]

While some states are principally suppliers of migrant labour, Saudi Arabia and Israel are perhaps the largest markets for migrant labour around the Red Sea. According to the 1992 General Census, there were 4,624,459 foreign nationals in Saudi Arabia, or 27.3 per cent of the total population. By the 2009 Census, the expatriate population had grown dramatically to 8.4 million, in a total population of 27.1 million. The expatriate population thus has grown at twice the speed of Saudi nationals in the 2000s,[48] and was now accounting for nearly a third of the total population of the Kingdom. Even these figures may be underestimates as the issue of dependence on foreign labour is now such a sensitive subject that it is assumed that the government would have massaged the true numbers downwards. While the early years of the oil bonanza saw a political and social preference for Arab migrants to fill menial, domestic and blue-collar employment posts, more skilled labour inevitably came from the United States and (to a lesser degree) Europe. In recent years, however, Saudi Arabia has had to deal with unpleasant repercussions of both labour sources. American managers and technicians are seen as evidence of intrusive Western culture and economic superiority. Arab workers are seen as potentially politically subversive and relatively expensive. Today the Saudi government is therefore keen to seek alternatives to both labour sources (see below) with far more serious repercussions for the economies of poorer Red Sea neighbours than for America or Europe. At the same time, new labour exporters have emerged, particularly from the Indian subcontinent and from the Far East, able to export both skilled and unskilled labour at competitive prices and with minimum political baggage attached. Inevitably, the tendency has been to seek 'replacement labour' as well as the 'nationalisation' of the labour force.

Unconnected to its neighbouring Arab world for over 50 years, Israel was nonetheless the destination for over 107,000 foreign workers in 1995. While cheap Palestinian labour was drawn from the Occupied West Bank and Gaza Strip from 1967 until 1987, the Palestinian Intifada (or Uprising) dramatically reduced that number. When the Oslo Peace Accords opened the way for a formal return of that labour force, it was evident that Israel had already begun to look further afield for less politically sensitive sources of cheap manual labour. In 1994, of a total 97,000 migrant labourers working in Israel, only 69,000 were Palestinians, while 28,000 came from Eastern Europe, Turkey and Asia. By 1997, the number of Palestinians working in Israel had been reduced, through a combination of registration measures and closures of the Occupied Territories, to just 35,000.[49] Unlike Saudi Arabia, opportunities for labour migrants in Israel are confined to manual and domestic positions, as well as the rapidly growing sex trade which draws thousands of women from the former Soviet Union every year. Yet like Saudi Arabia, such workers are endowed with minimal rights, often amounting to little more than slavery. For Palestinians, meanwhile, the ever-deteriorating Palestinian economy, squeezed since the Oslo Accords between Israeli efforts to curtail and control its development to their own advantage, and by the corrupt and inefficient management of the Palestinians' own leadership, has meant that long-established patterns of labour migration away from the West Bank and Gaza Strip are being maintained and even reinforced despite the prospects of a peace process opening up new employment opportunities. Opportunities in the Arab world fluctuate and, as such, the search for work must not only carry Palestinians further afield but also increasingly risks political obstacles to return being imposed by Israeli authorities.

Labour migration between Red Sea countries, on the one hand, and the wider world, on the other, takes a variety of forms. This is not the place to catalogue the full profile of such labour –suffice to say that a number of trends can be identified which correspond to the increasing integration of Red Sea states into the global economy. David McMurray has highlighted, for example, the feminisation of migration as more women seek to move into the MENA labour force (Russian prostitutes and Sri Lankan housemaids being prominent examples) even as more Middle Eastern women join the exodus in search of paid work in Europe.[50] A second trend is that of so-called 'replacement migration' mentioned earlier. In this case, workers from non-Arab states are sought to replace migrant workers from Arab states who have previously been able to find employment within the Arab world. Saudi Arabia and Kuwait, for example, have been keen to find less politically and financially demanding migrant labour than those Yemenis, Egyptians, Jordanians, Syrians and Palestinians who previously provided the backbone to the lower end of the employment market. Third, the GCC states in particular have been eager to 'nationalise' their labour forces as far as possible, reducing the overall number of foreigners in order to provide employment opportunities for their own growing labour forces. Saudi Arabia, for example, is acutely aware that 69 per cent of its labour force was non-Saudi in 1999.[51] If we are to draw a conclusion, then, about labour migration around the Red Sea, it would be this: that there is a general and inevitable trend for labour to move from the poorer states to richer neighbouring states, despite the problems which this can create for both source and destination economies. Increasingly, however, the advantages which such Red Sea labour had in terms of geographical proximity and Arab cultural affinity, are being eroded by more global labour trends that make cheaper and politically less sensitive foreign labour available for the lower end of the market, and national labour preferable for the higher end.

Aid and investment

As well as goods and people, capital flows also link the economies of the Red Sea, both to one another and to the regional and international economies. In general, these take three forms: labour remittances, investment capital, and financial assistance. Table 6.9 shows the Red Sea nations among the top 70 aid recipients in 1996.

Aid flows may be broadly categorised into those determined by strategic interests (which are largely bilateral) and those which serve developmental purposes (which are more frequently multilateral but which may also be bilateral) (Table 6.10). In the first category, the strategic importance of the Red Sea area has been reflected in the fact that Israel, Egypt, Jordan have received the bulk of American overseas aid for over 20 years, and that and more recently Yemen has been added to this list. Indeed, we

Table 6.9 Ranked Red Sea countries among top 70 recipients of aid, 1996 ($ million)

Country	Amount	Aid per capita	Ranking
Egypt	2,695	47	2
Israel	1,237	228	9
Ethiopia	1,070	–	11
Somalia	538	59	30
Sudan	412	–	40
Jordan	370	88	42
Yemen	172	–	69

Source: *Economist* (1996).

Table 6.10 Net development assistance to Red Sea countries in late 2000s ($ million)

Country	2006	2007	2008
Djibouti	115	112	121
Egypt	873	1107	1348
Eritrea	126	157	143
Ethiopia	1941	2563	3327
Jordan	580	529	742
Palestine	1450	1873	2593
Sudan	2044	2112	2384
Yemen	280	236	305

Sources: OECD and World Bank databases (various years).

should note that five of the top ten recipients of US aid in 2009 were Red Sea states, with Israel topping the bill ($3.1 billion), then Egypt ($1.86 billion), Jordan ($1 billion), the Palestinian national authority ($910 million), and Ethiopia ($575 million).[52]

As we see, US aid to Israel has been particularly marked, amounting to around $3 billion a year ($1.8 billion of which was in military aid) or 12 per cent of Israel's GNP.[53] This has enabled Israel to service large military debts, to settle new immigrants, and to sustain a generally high standard of living. Since the mid-1990s, the amount of US aid had levelled off as other client arenas made greater demands on the US budget, as the need to deter Soviet expansionism in the region has been removed, as the USA has been more prepared to trade its aid for advances in the peace process, and as Israel itself has become aware of the inflationary and distortionary effects of aid recipientship. By the end of the 1990s, the aid package represented just 3 per cent of Israel's GNP, and has continued at around this level into the new century. Egypt has meanwhile benefited since signing the Camp David Accords in 1979 from both US military aid and project aid, almost entirely in the form of grants. In the early 1980s, the combined contribution to the Egyptian economy was around 8 per cent of GNP per annum. Economic aid has been in the form of cash assistance, development project aid and a commodity import programme, some of which has been tied to economic reform programmes. Again, by the early 1990s, pressure mounted in the US Congress to reduce this aid in favour of redirecting it towards support for Jordan, as that country engaged in a peace process with Israel.[54] The post-Oslo peace process generated new aid flows to the northern end of the Red Sea as a whole. One of the five tracks of the multilateral talks was devoted to fostering regional economic integration and development to underpin political processes. The Regional Economic Development Working Group (REDWIG) was established to both promote regionwide economic prosperity, and to directly support Palestinian economic recovery. Despite some promising early initiatives, its utility was seriously hampered by competition between the United States, on the one hand, and the European Union, on the other, the latter having spent the 1990s working hard to generate its own collective policy towards the MENA region as a whole. Thus, while the USA preferred to take the major role in convening donor conferences (including an initial conference at which a total of $2.8 billion was pledged to be disbursed over a five-year period) and MENA economic summits, the Europeans preferred to see these tasks undertaken by multilateral agencies such as the World Bank. It has itself provided significant project funding, offering, for example to fund a regional desalination plant to ease pressures on water sharing between Israel, Egypt, Jordan and the Palestinians. In the event, however, and although significant amounts of aid have been channelled through to the Palestinian Authority and some regionwide activities have been initiated, the stalling of the peace process in the mid-1990s and the corruption and inefficiency of the Palestinian Authority both worked to undermine the quantity of aid disbursed and the quality of its achievements. This has been disastrous for the Palestinian economy; about 80 per cent of the 1998–2000 Development Plan budget of $3.47 billion required foreign financing. Moreover, the clearly political ambition of donors, to use aid as a way of advancing an inherently flawed political process, and their own competition for influence in the region, also served to highlight the weaknesses of strategic aspects of aid-giving to Red Sea states.

As already noted, the addition of Yemen to the list is noteworthy, for it is completely driven by security, or rather due to the consequences of insecurity in Yemen for the rest of the sub-region. Thus, the $63 million per year of US aid to Yemen was increased in 2009 to over $70 million and doubled to $140 million for 2010.[55] Thus, by the end of 2010, the USA had completed the transfer of $155 million worth of military aid to Yemen.

External aid interests are not always tied solely to direct strategic interests. In the case of Djibouti, France has historically provided its former colony with aid that has been crucial to its economic survival. France's aid package of around $55 million per year in the late 2000s has dwarfed others' contributions. Today, however, and despite having committed itself to providing budgetary aid, France is unwilling to give additional aid without a structural reform programme in place. In the meantime, aid from Japan and international organisations such as UNICEF remains vital. Yemen has also been heavily dependent on foreign aid – notably from the West (Germany, the Netherlands and Japan), the United Nations and multilateral donors. Indeed in the 1990s, the total annual revenue from Western bilateral and multilateral loans and grants nearly matched the annual oil export revenues of the country.[56]

The wealthy Gulf states have also been generous aid donors to their poorer neighbours. In the past, this has often been through forums such as the Arab Fund for Economic and Social Development (AFSED), the League of Arab States, the Arab Monetary Fund (AMF), and the Islamic Development Bank. The AFSED provides a good example of inter-Arab economic assistance through project lending and concessionary loans. Its members include all 21 Arab countries, and all the Red Sea states except Eritrea and Israel. Lending inevitably goes predominantly towards the poorer states, although criteria for project viability mean that the very poorest are less able to compete for loans than countries such as Egypt and Libya. So, for example, in 1997 Jordan received 7.4 per cent of all net loans, Sudan received 4.1 per cent, Egypt 15.1 per cent, and Yemen 7.5 per cent, but Palestine received only 0.5 per cent and Djibouti 0.5 per cent.[57] The African states of the Red Sea have also benefited from loan facilities available through organisations such as the African Union and the African Development Bank.

Bilateral aid has also figured strongly, with Saudi Arabia, for example, contributing heavily to development in the Horn of Africa and Yemen in particular, although here again one can see strategic interests at play. Egypt (especially during the 1960s) and Israel, who are less able to extend financial aid than Saudi Arabia, have both provided technical forms of aid to regional allies, notably expertise and, in Israel's case, military assistance, in their efforts to enhance their own regional positions. In general, however, we may say of aid that most Red Sea states are recipients of either or both multilateral aid (due to weak economic performances) or bilateral aid (due to strategic interests). Both international aid and aid provided by Red Sea donors themselves have focused on these two requirements, with strategic interests generating most donor interest. Inevitably the economic weaknesses of many Red Sea states, and their engagement in many and varied conflicts, have made them vulnerable to the ambitions of both external and regional players expressed through aid-giving.

Investment capital flows between Red Sea states are less significant compared with labour remittances and aid in terms of contribution to national economies. In general, MENA states have proved to be poor at attracting foreign direct investment (FDI) from any sources. According to the IMF, in the first half of the 1990s, the MENA states (including Turkey, Israel, and the Arab states along the Mediterranean littoral) received only 1 per cent of total FDI in the world, amounting to less than 1 per cent of the GDP of the region.[58] It has been pointed out that there has been less FDI in the Middle East than in any other region of the Third World, apart from Sub-Saharan Africa, as a result of political uncertainty.[59] Added to this have been the slow rate of privatisation in economies in which the state has historically played a heavy role, inadequate currency exchange and banking facilities, and the inadequacy of legislative protection for foreign investors and their assets. Although the Red Sea states are all working to remedy these structural defects, few offer promising investment opportunities, the exceptions being Israel, Egypt and possibly Saudi Arabia.

Saudi Arabia, however, has emerged as a significant investor in its own right in the Red Sea sub-region. The Kingdom has substantial investments in Egypt. 'The number of investment plans involving Saudi capital in Egypt has reached approximate 2,268 projects' in 2010, according to the Egyptian Trade Minister Rachid Mohamed Rachid, with capital exceeding E£86 billion ($15.6 billion). Thus, Saudi Arabia now occupies the first place for Arab investment in Egypt, and Egyptian land in turn produces wheat and poultry for Saudi consumption.[60] Saudi investments in Jordan (to the tune of $2 billion in 2010) have also grown dramatically over the past 10 years. But it is in the Sudan that Saudi Arabia has emerged as one of its top investors. According to Sudan's Ministry of Investment, Saudi Arabia had financed 341 projects (212 service projects, 107 industrial projects, 22 agricultural projects) in that country between 2000 and 2007 with an accumulated investment of $4.3 billion during this period.[61] Less than two years later Saudi investments had grown to $8 billion in 737 projects. Of particular interest has been Sudan's courting of Saudi investment in its agriculture sector through which Sudan's land will aim to meet some of the Kingdom's demand basic food stuffs.

Given the relatively small size and social vulnerabilities of these economies, Saudi investment can make a very direct difference to their well-being. But in the process it can also help shape some of their attitudes and business cultures.

Sudan, of course, as an exporter of hydrcarbons in its own right – with an average production of 410,000 barrels/day in the second half of the 2000s and high of 480,000 barrels a day in 2008 according to the US Energy Administration Information department – and as a trade hub for Ethiopia, Chad and Uganda – has received attention from a number of potential investors, notably Chinese and Canadian firms. While Israel has potentially the most attractive economic profile, Arab states and firms are still reluctant to invest in Israeli companies, just as Israel has been cautious in its privatisations to secure strategic companies from potentially hostile purchasers. Like Israel, Egypt has a flourishing stock exchange, which has attracted international finance in recent years, but this remains subject to the continued implementation of the reform process and is still hampered by weaknesses in the banking sector, corruption and financial mismanagement. However, FDI has seen dramatic growth since the introduction of economic reforms and market liberalisations in the 2000s, leading to a tenfold increase in FDI from just $500 million in 2001 to over $6.5 billion in 2008 – the year before the global financial crisis. Saudi Arabia, which has the lion's share of investment capital among the Red Sea states, has in the past shown a greater preference for investing outside the region, where returns were generally better and carried fewer risks. But as we have seen since 9/11 and also with greater opportunities within the region itself, Saudi capital has been much more in evidence in Egypt, Jordan, Sudan and, most recently, Yemen.

In sum, while labour remittances and aid flows bring capital into parts of the Red Sea sub-region, investment flows generally follow a reverse pattern. Migrant labour, and to a lesser extent intra-regional aid, facilitate the transfer of financial resources between Red Sea states, but they also – and possibly to an overall greater extent – combine with investment flows to link Red Sea states first and foremost with each other, and then with wider MENA region and the international economy (Table 6.11).

Table 6.11 Selected balance of payment figures, 1995 ($ million)

Country	Current transfers received	Current transfers paid	Direct inv. abroad	Direct inv. from abroad
Djibouti	85.4	−18.4	–	3.2
Egypt	4,284.0	−253.0	−93.0	598.0
Israel	6,123.0	−251.0	−606.0	1,548.0
Jordan	1,591.8	−147.6	27.3	13.3
Saudi Arabia	–	−16,916.0	–	−1,877.0
Sudan	84.9	–	–	–
Yemen	1,120.5	−16.6	–	−217.7

Source: Europa (1998a, 1998b).

Note: In the same year, Eritrea enjoyed private unrequited transfers amounting to $215 million, and net official unrequited transfers of $73 million.

It is clear from the discussion above that the Red Sea states do not yet combine in any particular economically distinct grouping and the disparities in wealth, natural resources, infrastructure and geography mitigate against 'bloc' convergence. Yet, the data clearly show that over the past 20 years interaction between some of the Red Sea economies has grown quite considerably, as indeed have interdependencies. Growing economic contacts among the African Red Sea states is a case in point, through which Sudan, Ethiopia, Djibouti, Egypt have all entered into closer economy-based relationships. It is also evident that Saudi Arabia as the economic powerhouse of the Red Sea has a critical role to play in weaving sub-regional interdependencies.

The Red Sea states are clearly divided between the haves and the have-nots, between the resource-rich and the resource-poor, with the majority falling into the latter category. As we have seen, three states clearly have economic advantages over their neighbours: Israel, Egypt and Saudi Arabia, although the nature of those advantages is dramatically different in each case. While Egypt and Saudi Arabia have so far been able to capitalise on their strengths to develop regional economic roles, Israel has been largely unable to do so because of the Arab boycott and continuing Arab hostility to doing business with the Jewish state. Although this is gradually changing, and is likely to fundamentally alter in the medium-to-long term, in the meantime, Israel has utilised technical and military aid packages as a principal means of extending influence down the Red Sea. It has been able to do this not least because of its own industrialised status in the international economy, now also a member of the OECD, and its position as major beneficiary of US military and economic aid. Egypt and Saudi Arabia have developed their sub-regional economic roles through a combination of trade, labour migration (either as a source of, or destination for, migrant labour) and hydrocarbons production and export. In recent decades, smaller sub-regional economies have become more or less dependent on these larger economies while the larger economies have focused on integrating themselves into the global economy. We can argue, then, that, on balance, the smaller Red Sea states have a greater sub-regional economic dependence and interest than the larger economies, but also that the larger economies have been able to capitalise on this fact to extend their own influence over their neighbours. This relationship takes place within the context of specific economic ties between both larger and smaller economies, on the one hand, and the global economy and international players, on the other. The sub-regional ties include aid dependency, labour migration, trade, and increasingly direct investment, demonstrating a general convergence of the sub-region compared with the immediate period post-Cold War period. Growing policy maturity, combined with greater business opportunities, is producing a string of interesting and unexpected interdependencies of a kind among the Red Sea states that we simply have not experienced elsewhere in the MENA sub-system.

7 Red Sea networks

Regional and international transport

Inevitably, access to the Red Sea itself is perhaps the major transport asset of all the Red Sea states, although some have developed their internal and international infrastructure more than others. While Saudi Arabia and Israel may be said to possess modern facilities for both domestic use and for international passengers and freight, the others lag behind considerably. For some, like Djibouti, Eritrea and even Jordan, their location on the Red Sea should enable them to enjoy the economic fruits of transit trade. For Ethiopia, access through its neighbours is vital. For Egypt, Sudan and Yemen, the Red Sea provides export routes for domestic products, as well as a source of port revenues for traffic. For Egypt in particular, the Suez Canal is a major source of budget revenue. Yet, for reasons outlined below, none of these countries have as yet realised the full potential of such activity. Moreover, in many instances the Red Sea states' internal transport networks are poor, hindering both internal movement of goods and the potential for international trade via non-maritime routes. In particular, the road and rail linkages between the Red Sea states themselves are virtually non-existent, hindering sub-regional trade and economic co-operation, as well as competitive trading with the wider MENA and African regions. Most Red Sea states are thus overly dependent on the Red Sea itself, limiting their economic potential even as they are able to benefit from it.

Maritime transport

The desire to modernise and upgrade port facilities is perhaps one of the strongest investment impulses of Red Sea states. Not only do such facilities increase their own import and export capacities, but they also allow the states to act as entrepôts or conduits for trade between themselves and third countries (Table 7.1). Moreover, as the need for intra-regional integration and trade becomes ever more obvious, states are competing for this role, even as global interest in accessing Middle Eastern markets is rising. Leading Asian carriers in particular have indicated a growing interest in the Middle East 'box' and the Red Sea in particular, identifying it as niche market in the main haulage trade.[1]

Table 7.1 International seaborne freight traffic ('000 metric tons excluding petroleum) and vessels in merchant fleet, 1996

Country	Goods loaded	Goods no. unloaded	Vessels	Displacement (000 grt)
Djibouti	–	–	4	–
Egypt	–	–	375	1,230
Eritrea	–	–	4	0.83
Israel	25,900	10,680	54	679
Jordan	739*	514*	4	40
Saudi Arabia	214,070*	46,437*	276	1,208
Sudan	1,543**	4,300**	10	54
Yemen	1,936*	7,829*	42	25.1

Source: Europa (1998a, 1998b).

Note: * Figures for 1990. ** Figures for 1993.

Table 7.2 Freight handling of major Saudi Arabian sea ports, late 1990s

Port	No. ships	Exports (tons)	Imports (tons)
King Abdul Aziz Dammam	2,091	2,191,006	5,387,115
Jubail Commercial	134	740,665	518,797
King Fahd Industrial Jubail	63	23,686,374	3,455,560
Yanbu Commercial	1,233	94,295	851,009
King Fahd Industrial Yanbu	991	24,674,756	454,647
Jizan	991	13,801	227,604
Duba	419	12,756	34,736
Jeddah Islamic	4,205	3,309,510	13,781,814

Source: Saudi Arabian Monetary Agency (various years).

Note: Figures exclude crude oil.

In terms of port facilities, the Red Sea already possesses numerous facilities. Saudi Arabia has the greatest capacity, with eight major commercial and industrial sea ports handling a total of 87.4 million tons of trade in 1996 via 183 piers (as well as 14 smaller ports and harbours). In the 1990s, the two largest ports, King Fahd Industrial Port at Jubail and the King Fahd Industrial Port at Yanbu, between them handled 66 per cent of total operations, acting as the main export outlets for goods other than hydrocarbons.[2] In total, 95 per cent of all the Kingdom's imports and exports go through these ports, with 12,000 ships being received every year.[3] Of the eight ports listed in Table 7.2, the last five are situated on the Red Sea, accounting for 55 per cent of total trade (excluding crude oil exports) going through ports.

Over a decade later, in 2010, Jeddah was still taking the biggest share of the Kingdom's cargo traffic, 10.19 million tons to be precise, and King Fahd Indistrial Ports at Jubail and Yanbu were together responsible for just over 16.0

million tons of cargo, 10.6 million and 5.9 million respectively.[4] Jeddah has some 58 berths of international standing in service today, compared with just six births at Yanbu commercial port.

An ongoing programme of port modernisation and expansion since the 1970s by the Saudi Ports Authority has left Saudi Arabia with advanced handling and storage facilities, with Jeddah being known as 'The Pearl of the Red Sea', acting as the commercial hub of the country (and most of the major trading families being based there). The Kingdom's plans in the twenty-first century are even more ambitious, founded around the construction of the country's largest and newest metropolis on the Red Sea coast, the $130 billion King Abdullah Economic City (KAEC) near Rabigh. Once completed by 2030, the KAEC will accommodate a 60-square kilometre industrial zone (to include an aluminium smelter, a new oil refinery, and a huge new port facilties for trans-shipment), and a further 100-square kilometre residential, educational and research, and tourist development. North of Jeddah will also be located the campus of the proposed research-intensive King Abdullah University for Science and Technology as a new R&D facility serving the country.

The new $1 billion Knowledge Economic City near Medina is another Red Sea coast project, which will eventually have a population of 150,000. The KEC will be complemented by the Jizan Economic City near the Yemeni border, with another major port, a petrochemicals complex, power desalination plant and another aluminium smelter. The JEC will have a population of 250,000 on completion. These projects combined decisively will shift the Kingdom's industrial and transport infrastructure and resources westwards to the Kingdom's Red Sea coast, accounting for an initial investment of over $200 billion. On completion, by the 2030s, Saudi Arabia will become the sub-region's greatest industrial and economic powerhouse, and its most influential socio-economic hub. These new and vibrant developments will be supported by a $5 billion high-speed rail link running the length of the Kingdom's Red Sea coast, with Jeddah, Yanbu and Jubail as other beneficiaries of the country's most ambitious economic development plans to date.

By mid-century, therefore, the Kingdom will be the Red Sea sub-region's greatest industrial power for whom this sea will arguably be an even more significant transport route for the Persian Gulf. Given the scale of investments and financial commitments being made, the interests of the other Red Sea states will equally be influenced by the development projects in Saudi Arabia.

With Saudi Arabia emerging as the Red Sea's emerging industrial power, we should not lose sight of the other two big players, namely, Israel and Egypt. Israel has modern port facilities, although only one of its six sea ports, Eilat, at the northern tip of the Gulf of Aqaba, lies on the Red Sea. While the largest port facilities are at Haifa, and given that expansion is focused on those facilities on Israel's northern Mediterranean coast, Eilat retains its importance if only because of the historical lack of transit routes across the territory of neighbours has meant that Israeli exports and imports have been dependent on maritime and air transport. A massive investment drive was launched in the late 1990s aimed at improving facilities across the board, taking advantage of peaceful relations with Jordan and the possibilities for regional trade which they offer. Article 14 of the Jordan–Israel peace treaty stipulated that both countries would recognise the rights of the other's vessels to passage through its territorial waters and that their ports would grant those vessels and their cargoes normal access. Article 23 dealt solely with an agreement to negotiate on arrangements for the joint development of Aqaba and Eilat, including tourism development, joint customs posts, a free trade zone, prevention of maritime pollution and co-operation in aviation. The development of these facilities, of course, have been affected by lack of progress in the peace process and it is interesting that the re-launch of direct talks between the two sides in September 2010 in Washington was underlined by the necessity of the parties agreeing to accelerate economic co-operation bilaterally and multilaterally.

Jordan itself shares the head of the Gulf with Israel, with the port of Aqaba lying next to Eilat. The port has for many years provided access to the Red Sea for trade from Syria, Lebanon and further afield, as well as for Jordan itself. During the 1980s the port was able to expand rapidly on the back of trade with Iraq, which was itself suffering from closure of traditional transport routes through Syria and the Gulf. By the end of the1990s, the port included 20 berths, a container terminal, and 299,000 square metres of storage facilities. The imposition of sanctions on Iraq in the 1990s killed off most of this trade, seriously reducing cargo-handling levels in the port. In 1989, Aqaba had handled 18.7 million tons of cargo, of which 11.2 million tons were Jordanian imports and exports and the rest was transit cargo. By 1992, the cumulative loss of transport revenues incurred as a result of lost trade amounted to $570 million, with only 2.1 million tons of transit cargo passing through the port. Much of this was Iraqi imports of basic foods, while Iraqi exports (which had amounted to 1.15 million tons a year before the sanctions) have virtually ceased entirely. Even transit cargo from or to other countries was redirected away from Aqaba port by shipping companies who were reluctant to subject themselves to the lengthy delays caused by UN monitoring of Aqaba-bound cargo.[5]

However, things began to change very rapidly in the new century, with massive investment preceding the rejuvenation of this strategic port. Post-2003 and regime change in Iraq, Aqaba's economy has been growing rapidly. Construction of new resorts, residential units, and business parks are having a major impact on the country's relationship with its only port. Emergence of high profile projects such as Tala Bay and Saraya al Aqaba are visible examples of the $20 billion worth of investments made in the Special Economic Zone between 2001 and 2010 that are rejuvenating the Aqaba region. Not unlike Saudi Arabia, Jordan is also banking on becoming a handy transport and logistics hub for the Palestinian territories, Syria and also Lebanon. Interestingly, the transformation of Aqaba since 2001 has begun to overshadow Eilat, the prosperous Israeli Red Sea resort only several miles away. The Oxford Business Group has noted that by 2006 the ASEZ had attracted some $8 billion in committed investments, far exceeding its $6 billion target by 2020 by a third and more in under 10 years. In 2009 alone, deals worth $14 billion had been agreed, including a major $5 billion port relocation investment through which the current port would be relocated to the southernmost part of the province near the Saudi border. Its capacity will surpass that of the current port. The project costs $5 billion, and it will be completed by 2013. Aqaba will be connected by the national rail system which is scheduled to be completed by 2013. Tellingly, the Aqaba Container Terminal handled a record 587,530 20-foot equivalent units in 2008. By mid-decade Aqaba port had received nearly 3,000 ships, and Jordan is again in the frame as far as trade with Iraq is concerned and its plans for upgrading the King Hussein International Airport and the development of a logistics centre are expeced to help position Aqaba as a regional hub for tourism, trade and transport.

Egypt has three of its nine major ports and harbours on the Red Sea, at Al Ghardaqah, Bur Safajah and Suez. In total, it has 34 sea ports, 13 general commercial ports and 21 specialised ports. It also has a relatively large merchant marine fleet which contributes to Egypt transporting 90 per cent[6] of its international trade via maritime transport. Since the early 1990, efforts have been made to expand and modernise the ports, especially Alexandria on the Mediterranean, Damietta and Safajah on the Red Sea, with attention being paid to export cargo facilities rather than passenger facilities. However, since 1985, a ferry service has crossed from Nuwiebeh to Aqaba, run by the Arab Bridge Maritime Company, and carrying over one million Egyptian workers annually en route to the GCC states or, in the case of 1990, back from Kuwait. Even so, and despite state claims to have spent E£4.3 billion on improving port infrastructure and services between 1981 and 1997, Egyptian ports are in urgent need of upgrading to accommodate a wider range of transport activities, to establish greater storage, to allow for repairs and maintenance of ships and to develop container quay capacity. Moreover, while Egypt's commercial shipping fleet is still numerically the highest among Arab states, the ships are frequently old and antiquated, often too fragile to venture into overseas operations.

Of more interest has been foreign investment entering Egypt's maritime infrastructure. A good example is the DP World's bid to buy into Egypt's Red Sea port infrastructure with an initial investment of $670 million in 2008, which was to grow to $2 billion by 2010.[7] DP World had initially announced that it would invest close to $8.7 billion in Egypt to develop a sea port and other industrial projects. The total investment is said to include the development of a container terminal at Eastern Port Said ($3.5 billion) and associated infrastructure to facilate movement though the Suez Canal ($5.2 billion).[8] Through the investment in Sokhna Port, DP World intended to integrate this port's activities into its worldwide 42 terminals network. As part of its port improvements, Port Said has also been expanding into a transhipment hub, with an investment promise of $5.8 billion by the state. Port Said already accounts for 40 per cent of Egypt's container traffic.

Further south, Sudan has two major sea ports, both on the Red Sea and located at Port Sudan and Sawakin. Both possess some modern port equipment but most cargo handling is manual. In 2007, Port Sudan handled a total of almost 8 million metric tons of cargo, including 1.7 million tons of imports and 6.2 million tons of exports. Accoding to World Port Source, Port Sudan handled over 2 million TEUs of containerised cargo, including 1.5 million TEUs for export and 588,000 TEUs for import.[9] Signifying the growing importance of hydrocarbons to the Sudanese economy, the port has also handled more than 1.3 million metric tons of petroleum in 2007, including 760,400 tons of exports and 550,900 tons of imports. Port Sudan's primary exports are cotton, oilseed, senna, gum Arabic, and hides and skins; and its major imports include fuel oil, machinery, construction materials, and vehicles. The port's capacity has increased since the early 2000s to now process cargo through 15 dedicated berths. Indeed, the China Harbour Engineering Co. was given the contract in 2009 to build a two-berth container terminal at Sudan's Digna port at a cost of $100 million. The new Suakin International Container Terminal's berths will be able to handle 100,000-ton ships by 2012.

But the country's merchant fleet remains small, with no more than 10 vessels available, of which a smaller proportion are deemed to be seaworthy ships, perhaps giving the country a maximum of 122,200 tons. Its small fleet operates between Red Sea, Mediterranean and European ports and, like much of Egypt's fleet, is outdated and in many cases barely seaworthy.

Eritrea, whose independence swallowed all of Ethiopia's coastline, also has two sea port facilities, Massawa and Assab. Massawa was heavily damaged by bombing raids between February 1990 and May 1991 and, according to Eritrean sources, was badly neglected during the period of Ethiopian administration.[10] It would require considerable investment before it can be utilised to its full capacity. Meanwhile the World Bank and the Italian government have been funding a $57.6 million project to improve the productivity and capacity of both ports, which together have handled much of Ethiopia's, as well as Eritrean, exports.

Djibouti, of course, is almost entirely dependent on Djibouti Port for its economic well-being. In an effort to counter competition from other emerging Arab ports, Djibouti was made a free port in 1981. A deep-water container terminal was added in 1985 with roll-on-roll-off facilities and a refrigerated warehouse. The berth facilities were improved and the port was dredged to take larger vessels. Although the port lost Ethiopian trade to Eritrean ports during the Ogaden war, it was to benefit from conflict in the Gulf in 1990/91, with traffic almost doubling in two years. Today, its facilities are more modern than those of Eritrean ports although Eritrean analysis has suggested that Djiboutian port services are 'at least 400% to 500% more expensive' than those of Assab.[11] Nonetheless, Ethiopia has in recent times and as part of the escalating crisis with Eritrea, encouraged firms to boycott Eritrean ports in favour of Djibouti. New facilities have been added at Dorale, about 7 km from the main port, in order to provide new capacity to service trade with Ethiopia. Thus, today, Ethiopia accounts for 85 per cent of the port's activities, representing further evidence of sub-regional integration.

The future of Red Sea maritime transport facilities, which in total are not sufficient for the needs or potential of most Red Sea states, may well depend on moves to privatise what are usually state-owned and managed assets, or at least to allow greater private sector participation. Nearly half of the Egyptian commercial ship-ping fleet is now privately owned.[12] Although the absolute number of ships in the fleet is decreasing, private investment has allowed the gross tonnage capacity to increase, helping Egypt to sustain itself as the Arab country with the largest ship-ping fleet, outmatched only by Kuwait in tonnage capacity. As we have seen, pri-vate investment has also been sought in the provision of new facilities. For example, Egypt is currently trying to build a hub port and development zone at the entrance to the Suez Canal, awarding concessions to private firms to dredge the Canal, to construct a new breakwater and quays, and to build and operate a new east Port Said container terminal.[13] A second new hub port will be built at Ain al-Sukhna on the west coast of Suez. In Saudi Arabia, 10-year contracts have already been offered for the leasing of a general cargo station at Dammam on an income-sharing basis with the Saudi Seaports Authority. A similar 20-year arrange-ment is in place for Jeddah Islamic Port and leases have been issued to operate Jeddah's General Cargo Station, roll-on-roll-off services and the container station at Riyadh railway terminus. Jordan is also offering out the construction and opera-tion of a new industrial jetty at Aqaba. Most Red Sea states acknowledge that enlarging and improving container port facilities are essential if they are to deal with the commercial demands of the future, and that the public sector has in the past proved incapable of finding sufficient investment capital or meeting the demand effectively and efficiently. Nonetheless, Egypt has stressed that the Suez Canal Authority and major maritime companies will stay in state hands due to their strategic importance.

A final aspect of waterway transport is the use of the Nile River as a transport route. Sudan has 5,310 km of navigable waterway while Egypt has 3,500 km including the Alexandria–Cairo waterway, the Suez Canal (193.5 km including approaches) and numerous smaller canals in the Nile Delta. Both countries have cargo handling facilities at points along the Nile (for example, Egypt at Asyut and Aswan and Sudan at Khartoum, Kusti, Juba and Nimule), but only a small portion of freight transport utilises this route (in Egypt's case just 3 per cent of domestic freight transport is carried on the river). Egypt seeks to expand river transport to relieve the pressure on land-based internal transport systems. In Sudan, river transport is minimal on the 4,068 km of the navigable Nile. A section between Karima and Dongola on the White Nile is most used but government plans since 1981 to remedy years of neglect by dredging rivers and constructing quays and navigation aids, have fallen behind schedule. Moreover, river transport in the south of Sudan has been disrupted for a prolonged period by the civil war. More positively, a joint Egyptian–Sudanese company is now providing river transport, linking Wadi Halfa and Aswan across Lake Nasser after a three-year disruption caused by poor relations between the two countries.

Road transport

Here again, some countries have invested proportionately more in their road net-works than others. The primary means of transportation within Red Sea states, as elsewhere in the MENA region, is road transport. As Rodney Wilson has pointed out, road networks in the Middle East and North Africa have been planned on a purely national basis 'and there is no inter-state road system similar to that found in North America or the European Union'.[14]

In Egypt, road haulage accounts for 90 per cent of domestic freight movement, with 17,000 km of roads being inter-city highways.[15] Given the reliance of the haulage industry on the roads, these have grown considerably since the late 1990s, so by 2009 31,500 million tons/km were being carried on 92,370 km of roads.[16]

In Saudi Arabia, road-building has been a priority. Until 1964, the only surfaced roads were in the Jeddah–Mecca–Medina areas but the rapid increase in international trade, in urbanisation, development and consumption, have all demanded that a sophisticated road network be constructed quickly that can transport goods and people across the vast distances of the country. Moreover, plans for regional and agricultural development have meant that such networks have to be extended into the hinterland and include more than just inter-city carriageways. Consequently, road building was given priority in early development plans. During the Fifth Development Plan alone (1990–95), over 35,000 km of new roads were constructed. Work has been underway for another 990 km main, 340 km secondary and 2,500 agricultural roads and in the 1999 budget SR4.6 billion was earmarked for road construction, to include the completion of 820 km of the Qassim–Medina–Yanbu–Rabigh–Thoual expressway. By 2010, the Kingdom had built a total road network of 152,044 km, the most complex among the Red Sea states, carrying 84,473 million tons/km of cargo.

Israel also has a well-developed domestic road network, but one legacy of its continuing dispute with its Arab neighbours is that these roads are to a large extent isolated within the country. Road crossings to Egypt via Gaza and the Sinai, and to Jordan via the West Bank, have been maintained but in no sense amount to inter-state highways. Regional isolation has historically meant that Israel has relied on maritime and aviation transport for its international trade. New road investments are concentrated on providing a system of bypasses around Palestinian population centres in the West Bank and service the needs of Israeli Jewish settler communities rather than domestic or international trade.

For Djibouti, Eritrea, Sudan and the Yemen, budgetary constraints have clearly limited investment in road transport. The consequences can be disastrous, as the 1984–85 and 1990–91 droughts in Sudan illustrated, when the road system was inadequate for the distribution of food and relief aid. Some efforts are being made to improve inter-urban systems, especially since the rail system has become progressively more outdated and inefficient, with Iran paying for the construction of a highway between Rabak and Juba, for example, which will link north and south Sudan. The road will be particularly useful for the oil sector. It has also been suggested that the road could be extended into East Africa.[17] Internally, oil income has proved very helpful in this regard and by 2010 Sudan had built an 11,900-km road network, but the railways remained central to the country's transport infrastructure, as we will see later.

Eritrean ports have historically been serviced primarily by railroads, but today two-thirds of the transport budget is destined for road repair and construction. Road building is cheaper than port and airport construction, while road transportation is faster than maritime transport and less costly than air freight. Given the need to revive agriculture and trade, the establishment of a modern road infrastructure is therefore seen as vital to development interests. As yet, however, the country remains poorly served. Djibouti, which is reliant upon its port as a source of income and employment, has similarly few surfaced roads, most of which are anyway narrow and in need of repair. Inevitably, this limits Djibouti's potential as a gateway to and from African markets, restricting its services to Ethiopia and Somalia which whom it shares railway connections but no all-weather roads. One major project underway, however, is a 114-km 'unity' highway to link Djibouti with northern Somalia. Moves to provide better road transport between Ethiopia and Djibouti port have also been developed.

Yemen has been largely dependent on foreign assistance for the development of its road network. The main inter-urban highways were built with Chinese (Sana'a-Hodeida, Sa'ada-Saudi border, Amran-Hajjah), US (Sana'a-Taiz-Mocha), UAE (Sana'a-Marib) and German (Taiz road and Al-Mahweet road) aid. Repair and maintenance remain a problem, however, since neither equipment nor expertise is locally available. While road construction is a developmental priority, particularly since linkages between the north and south of the country remain weak, there are signs of nervousness that, while asphalting existing gravel feeder tracks can assist in getting agricultural products to markets and ports, the newer roads which link Yemen to Saudi Arabia are being used as a means for the larger state to dump its own exports in Yemen. In April 1998, the *Yemen Times* reported that 54 huge trailers and trucks were crossing one border point at Haradh every day, bringing in Saudi foodstuffs, manufactured goods, beverages and industrial materials. The report asserted that 'the volume of Saudi exports to Yemen rose by 88 per cent in 1997, compared to 1996' and quoted one Yemeni official as having said that 'We are expecting them to almost double again this year'.[18]

Table 7.3 shows the road network in the Red Sea states in 2005. Some states, such as Jordan, have developed their freight-carrying fleets to dominate the region's transport. While Egypt has just 758 refrigerated road trucks, Jordan can boast of over 2,000 and a total fleet of over 10,000 trucks. Jordan's geographic location and lack of natural resources have ensured that facilitating transit trade (particularly to and from the Gulf Arab states) has become a major business activity for the private sector. Egypt, by contrast, has little trading contact with its direct neighbours and has a sufficiently large market to be a direct target for other nations' exports, making transit trade less attractive and viable as a business opportunity.

Data from the CIA factbooks for the 2000s decade indicate that the trend of road construction in the larger states continued unabated. In Saudi Arabia, for example, the total road network has expanded to 221,000 km, Egypt's to 92,300 km, Yemen's to 71,300 km, and Jordan's to 7,700 km. Ethiopia's road network

Table 7.3 Road networks in the Red Sea states, 2005 (in km)

Country	Paved	Non-paved	Total	% paved
Djibouti	364	2,526	2,890	12.6
Egypt	49,984	14,016	64,000	78.1
Eritrea	874	3,136	4,010	21.8
Israel*	15,065	0	15,065	100.0
Jordan	6,640	0	6,640	100.0
Saudi Arabia	69,174	92,826	162,000	42.7
Sudan	4,320	7,580	11,900	36.3
West Bank	2,700	1,800	4,500	60.0
Yemen	5,243	59,482	64,725	8.1

Sources: *CIA Factbook* (various years), Jane's Information Group, and national sources.

Note: * Does not include the Gaza Strip.

has also increased to 36,500 km to account for the need to develop its transportation links with Djibouti.

Lack of an inter-state road network is true also of the states of the Horn of Africa and this undoubtedly hinders trade between the Red Sea states, or at least prevents it from reaching its full potential, although one can also argue that trade interests often lie with external rather than local partners. Following the initiation of the Madrid Peace Process in 1991, and particularly after the signing of an Interim Accord between Israel and the Palestinians in 1993, a number of new initiatives have been taken to try to correct this problem, with numerous proposals for new road schemes that could create a regional network and facilitate better intra-regional trade. Most of these have inevitably focused on Egypt, Israel, Jordan and Saudi Arabia, with few initiatives considering the more southerly needs of the Red Sea. Proposals have included an 'Eastern Mediterranean Corridor' which would upgrade and link existing coastal roads right around the Mediterranean from Morocco to Turkey via a new bridge to be built across the Suez Canal. A smaller version, the Mediterranean Coastal Highway, would run from Syria through Lebanon, Haifa, Ashdod and Gaza to Egypt. Another plan was the Aqaba Regional Road, a smaller undertaking which would run from Cairo through Suez, Taba, Eilat to Aqaba. The so-called Central Corridor would link Syria, Lebanon, Jordan, Israel, the Palestinian Areas and Egypt with a 1,700 km expressway starting at the Syrian–Turkish border and ultimately extending to Saudi markets. Finally the East–West Connection would entail building a 500-km highway linking Jordan with the Egyptian Mediterranean ports via Israel as part of a larger integrated transport network. Given the recent collapse of any meaningful movement in the Arab–Israeli peace process, the more ambitious of these projects have fallen by the wayside, although the EU is committed to funding a $1 billion road link between Egypt and Jordan via Israel and the Palestinian Areas. Some developments between Israel and Jordan have been initiated but Arab countries have preferred to concentrate on developing transport linkages between themselves, such as the North Africa Coastal Road. Egypt is meanwhile planning a new Build-Own-Operate-Transfer (BOOT) road tunnel crossing the Suez south of Port Said, and is considering the construction of a causeway to link Egypt and Saudi Arabia directly.[19] At the multilateral level, the Arab Economic Union Council, at a special meeting of the Council of Ministers in 1994, argued that the development of a common road network should be prioritised, with a joint company being set up to specialise in land transportation. Thus, as part of the plans for an Arab Free Trade Area, all countries should be required to upgrade those parts of their road networks which can be linked, border crossing proce-dures should be simplified, a common Arab passport for vehicle transports should be introduced (Egypt, Lebanon, Libya, Sudan and the Palestinian Areas have already signed up to this) and a unified data centre should be established. Most of this remains on the drawing board, however, and is likely to do so for some time. Those projects which have actually been started, such as the shuttle bus service between Israel and Jordan, have attracted little custom and remain prey to regional insecurities.[20] It would be tragic for the region if they were to remain so, especially given the increasing propensity for Europe to look south to its neighbours as trading partners. As Geoffrey Kemp and Robert Harkavy have remarked:

> If a well-developed road network between Europe and the Middle East were built, land traffic through the region could expand geometrically. It is worth noting that Turkish road links with Central Asia have become a key element of the economic changes underway in the Caucasus and Central Asia.[21]

Rail transport

In the absence of regional road networks, one might hope that rail networks were sufficiently developed to act as an alternative, but the reverse is unfortunately true. There has been little investment in rail tracks, with no high-speed inter-city connections either within or between countries and few modern upgraded tracks like the one between Riyadh and Damman.[22] An additional problem for any future plans to integrate rail networks is that existing networks do not utilise the same gauge tracks – indeed, even within countries there are significant variations – which make systems incompatible (Table 7.4).

Egypt's railways are the oldest in the region – over one-third of existing track was in place before 1869. Due to the dilapidated nature of much of the track and rolling stock, only 7 per cent of domestic freight travels by rail (although the government plans to raise this to 50 per cent)[23] and the network is badly in need of modernisation 'if it is to realise its potential for containerised transport from Egyptian ports to continental Africa and increase its share of domestic freight transport'.[24] Egypt has invested, however, in a 4.2-km Cairo Metro system to service passenger needs in and around Cairo and in recent years loans have been sought to modernise lines in Upper Egypt, in the south and to connect mineral deposits in the Western Desert with Cairo. Unlike Egypt, most of whose line is of

Table 7.4 Railway transport networks in the Red Sea states, mid-1990s

Country	Track in operation (km)	Gauge*	Freight (tons/km) million	Passenger (km) million
Djibouti	97	narrow		
Egypt	4,751	standard	3,621	50,665
Eritrea	307	narrow	–	–
Israel	610	standard	1,251	294
Jordan	676	narrow	676	2
Saudi Arabia	1,390	standard	1,610	547
Sudan	5,516	narrow	2,240	1,183
Yemen	0	N/A	N/A	N/A

Notes: * This figure applies to the predominant gauge used.

The West Bank and Gaza have only inoperable out-of-date lines and so have been excluded from this table.

standard gauge, Sudan operates 4,725 km of narrow gauge rail track, expanded to nearly 6,000 km by 2009, carrying 766 million tons/km of goods. But a significant proportion of its rolling stock is out of service and this is being reduced as a rehabilitation scheme is being introduced. Despite a substantial loss of rail traffic to roads in the mid-1970s, rail transport has remained important for the movement of agricultural exports and the inland delivery of heavy capital equipment, construction materials and economic development goods.[25] More recently the government has decided to transport crude oil to refineries by rail and recently completed construction of a new line between Muglad and Abu Jabra to service the refinery at Abu Jabra. New lines are principally designed to also allow the army improved access to the south of the country. A loan from the Islamic Development Bank in 1998 enabled the Sudan Railway Corporation to purchase up to 700 new railway carriages.

Saudi Arabia's railway network is limited to a few major lines between Damman and Riyadh, Riyadh and Hofuf and a planned link between Damman and Jubail (including a link to the port itself). There are no other railway lines on the Arabian Peninsula, including Yemen, and thus inter-state networks would have to be initiated from scratch. Not surprisingly, investments are concentrated on road, air and maritime transport where facilities are already available and, in the case of Yemen, where mountainous terrain permits. Jordan is seeking to expand its network, however, encouraging private sector involvement. The historic Hedjaz railroad runs from the Syrian to the Saudi border, with an extension to a phosphate terminal at Aqaba having been added in the 1970s. Not surprisingly, the railroad has primarily oriented towards freight rather than passenger trade and Jordan has been eager to extend its possibilities where possible. At one point in the late 1980s an agreement was reached to construct a line from Aqaba to Baghdad, although the plans fell through with the onset of the Iran–Iraq War. The problem for Jordan has always been investment capital, and so in 1988 it opened negotiations for concessions to operate the Aqaba Railways Corporation (ARC), one of the conditions of which would be expanding the line to serve the Shidiyeh mine close to the Saudi border and an industrial complex near Aqaba. In return for investment of up to $120 million, the government would absorb ARC debts of $99 million. It is anticipated that such an expansion could increase annual rail shipments from 3 million tons to 10 million.[26] Jordan has also been studying the feasibility of a railway link with Israel, connecting their potash factories in the Dead Sea area with port facilities at Aqaba and Eilat. The line may be extended to link Jordan to Israeli free trade zones.[27] Israel's own lines service the main cities, running from Nahariya in the north, through Haifa and Tel Aviv, to Jerusalem and then Beersheba in the south. An extension into Eilat is anticipated to carry freight to an expanding port which can benefit from peace with Jordan and regional economic co-operation and integration. In general, however, the regional isolation of Israel has ensured that lines remain domestically oriented and even links with Jordan are limited by the different gauges of existing tracks. Djibouti, ever conscious of the importance of the Djibouti–Addis Ababa railway to its economic health, has been seeking and receiving funding pledges from international donors for its rehabilitation. Indeed, the decision by the governments of Ethiopia and Djibouti in 2005 to seek private sector management of the 781-km Djibouti–Addis Ababa railway may have cemented the Djibouti Port's position as the main port for Ethiopia.

Ethiopia has been similarly keen to improve its own options for getting exports to Red Sea access points other than through Eritrea. The two countries have been trying since a railway agreement in 1981 to organise and arrange funding for the railway's rehabilitation, although efforts have foundered on poor communications, inadequate funding, theft of railway stock, damage to bridges, and other technical hitches. In 1997, however, both countries agreed to hand over autonomous management of the railway to the railway company itself, opening the way to private sector participation and reviving international interest in providing financial support. Eritrea, while possessing track of a similar narrow gauge to Djibouti's linking Ak'ordat, Asmara and the port of Massawa, has seen most of its track become inoperable, not least since much of the iron was torn up during the war with Ethiopia. A 5-km stretch serving the port was reopened in 1994 and plans to rehabilitate the remainder are underway.

In summary, rail networks in the Red Sea states are under-developed and, where they do exist, they are generally out-dated and even inoperable. Although some states are keen to develop rail transport for freight carriage, the problems remain of limited cross-border possibilities that inhibit the usefulness of rail transport for trade. Rail networks cannot be said to link Red Sea states together, nor in their existing form to offer the potential for Red Sea states to act as serious entrepôts for access to and from the African or Asian hinterlands. Inevitably the cheaper investment option of road construction and transport is generally likely to attract more public and private interest in the future.

Aviation

Given the overall inadequacy of both road and rail transport for international trade and passage in and out of Red Sea states, aviation transport has become a viable, although expensive, substitute. In the wider MENA region, airports and services are comparable with others elsewhere in the world and air is the preferred method of intra-regional travel. Table 7.5 shows the airport and carrier provision of the Red Sea states, in the late 1990s. Table 7.6 shows the Red Sea airlines servicing major Red Sea airports, in the mid-2000s.

Table 7.5 Airport and carrier provision of Red Sea states, late 1990s

Country	National carrier	Airports (paved)	Freight handled (million tons/km)*	Passengers through airports**
Djibouti	Air Djibouti (Red Sea Airlines)	2	–	124,221
Egypt	EgyptAir	70	606 (1993)	2,881,000
Eritrea	Eritrean Airlines	2	–	–
Israel	El Al	31	1,832	2,980,000
Jordan	Royal Jordanian	14	627	1,220,000
Saudi Arabia	Saudi Arabian Airlines 70	2,477	12,142,000	
Sudan	Sudan Airways	12	96	432,000
Yemen	Yemenia	11	119	791,000

Sources: http//www.odci.gov/cia/publications/factbook/html, 30 March1999; *UN Statistical Yearbook*, as quoted in Europa (1998b).

Table 7.6 Red Sea airlines servicing major Red Sea airports, mid-2000s

Djibouti International Ambouli	Air Djibouti, Daallo Airlines, Egyptair, Ethiopian Airlines, Yemenia, Yemen Airways
Cairo International	Air Djibouti, Air Sinai, Egyptair, El Al Israel Airlines, Ethiopian Airlines, Royal Jordanian, Saudia, Sudan Airways, Yemenia, Yemen Airways
Asmara International	Air Djibouti, Daallo Airlines, Egyptair, Saudia, Yemenia, Yemen Airways
Ben Gurion (Tel Aviv)	Air Sinai, Arkia Israel Airlines, El Al Israel Airlines, Ethiopian Airlines, Royal Jordanian, Samara Airlines
Queen Alia International	Egyptair, El Al Israel Airlines, Royal Jordanian, Saudia, Sudan Airways, Yemenia, Yemen Airways
Jeddah King Abdulaziz International	Air Djibouti, Daallo Airlines, Egyptair, Ethiopian Airlines, Palestinian Airlines, Royal Jordanian, Saudia, Sudan Airways, Yemenia Yemen Airways
Riyadh King Khaled International	Egyptair, Ethiopian Airlines, Royal Jordanian, Saudia, Sudan Airways, Yemenia

Djibouti, the smallest state, has one modern airport, Ambouli, which can accommodate large jet-engined aircraft, and six other smaller airports providing regional services. The Ambouli airport has been developed as the largest and most modern airport in the southern Red Sea area, focusing on freight cargo and contributing to the country's profile as a hub for regional and international transport.

Sudan, Yemen and Eritrea have more airport facilities but all face the problems of an absence of modern services and ageing national carrier fleets. Sudan has 12 airports with permanent surface runways, with Khartoum International as the country's principal airport. Interestingly, freight has dropped considerably since the 1990s and in the mid-2000s was standing at just 43.12 million tons/km, but passenger numbers have gone up to over 500,000 a year.

Eritrea has one international airport at Asmara and has since 1996 been busy constructing a second at Massawa. Yemen has six international airports and a large number of unsurfaced regional strips which provide air transport between most towns. By 2005, Yemeni airports were carrying over one million passengers a year, well up on the figures in the 1990s. Jordan, Israel and Egypt all have more developed airport facilities, not least because they are all major tourist destinations. For Jordan, passenger numbers are growing, standing at 1.74 million a year by 2005, and freight carriage is recovering after the 2003 war in Iraq to double compared with the late 1990s, to stand at 224 million tons/km. The main international airport, Queen Aliya, is located 40 km from Amman, while Israel's main international airport, Ben Gurion, is located outside Tel Aviv. The Aqaba airport in the south of Jordan has also come to service Israeli needs in a pilot scheme which will see separate terminals on either side of the border sharing the same airport facilities. Eilat's own airport can only handle medium-sized aircraft, being located in the centre of Eilat and being subject to noise restrictions.[28] Cairo Airport accounted for 7 million of the 11 million passengers who passed through Egyptian airports in the mid-1990s, and Cairo Airport has continued to dominate the air transport network of the country. Unsurprisingly the government's keenness to develop a third terminal at the airport has borne fruit, for which BOOT contracts have been awarded, adding new and modern facilities to the airport.

All three countries utilise air transport for freight trade purposes, in particular for the transport of fresh flowers, perishable foods and luxury items, although Saudi Arabia sends and receives a far greater amount of freight cargo by air. Saudi Arabia also receives millions of passengers visiting the country for the annual *hajj* by air. Unlike its smaller or poorer neighbours, Saudi Arabia also sees a large amount of internal travel by air, with heavily subsidised internal flight prices. Three international airports and 19 regional hubs saw almost 25 million passenger embarcations alone in 1995.

Despite the convenience of, and available facilities for, air transport around the Red Sea, all is not well in the aviation sectors of these countries. Existing Middle Eastern air fleets have an uncommon and inefficient number of large aircraft – the typical size of aircraft operated by the region's airlines is 18 per cent above the world average – although demand has not always reached capacity, making airlines costly to run (although current purchases of more Airbuses is bringing that down). The level of service provision among national air carriers is variable, not least since historically they have been public sector companies and subject to inefficiency, poor management and debts. For some, the answer lies in privatisation. Royal Jordanian, for example, with debts of over $846 million, has had to restructure with a view to future privatisation. In the meantime, Royal Jordanian is already withdrawing from expensive long-haul routes and is replacing its ageing Tristars with leased Airbuses.[29] In Sudan too, the 1996 IMF deal specified that the airport company should be restructured.

Leasing rather than purchasing new aircraft provides one solution in the struggle to modernise fleets, an essential task for those countries like Egypt and Israel which require modern passenger facilities to service the needs of the burgeoning tourist sector, or Sudan and Yemen which are also struggling to update their fleets. Egypt, however, has so far excluded EgyptAir from privatisation schemes on strategic grounds, and in the case of Saudi Arabia guarantees of low cost internal passenger flights make the process awkward, although deregulation is an option. In the case of Yemen, however, where Saudi Arabian Airlines hold 49 per cent stake in Yemenia, government fare subsidies have been reduced considerably in recent years.

It is not only national carriers which are subject to privatisation, but increasingly airport facilities themselves. Egypt, for example, has already awarded a number of BOOT contracts for development of airports in Red Sea coastal areas and is considering the possibilities of a privately run third terminal at Cairo Airport.[30]

Meanwhile, efforts to rationalise regional transport have led to efforts at co-operation. The major national carriers in Egypt, Jordan, Saudi Arabia, Sudan and Yemen all belong to the Arab Air Carriers Organisation which, in a pioneering move in 1998 that recognised the benefits and difficulties of a common language group of airlines, agreed to co-operate on joint handling of aircraft at London airports, then other locations. Ultimately it is intended to jointly contract out the task of handling baggage, passengers, cargo and mail and other ramp services.

The Suez Canal

Ever since its nationalisation in 1956, and with the exception of periods of closure due to hostilities with Israel, the Suez Canal has been a major source of revenue for the Egyptian government and a jewel in its economy. The development of Gulf oil fields led in the 1970s to increased demand for a shipping route which would take the oil easily to European markets and beyond via the Mediterranean. Equally the canal has been a nexus point in international East–West trade, linking the growing industrial production centres of East and South East Asia with Western markets and sources of technology. Canal dues rose sharply for 20 years, from E£33.2 million in 1975 to E£6,692 in 1995,[31] with oil cargoes accounting for around 25 per cent of revenue and dry cargo for the rest. The Suez Canal Authority was continually under pressure to deepen the canal to accommodate new generations of tankers. In 1970, it was dredged to sufficient depth to allow

Table 7.7 Suez Canal traffic comparison by ship type (numbers of ships), 1995–98

Ship type	1995	1996	1997	1998
Tankers	2,473	2,309	2,255	2,135
Bulk carriers	3,114	2,959	2,994	2,400
Combined carriers	141	102	89	74
General cargo	3,326	3,057	2,788	2,536
Container cargo	3,765	4,082	4,012	4,049
Lash	41	33	33	35
Ro/Ro	354	339	299	285
Car carriers	660	729	870	969
Passenger ships	78	69	76	118
Warships	168	136	174	158
Other	931	916	840	713
TOTAL	15,051	14,731	14,430	13,472

Source: Compiled from *Suez Canal Report*, various months and years.

passage of supertankers, but by the mid-1990s the trend towards ever larger vessels meant that many were unable to manage the 195 km run fully laden. Consequently, plans were made to deepen the canal still further to 62 feet by the year 2000, which has enabled the largest bulk carriers to use the canal although it will still not accommodate the latest very large crude carriers (VLCCs) which need between 68 and 72 feet when fully laden. Despite these investments, and the establishment of major industrial areas and tax-free zones at Ismailia and Port Said, traffic through the canal has declined in recent years. The Kuwait Crisis of 1990/91 provided a temporary boost as oil was piped across Saudi Arabia to the Red Sea rather than risking the Persian Gulf route. By the mid-1990s, however, the canal was facing the twin challenges of increasing use of the Suez-Mediterranean (SUMED) pipeline for the carriage of oil to Europe, and an overall drop in dry cargo traffic between East and West which deepened with the East Asian financial crisis in the second half of the decade. The number of vessels passing through the canal fell from 19,791 in 1985 to 13,472 in 1998. Table 7.7 shows the Suez Canal traffic by ship type in the period, 1995–98.

In particular, northbound oil tanker traffic, which accounted for a third of the $2 billion in annual revenues from the canal, dropped by almost a third between 1991 and 1995 as oil showed a preference for pipeline transportation.[32] Total canal revenue slipped to $1.8 billion in 1996 from a record of $1.96 billion in 1993, not least due to a 5.3 per cent decline in the value of IMF Special Drawing Rights, in which canal tolls are denominated against the dollar. The Suez Canal Authority's (SCA) answer has been to freeze and even reduce tolls for passage, as well as to continue its development plans for the Canal Zone and to extend its dredging activities with the intention of establishing a depth of 72 feet as soon as possible. Since then revenues have recovered, to reach $5.38 billion in 2008. But due to the financial crisis of the late 2000s, revenue from the canal plunged

Table 7.8 Region of origin and destination for cargo traffic through the Suez Canal, 1998

Region	Northbound (% of total)	Southbound (% of total)
Red Sea ports	19.7	28.1
East Africa and Aden	2.3	0.6
Persian Gulf	9.3	9.1
South Asia	13.8	14.6
South-East Asia and Far East	34.8	38.3
Australia	20.0	9.1
TOTAL	100.0	100.0

Source: Compiled from *Suez Canal Report*, various years and months.

20 per cent to stand at $4.28 billion in 2009, very much underlining the vulnerability of strategically placed Red Sea states to international trends. By 2005, there were 18,700 ships crossing the canal, accounting for 7 per cent of global maritime trade. Number of vessels passing through the canal had again grown by the end of the decade, standing at 34,456 in 2009. Significantly, the canal was responsible for transiting nearly 600,000 barrels of oil a day, and a further 17.5 million metric tons of LNG to Western markets (including Yemeni gas to Europe) by the end of the decade.[33]

But the Suez Canal provides revenue for Red Sea states other than Egypt as well. Shipping companies are eager to offset the cost of tolls through the canal by maximising their loads both ways through, providing business for the cargo and container ports along the Red Sea. The importance of these ports can be seen from Table 7.8. Red Sea ports come second only to those of South-East and Far East Asia in terms of loading and unloading cargoes which have been transported through the Canal. In the cases of Saudi Arabia and Israel, the cargo serves domestic markets, for smaller economies such as Djibouti, Eritrea, Jordan and Sudan, transit trade makes up the bulk of goods loaded and unloaded.

Energy networks and pipelines

An alternative transport method for crude hydrocarbons and one which appears to have growing appeal is the use of pipelines. They have the benefit of providing relatively cheap shipment, but the disadvantage of being strategically vulnerable. The closure by Syria of the Banias pipeline which carried Iraqi oil to the Mediterranean was a good example of the political problems associated with pipelines which cross borders.

Saudi Arabia constructed its first major oil pipeline in 1981, the TransArabian which carries oil from Abqaiq and the Eastern oil fields to a tanker terminal at Yanbu on the Red Sea coast and which has a capacity of close to 5 million barrels per day. From 1985 until 1989, Iraqi oil also passed through this line after a link with Iraqi oil fields was constructed. It was planned that a new pipeline should be completed to carry Iraqi oil directly to Yanbu, although recent sanctions have put paid to that scheme. Saudi also has a pipeline connection with Jordan and Lebanon, although this is only partly in use, and is planning a new 635-km pipeline to connect the Shaybah oil field on the border with the United Arab Emirates to the Abqaiq terminal.

Egypt has developed a real interest in pipelines in recent years. Most recently it has employed an Italian firm, ENI, to construct the so-called 'peace pipeline', which will bring gas from Egypt's offshore fields in the Mediterranean to the town of El Arish, with the ultimate goal of extending the line into Israel and Jordan. Agreement has already been reached for the Gazan leg of the pipe, which will carry gas to the Palestinian enclave.[34] In the meantime, Egypt's major oil pipeline, the SUMED, carries Saudi and other Gulf oil, this time from the Gulf of Suez to Sidi Kreir on the Mediterranean. Ownership is split – with Egypt owning half and the five main Gulf oil producers owning the other half. The Gulf Arab states are keen to develop the pipeline, although Egypt inevitably has reservations about drawing business away from the Suez Canal, and the capacity of the pipeline was recently upgraded to 2.5 million barrels per day. In 2008, SUMED carried 2.1 million barrels of oil a day, though, reflecting market conditions, this dropped to 1.1 million b/d a year later, according to Business Monitor International.[35]

Arab states are less keen on the Israeli Tipline, which has a capacity of 0.7 million barrels per day and can carry oil from Eilat to the Mediterranean, although this might change if significant advances in the Arab–Israeli peace process were achieved. Jordan has two pipelines passing through its territory, one which used to carry Iraqi oil to Haifa until 1967. The other is a 177-km stretch of the TransArabian 'Tapline' which stopped pumping Saudi oil to Lebanon and Syria in 1983. Oil is still pumped through it for Jordanian use, but attention now is turning to the probability that a new pipeline will be constructed by an Amoco-led consortium to carry Egyptian natural gas to Jordan for its own domestic use. The deal proposed that Jordan purchase up to 350 million cubic feet a day of gas, with Aqaba being supplied by 2000 and Amman by 2002.

In Sudan, the process of pipeline construction is being given new momentum as cheap transport for developing oil exports is sought. In 1999, it was reported that the China National Petroleum Company (CNPC), Petronas of Malaysia, the Sudanese state-owned Sudapet and Talisman of Canada were collaborating on a new 1,600-km pipeline to carry oil from southern oil fields to Port Sudan, to be completed by the end of the year. Another report in July 1999 announced that a similarly lengthened pipeline (possibly one and the same), this time funded by a conglomeration of Chinese, Malaysian, British, German and Argentine companies and carrying crude oil from Hejleej in Western Kordofan to Bashair on the Red Sea, was inaugurated in 1999 by President al-Bashir.[36] An earlier 815-km pipeline had been constructed between Port Sudan and Khartoum in 1976 with a capacity ultimately upgraded to 1 million barrels per day, carrying refined products including gasoline, gas oil, kerosene and aviation fuel. Overall, Sudan today has a pipeline network of 2,365 km, carrying crude oil and 810 km of pipelines carrying refined products.

Meanwhile, Yemen's main pipeline, the Marib Pipeline, carries 170,000 barrels per day of crude oil 420 miles from Marib (105 miles east of Sana'a) to the Red Sea port of Ras Isa. This amounts to almost a half of the country's oil output and the strategic importance of the pipeline has been evident not least in the number of attacks made upon it by disgruntled tribesmen seeking to pressure the government. As Yemen's oil exploration activities have increased in the twenty-first century, so too has its pipeline infrastructure, which by 2005 included 1,174 km of pipeline carrying crude oil.

Gas is also increasingly being piped around the Red Sea, notably with Egypt as the principal regional supplier. Italy's ENI gas and oil company, Repsol of Spain and Edison International of the United States, have all been involved in projects to supply Egyptian gas by pipeline from fields north of Port Said to El-Arish and thence to the Palestinian Authority areas of Gaza. A new pipeline is also being built to carry Egyptian gas to Jordan. The US oil group, Amoco, has built a pipeline from Ain Musa in the Gulf of Suez to Aqaba, with first gas deliveries taking place in 2000. Eventually, Egyptian gas is also likely to fuel the Israeli economy, but that will depend on the political conditions on the ground. Egypt has planned to export 25 per cent of its gas output by the mid-2000s, with Red Sea states being the most proximate and likely recipients.[37]

Oil and gas pipelines allow exporting countries to transport exports to markets further afield. In some cases the markets may indeed be local, for example, the pumping of Saudi oil to Jordan or the distribution of Egyptian oil across the national market. In most cases, where major pipelines are concerned, however, the pipelines link the Red Sea states to markets further afield, although transit across borders does create common economic and strategic interest among Red Sea neighbours. While Saudi Arabia and Egypt are to some extent in competition over use of the Canal versus the SUMED pipeline, they also share an interest in creating secure and competitive routes for hydrocarbon transportation from the Persian Gulf to the Mediterranean.

Summary

It is worth noting that some Arab countries are also busily engaged in developing cross-border energy networks that link their existing national supply and distribution networks. In March 1999, for example, Egypt and Jordan connected their electricity power systems in a $229 million project funded by the Arab Fund for Economic and Social Development (AFESD). The link is expected to be expanded into the Five Countries Interconnection Project (FCiP), which will include Egypt, Jordan, Saudi Arabia, Syria-Lebanon and Turkey. At a later stage it is envisaged that even Iraq might be included in this project. The interlinkage will not stop there. Already Libya and Tunisia have connected their own networks. Tunisia has linked up with Algeria and Morocco, as have Libya and Egypt.

Ultimately Algeria, Morocco and Spain will be connected and by 2002 there has existed a greater Mediterranean Sea Power Pool Project. A third scheme, the Pan-Arab Interconnection Project, which will link Egypt, Jordan and Saudi Arabia to the other Gulf Arab states (the GCC states having already agreed in principle to link their power networks) will complete a grid which will join the three continents of Africa, Asia and Europe in one mammoth electricity network. The focal point of this, and the largest producer of energy in Africa, will be Egypt. With their hydrocarbon assets, the other Arab states will not be far behind. At the moment, only Israel is excluded, although in the much longer term it is likely to be integrated through the FCiP network. While this networking will obviously extend vastly beyond the confines of the Red Sea, it should be noted that Red Sea states have been at the forefront of its initiation, will be geographically central to the project, and will be major suppliers of the electricity that powers the greater grid.

But the most ambitious sub-regional project must be the proposed $20–30 billion six-lane road and four light rail bridges project across the Bab el-Mandeb through Yemen and Djibouti. This 28.5-km project, launched in 2008, will, if and when inaugurated around 2020, provide the most visible feature of sub-regionalisation of the Red Sea through networks that we will have seen.[38] Linking Africa with the Arabian Peninsula in this manner will generate direct employment for around 1.5 million in Yemen and Djibouti. But the bridge will present huge trade, investment and migration opportunities, tying the interests of the southern Red Sea countries ever closer together. As it does so, it will also raise their interest in the security and stability of the Horn's hinterland – shared interest will also generate shared responses when the stakes grow.

In sum, trans-Red Sea transport systems, as a feature of regionalisation, has been increasing since the end of the 1990s and by 2010 had entered a new phase, in which interdependencies had grown and with it reliance on the Red Sea for cross-border traffic. As we have seen, efforts are increasingly being made to rectify transport and cross-border trade deficiencies across the sub-region, but clearly with mixed results. Maritime transport, which has been the principal and most income-generating connection for these states to the international economy, has perhaps developed most and is now certainly the object of growth-oriented investment plans that seek to consolidate and build on the Red Sea's strategic position in international trade. Collective interests in developing the capacity of the Red Sea maritime transit route are increasingly being recognised, as are the benefits of enhancing trade around the sea itself. The smaller states are necessarily the more interested parties in this, but even for the larger economies there are clear benefits to be gained. Tourism in particular requires enhancement of land connections and air links. The so-called TEAM project (the Taba-Eilat-Aqaba Macro Area) is one example of an effort to simplify procedures for tourists crossing borders between Egypt, Israel and Jordan. Road construction projects and plans are also evidence that most states can envisage harnessing new tourism or trade potential from upgrading and integrating transport systems.

Inevitably, the decisive factor in implementing the many planned projects will be investment income, including international and bilateral assistance. Some sectors, such as energy transport systems, will take priority over others. But while the sub-region has in the past suffered from a lack of recognition of the virtues of compatible and up-to-date intra-regional transport systems, this is evidently no longer the case. Here we have tangible and concrete evidence of sub-regionalisation taking route, irrespective of security challenges and continuing political instability.

Conclusion
Regionalising the Red Sea

Few would dispute that new regional situations were brought about by the dramatic sea change in the relations between the superpowers at the end of the 1980s. As Hobsbawm has observed, 'The Cold War had frozen the international situation, and in doing so had stabilized what was essentially an unfixed and provisional state of affairs'.[1] The end of the Cold War, he elaborates, 'suddenly removed the props which had held up the international structure and, to an extent not yet appreciated, the structures of world's domestic political systems'.[2] The MENA regional system was clearly deeply affected by the retreat of one superpower from active intervention in regional affairs, and the alterations in the regional balance of power. In interactions between regional states and in the domestic construction of states themselves, the transformations were unsurprisingly passed on to the sub-system's sub-regions. Indeed, they were to shape the sub-regions themselves through the creation of new imperatives for alliance building, on the one hand, and the assertion of spheres of influence by regional powers, on the other. The loosening of the superpower grip unleashed previously dormant local conflicts which required responses from new 'external' powers, only this time the players were not external only to the sub-regions but were located within the wider regional system itself, one result being that sub-regions became interdependent theatres of activity. Within this context one can see the critical role played by Red Sea states, not only in the development of sub-regional dynamics between them, but also in terms of the influence of the Red Sea (and its internal relations) upon the MENA sub-system as a whole *and* upon other arenas of regional conflict.

The Red Sea sub-region

Before advancing with this argument, it is necessary to backtrack a little and review the utility of the term 'sub-region' when discussing the Red Sea states. The term was initially chosen more as an operating tool than as a definitive label. The preceding text indicates that the requisite conditions initially outlined for the existence of a sub-region have been fulfilled but there are equally clear grounds for reservation in using the term. During the Cold War era, the Red Sea states showed some inclinations towards behaving as a sub-region of the MENA region, which was itself a sub-system of a bipolar international system. However, super-power penetration of, and competition within, the region created stronger alternative connections between Red Sea states, on the one hand, and external players (notably but not exclusively the superpowers), on the other, serving to create obstacles to closer inter-Red Sea relations rather than to foster them. Other hindrances resulted from incompatible political ideologies, hostile political systems, and economic development strategies that sought to foster independence rather than inter-dependence. In the post-Cold War era, the withdrawal of superpower rivalry removed some of the constraints that both prevented greater regional interaction and contained regional conflicts. In the wake of the Soviet withdrawal and newly defined American interests, regional powers have sought to assert themselves more influentially. Sub-regional arenas have become more important to the strategic ambitions of such states, and both regional and sub-regional alliances have assumed a much greater role for both stronger and weaker states alike as they seek to protect their interests and fend off the possible encroachments of others. Although this generates some dynamics for sub-regional consolidation, it also means that states are more inclined to respond to broader MENA developments in order to multiply their options and improve their power relative to one another. Thus greater sub-regional coherence is matched by sub-regional interdependence. External penetration by regional powers replaces that by superpower competition (although not forgetting that the United States is still very active in the region and, given the scale of its military and security presence, has been described as being to all intents and purposes a regional power itself).

The Red Sea states today undoubtedly demonstrate a series of sub-regional tendencies. They increasingly recognise their collective interests through institutional and organisational gatherings, although these remain impeded by the high level of conflict between the states and have never assumed comprehensive proportions. More importantly, they increasingly act with reference to one another. In particular, a pattern has emerged whereby three regional powers (Israel, Egypt and Saudi Arabia), all of whom are Red Sea states of note in their own right, seek to establish their influence over the sub-region as part of both sub-regional and regional strategies for power projection. The smaller Red Sea states, many of whom are weak domestically, or heavily engaged in conflicts or disputes with one or more of their neighbours, cannot stay immune from the efforts of the larger states, given their domestic political, military and economic vulnerability. Thus, they too must engage in alliance building at both sub-regional and regional levels in order to stave off the ambitions of their neighbours. In sum, the consolidation of the sub-region goes hand in hand with intensive alliance building, greater integration into the regional system, and a corresponding sub-regional interdependence being driven by economic and socio-economic forces.

Alliance building

Of course, security-oriented regional alliances are not a new feature of the MENA sub-system, but existed throughout the Cold War era. On occasion, alliance blocs emerged that adopted mutually hostile ideological positions, while at other times external forces provided the impetus for the establishment of strategic alliances of unlikely partners. The Syrian–Iranian alliance presents a good example of the latter, forged from a common fear of Iraq and now established as a regional bulwark against American pressure in the region and as a regional counter-weight to Israel. Opportunistic alliances may be said to have become more prevalent in recent years, particularly since the Arab states have discovered the virtues of a territorially-based 'national interest' as opposed to the pan-Arabist tempo of the past. The GCC countries' ability to invite and absorb security umbrellas from several Western countries simultaneously since the end of the Cold War is indicative of how far the pursuit of the national interest is affecting MENA countries' relations with each other as well as with the outside world. The impetus for alliance building has come, not least, as a reaction to the numerous profound 'shocks' which the region has experienced in the last decades of the twentieth century and the first decade of the twenty-first. Recent regional traumas have included the Arab–Israeli war of 1973, the Iranian revolution (1979), the Egyptian–Israeli peace agreement (also in 1979), the Iran–Iraq War (1980–88), the Israeli invasion of Lebanon (1982), the withdrawal of the Soviet Union (late 1980s) and the Iraqi invasion of Kuwait (1990), 9/11 (2001), violent regime change in Iraq (2003), the Israel–Hezbollah war (2006), all of which have led to the reconfiguration of regional alliances. The 1973 war, for example, joined Syria, Egypt and Saudi Arabia in an uneasy Arab front. The Iranian revolution challenged and disrupted the growing Iranian–Saudi–Egyptian axis, not to mention the Iranian–Israeli alliance, and encouraged omni-balancing among surrounding Arab states. Egypt's peace with Israel ended the triple alliance and hopes for a united Arab front, while the Iran–Iraq War saw Ba'athist Syria line up with Shi'a Iran against its more 'natural' Iraqi sister Arab state. The war also saw the formation of the GCC as the Persian Gulf monarchies became more intensely aware of their own collective vulnerabilities and the unlikelihood that they would find protection in the collective of Arab states. The withdrawal of the Soviet Union from the MENA arena saw those states which had previously sheltered under its umbrella lining up to reposition themselves in a mainstream, pro-American Arab camp, while the Iraqi invasion of Kuwait saw the final fragmentation of any united Arab and Arabist front. Those states (and the PLO) which aligned themselves with Saddam's Iraq, were to pay dearly for their choice and found themselves after the war at pains to prevent their total exclusion from George W. Bush's New World Order. Meanwhile new security arrangements for the region found Egypt and Syria aligned with the GCC states, although in a format that was essentially meaningless without the patronage of over-the-horizon guarantors. The post-Kuwait War Middle East, in the context of 9/11 and the removal of the Ba'ath regime in Iraq, have also seen the revival of non-Arab MENA powers as pivots for regional developments, one aspect of which has led to the emergence of a powerful Israeli–Turkish alliance in the 1990s and 2000s which sought to contain in one sweep Iran, Iraq and Syria. Since 2008, however, this alliance has been much weakened as Turkey proceeded to take advantage of regime change in 2003 to exert greater regional influence, and moved to rebuild bridges with its Arab neighbours and also Iran. Iran, now a close ally of Shi'a-dominated Iraq, has been extending its influence beyond the Persian Gulf precisely because the barriers to its presence in the Levant have been lowered, to the dismay of Israel, Saudi Arabia and Egypt – our three powerful Red Sea actors.

Economic divisions between the MENA region's rich and poor states have further replaced ideological differences in dividing the states of the area – and in underpinning alliances. With these divisions have come higher premiums on reliable allies, particularly with those which are better endowed economically. So, we see that since the 1980s the more vulnerable Arab states have developed the habit of relying on assistance from regional supporters: Kuwait from Egypt, Saudi Arabia and Syria, for instance; Palestine from Egypt; and, Sudan from Iran.

If the MENA region has for decades demonstrated this propensity for tactical alliance building, it has done so in a more exaggerated manner in the post-Cold War era with specific effects on, and challenges for, the security of the Red Sea. Not least since inter-state conflict and civil war in the sub-region itself have drawn in sometimes unexpected responses from MENA powers and given rise to interesting new partnerships.

Two post-Cold War regional alliances have posed particular dilemmas for the sub-region and offered key regional players opportunities to advance their own agendas. First, the Sudanese partnership with Iran, which developed in 1995, and which provided Iran with access to Sudan's naval facilities at Port Sudan has given Iran the potential to disrupt shipping in the Red Sea, to assist its allies in Palestine more easily, or to threaten directly Israel, Egypt or Saudi Arabia. Second, the Eritrean–Israeli partnership which lasted well into the twenty-first century, has given the Jewish state a major strategic advantage in this strategic waterway, strengthening its role on the Arab periphery, enabling it to keep a close eye on Saudi Arabia and Sudan and Yemen, and challenging the hostile Islamist and Arab forces resident in Sudan and elsewhere in the Red Sea.

A third alliance can also be mentioned here, that of the East African Front of Uganda, Ethiopia and Eritrea against Sudan's Islamist-leaning regime, although the efficacy of this relationship was recently diminished by the war between Ethiopia and Eritrea. In this instance, as with Yemen's moves to form closer bonds with Djibouti (with which it signed a Brotherhood Agreement in early 1997 and is hoping to establish a 'bridge border' across the Red Sea by 2020), the parties involved do include states which play a large role in the sub-regional balance of power. One may note, then, that it is not just the regional powers which may threaten or determine regional and sub-regional security, but that there are also weaker but nonetheless key states whose domestic and foreign-policy orientations are particularly central to the dynamics of that security. For example, Jordan's preparedness, despite strong opposition from the Arab world, to participate (as an observer) in the January 1998 exercises among three strategic allies

(Israel, Turkey and the USA) set a deeply significant (and for the Arab states a worrying) precedent, despite the relative military weakness of the Hashemite state. Equally, it demonstrated how new security partnerships initiated by some Red Sea states can suck in other countries, and create counter-balancing pressures elsewhere in the region and sub-region.

The increasing interdependence of sub-regions within the MENA sub-system has also been in part a result of the dynamics of alliance building and the assertion by regional powers of spheres of influence as the superpower containment of conflicts has declined. The process clearly began in the 1980s when the two most pertinent theatres of activity in the region, and those which between them draw in all our Red Sea states in one way or another, were the Arab–Israeli conflict and the Persian Gulf crisis. The nature of the split in Arab ranks in the 1980s was such that these theatres operated in essentially competing orbits, with a rise in the prominence of one signalling a decline in attention given to the other. For different reasons, almost all parties to the Arab–Israeli conflict tried their luck in the Gulf crisis of the 1980s: Israel provided secret assistance to Iran, while Egypt, Jordan and the GCC countries weighed in on Iraq's side. All of this was at the expense of the traditional Arab preoccupation, the Palestinian issue. So much so that the 1987 Extraordinary Arab Summit held in 'front-line' Amman concentrated almost exclusively on the Persian Gulf crisis, while its final communiqué spoke mainly of the threats to the Arab world from Iran.[3] The problems of the Iran–Iraq War were not to be confined to that sub-region, however, spilling over as they did to affect the internal politics of Sudan as well as to unsettle the two Yemeni states.

First, let us deal with the case of Sudan, which was regarded as an important strategic prize. This country found itself being courted by both Iran and Iraq, who were keen to gain the upper hand in a country which provided access to both the Arab world and Africa and one close to the Horn, and also a neighbour of Egypt and Saudi Arabia. The struggle for influence in Sudan continued until 1990, by the end of which time Iraq had been vanquished as a strong Arab military force and Iran had emerged as a friend of the new Islamist regime in Khartoum. Iraq, thanks to the pipeline which carried Iraqi oil through Saudi Arabia to the Red Sea, did develop a unique dependency on the Red Sea in the mid-1980s, but since the emergence of the Shi'a-dominated regime in Iraq post 2003, it is unlikely that this pipeline system could resurface in the next few years as an alternative route for Iraq's oil exports to Western markets. But were war to break out between Iran and the US/Israel over the former's nuclear programme, then one can anticipate the re-emergence of the Red Sea as a strategic oil supply route for more than one Persian Gulf oil exporter.

As for the Yemens, for the best part of the 1980s, the two countries adopted directly opposing policies towards Iran and Iraq: Marxist South Yemen came out in support of Islamist Iran while conservative North Yemen gave strong backing to Arab nationalist Iraq. Indeed, the support which Iraq received from the Red Sea Arab countries was so significant that in 1989 Jordan, Egypt and North Yemen joined hands with Iraq to form a new all-Arab regional organisation named the Arab Co-operation Council (ACC). Though short-lived and riddled with problems,[4] the ACC's birth symbolised the ease with which inter-theatre linkages could emerge from crisis in one sub-region, and also highlighted the narrowness of the gap which separated the Persian Gulf sub-region from the Red Sea countries.

The logic for sub-regional interdependence was already in place, therefore, by the end of the Cold War and the advent of the Kuwait crisis in 1990. What then changed with the Kuwait crisis, and how did this crisis manage to reformulate the regional equation? The answer to this question lay in the nature of the Kuwait crisis itself. Far from being seen as purely an intra-Arab conflict of Arabs against the 'imperialists', Iraq's occupation of Arab Kuwait opened a Pandora's box of inter-related issues which found their roots not in radical or moderate, fundamentalist or modernist camps, but in much deeper wounds stemming from the colonial division of the old Ottoman Empire into arbitrarily created independent nation-states in the aftermath of the Great War.[5] Several Middle Eastern countries saw the Kuwait crisis as a statement about their own sovereignty, and a challenge to that of their regional enemies.

The interdependence of sub-regions was also tested in practical ways in 1990 as the Red Sea states found themselves entangled in the net that the new crisis was spreading. Although this crisis was perhaps a product of the instabilities which had been around in the Persian Gulf sub-region since about 1970,[6] the parties which were directly affected by it included several non-Gulf states. Iraq's surface-to-surface missiles raining down on Israel was a case in point. The Iraqi attacks on Israeli urban centres showed how easily any dispute, in this case an essentially inter-Arab one, could get out of hand and threaten the security of other regional actors. Saddam Hussein himself attempted to create a direct comparison and linkage between his own occupation of Kuwait and the Israeli occupation of Palestine, a notion which was rejected in principle by the Western forces but the salience of which became evident when American President George W. Bush was forced to promise a new peace initiative for the Arab–Israeli arena in return for Arab participation in the Allied coalition. The participation of Egyptian forces in that coalition, the isolation of Jordan after its expression of sympathy with Iraq, the forced expulsion of Palestinian and Yemeni migrant labour from the Gulf for the same reason, all indicated that Red Sea states were as much party to the crisis in the Persian Gulf as the GCC states themselves.

The main lessons in security terms that regional powers learnt from the Kuwait crisis were that, first, today's weaponry has a long reach, and, second, that geopolitical linkages, which have been a feature of the modern Middle East, have infiltrated the infrastructure of the sub-system so profoundly that every state seeking an advantageous position can easily find itself against an equally determined opposition. The Red Sea powers, Egypt, Jordan, Israel, and Saudi Arabia, have also learnt that in a post-Cold War regional environment it pays to develop contingency plans that can respond to challenges arising from any quarter in the sub-system. Increasing strategic interdependence in the sub-system, in other words, has been accompanied by increasing insecurity.

The challenge for regional players in the sub-region now is to predict where the future threats to security will emerge. Will they come from Iran, a coalition of Islamist forces co-led by Iran and Sudan, piracy around the Horn of Africa, state implosion, or as a result of conflict between neighbours over the control of Red Sea resources? Sub-regional proximity (the Red Sea straddles several conflict theatres), compounded by Middle East sub-system interdependence, means that any threat to Red Sea security is likely to be multi-dimensional and multi-faceted, and is likely to pitch one or more of its states against another.

We can begin to understand the assessments by the Red Sea states as to where this challenge will emanate from if we briefly look at the alliances which are forming today, particularly those of the three regional powers: Egypt, Israel and Saudi Arabia.

Egypt

Egypt has been at the forefront of alliance building in the MENA sub-system. Since Nasser's death, Cairo's aim has been to find partners among the moderate Arab states and their Western backers. Although for a period, after its peace treaty with Israel, Egypt was an isolated Arab state, since 1987, and more emphatically since the Kuwait crisis of 1990/91 and the end of the Cold War, Cairo has been displaying a strong desire to develop its Arab and African zones of influence through co-operation with several other regional countries. In the Red Sea sub-region, Saudi Arabia has been the key Arab partner which Egypt has been courting. In the peace process, with regard to developments in Lebanon, over Iran, and also Israel's actions against Gaza, Cairo has managed to find common cause with Riyadh and has used various crises to cement its ties with the Kingdom, notably in countering al-Qaeda terrorism and in its projection into the region of non-Arab Iran and Israel, which have used Arab divisions to develop and expand their own zones of influence in the sub-system. Their deeper penetration of the Arab world has weakened Egypt's grip on it.

Aftandilian notes that the regional situation from the start of the 1990s was conducive to Egypt's regional ambitions.[7] Not only had the Arab region been largely de-radicalised, which suited Egypt's foreign policy, but also Cairo had emerged from the 1980s as a close friend of Iraq and in 1990 a regional partner of Syria. Although Iraq's invasion of Kuwait in 1990 was a radicalising factor, it did not lead to a broad radicalisation of the entire sub-system. In effect, it merely accelerated the process of diffusion of power in the Arab world. This of course allowed Egypt to reassert its regional leadership role without facing a serious challenge from any other Arab state; in the Mashreq, Syria was already a partner and Iraq too weak and isolated to pose any challenge; in the Maghreb, Libya was too dependent on Egypt's good will to try and undermine its position. Moreover, as both the United States and Israel were dependent on Egypt to steer the Arab ship in the delicate peace process with Israel, Washington chose to bolster its Arab role by giving it more credit in the negotiations and more aid as well.

But, at the same time, the very divisions and polarities in the Arab world, which Egypt had been trying to capitalise on in the 1990s and 2000s, also acted as a barrier in the way of Cairo; unlike the 1950s and 1960s, Egypt's needle (its resources and influence) today is not sufficient to repair and reweave the strained fabric which encompasses the Arab space which Cairo wants to control. Lack of cohesiveness in the Arab order, thus, has hindered Egypt in terms of it not being able properly to head a divided 'tribe', so to speak, and has worked to its advantage at the same time, in terms of enabling it to carve a broader zone for itself without, for a time, facing countervailing pressures from other Arab states. The Arab region has grown in importance for another important reason: trade and investment. Not only does Egypt act today as a prominent host for Arab investors, its trade with its Arab partners has also grown considerably since 2000 – to the point where the Arab world now represents Egypt's second largest market in the world. Thus, by 2006, it was exporting some $2.2 billion worth of goods to the rest of the Arab region, up from just $600 million in 2000.[8]

Saudi Arabia

Saudi Arabia, the third important alliance builder in the Red Sea, is something of a newcomer to this game, having never really felt the need to prepare against the potentially aggressive intent of its neighbours until the 1980s and 1990s, by which time the Iran–Iraq War (to which Saudi Arabia was an interested bystander) and the Kuwait crisis (in which Saudi Arabia was an active participant) provided the tasters for future problems.[9] Apart from its close ties with the USA, since 1990, Saudi Arabia has invested heavily in co-operative ties with Egypt in particular, and to a lesser degree with Syria. These are the two countries with which it had managed to found a short-lived but profitable triangular relationship in the 1970s. Of the earlier alliance, Taylor says:

> The trilateral states were unmatched in inter-Arab politics. They remained the dominant force in the system from 1971 until ... the interim Sinai agreement [between Egypt and Israel] in September 1975. They continued to exert considerable influence until the alliance was disbanded two years later.[10]

Having secured its supreme position on the Arabian Peninsula and in the Persian Gulf, discernible patterns in the aftermath of the Cold War clearly illustrate that the Kingdom has been keen to extend its presence to neighbouring regions, most notably around the Red Sea area. A bigger role here, of course, has been an old Saudi aspiration, dating back at least to the middle of the twentieth century. Riyadh's efforts, however, were thwarted by the Soviet presence in the 1970s and 1980s, and have often produced an unfavourable response from Israel. With the Soviet Union no more, and former Soviet allies in the Red

Sea highly vulnerable, Saudi Arabia has felt more confident in launching its bid for the creation of an Arab Red Sea security forum. In this exercise, it has received support from Egypt, which is clearly conscious of the havoc even a weak country like Sudan can cause if armed with such contrary ideologies as political Islam. Riyadh's role in the stabilisation of Yemen is also significant, in that the Kingdom has been actively involved since mid-2000s in countering al-Qaeda's growing presence in Yemen and also in providing material and political support for the unpopular and rather ineffective government of President Abdullah Saleh.

Saudi Arabia's assertiveness in response to regime change in Iraq in 2003 and fear of a more influential Iranian presence in the Arab East, have meant that Egypt could no longer pretend to be leader of the Arab region when it was Saudi Arabia which was clearly exerting far greater influence, in terms of being the Arab region's G-20 member and also in its efforts to contain Iran while also underwriting the Arab Peace Plan which it itself sponsored from the early 2000s. Saudi Arabia today has the resources, the international partnerships, and the legitimacy to act regionally – despite its many domestic socioeconomic problems (unemployment, residual Islamic militancy, population growth, challenges of economic reform …).[11] From outside the region, it is of course the United States which has been trying to strengthen Saudi Arabia's regional position and has been supporting Riyadh's policies in the Red Sea.

Israel

Egypt's Sinai neighbour, Israel, developed the taste for alliance building early on in its life. While in the 1950s it was France and Britain who provided it with strategic support, Israel's survival tactics have dictated that it cultivate close relations with the US superpower. That Israel has been extremely successful in nurturing this alliance is evident in the close military and political contacts which have marked the two states' relations since the 1970s, and more so since 1980, the year when the American electorate chose the country's most pro-Israeli president of the Cold War era, and turned its back on the architect of Camp David Accords which had brought security to Israel's western borders and peace with its most powerful Arab enemy.

In addition to its warm relations with the USA, however, Israel has been quite active in forging alliances closer to home as well. Israel's established regional strategy, encapsulated as the Ben Gurion Doctrine, has always required of the Israeli government to try and minimise the negative impact that any Arab bloc might have on the country by creating co-operative structures with the subsystem's non-Arab members, who also happen to mark the geographical boundaries of the Arab world. The most successful of Israel's regional alliances has been with the two non-Arab states of Iran and Turkey. While its alliance with the former served Israel's interests in the Cold War years and at the height of its regional isolation, in the uncertain setting of the post-Cold War regional order it has been its burgeoning relationship with the latter which has given Israel the opportunity to expand its regional influence and drive home its strategic advantages against a wholly divided and leaderless Arab world. The Turkish–Israeli military relationship (based on several signed agreements on joint training and exercises, intelligence co-operation, and right of access to each other's territories), which came to light in 1996, was expanded in the early 2000s to include several joint military research and development and production arrangements. Israel has entered the Turkish arms market as a strategic partner of Turkey, offering a range of weapons and services to the Turkish military (which is still one of NATO's largest), including the transfer of the Merkava main battle tank and a new standard issue rifle to the Turkish army, the overhaul of its F-4 Phantom combat aircraft and the refit of its F-5 Tiger fighters, the joint production of such weapons systems as Israel's Popeye II missile and the long-range Delilah missile, and assisting the Turkish military in developing military aviation systems.[12] Political disputes since 2008 do not seem to have adversely affected the military links between the two countries, but Israel has already tried to compensate for the 'loss of Turkey' by drawing closer links with Greece, Azerbaijan and other willing Central Asian states.

Israel, moreover, has had a particular interest in developing links with the southern Red Sea countries. Its key targets have been Ethiopia and Eritrea, plus Yemen as well as Sudan. Militarily speaking, by the early 1980s Israel was already on the scene. In return for a closer relationship with a non-Arab Red Sea state and the emigration of Ethiopian Jews to Israel, it was ready to provide both weapons and advisers to the Ethiopian armed forces. Israel's assistance included aircraft technicians to service the Ethiopian Airforce's ageing MiG-21 and MiG-23 fighters.[13] Military links with Eritrea for a period in the 2000s, such as naval access to its strategic islands, did extend to Israel unprecedented access to the Red Sea and Bab el-Mandeb.

Furthermore, Israel also managed, in the 1990s, to carve out of the Arab world security relations with three neighbours: Egypt, Jordan and the Palestinian Authority. With Jordan, Israel can boast of close relations on all fronts, going as far as acting as a *de facto* protector of the Hashemite Kingdom; with the PA, it can exert considerable influence and manipulate wider PA–Arab relations; and, with Egypt it can take comfort in being able to work closely on sub-state threats to regional security as well as the perennial problem of radical Islamist challenges to the status quo. With three out of its five Arab neighbours, in other words, Israel can be said to be working closely. The end of the Cold War accelerated the pace of change in Israel's relations with its closest Arab neighbours. Speaking of the first Netanyahu government, Ephraim Sneh (a Labour Party defence expert), argued that the policies of his Likud government had begun undoing the post-Cold War strategic alliances the Labour government had tried to establish with the Arab world. In his words, 'peace with the Palestinians was the clue to a different regional equation', a crucial part of 'a new alliance configuration' (against hostile countries such as Iran):

The inner core would consist of Egypt, Jordan, Israel and the Palestinian Authority ... the periphery would include Turkey, the Gulf states and the Maghreb. Under Netanyahu, this configuration is being dismantled because he does not understand the wider regional implications of relations with the Palestinians.[14]

The Likud-led government of Prime Minister Netanyahu has found it much harder upon returning to power in 2009 to nurture Sneh's new 'regional equation', dependent as it is domestically on Right-wing pro-settler political forces.

Hashemite Jordan is another link in the strategic chain. Jordan has been experiencing dramatic changes since the death of King Hussein at the end of last century. It has experimented with limited political liberalisation in the 2000s and has also attempted to deepen citizen participation and commitment to the state through its 'Jordan First' campaign of the early 2000s. But geo-political and security constraints have left a negative mark on the young monarch's efforts to modernise and liberalise his country. Though the country has taken many positive strides towards an improved economic environment, particularly with regard to the development of the Aqaba region on the Red Sea, since taking power in 1999, King Abdullah II has had to contend with many other problems: the impact of the 2000 Palestinian *intifada*, violent regime change in its long-standing economic partner Iraq in 2003, the transformation of Iraq into a Shi'a-dominated polity since the fall of Baghdad to US forces, terror attacks in Amman in 2005, the Israel–Hezbollah war in neighbouring Lebanon in 2006 in which the leader of this Shi'a organisation (Sheikh Nasrallah) emerged as an Arab hero on the 'Arab street', and the emergence of Hamas as a political force since its electoral successes in 2006 in Gaza and the West Bank. In the absence of warm peace with Israel, Jordan has used the post-Saddam era to rebuild relations with its Red Sea neighbours, Egypt and Saudi Arabia, around the need to contain a purported Iran–Iraq-supported 'Shi'a crescent' rising in the heart of the Arab world. It has also deepened its security partnership with the United States over the first decade of this century, acquiring many major weapons systems from the USA and also extending its intelligence partnership with the superpower in the aftermath of the war in Iraq and Iraq-based terror attacks in Jordan.

Southern Red Sea alliances

In the southern Red Sea, alliances have been much more fluid, tempered by cross-border tensions, territorial disputes, strong regionalism within each country, and the absence of effective central government authority. The fallout of the break-up of Ethiopia and the Somali civil war continue to reverberate throughout the region, as indeed have done regime weakness in Yemen and the strengthening of al-Qaeda and Shi'a forces there. Such developments have directly affected Red Sea security and have caused severe tensions as Israel and other African and Arab actors have rushed to take advantage of southern Red Sea instabilities by establishing footholds on its shores.

Another upshot of Horn tensions has been the emergence of some unusual partnerships (though certainly not alliances); Eritrea has moved closer to the Libyan-sponsored Sahel-Sahara regional grouping (which also includes Sudan), for instance, and Ethiopia has tried to keep close contacts with both Sudan and Israel. Libya, in turn, has been busy investing some $100 million in Ethiopia.[15]

In the Ethiopian–Eritrean case, suspicions between the two countries has encouraged each party to look for friends from any quarter possible. But in practice neither has been able to forge close alliances with either the more powerful northern Red Sea states, nor with the instrumental African powers south and west of the Horn. Ironically for the United States, this conflict between its two promising Red Sea friends has dissolved other regional alliances and has unravelled its patiently created network of regional partnerships against the Islamist government in Sudan. By the end of the 1990s, both Ethiopia and Eritrea were attempting to mend fences with Khartoum, and in the process managed to undo the chain that had been thrown around that country.[16] Sudan, therefore, despite the Darfur crisis and the South's separation efforts, has remained an influential actor in the sub-region and East Africa more broadly. Indeed, the 2005 Comprehensive Peace Agreement with the South gave Khartoum badly needed breathing space to rebuild its forces and try and consolidate power. The relative success of this strategy has been as much due to geopolitics as Sudan's growing oil-generated income and well-publicised investment and exploration opportunities. But, as we look forward, we can see regional tensions rising again were the Sudanese state to disaggregate after the referendum in the Christian-dominated south of the country in January 2011. The new post-Sudan entity will seek to establish a new authority for itself, but it will also be deeply dependent on its African neighbours for economic and social development, even if it manages to carve into its territory some of Sudan's oil-rich Abyei region. It is worth noting again that oil has become central to Sudan's political economy since the mid-1999s and in 2008 oil income represented 95 per cent of the country's export revenues and as much as 60 per cent of central government revenues.[17] In the South, oil income has been even more important, having accounted for 98 per cent of the region's total revenues in that same year.

Furthermore, except for Djibouti, which has the strategic ear of France and also the United States, no other southern Red Sea country has managed to recruit an over-the-horizon ally. Ironically, the continuing conflict between Ethiopia and Eritrea and those between Ethiopia and the Somali warlords, and the rapid rise in piracy off the Horn have ensured that the southern Red Sea zone remain an arena for powerful states to extend their presence in. Ironically, the combination of intra- and inter-state conflicts has in turn hindered the emergence of regional alliances in the Horn of Africa.[18] From these tensions has flowed even more troubling developments, where Ethiopia and Eritrea seem to have found it prudent to pour arms into government-less Somalia in a vain attempt to recruit friends in this strategic but troubled land.[19] As we have seen, these developments are in sharp contrast to the unfolding events in the northern Red Sea, where three core players continue to show the potential to make advances in economic, political and strategic realms.

Sub-regionalism lite?

We have argued here that the propensity for alliance building, which both links Red Sea states to one another and ties them increasingly to more region-wide and international geopolitics, acts, on the one hand, to foster a sub-regional consciousness but, on the other, to simultaneously inhibit the emergence of a distinct sub-regional identity. We therefore accept that there are limits to the usefulness of the term sub-region when referring to the Red Sea. Michael Hudson has argued that a sub-region must display four characteristics: (1) geographical contiguity; (2) a minimum of social communication; (3) recent shared history that can be drawn upon; and (4) the prevailing standard of modernisation.[20] We maintain that the first three of these are clearly in evidence and our own analysis of the Red Sea states has shed concrete light on this, but there is a clear deficiency when it comes to the last, given the variations in levels and bases of economic development among the states. Our chapters on the economics of the Red Sea illustrated the fact that their disparate economic status has meant that some Red Sea states have been much more dependent on their sub-regional links than others, obstructing commonality. But, on the other hand, we have also illustrated the rapid growth in economic partnerships between most Red Sea countries.

More importantly, perhaps, Bassam Tibi argues[21] that a further criterion must be the self-perception of inhabitants that they distinguish themselves with a collective sub-regional identity. The Red Sea states not only have geopolitical alliances which link them to other regional axes – they also possess a myriad of identities – Arab, Muslim, Christian, Jewish, African, etc., which cut across any emerging or nascent Red Sea collective consciousness and undoubtedly at this point in time outweigh any such sentiments. But the same can also be said of the geopolitical situation along the MENA's other dynamic sub-region, namely, the Persian Gulf. There too, one is increasingly struck by the complexity of identity politics and its adverse effects on sub-regional identity building.[22] Since 2003, in particular, the Iran-Arab divide has been deeply influenced by a Sunni-Shi'a one as well, putting more distance between the GCC and the other members of the sub-region.

Thus, while sub-regional tendencies have been evident among Red Sea states, and increasingly so since the end of the Cold War, and burgeoning economic and transport links are creating chains of dependencies, the area is still witness to many divergent and often competing dynamics. The competing forces make it difficult to easily single out sub-regionalism as the defining characteristic of the collectivity of states – a regionalist order is not in the making yet. As an analytical tool, however, we believe we have demonstrated its utility, despite the absence of institutional scaffolding holding the qualifying states together, and the time will come for the term 'sub-region' to be used to describe the totality of relationships between these states, and indeed between them and the wider world.

One could argue, moreover, that the same dynamics which work to obstruct the consolidation of an emerging sub-region around the Red Sea are equally at work on more established sub-regions. In North Africa, for example, the member states have been eager in the wake of the closing of the Cold War chapter, to establish security-minded and economic partnerships with states and international organisations beyond their own community, most particularly the European Union. The institutional representation of the sub-region, the Arab Maghreb Union, has been largely ineffective compared to the developing links between individual states and the EU, for example, through the Euro-Mediterranean Partnership Programme. Nonetheless, efforts to revive it in the last year or so have seen not only Egypt but also Senegal, both of which states have significant regional interests of their own and elsewhere, showing an interest in joining the organisation as they seek to maximise their access to markets, international finance, and communication networks. Likewise the Gulf Co-operation Council has been insufficient in itself to satisfy either the security or economic interests of the Gulf Arab states. The early-1990s 'six-plus-two' formula of the Damascus Declaration foundered on its own failure to recognise the conflicting interests of its partner states, but defence agreements with over-the-horizon actors and efforts to expand international economic ties through albeit limited liberalisation packages, are all symptomatic of broader global dynamics which are affecting regions and sub-regions, however distinct and 'free-standing' they might have seemed in the past. Discernible patterns in the Middle East sub-system show therefore that the uneven international division of labour has a direct impact on the positioning of the MENA states in the international system, producing an often diverging variant of the intra-sub-system relationship. The global dimension continues to have a major influence on MENA countries' regional role as well, which, ironically, has been amplified since the end of the Cold War and the period of intense superpower competition in this region. As such, 'regional alignments in the Middle East remain largely derivative of the international relations of individual states, for which the overall trend remains to be integrated, separately and to unequal degrees, into the wider international system'.[23] Yet, as Acharya points out, 'superpower retrenchment' has caused a shift in balance of power at local and regional levels, 'creating opportunities for locally dominant actors to step' into the vauum.[24] Such states, with the appropriate resources at their disposal, can in turn carve regional hubs of their own. In a classic sense, this is exactly the pattern which may be unfolding in the Red Sea sub-region, with the big players creating what can best be described as degrees of sub-regional dynamism.

But, at the same time, smaller powers – indeed even sub-national forces – too have become more emboldened since superpower entrenchment. Eritrea's regional policies since the mid-1990s illustrate the first point, and the challenges that Darfur and the SPLM have been posing to Sudan's central authority in the 2000s the second. Ethnic tensions, as a consequence, have grown, particularly in a multi-ethnic region such as the Red Sea. Moreover, this situation has been compounded by the recognition that, post-Cold War, few can really rely on security protection from a great power. This reality has imposed unpalatable choices on the local actors. A direct consequence has been rapid rearmament by the parties and a subsequent regional arms race. But as we have seen, the arms race itself is complex and uneven, and where national resources or indeed foreign military assistance have permitted (as in Israel, Egypt and Saudi Arabia), the quantitative build-up has been compounded by a qualitative one as well. All Red Sea states, however, have upgraded their military forces since the late 1990s and more than half have demonstrated the propensity to use force across their own borders or within them.

Also, superpower retrenchment should not be confused with abandonment, lack of interest or indeed absence from strategic regions! In the case of the United States, for example, we have seen, if anything, renewed activism on the global scene, largely driven by the US national security calculations and the strategic desire to remain the global premier well into the twenty-first century. The Red Sea sub-region, of course, accounts for the US post-Cold War role rather well, for despite some setbacks (notably in Somalia and Sudan in the 1990s), since that decade the United States has in fact intensified its interaction with Africa, and the Red Sea sub-region more specifically: the Arab–Israeli peace process, counter-terrorism, close security relations with a group of allies (Israel, Saudi Arabia, Egypt and Jordan), a security presence in Djibouti and Yemen, containment of the crisis in Sudan, and a military presence off the coast of Somalia, are all evidence of an engaged superpower. It has then continued to play a central role across the Red Sea's zones of conflict, and given this wider context, the actions of smaller states and sub-national actors can also be seen as resistance from below against regionalisation, on the one hand, and struggle against a perceived hierarchy of power, on the other.

We also subscribe to the view that 'integration proceeds at different rates and through different mechanisms, since the states of the [Middle East] region have evolved along distinct, at times dissimilar, historical, social, and institutional paths'.[25] Nowhere can this astute observation be better understood than in the Red Sea. The inter-state relationships that we have unearthed highlight the Red Sea actors' different origins as much as their often competing paths towards state formation. This in itself may not be important, but when different national starting points define so-called national characteristics and 'otherness', then we can see the pursuit of sovereign aims having a detrimental effect on sub-regional security. Their national differences have inevitably left their mark on the Red Sea states' policies and their role perceptions, which inhibited sub-regionalisation during, and in the immediate period following the end of, the Cold War. But at another level, interdependencies have emerged surprisingly rapidly since the mid-1990s, and have accelerated even since 2000. Indeed, examples abound in this study of what we might call 'meso-sub-regionalisation',[26] which has proceeded well precisely where interest and necessity have been complemented by empathy.

Convergence is preceding integration, not unlike the other self-aware regional or sub-regional entities populating the international system. The impetus towards sub-regionalisation is being provided by these emerging and consolidating inter-actions, in spite of the many dysfunctional relationships acting as inhibitors. The point surely is not whether we see consciousness of shared destiny in terms of integration or regionalisation. Rather – in highlighting both the utility and defi-ciencies of the concept of the sub-region for understanding the political relation-ships and international politics of the Red Sea – we have aimed to make the case for focusing on the processes at work as manifestations of collective communities defining regional relationships through direct action. This may not be pure regionalisation or regional institutionalism, but it is sub-global convergence, which is, of course, itself increasingly characteristic of a new age of international relations.[27]

Notes

Introduction

1 Albert Hourani, *A History of the Arab Peoples* (London: Faber and Faber, 1991), p. 111.
2 Ibid., p. 225.
3 Bernard Lewis, *The Middle East: Two Thousand Years of History from the Rise of Christianity to the Present Day* (London: Phoenix, 1996).
4 Carol Zeman Rothkopf, *The Opening of the Suez Canal* (New York: Franklin Watts, 1973), p. 13.
5 A. H. Trapmann, 'The First Phase of Turkey's Share in the War', *The Great War*, Part 34, Chapter XLVIII, April 1915, p. 40.
6 J. A. Hail, *Britain's Foreign Policy in Egypt and Sudan, 1947–1956* (Reading: Ithaca Press, 1996), p. 13.
7 Peter Hahn, 'National Security Concerns in U.S. Policy Toward Egypt, 1949–1956', in David W. Lesch (ed.) *The Middle East and the United States: A Historical and Political Assessment* (Boulder, CO: Westview Press, 1996), p. 92.
8 In an otherwise excellent and detailed chapter on trans-state integration in Africa by Daniel Bach, the Red Sea states barely get a mention, let alone undergoing rigorous analysis. Daniel C. Bach, 'Regionalism versus Regional Integration: The Emergence of a New Paradigm in Africa', in Jean Grugel and Will Hout (eds) *Regionalism Across the North–South Divide: State Strategies and Globalization* (London: Routledge, 1999), pp. 152–66.
9 Geoffrey Kemp and Robert E. Harkavy, *Strategic Geography and the Changing Middle East* (Washington, DC: Brookings Institution Press, 1997), pp. 13–15.
10 For a concise, competent and thorough discussion of the concept of a Middle East system, see F. Gregory Gause, 'Systemic Approaches to Middle East International Relations', *International Studies Review*, Vol. 1, No. 1, Spring 1999.
11 Kenneth Waltz, *Man, the State and War* (New York: Columbia University Press, 1959).
12 Morton Kaplan, *Systems and Process in International Politics* (New York: Wiley, 1957).
13 Paul Noble, 'From Arab System to Middle East System?: Regional Pressures and Constraints', in Bahgat Korany and Ali E. Hilal Dessouki (eds) *The Foreign Policies of Arab States: The Challenge of Globalization* (Cairo: American University of Cairo Press, 2008), pp. 67–165.
14 See Leonard Binder, 'The Middle East as a Subordinate International System', *World Politics*, Vol. 10, April 1958, pp. 408–29; B. M. Russet, *International Regions and the International System* (Chicago: University of Chicago Press, 1967); Louis J. Cantori

and Steven L. Spiegel, *The International Politics of Regions: A Comparative Approach* (Englewood Cliffs, NJ: Prentice-Hall, 1970); William R. Thompson, 'The Regional Subsystem: A Conceptual Explication and a Propositional Inventory', *International Studies Quarterly*, Vol. 17, No. 1, March 1973.

15 Barry Buzan, 'The Level of Analysis Problem in International Relations Reconsidered', in Ken Booth and Steve Smith (eds) *International Relations Theory Today* (Cambridge: Polity Press, 1995), p. 202.

16 Ibid., p. 202.

17 Ibid., pp. 204–5.

18 Barry Buzan and Ole Waever, *Regions and Powers: The Structure of International Security* (Cambridge: Cambridge University Press, 2003), p. 216.

19 These conditions are drawn from the literature on regional systems.

20 Syed Farooq Hasnat, 'The Persian Gulf as a Regional System: Its Operations in the New World Order', *Strategic Studies*, Vol. XIII, No. 4, Summer 1989, p. 24.

21 Jordan moved to reintegrate Egypt into the Arab system at the Amman Arab summit, and Kuwait invited it to the Islamic summit, both in 1987.

22 *Middle East News Agency* (MENA), 1 March 1977.

23 The US amphibious force had passed through the Suez Canal on 27 October 1980. See Edgar O'Ballance, *The Gulf War* (London: Brassey's, 1988).

24 Joseph G. Whelan and Michael J. Dixon, *The Soviet Union in the Third World: Threat to World Peace?* (London: Brassey's, 1986), p. 210.

25 Samuel M. Makinda, *Security in the Horn of Africa*, Adelphi Paper 269 (London: Brassey's for IISS, 1992), p. 64.

26 Joel J. Sokolsky, 'The Superpowers and the Middle East: The Maritime Dimension', in Aurel Braun (ed.) *The Middle East in Global Strategy* (Boulder, CO: Westview Press, 1987), p. 127.

27 Yezid Sayigh, 'System Breakdown in the Middle East?', in *Middle Eastern Lectures 2* (Tel Aviv: Tel Aviv University, 1997), pp. 57–68.

28 Ghassan Salamé, 'Inter-Arab Politics: The Return of Geography', in William B. Quant (ed.) *The Middle East: Ten Years after Camp David* (Washington, DC: Brookings Institution, 1988), pp. 319–53.

29 Louise Fawcett, 'Alliances, Cooperation and Regionalism in the Middle East', in Louise Fawcett (ed.) *International Relations of the Middle East* (Oxford: Oxford University Press, 2005), p. 189.

30 Allen J. Scott, *Regions and the World Economy: The Coming Shape of Global Production, Competition, and Political Order* (Oxford: Oxford University Press, 2000).

1 Weakness and instability: national politics and their sub-regional impact

1 Jim Paul, 'Struggle in the Horn', *MERIP Report*, No. 62, November 1977, Vol. 7, No. 9.

2 David McClintock, 'The Yemen Arab Republic', in David Long and Bernard Reick (eds) *The Government and Politics of the Middle East and North Africa* (Boulder, CO: Westview Press, 1980), p. 170.

3 Hisham Shirabi, 'The Transformation of Ideology in the Arab World', in Irene L. Gendzier (ed.) *A Middle East Reader* (New York: Pegasus, 1969), p. 73.

4 Roger Owen, State, *Power and Politics in the Making of the Modern Middle East* (London: Routledge, 1992), p. 19.

5 Yezid Sayigh, *Armed Struggle and the Search for the State: The Palestinian National Movement, 1949–1993* (Oxford: Oxford University Press, 1997), pp. 5–6.

6 Derek Hopwood, *Egypt: Politics and Society 1945–1984* (Winchester, MA: Allen and Unwin, 1985), p. 99.

7 Jeffrey A. Lefebvre, 'Middle East Conflicts and Middle-Level Power Intervention in the Horn of Africa', *Middle East Journal*, Vol. 50, No. 3, Summer 1996, p. 390.

8 Malcolm H. Kerr, *The Arab Cold War: Gamal 'Abd al-Nasir and His Rivals 1958–1970* (Oxford: Oxford University Press, 1971), pp. 40–1.

9 Ibid., p. 5.

10 Peter Schwab, *Ethiopia: Politics, Economics and Society* (London: Pinter Publishers, 1985).

11 Jim Paul, op. cit.

12 Bereket Habte Selassie, *Conflict and Intervention in the Horn of Africa* (New York: Monthly Review Press, 1980), pp. 63–4.

13 Ibid., p. 147.

14 Lefebvre, op. cit., pp. 392–3.

15 Ibid., p. 195.

16 Derek Hopwood, *Egypt Politics and Society, 1945–1984* (London: George Allen and Unwin, 1985), p. 100.

17 R. Hrair Dekmejian, *Egypt under Nasir* (London: University of London Press, 1972), p. 67.

18 John Waterbury, *The Egypt of Nasser and Sadat* (Princeton, NJ: Princeton University Press, 1983), p. 360.

19 Beverley Milton-Edwards, 'Climate of Change in Jordan's Islamist Movement', in Abdel Salam Sidahmed and Anoushiravan Ehteshami (eds) *Islamic Fundamentalism* (Boulder, CO: Westview Press, 1996), pp. 123–42.

20 Iyad Barghouti, 'Islamist Movements in Historical Palestine', in Abdel Salam Sidahmed and Anoushiravan Ehteshami (eds) *Islamic Fundamentalism* (Boulder, CO: Westview Press, 1996), pp. 163–77.

21 Quote taken from an article in *al-Sirat*, the Islamist weekly, by Jacob Landau, *The Arab Minority in Israel, 1967–1991* (Oxford: Clarendon Press, 1993), p .42.

22 Jacob M. Landau, *The Politics of Pan-Islam* (Oxford: Clarendon Press, 1994), p. 255.

23 Nazih Ayubi, *Overstating the Arab State* (London: I.B. Tauris, 1995).

24 Lefebvre, op. cit., p. 388.

2 International politics of the Red Sea in the Cold War era

1 John Mason has argued that Poland was at the centre of the origins of the Cold War. While this may be true, it was over Azerbaijan that the danger of a confrontation between the two old war allies actually surfaced. John W. Mason, *The Cold War, 1945–1991* (London: Routledge, 1996).

2 Louise Fawcett, *Iran and the Cold War: The Azerbaijan Crisis of 1946* (Cambridge: Cambridge University Press, 1992), p. 122.

3 Fred Halliday, 'The Middle East, the Great Powers, and the Cold War', in Yezid Sayigh and Avi Shlaim (eds) *The Cold War and the Middle East* (Oxford: Oxford University Press, 1997), pp. 6–26.

4 Gregory Treverton, 'Introduction', in G. Treverton (ed.) *Crisis Management and the Super-powers in the Middle East* (Aldershot: Gower, 1981), p. 1.

5 Colin Legum and Bill Lee, *Conflict in the Horn of Africa* (New York: Africana Publishing Company, 1977), p. 5.

6 See, for example, Eric Hobsbawm, *Age of Extremes: The Short Twentieth Century 1914–1991* (London: Abacus, 1995).

7 Guy Wint and Peter Calvocoressi, *Middle East Crisis* (London: Penguin, 1957), p. 108.

8 Leo Silberman, 'Ethiopia: Power of Moderation', *Middle East Journal*, Vol. 14, No. 2, Spring 1960, pp. 141–52.

9 The US–Ethiopian agreement for a 25-year lease of the station was signed in 1953.

10 Marina Ottaway, *Soviet and American Influence in the Horn of Africa* (New York: Praeger, 1982).

11 Benjamin Beit-Hallahmi, *The Israeli Connection: Whom Israel Arms and Why* (London: I.B. Tauris, 1988), p. 48.

12 See Bernard Reich, 'Israel's Policy in Africa', *Middle East Journal*, Vol. 18, No. 1, Winter 1964, pp. 14–26.

13 Egypt signed its first trade treaty with Ethiopia during the Ethiopian leader's visit to Cairo in 1959, and it began sending nearly 100 teachers to shore up the newly-independent Somalia's educational system soon after the country's independence from Britain in 1960.

14 Jeffrey A. Lefebvre, 'Middle East Conflicts and Middle-Level Power Intervention in the Horn of Africa', *Middle East Journal*, Vol. 50, No. 3, Summer 1996, pp. 387–404. The ELF moved its HQ to Damascus in 1964 after the break-up of the United Arab Republic.

15 Rodinson notes that in 1965 Aramco paid the Saudi government $618.4 million in taxes and loyalties. Maxime Rodinson, *Israel and the Arabs* (London: Penguin, 1968), p. 120. This income was over 10 times greater than what Egypt received from the World Bank in 1959.

16 Colin Legum and Bill Lee, *Conflict in the Horn of Africa* (New York: Africana Publishing Company, 1977), p. 5.

17 Moscow recognised the republic almost immediately (in October 1962) while Washington refused to do so. Washington finally recognised the Yemen Arab Republic in December 1962.

18 Fawaz A. Gerges, *The Superpowers and the Middle East: Regional and International Relations, 1955–1967* (Boulder, CO: Westview Press, 1994), p. 151.

19 See ibid.

20 Ibid., p. 191.

21 Israel's successful bombing of the Egypt's Hurghada and Ras Banas air bases on the country's Red Sea coast on 5th June 1967 also illustrated the progress of Israel's modern military machine in the later 1960s and its ability to strike at targets along the Red Sea many hundreds of miles from its own territory. Egypt, for its part, had amassed an impressive naval force in the Red Sea on the eve of the June war, though the country's naval superiority was not fully exploited during the conflict itself. Three destroyers, two submarines, one frigate, and a large number of missile and torpedo boats were stationed in the Red Sea theatre during the war. See Ashraf Rifaat, 'Two If By Sea', *Al-Ahram Weekly*, 4–10 June 1998.

22 Total US aid to Ethiopia between 1953 and 1970 stood at $387 million. See Marina Ottaway, *Soviet and American Influence in the Horn of Africa* (New York: Praeger, 1982).

23 J. Bowyer Bell, *The Horn of Africa: Strategic Magnet in the Seventies* (New York: National Strategy International Center, 1973).

24 Haggai Erlich, *Ethiopia and the Middle East* (Boulder, CO: Lynne Rienner, 1994), p. 151.

25 Ibid.

26 Gorman defines a hot spot as a 'tension-prone area of the world that experiences intermittent outbreaks of overt hostilities involving conflict between conventional and/or guerrilla forces'. See Robert F. Gorman, *Political Conflict on the Horn of Africa* (New York: Praeger, 1981), p. 5.

27 See Legum and Lee, op. cit.

28 John C. Campbell, 'The Soviet Union in the Middle East', *Middle East Journal*, Vol. 32, No. 1, Winter 1978, pp. 1–12.

29 As US-Ethiopian relations deteriorated rapidly in 1977 only a small portion of this new military equipment was in fact delivered. See Peter J. Schraeder, *United States Foreign Policy toward Africa: Incrementalism, Crisis and Change* (Cambridge: Cambridge University Press, 1994).

30 Greg Shapland, *Rivers of Discord: International Water Disputes in the Middle East* (London: Hurst, 1997), p. 79.

31 As much as one billion worth of Soviet weapons was transferred to Ethiopia during the Ogaden war. See Bruce D. Porter, *The USSR in Third World Conflicts: Soviet Arms and Diplomacy in Local Wars 1945–1980* (Cambridge: Cambridge University Press, 1984).

32 Galia Golan, *Soviet Policies in the Middle East: From World War II to Gorbachev* (Cambridge, Cambridge University Press, 1990).

33 Yemen was discussing the prospect of a union of radical Red Sea states under Moscow's supervision when Saudi Arabia was searching for a pan-Arab Red Sea pact.

34 A word of caution is needed here about US strategic aims in the Horn in the mid-1970s. It would be incorrect, as Habte Selassie and Halliday have pointed out, to view the American position in the 1974–77 period as one of automatic opposition to Addis Ababa for its more pro-Soviet stance. For the USA, Ethiopia remained the 'strategic prize' in the Horn and Washington remained engaged with the country until 1979, when Mengistu emerged as Moscow's man in the leadership and the Carter administration found itself engaged in a major crisis in the Persian Gulf. American policy until then had been based on the expectation that the Soviet presence in the country would prove to be a temporary one. See Bereket Habte Selassie, *Conflict and Intervention in the Horn of Africa* (New York: Monthly Review Press, 1980); Fred Halliday, 'U.S. Policy in the Horn of Africa: *Aboulia* or Proxy Intervention?', *Review of African Political Economy*, No. 10 (September–December 1978).

35 Fred Halliday, *Cold War, Third World: An Essay on Soviet-American Relations* (London: Century Hutchinson, 1989), p. 68.

36 Porter, op. cit., p. 213.

37 Alexei Vassiliev, *Russian Policy in the Middle East: From Messianism to Pragmatism* (Reading, MA: Ithaca Press, 1993).

38 IISS, *The Military Balance* (various years).

39 On the RDF and its successor, CENTCOM, see Amitav Acharya, *U.S. Military Strategy in the Gulf* (London: Routledge, 1989); Jeffrey Record, *The Rapid Deployment Force and U.S. Military Intervention in the Persian Gulf* (Cambridge, MA: Institute for Foreign Policy Analysis, 1981); Leila Meo (ed.) *U.S. Strategy in the Gulf: Intervention against Liberation* (Belmont, MA: Association of Arab-American University Graduates, 1981).

40 Anthony H. Cordesman, 'The Regional Balance', in Hans Maull and Otto Pick (eds) *The Gulf War* (London: Pinter Publishers, 1989), p. 83.

41 Geoffrey Godsell, 'Containing Soviet Power: Once Again the Top US Priority', *Christian Science Monitor*, 13 March 1981.

42 Ned Temko, 'Red Sea Crisis Boosts US', *Christian Science Monitor*, 15 August 1984. Both Iran and Libya were accused of laying the mines by Cairo. Interestingly, the mining of the Red Sea occurred at the height of the 'tanker war' between Iraq and Iran in the waters of the Persian Gulf.

43 Schraeder, op. cit.

44 Ibid., p. 183.
45 Jeffrey A. Lefebvre, 'Middle East Conflicts and Middle-Level Power Intervention in the Horn of Africa', *Middle East Journal*, Vol. 50, No. 3, Summer 1996, p. 388.

3 Red Sea sub-regional developments in the post-Cold War era

1 Jeffrey A. Lefebvre, 'Middle East Conflicts and Middle-Level Power Intervention in the Horn of Africa', *Middle East Journal*, Vol. 50, No. 3, Summer 1996, p. 388.
2 In the early 1990s, Iran targeted Sudan as a potential ally and a base to conduct its regional affairs. To this end, Sudan became the grateful recipient of one million tons of oil per year from Iran, military advisers and assistance, and also finance from Tehran for its arm imports from China. Iran also built a military airfield and a naval base at Port Khartoum, directly opposite Saudi Arabia's industrial hub on the Red Sea.
3 For Egypt, Sudan is not only a large neighbour through which flows the Nile, but also a strategically located neighbour which commands the western flank of the Red Sea, as well as Egypt's contact with African nations to the south.
4 *ArabicNews.com*, 2 February 1999.
5 From early 1997 co-ordinated NDA military offensives, spearheaded by the SPLA forces, were reaching strategic targets in the northern parts of the country. In mid-January 1997, for instance, SPLA forces seized three towns near the Ethiopian border and advanced on Damazin, just 480 km south of Khartoum. Damazin is home to the hydro-electric plant which supplies 80 per cent of Khartoum's electricity.
6 Pointedly, prior to the opening of the conference in August President Mubarak of Egypt held a private meeting with the three most important Sudanese opposition leaders, Mahdi, Mighani and Garang. Khartoum's response was swift: it would plan a conference of its own in Khartoum of Egypt's 'armed (opposition) groups'. 'Taking Sides in Sudan War', *Guardian Weekly*, 23 August 1998.
7 Elements in the north complained of the 'liberal' ways of the southern Yemenis and their 'immoral' attitude towards such important matters as the role of women in society, consumption of alcohol and social interactions. Southern Yemenis, for their part, expressed concern about the 'tribal' nature of Northern Yemen, the role of the religious establishment in national affairs, and the proposals by several leading individuals in the North to use Sharia'a law as the basis of united Yemen's Constitution.
8 The GPC won 123 seats of the newly-created 301 seat House of Representatives, the YSP secured 56 seats and the Islamist Yemeni Islah Party won 62 seats. The five-man Presidential Council, headed by General Ali Abdullah Saleh of the North, was aided in its efforts by another new body, the 45-member Advisory Council. The Advisory Council's membership consisted of 25 individuals from the YAR and 20 from the PDRY.
9 Gerd Nonneman, 'Key Issues in the Yemeni Economy', in E. G. H. Joffé, M. J. Hachemi and E. W. Watkins (eds) *Yemen Today: Crisis and Solutions* (London: Carvel Press, 1997), pp. 89–109.
10 Income from oil exports in the mid-1990s was around $1.5 billion per year.
11 Another interesting development of the mid-1990s was the way in which the United States emerged as Yemen's largest trading partner. Nonneman's figures indicate that in 1994 bilateral trade had stood at $377 million. See Nonneman op. cit.
12 *Yemen News*, 7 May 1999.
13 According to *Asharq al-Awsat* (13 April 1999), dozens of Islamist activists were extradited to Egypt between early 1998 and mid-1999.

14 Paul Henze, 'Ethiopia and Eritrea: The Defeat of the Derg and the Establishment of New Governments', in David R. Smock (ed.) *Making War and Waging Peace: Foreign Intervention in Africa* (Washington, DC: United States Institute of Peace Press, 1993), pp. 53–77. See also, 'Weather and War Conspire against Ethiopians', *Financial Times*, 27 March 1990.

15 The post-Dergue government of Meles Zenawi in Ethiopia agreed to autonomy for Eritrea in 1991 and possible independence subject to a favourable result in the planned referendum which was held in April 1993. Egypt and Sudan, active in African politics and dependent on the Nile, both expressed concern about the wisdom of one of Africa's oldest states breaking up. For the Sudanese government, embroiled in its own civil war, the reality of territorial division just next door along ethnic/religious lines was clearly hard to bear. Other African countries, equally mindful of the fragility of Africa's other multi-ethnic/multi-religious states, adopted similar positions on Ethiopia's territorial division.

16 See *Survey 1997/98* (Oxford: Oxford University Press, 1998).

17 Yemen, which had been suspected of building a secret channel with Israel, was adamant that it had suspended all contacts with the Netanyahu government after new tensions had crept into the peace process. Israel had approached Yemen in the Spring of 1998 to relaunch bilateral discussions. Israel had presented Yemen with a list of requests and suggestions: Sana'a should allow Jews and Israelis to visit Yemen, they should grant automatic over-pass through Yemen's air space, Yemen should allow telephone calls to Israel to go through. *Yemen Times*, 19 April 1998.

18 See Richard Schofield, 'The Last Missing Fence in the Desert: The Saudi–Yemeni Boundary', in E. G. H. Joffé, M. J. Hachemi and E. W. Watkins (eds) *Yemen Today: Crisis and Solutions* (London: Carvel Press, 1997), pp. 213–68.

19 Ann Mosely Lesch, 'External Involvement in the Sudanese Civil War', in David R. Smock (ed.) *Making War and Waging Peace: Foreign Intervention in Africa* (Washington, DC: United States Institute of Peace, 1993), pp. 79–105.

20 Yehudit Ronen, 'Sudan', in Bruce Maddy-Weitzman (ed.) *Middle East Contemporary Survey Volume XIX: 1995* (Boulder, CO: Westview Press, 1997), p. 581.

21 Ibid.

22 Zenawi's mother is Eritrean and Afeworki's mother is from Tigray in Ethiopia.

23 The introduction of the Nakfa in Eritrea meant that Ethiopia ended up paying more for the use of Eritrean ports. Addis Ababa's response was to reroute all its maritime trade to the neighbouring country of Djibouti. While Djibouti was set to benefit from this new relationship, in practice both Ethiopia and Eritrea stood to suffer economically. For Eritrea it was payments for the use of its port facilities, and for Ethiopia higher costs associated with distance and longer loading and unloading periods. The other ever-present danger was that tiny Djibouti, sandwiched between the warring countries, could find itself embroiled in this new Horn conflict.

24 'Prickly Horn of Africa States Threaten to Fight Over Border', *Financial Times*, 21 May 1998. Ethiopia also found it very hard to accept the Eritrean proposal that its new currency be traded at parity with the Birr.

25 Cathy Jenkins, 'Ethiopians Target Port Area', *BBC News* (online), 15 February 1999. For a detailed Eritrean response to Ethiopia's moves on the economic front, see Gebremichael Mngistu, 'Do Ethiopia's Recent Claims and Allegations on the Economic Relationship that Existed Between Eritrea and Ethiopia Hold Water?', *Eritrean Network Information Center* (online), 1998.

26 *International Herald Tribune*, 25 June 1998.

27 Since the start of hostilities, both countries have grown more reliant on their nationals living abroad to part-finance the war. In Eritrea's case, its citizens residing overseas are expected to provide the state with 2 per cent of their income to finance the war effort.

28 At least one source has alleged that Yemen, in an attempt to form a three-way relationship with Eritrea and Somalia's Aideed, may have become Eritrea's main supplier of weapons, possibly including the six MiG-29s in its armoury, since July 1998. See 'Yemen and War in the Horn of Africa', *Yemen News*, 15 February 1999.

29 *APS Diplomat*, 22–29 March 1999. Israel is also said to have been assisting both sides, largely Eritrea in return for the right to gather intelligence on Sudan and other neighbouring Arab states from Eritrean territory. It has also been reported that Asmara may have provided Israel with military facilities on some of its Red Sea islands.

30 The aircraft deals alone cost these two poor African countries some $310 million. See Patrick Gilkes, 'Analysis: Arms Pour in for Border War', *BBC News* (online), 16 February 1999.

31 Dan Connell, 'Behind the War in the Horn of Africa', *Middle East International*, No. 595, 12 March 1999, pp. 20–2.

32 For Yemen, which was increasingly worried about the deepening of a powerful US/Israel-backed Ethiopian–Eritrean axis, the Eritrean–Ethiopian conflict could not have happened at a better time.

33 Ethiopia had already accused Eritrea of rearming the anti-government Ogaden National Liberation Front. Eric Watkins, 'Yemen and War in the Horn of Africa', *Yemen News*, 15 February 1999.

34 News that Yemen, or 'Yemenis in uniform', were engaged in arms-trafficking to Eritrea, had been in circulation for some time. See *Yemen Times*, 15–21 March 1999.

35 Quoted in Dina Ezzat, 'Holding off the Horn', *Al-Ahram Weekly*, 18–24 June 1998.

36 Israel Foreign Ministry statement, 7 February 1999.

37 Both sides submitted their appeals to the court of arbitration in London on 9 April 1999.

38 Yemen has had the upper hand for another reason as well: the court of arbitration had already established Yemen's sovereignty over the Hanish archipelago (its verdict was issued on 9 October 1998) and the discussions were not concentrating on the demarcation of the maritime boundary.

39 *Yemen Times*, 16–25 April 1999.

40 One graphic report of the fighting explains that:

> Eritrean defences on the Badme front had been thought impenetrable: the Ethiopian forces would find themselves running into a brick wall. They did, but they were prepared to sacrifice tens of thousands of men in an all-out bid to recapture Badme. After their initial forays were repulsed, the Ethiopians launched a barrage of air strikes from bombers, fighters and helicopter gunships. They then threw division after division at the Eritrean frontline. Eventually, the line buckled and the Eritreans were driven out of the Badme area. Ethiopia then claimed victory.
>
> (*The Economist*, 'Ethiopia and Eritrea: Trench Warfare', 13–19 March 1999, p. 90)

41 *New York Times*, 29 March 1999; *APS Diplomat*, 27 March–3 April 1999. Independent sources have spoken of 20,000 Eritreans killed. See *The Economist*, 'Eritrea: Carnage on the Plain', 17–24 April 1999.

42 *ArabicNews.com*, 8 February 1999. Western diplomats reported that as many as 10,000 Ethiopians may have been killed in less than two months of fighting.

43 Ibid.

44 Both sides had already succumbed to bombing civilian targets and facilities since the fighting started in 1998, and in April 1999 Eritrea accused Ethiopia of using napalm. *International Herald Tribune*, 4 April 1999.

45 The Amhara carry a big grudge against their own government as much as against the Eritrean government, for since the early 1990s they have suffered at the hands of both. After 1993, for instance, the Ethiopian government sat back while Asmara set about expelling non-Eritrean settlers, the bulk of whom were Amharans and seen as locally-based tools in the hands of the Imperial and Marxist regimes in Addis Ababa, from the new country.

46 Mohammed Ali, *Ethnicity, Politics, and Society in Northeast Africa: Conflict and Social Change* (Lanham, MD: University Press of America, 1996).

47 Berouk Mesfin, 'The Eritrea-Djibouti Border Dispute', *Situation Report*, 15 September 2008.

48 Joshua Teitelbaum, 'Saudi Arabia', in Bruce Maddy-Weitzman (ed.) *Middle East Contemporary Survey, Volume XIX: 1995* (Boulder, CO: Westview Press, 1997), pp. 532–61.

49 Yemeni forces retook the island from Saudi troops after two days of naval battles and troop landings. Yemen accused the Saudis of aggression. *CNN.com*, 23 July 1998.

50 There has been much talk of the richness of the southern Red Sea in terms of tourist and fishing potential of the surrounding waters, as well as the significant quantities of hydrocarbons and minerals beneath it. *Financial Times*, 10 January 1996.

51 Statement of the Israeli Foreign Ministry. *APS Diplomat*, 3–10 February 1996.

52 BBC, SWB ME/2491, 18 December 1995; *Al-Hayat*, 19 December 1995; *APS Diplomat*, 3–10 February 1996.

53 *Saudi Gazette*, 5 January 1996.

54 Based on private discussions with Saudi and Egyptian commentators.

55 *Yemen Times*, 19–25 October 1998.

56 The Northern region of Somalia tried to separate itself from the rest of the country in 1991, giving itself the name of Somaliland.

57 In Somalia, the legacy of direct superpower intervention had left the country in total disarray. The end of the Cold War seemed to have had little effect on the civil war, causing the USA to take direct action through military intervention in 1993. The outcome of this bold American move was further tensions in this strategically located country and in the Horn as a whole. The rather sudden departure of American forces from the country soon after their arrival left an even bigger political vacuum in the country which only served to widen the civil war.

58 *Somalia After Aideed* (London: Liberty for the Muslim World, no author or date given). Apparently, in his dealings with Israel, Egal has made much of his willingness to confront Arab and Islamist influence in the Horn. Egal's letter to Prime Minister Rabin of Israel dated 3 July 1995 is reproduced in above. In the letter, Egal offers to enter a 'strategic partnership' with Israel against Arab influence in the Horn.

59 One such report from August 1996 spoke of Ethiopian helicopter gunships, tanks and artillery being deployed against the al-Ittihad forces, which have developed a stronghold on Somali territories near the Kenyan border since 1993. *The Times*, 12 August 1996. Al-Ittihad has been accused of carrying out bombing campaigns in Ethiopia and kidnapping of Ethiopian citizens in Somalia.

60 *APS Diplomat*, 22–29 March 1999, Vol. 50, No. 12.

61 General Aideed died of gunshot wounds in August 1996. His son, Mohammed Farah Aideed stepped into his father's shoes.

62 Sudan joined the Libyan-sponsored Community of Sahel and Saharan States at its inception in 1998.

63 *Yemen News*, 3 April 1999. Reports continue to circulate that Yemeni military planes help in transporting Eritrean arms to anti-Ethiopian Somali factions and that some of these factions, like the Islamist Oromo Liberation Front, are sheltered in Yemen.

64 *Associated Press*, 2 January 1996.

65 Mohammed al-Kibsi, 'Saudi Authorities Erect Barriers on Yemeni Border', *Yemen Today*, 12 January 2008.

66 Ibid.

67 *World Tribune*, 5 December 2009.

68 International Criris Group, *Eritrea: The Siege State* (Brussels: ICG Africa Report No. 163, 2010).

69 Ibid., p. 1.

70 'On Piracy and the Afterlives of Failed States', *Middle East Report*, No. 256, Fall 2010, p. 7.

71 For details, see IGAD's *2009 Annual Report* (Djibouti: IGAD, 2009).

4 Security, militarisation and arms flows

1 *MEED Special Report: Saudi Arabia*, August 1982, p. 163.

2 Directorate General for Yanbu Project, *Investment Opportunities: Industry* (Yanbu: Saudi Arabia, n.d.), p. 5.

3 Daniel, 'Why Iran–Iraq War Hasn't Had Greater Worldwide Impact', *Christian Science Monitor*, 29 August 1984.

4 Iran had loaned Egypt one billion in 1974 for its Suez-related projects. See Samuel Segev, *The Iranian Triangle: The Untold Story of Israel's Role in the Iran-Contra Affair* (New York: Free Press, 1988).

5 *Gulf States Newsletter*, Vol. 12, No. 548, 4 November 1996.

6 *Exploiting Grievances: Al-Qaeda in the Arabian Peninsula* (Washington, DC: Carnegie Endowment for International Peace, 2010).

7 IISS, *The Military Balance* (various years) (Oxford: Oxford University Press).

8 Jaffee Center for Strategic Studies, *The Middle East Military Balance, 1987–1988* (Jerusalem: Jerusalem Post Press, 1988), p. 147.

9 Ibid., p. 155.

10 Aharon Levran, *Israeli Strategy After Desert Storm: Lessons of the Second Gulf War* (London: Frank Cass, 1997).

11 *Middle East Security Report*, 1 April 1998.

12 Quoted in Areih O'Sullivan, 'A Nuclear Cloud over the Middle East?', *Jerusalem Post*, 5 June 1998.

13 Levran, op. cit., p. 155.

14 Quoted by Judy Dempsey, 'Israel: Iran's Missile Capability Source for Worry', *Financial Times*, 12 November 1997.

15 Data is compiled from various editions of *The Military Balance* and *The SIPRI Yearbook*.

16 *Mid-East Realities*, 1 July 1998.

17 http://www.nandotimes.com, 16 July 1999.

18 See Areih O'Sullivan, 'A Nuclear Cloud over the Middle East?', *Jerusalem Post*, 5 June 1998.

19 *Associated Press*, 12 March 1999.

20 Our calculation of Saudi Arabia's military-related expenditures in the 1980s is based on the wealth of data provided by ACDA, IISS, CIA and SIPRI. None of these sources, however, agree on Saudi Arabia's aggregate military expenditures.

21 Anthony H. Cordesman, *Saudi Arabia: Guarding the Desert Kingdom* (Boulder, CO: Westview, 1997).

22 *Gulf States Newsletter*, Vol. 21, No. 550, 2 December 1996.

23 Anthony H. Cordesman, Ibid., p. 160. Cordesman goes on to say that 'no nation other than the US could alter the software on the F-15S, and it had no software optimized to attack US or Israeli air and air defense systems' (p. 161).

24 As reported by Khaled Bin Sultan (the Saudi Joint Forces Chief) in *Desert Warrior* (London: HarperCollins, 1995), p. 20.

25 *The Military Balance 1997/98* (Oxford: Oxford University Press, 1997).

26 *The APS Diplomat*, Vol. 47, No. 26, 29/31 December 1997.

27 *Jane's Defence Weekly*, 22 September 1999; *Financial Times*, 8 October 1999.

28 *Airforces Monthly*, November 1997.

29 *The Independent*, 4 March 1999.

30 Alex Duval Smith, 'Killing Field Barricaded with Corpses', *The Independent*, 17 July 1999.

31 Karl Vick, 'On the Road to "Mega Tragedy"; Ethiopia, Eritrea Put Progress at Risk as They Move Toward "Full-blown War"', *Washington Post*, 10 January 1999.

32 *Jerusalem Post*, 8 January 1998.

33 *Gulf States Newsletter*, Vol. 20, No. 520, 24 September 1995.

34 It now stands at around 1,800 men.

35 *The Military Balance, 1991–1992* (London: Brassey's, 1990).

36 *Yemen News*, 5 October 1999. The same reveals that Yemen has actively been seeking access to such Russian hardware as BMP-1 and BMP-2 armoured personnel carriers, and BTR-70 armoured vehicles.

37 *SUSRIS Newsletter*, August 2010.

5 Land boundaries, maritime borders and territorial issues

1 Ian Brownlie, *African Boundaries: A Legal and Diplomatic Encyclopaedia* (London: C. Hurst, 1979), p. 111.

2 *Financial Times*, 4 February 1992.

3 *MENA News Agency*, Cairo, 27 January 1997. *SWB ME/2828*.

4 'The Violet Line was an arbitrary straight-line extension of the Anglo-Ottoman boundary delimited between 1903 and 1905 basically to separate the wilayat of Yemen from the nine loosely federated cantons of the Aden Protectorate'. Richard Schofield (ed.) *Territorial Foundations of the Gulf States* (London: University College London, 1994), p. 42.

5 Where American companies were concerned, a memorandum was passed to the United States state department. Richard Schofield, Ibid., p. 26.

6 *Yemeni Radio*, SPA, Riyadh, 8 December 1994. *SWB ME/2174*.

7 *Al Quds Al'Arabi*, London, 5 June 1997.

8 John Duke Anthony, 'The Red Sea: Control of the Southern Approach', *Middle East Problem Paper No. 13* (Washington, DC: The Middle East Institute, 1975).

9 Clive Schofield and Martin Pratt, 'Eritrea and Yemen at Odds in the Red Sea', *Jane's Intelligence Review*, Vol. 8, No. 6, June 1996, p. 264.

10 *Oil and Gas Journal*, 9 October 1995, p. 39.

11 Andarko Petroleum representatives said that their early test drilling in the Red Sea had revealed geological formations similar to those found in the Gulf of Mexico. Salt structures suggested the possibility that what they believed to be 'one of the few underexplored areas remaining in the world today' might ultimately produce significant quantities of petroleum. *New York Times*, 29 September 1995.

12 Eritrean Foreign Ministry Statement, 17 December 1995.

13 Address by the President of the Republic of Yemen on the Dispute between the Republic of Yemen and Eritrea, 20 December 1995.

14 *Yemeni Republic Radio*, 17 December 1995.

15 *Al-Sharq al-Awsat*, 18 December 1995.

16 According to Ahmad Salahuddin in the Saudi newspaper *Al-Madinah Arabic*, an Ethiopian weekly magazine disclosed in 1998 that Israel was constructing a military base on the island of Dahlak, with a harbour that could service up to three submarines simultaneously. It further claimed that Eritrea had agreed to grant Israel free movement to operate in the Red Sea and spy on Arab countries. Moreover, Mossad agents were free to deploy in the Horn of Africa and the Great Lakes region in order to secure Israeli trade and traffic to Asia and the Far East. *Arab View*, http://www.arab.net/arabview/articles/ahmadsalah1.html, 12 April 1998.

17 Suspicions regarding the development Eritrean–Israeli relationship had emerged earlier when Eritrean President Isayas Afewerki had visited Israel immediately after his country had won its independence, according to Yemen in order to formalise a partnership secretly cemented in 1990. His failure to take Eritrea into the Arab League as had been expected in 1993 was considered to be further evidence of Israeli influence. Israel for its part denied direct involvement in the islands dispute but admitted that it viewed Eritrea as a 'peripheral ally' because 'it sits close to the Red Sea's southern entrance, which controls one of the world's major shipping lanes and can counterbalance fundamentalist Sudan'. Quote attributed to the then-Health Minister, Ephrain Sneh, *Middle East Mirror*, 21 December 1995. Sneh also officially confirmed that the two countries had engaged in co-operation in a number of agricultural and health-related areas.

18 *SWB, ME/2492 MED/6*, 21 December 1995.

19 See *Boundary and Security Bulletin*, International Boundaries Resource Centre, Autumn 1998, pp. 51–4.

20 *Financial Times*, 10 January 1996.

21 *Gulf States Newsletter*, Vol. 22, No. 527, 15 January 1996.

22 Ali El-Hakim, *The Middle Eastern States and the Law of the Sea* (Manchester: Manchester University Press, 1979), p. 179.

23 Ali El-Hakim, ibid., p.187.

24 Nurit Kliot, 'The Evolution of the Egypt–Israel Boundary: From Colonial Foundations to Peaceful Borders', International Boundaries Research Unit, *Boundary and Territory Briefing*, Vol. 1, No. 8, 1995.

25 Information provided by the International Boundaries Research Unit, Durham University, UK, August 1999.

26 Avi, *Collusion across the Jordan* (Oxford: Clarendon Press, 1988).

27 *The Guardian*, 10 November 1992.

28 For a detailed account of the background to this part of the boundary dispute, see Elisha Efrat, 'The Israel-Jordan Boundary Dispute in the Arava Valley', *British Journal of Middle Eastern Studies*, Vol. 21, No .2, 1994, pp. 228–39.

29 'Israel Eyes the Greenhouse', *The Economist*, 20 June 1998, p .76.

30 For details see Jan de Jong, 'The Geography of Politics: Israel's Settlement Drive after Oslo', in George Giacaman and Dag Jørund Lønning (eds) *After Oslo: New Realities, Old Problems* (London: Pluto Press, 1998), pp. 77–120.

31 'Israel-Lebanon Summary', International Boundaries Research Unit, Durham University.

32 'Israel-Syria Summary', International Boundaries Research Unit, Durham University.

33 Egyptian *aide-mémoire* to the United Kingdom and United States, quoted in 'Sovereignty and Jurisdiction in the Strait of Tiran', International Boundaries Research Unit, Durham University, 1994.

34 See Ali El-Hakim, op. cit., Chapter IV, pp. 132–77.

35 Medhane , *The Eritrean–Ethiopian War: Retrospects and Prospects. The Making of Conflicts in the Horn, 1991–1998* (Addis Ababa: Mega Publishers, 1998).

36 Karl Vick, '2 Old Friends Went to War', *International Herald Tribune*, 18 June 1998.

37 *Associated Press*, 8 June 1998; *Reuters*, 15 June 1998. The pilot of the small Eritrean aircraft carrying the cluster bombs missed its target and delivered its cargo on a school, killing an estimated 48 during its two attacks.

38 Michela Wrong, 'Eritrea/Ethiopia: Saving Face, Losing All', *Financial Times*, 20 June 1998.

39 Pamela Constable, 'Area's Ethiopian Community Torn by War with Eritrea', *Washington Post*, 14 June 1998.

40 The Ethiopian ambassador to Yemen, Dr Teketel Forssidi, claimed, for example, that Yemen was involved in arms trafficking and gun smuggling to Eritrea, defying the UN Security Council arms embargo on shipments to either faction. *Yemen Times*, 15–21 March 1999.

41 *Radio France International*, Paris, 17 April 1996. *Reuters*, 16 May 1996 and *MENA News Agency*, Cairo, 4 June 1996.

42 Medhane Tadesse, 'The Djibouti–Eritrea Conflict', *InterAfrica Group Briefing*, October 2008.

6 The economics of the Red Sea: trade, migration and capital flows

1 For example, the 1991/92 harvest of wheat cost the government around $480 per tonne, compared to world prices of £100 per tonne.

2 See the *Oil and Gas Journal* (various issues).

3 *Al-Ahram Weekly*, 25–31 March 1999.

4 Agriculture accounted for 84 per cent of Egyptian water usage in 1990.

5 In the 1970s the Aswan High Dam provided up to half of the electricity needs of Egypt. By the mid-1990s this was down to less than one-fifth of consumption. In Sudan, the Sennar, Roseires and Khashm al-Girba dams produce around half the country's generating capacity. Greg Shapland, *Rivers of Discord: International Water Disputes in the Middle East* (London: Hurst, 1997), p. 65.

6 Work was suspended in 1984 due to attacks by the Southern Sudanese armed opposition. Relations between the two countries deteriorated after 1989.

7 Greg Shapland, op. cit., pp. 73–5.

8 Ashok Swain, 'A New Challenge: Water Scarcity in the Arab World', *Arab Studies Quarterly*, Vol. 20, No. 1, Winter 1998, p. 6.

9 *Financial Times*, 27 February 1997.

10 In 1999, Ethiopia announced a major study of the four water basins in Ethiopia, all of which are tributaries of the Nile, stating that a national water policy had been devised

which, when executed, would facilitate the cultivation of an additional 2 million hectares and the generation of 30,000 megawatts of electric power. Available at: http://AddisTribune.EthiopiaOnline.Net/Archives/1999/05/07.

11 For more information, see Arnon Soffer, *Rivers of Fire* (London: Rowman and Littlefield, 1999), pp. 119–204.

12 For more detailed information on efforts to resolve water disputes in the Jordan Basin, see J.A. Allan (ed.) *Water, Peace and the Middle East: Negotiating Resources in the Jordan Basin* (London: I.B. Tauris, 1996).

13 *The Jordan–Israel Peace Treaty: What is it?* (Amman: Jordan Media Group, 1995).

14 Hydrologists categorise a country as subject to 'absolute water scarcity' when the annual per capita fresh water availability goes below 500 cubic meters. At the beginning of the 1990s Saudi Arabia, Jordan, Yemen and Israel all fell within this category. See Ashok Swain, op. cit., p. 1.

15 These terms relate to proposals to build canals linking either the Red Sea to the Dead Sea, or the Mediterranean to the Dead Sea. As water effectively fell below sea water, it might theoretically generate the energy needed to desalinise it.

16 http://www.eritrea.org/EIB/Economy/EconomicProfile.html, 24 March 1999.

17 In 1970, the 165 plants employing 14,000 people on a permanent basis contributed up to 40 per cent of Ethiopia's entire manufacturing output. During the era of Ethiopian rule much of this industry was removed to Ethiopia and what was left suffered from insufficient energy and water supplies. In 1997, there remained only 39 plants which were utilising out-of-date technology and producing under capacity due to lack of spare parts, raw materials and skilled labour.

18 See Emma C. Murphy, 'Structural Inhibitions to Economic Liberalization in Israel', *Middle East Journal*, Vol. 48, No. 1, Winter 1994, pp. 65–88.

19 *Sudan Focus*, Vol. 6, No. 1, 15 July 1999.

20 The ultra-orthodox population, who devote their lives to Talmudic study, currently account for 7 per cent of the Israeli population, a figure which is growing quickly due to high birth rates. Israeli levels of non-participation in the workforce are now the highest in the developed world. *Financial Times*, 17 March 1999.

21 *Financial Times*, 19 January 1999.

22 *The Economist, A Survey of Egypt*, 20 March 1999.

23 Economist Intelligence Unit, *EIU Saudi Arabia: Country Report 1998–99* (London: EIU, 1998), p. 15.

24 Just $100 million in 1998. *Financial Times*, 10 February 1999.

25 Ibid.

26 These crops used to account for as much as 90 per cent of cultivated land. See J.E. Peterson, *Yemen: The Search for a Modern State* (London: Croom Helm, 1982), p. 16.

27 Yemen's foreign policy during the Gulf War resulted in losses to the economy of well over $1.5 billion in terms of labour remittances, over 500 million in direct Saudi aid and a similar amount from the other GCC states. *Yemen Times Business and Economy*, Issue 3, 19–25 January 1998.

28 When the removal of subsidies led to sharp wheat and flour price rises in 1995, the result was riots on the street. The reforms had been resisted by the southern party, the Yemeni Socialist Party, before they were defeated in the 1994 civil war. They had argued for a rapprochement with Saudi Arabia instead that would lead to renewed aid from that country.

29 A five-year reform package (1996–2000) includes floatation of the Yemeni riyal, reduction of food subsidies, and improved systems of government revenue collection. It also anticipates privatisation of up to 60 per cent of public sector businesses.

30 Economist Intelligence Unit, *Sudan: Country Profile 1998–99* (London: EIU, 1998), p. 18.

31 There is an estimated annual productive potential of 70,000 tons of edible produce, although stock are still recovering from over-exploitation by Soviet trawlers in the past.

32 It is too early to tell how the intensive fighting between Ethiopia and Eritrea in the late 1990s will affect these plans.

33 *The Economist*, 'Africa's Forgotten War', 8–14 May 1999.

34 *The Economist*, 17–23 April 1999, p. 80.

35 *Middle East Review 1981* (Birmingham: Kogan Page, 1982).

36 Despite periodic assertions of a large disguised trade between Israel and the Arab states, with estimates rising as high as $1 billion a year, there is no hard evidence that such clandestine transfers have actually taken place. For an analysis of Israeli and Arab trade statistics which confirms that any such trade, should it exist, must be of a very small magnitude, see Ephraim Kleiman, 'Is There a Secret Arab–Israeli Trade?', *Middle East Quarterly*, Vol. V, No. 2, June 1998.

37 *Gulf States Newsletter*, 28 June 1999.

38 *Iraqi News Agency* (INA) Baghdad, 31 October 1994, *SWB ME/2144*.

39 In January 1999, 14 Arab countries implemented an agreement to cut tariffs on goods traded among themselves by 10 per cent, following an initial 10 per cent cut the previous year. Trade between these states accounted for 90 per cent of inter-Arab trade.

40 Rodney Wilson, *Economic Development in the Middle East* (London: Routledge, 1995), p. 171.

41 Ibid., p. 70.

42 H.A. MacMichael, *A History of Arabian Sudan* (London: Frank Cass, 1967).

43 Strategic Studies, *Strategic Survey 1997/98* (Oxford: Oxford University Press, 1998), p. 248.

44 *Africa, South of the Sahara 1998* (London: Europa, 1998a), p. 400.

45 Gil Loescher, *Refugee Movements and International Security*, Adelphi Papers 268, Summer 1992, p. 72.

46 Rodney Wilson, op. cit., p. 70.

47 Victoria Bernal, 'Migration, Modernity and Islam in Rural Sudan', *Middle East Report*, Summer 1999, No. 211, p. 27.

48 *Jadwa Monthly Economic Bulletin*, September 2010.

49 *Middle East Economic Digest*, 17 July 1998, p. 10.

50 David McMurray, 'Recent Trends in Middle Eastern Migration', *Middle East Report*, Summer 1999, No. 211, pp. 16–20.

51 Op. cit., p. 19.

52 Casey Research on *Foreign and Budget Appropriations 2010*.

53 Patrick Clawson and Zoe Danon Gedal, *Dollars and Diplomacy* (Washington, DC: The Washington Institute for Near East Policy, 1999), pp. 55–6.

54 In March 1999, US Undersecretary of State for Near East Affairs, Martin Indyk, told a Senate Appropriations subcommittee, that Israel was now able to stand on its own feet economically, while the Arab partners in the peace process still faced daunting economic challenges which required US assistance. He submitted a $1.9 billion package to Congress to support the Wye River Accord which allocated $1.2 billion in foreign military financing to Israel, $400 million in economic support funds to the Palestinians, and $300 million to Jordan. Available at: http://www.arabicnews.com/ansub/Daily/Day/990326.

55 *Reuters*, 2 January 2010.

56 *Yemen Times*, 29 January 1999.

57 Available at: http://www.arabfund.org/loans.htm, 23 July 1999.
58 Roger Owen and Sevket Pamuk, *A History of Middle East Economies in the Twentieth Century* (London: I.B. Tauris, 1998), p. 233.
59 Rodney Wilson, op. cit., p. 197.
60 Meanwhile, Egyptian exports to Saudi markets have steadily increased, reaching $1.3 billion in non-oil exports alone in 2009, whereas such exports only accounted for $332 million in 2005. *Almasry Al-Youm*, 7 October 2010.
61 *Al-Sharq Al-Awsat*, 18 May 2008, *Sudan Vision*, 27 June 2010.

7 Red Sea networks: regional and international transport

1 Middle East Economic Digest, *Middle East Economic Digest Special Report*, Vol. 42, No. 6, 6 February 1998, p. 8.
2 Saudi Arabian Monetary Agency, *33rd Annual Report* (Riyadh: ASMA, 1997).
3 *Saudi Economic Survey*, Vol. XXXIII, No. 1606, 24 February 1999, p. 6.
4 *Saudi Port Authority News,* 10 May 2010.
5 Figures from the Jordan Shipping Agents Association in Europa Publications, *The Middle East and North Africa 1994* (London: Europa, 1993), p. 551.
6 *Al-Ahram Weekly*, 18–24 March 1999.
7 *Port World News*, 18 February 2008.
8 *World Cargo News*, August 2006.
9 Available at: worldportsourse. com_sudan.
10 Gebremichael Mengistu, 'Do Ethiopia's Recent Allegations on the Economic Relationship that Existed Between Eritrea and Ethiopia Hold Water?', available at: http://www.eritrea.org/EIB/News/0998/N091701.html., 10 February 1999.
11 Ibid.
12 Some 46 ships of the 97 operating in 1998 were privately owned. *Al-Ahram Weekly*, 18–24 March 1999.
13 *Middle East Economic Digest*, 15 January 1999, p. 14.
14 Rodney Wilson, *Economic Development in the Middle East* (London: Routledge, 1995), p. 34.
15 American Chamber of Commerce in Egypt, *Freight Land Transportation in Egypt: Present Status and Future Prospects* (Cairo: ACCE, January 1995).
16 World Development Indicators database.
17 The Economist Intelligence Unit, *EIU Country Profile: Sudan 1998–99* (London: EIU, 1998), p. 22.
18 *Yemen Times:* Front Page, http://www.yementimes.com/98/iss15/front.html.
19 In March 1999, a joint technical committee was set up by the two countries to consider a link from Sinai to the island of Tiran and by causeway to the Saudi side of the Gulf of Aqaba, a distance of about 15 km. *Financial Times*, 4 March 1999.
20 *Reuters*, 9 June 1996.
21 Geoffrey Kemp and Robert E. Harkavy, *Strategic Geography and the Changing Middle East* (Washington, DC: Brookings Institution Press, 1997), p. xii.
22 Rodney Wilson, op. cit., p. 34.
23 American Chamber of Commerce in Egypt, op. cit.
24 Economist Intelligence Unit, *EIU Country Profile: Egypt 1998–99* (London: EIU, 1998), p. 23.
25 Available at: http://www.milnet.com/milnet/pentagon/centcom/sudan/sudinf.html.

26 *Middle East Economic Digest*, 14 December 1998.

27 Available at: http://www.arabicnews.com/ansub/Daily/Day/980508/1998050807.html, 5 November 1998.

28 *Flight International*, 29 October–4 November 1997, p. 10.

29 Middle East Economic Digest, *Aviation Special Report: Middle East Economic Digest*, Vol. 42, No. 23, 5 June 1998, pp. 15–16.

30 *Middle East Economic Digest*, 12 March 1999, p. 3.

31 IMF, *International Financial Statistics Yearbook* (Washington, DC: International Monetary Fund, 1998).

32 *Financial Times*, 23 August 1996.

33 Data from the annual surveys of *Middle East Economic Digest*.

34 *Financial Times*, 13 October 1998.

35 Business Monitor International, *Middle East and Africa Oil and Gas Insights* (various issues).

36 *Sudan Focus*, Vol. 6, No. 1, July 1999.

37 *Financial Times*, 13 October 1998.

38 *Yemen Times*, 31 July 2008.

Conclusion: regionalising the Red Sea

1 Eric Hobsbawm, *Age of Extremes: The Short Twentieth Century 1914–1991* (London: Abacus, 1995), p. 252.

2 Ibid., p. 255.

3 Since 2003, the spectre of Iran as a direct threat to the Arab order has again been resurrected, this time in terms of a rising Shi'a crescent inspired, if not led, by Iran.

4 The ACC died a quick death in August 1990, when its members adopted conflicting positions in the Kuwait crisis: Egypt co-led the anti-Baghdad, Jordan gave tacit support to Iraq, and Yemen (now united as one state) sympathised with Iraq.

5 For a sound discussion of the related issues, see Bassam Tibi, *Conflict and War in the Middle East: From Interstate War to New Security* (London: Macmillan, 1998).

6 The birth of Washington's 'twin pillar' policy in the Persian Gulf in the early 1970s at once promoted Iran and Saudi Arabia as the protectors of Western interests there. The other major local actor – Iraq – sought (and found) support from the main global rival of the United States, the Soviet Union. Thus, a dynamic triangular relationship, reinforced by the two superpowers and their main allies, was born in the Gulf. Always unstable, it nonetheless remained intact for almost a decade. The 1979 Iranian revolution, however, transformed beyond recognition the security structures of the Persian Gulf.

7 Gregory L. Aftandilian, *Egypt's Bid for Arab Leadership: Implications for U.S. Policy* (New York: Council on Foreign Relations, 1993).

8 Ali E. Hillal Dessouki, 'Regional Leadership: Balancing off Costs and Dividends in the Foreign Policy of Egypt', in Bahgat Korany and Ali E. Hillal Dessouki (eds) *The Foreign Policies of Arab States: The Challenge of Globalization* (Cairo: American University of Cairo Press, 2008), pp. 167–94.

9 It has to be said, however, that Riyadh did spend much of the Arab Cold War years fighting off Nasser's encroachment on the Peninsula, most dramatically in the Yemen war of the mid-1960s.

10 Alan R. Taylor, *The Arab Balance of Power* (New York: Syracuse University Press, 1982), p. 52.

11 Paul Aarts and Gerd Nonneman (eds) *Saudi Arabia in the Balance: Political Economy, Society, Foreign Affairs* (London: Hurst, 2005); Tim Niblock, *Saudi Arabia: Power, Legitimacy and Survival* (London: Routledge, 2006).

12 *Turkish Daily News*, 14 October 1997.

13 IISS, *The Military Balance 1990–1991* (London: Brassey's, 1990).

14 Judy Dempsey, 'Israel: Iran's Missile Capability Source for Worry', *Financial Times*, 12 November 1997.

15 *Reuters Business Briefing*, 7 September 1999.

16 'Sudan Loses its Chains', *The Economist*, 12–18 June 1999, pp. 77–8.

17 See IMF's 2008 country report.

18 John Prendergast, 'Building for Peace in the Horn of Africa: Diplomacy and Beyond', *USIP Special Report*, 28 June 1999.

19 *The Indian Ocean Newsletter*, 15 May 1999.

20 Michael C. Hudson, 'The Middle East', in James Rosenau *et al.* (eds) *World Politics* (New York: The Free Press, 1976), pp. 466–500.

21 Bassam Tibi, op. cit., p. 54.

22 F. Gregory Gause, III, *The International Relations of the Persian Gulf* (Cambridge: Cambridge University Press, 2010).

23 Yezid Sayigh, 'Globalization Manqué: Regional Fragmentation and Authoritarian-Liberalism in the Middle East', in Louise Fawcett and Yezid Sayigh (eds) *The Third World Beyond the Cold War: Continuity and Change* (Oxford: Oxford University Press, 1999), p. 231.

24 Amitav Acharya, 'Developing Countries and the Emerging World Order: Security and Institutions', in Louise Fawcett and Yezid Sayigh (eds) *The Third World Beyond the Cold War: Continuity and Change* (Oxford: Oxford University Press, 1999), p. 80.

25 Ibid.

26 To coin a phrase from Ohmae. See Kenichi Ohmae, *The End of the Nation State: The Rise of Regional Economies* (New York: Free Press, 1995).

27 Kalevi J. Holsti, *Taming the Sovereigns: Institutional Change in International Politics* (Cambridge: Cambridge University Press, 2004).

Select bibliography

Arab Banking Corporation (1994) *The Arab Economies: Structure and Outlook*, Bahrain: ABC.

Acharya, Amitav (1989) *U.S. Military Strategy in the Gulf*, London: Routledge.

Acharya, Amitav (1999) 'Developing Countries and the Emerging World Order: Security and Institutions', in Louise Fawcett and Yezid Sayigh (eds) *The Third World Beyond the Cold War: Continuity and Change*, Oxford: Oxford University Press.

Aftandilian, Gregory L. (1993) *Egypt's Bid for Arab Leadership: Implications for U.S. Policy*, New York: Council on Foreign Relations.

Ali, Mohammed (1996) *Ethnicity, Politics, and Society in Northeast Africa: Conflict and Social Change*, Lanham, MD: University Press of America.

Allan, J. A. (ed.) (1996) *Water, Peace and the Middle East: Negotiating Resources in the Jordan Basin*, London: I.B. Tauris.

American Chamber of Commerce in Egypt (1995) *Freight Land Transportation in Egypt: Present Status and Future Prospects*, Cairo: ACCE, January.

Anthony, John Duke (1975) 'The Red Sea: Control of the Southern Approach', *Middle East Problem* Paper No. 13, Washington, DC: The Middle East Institute.

Ayoob, Mohammed (1995) *The Third World Security Predicament: State Making, Regional Conflict, and the International System*, Boulder, CO: Lynne Rienner.

Barghouti, Iyad (1996) 'Islamist Movements in Historical Palestine', in Abdel Salam Sidahmed and Anoushiravan Ehteshami (eds) *Islamic Fundamentalism*, Boulder, CO: Westview Press.

Beit-Hallahmi, Benjamin (1988) *The Israeli Connection: Whom Israel Arms and Why*, London: I.B. Tauris.

Bell, J. Bowyer (1973) *The Horn of Africa: Strategic Magnet in the Seventies*, New York: National Strategy International Center.

Bernal, Victoria (1999) 'Migration, Modernity and Islam in Rural Sudan', *Middle East Report*, No. 211, Summer.

Bilgin, Pinar (2004) *Regional Security in the Middle East: A Critical Perspective*, London: Routledge Curzon.

Binder, Leonard (1958) 'The Middle East as a Subordinate International System', *World Politics*, Vol. 10, April.

Bin Sultan, Khaled (1995) *Desert Warrior*, London: HarperCollins.

Blechman, B. M. and Luttwak E. N. (eds) (1984) *International Security Yearbook 1983/84*, London: Macmillan.

BP (2010) *BP Statistical Review of World Energy.*

Brown, L. Carl (ed.) (2001) *Diplomacy in the Middle East: The International Relations of Regional and Outside Powers*, London: I.B. Tauris.

Brownlie, Ian (1979) *African Boundaries: A Legal and Diplomatic Encyclopaedia*, London: Hurst.

Buzan, Barry (1995) 'The Level of Analysis Problem in International Relations Reconsidered', in Ken Booth and Steve Smith (eds) *International Relations Theory Today*, Cambridge: Polity Press.

Buzan, Barry and Waever, Ole (2003) *Regions and Powers: The Structure of International Security*, Cambridge: Cambridge University Press.

Buzan, Barry and Gonzalez-Pelaez, Ana (eds) (2009) *International Society and the Middle East: English School Theory at the Regional Level*, New York: Palgrave Macmillan.

Campbell, John C. (1978) 'The Soviet Union in the Middle East', *Middle East Journal*, Vol. 32, No. 1, Winter.

Cantori, Louis J. and Spiegel, Steven L. (1970) *The International Relations of Regions: A Comparative Approach*, Englewood Cliffs, NJ: Prentice-Hall.

CIA (1996) *Handbook of International Economic Statistics* Washington, DC: GPO, available at: http://www.odci.gov/cia/publications/factbook/html.

Clawson, Patrick and Gedal, Zoe Danon (1999) *Dollars and Diplomacy*, Washington, DC: Washington Institute for Near East Policy.

Connell, Dan (1999) 'Behind the War in the Horn of Africa', *Middle East International*, No. 595, 12 March.

Cordesman, Anthony H. (1989) 'The Regional Balance', in Hans Maull and Otto Pick (eds) *The Gulf War*, London: Pinter Publishers.

Cordesman, Anthony H. (1997) *Saudi Arabia: Guarding the Desert Kingdom*, Boulder, CO: Westview Press.

de Jong, Jan (1998) 'The Geography of Politics: Israel's Settlement Drive After Oslo', in George Giacaman and Dag Jørund Lønning (eds) *After Oslo: New Realities, Old Problems*, London: Pluto Press.

Dekmejian, R. Hrair (1972) *Egypt Under Nasir*, London: University of London Press.

Directorate General for Yanbu Project (n.d.) *Investment Opportunities: Industry*, Yanbu, Saudi Arabia.

Economist, The (1996) *Pocket World in Figures 1997*, London: Profile Books.

Economist Intelligence Unit database, http://www.odci.gov/cia/publications/factbook/er.html.

Economist Intelligence Unit (1998) *EIU Country Profile: Egypt 1998–99*, London: EIU.

Efrat, Elisha (1994) 'The Israel-Jordan Boundary Dispute in the Arava Valley', *British Journal of Middle Eastern Studies*, Vol. 21, No. 2.

El-Hakim, Ali (1979) *The Middle Eastern States and the Law of the Sea*, Manchester: Manchester University Press.

Erlich, Haggai (1994) *Ethiopia and the Middle East*, Boulder, CO: Lynne Rienner.

Europa (1998a) *Africa, South of the Sahara 1998*, London: Europa.

Europa (1998b) *The Middle East and North Africa 1999*, London: Europa.

Ewing, Jonathan (2008) 'Ethiopia and Eritrea in Turmoil: Implications for Peace and Security in a Troubled Region', *Situation Report*, 1 December 2008.

Faringdon, E. (1989) *Strategic Geography: NATO, Warsaw Pact, and the Superpowers*, London: Routledge.

Fawcett, Louise (1992) *Iran and the Cold War: The Azerbaijan Crisis of 1946*, Cambridge: Cambridge University Press.

Fawcett, Louise (ed.) (2005) *International Relations of the Middle East*, Oxford: Oxford University Press.

Fawcett, Louise and Hurrell, Andrew (eds) (1995) *Regionalism in World Politics: Regional Organization and International Order*, Oxford: Oxford University Press.

Gause, F. Gregory, III (1999) 'Systemic Approaches to Middle East International Relations', *International Studies Review*, Vol. 1, No. 1, Spring.

Gause, F. Gregory, III (2010) *The International Relations of the Persian Gulf*, Cambridge: Cambridge University Press.

Gerges, Fawaz A. (1994) *The Superpowers and the Middle East: Regional and International Relations, 1955–1967*, Boulder, CO: Westview Press.

Godsell, Geoffrey (1981) 'Containing Soviet Power: Once Again the Top US Priority', *Christian Science Monitor*, 13 March.

Golan, Galia (1990) *Soviet Policies in the Middle East: From World War II to Gorbachev*, Cambridge: Cambridge University Press.

Gorman, Robert F. (1981) *Political Conflict on the Horn of Africa*, New York: Praeger.

Hahn, Peter (1996) 'National Security Concerns in U.S. Policy Toward Egypt, 1949–1956', in David W. Lesch (ed.) *The Middle East and the United States: A Historical and Political Assessment*, Boulder, CO: Westview Press.

Hail, J. A. (1996) *Britain's Foreign Policy in Egypt and Sudan, 1947–1956*, Reading, MA: Ithaca Press.

Halliday, Fred (1978) 'U.S. Policy in the Horn of Africa: *Aboulia* or Proxy Intervention?', *Review of African Political Economy*, No. 10, September–December.

Halliday, Fred (1989) *Cold War, Third World: An Essay on Soviet-American Relations*, London: Century Hutchinson.

Halliday, Fred (1997) 'The Middle East, the Great Powers, and the Cold War', in Yezid Sayigh and Avi Shlaim (eds) *The Cold War and the Middle East*, Oxford: Oxford University Press.

Halliday, Fred (2005) *The Middle East in International Relations: Power, Politics and Ideology*, Cambridge: Cambridge University Press.

Harrison, Ewan (2004) *The Post-Cold War International System: Strategies, Institutions and Reflexivity*, London: Routledge.

Hasnat, Syed Farooq (1989) 'The Persian Gulf as a Regional System: Its Operations in the New World Order', *Strategic Studies*, Vol. XIII, No. 4, Summer 1989.

Henze, P. B. (1982) *Arming the Horn 1960–1980,* Washington, DC: International Security Studies Program, The Wilson Center.

Henze, Paul (1993) 'Ethiopia and Eritrea: The Defeat of the Derg and the Establishment of New Governments', in David R. Smock (ed.) *Making War and Waging Peace: Foreign Intervention in Africa*, Washington, DC: United States Institute of Peace Press.

Hobsbawm, Eric (1995) *Age of Extremes: The Short Twentieth Century 1914–1991*, London: Abacus.

Holsti, Kalevi J. (2004) *Taming the Sovereigns: Institutional Change in International Politics*, Cambridge: Cambridge University Press.

Hopwood, Derek (1985) *Egypt: Politics and Society 1945–1984*, Winchester, MA: Allen and Unwin.

Hourani, Albert (1991) *A History of the Arab Peoples*, London: Faber and Faber.

Hudson, Michael C. (1976) 'The Middle East', in James Rosenau *et al.* (eds) *World Politics*, New York: The Free Press.

IISS, *The Military Balance* (various years) Oxford: Oxford University Press.

International Institute for Strategic Studies (2010) *The Military Balance 2010*, London: Routledge.

Jordan Media Group (1995) *The Jordan-Israel Peace Treaty: What Is It?*, Amman: Jordan Media Group.

Kaplan, Morton (1957) *Systems and Process in International Politics*, New York: Wiley.

Kemp, Geoffrey and Harkavy, Robert E. (1997) *Strategic Geography and the Changing Middle East*, Washington, DC: Brookings Institution Press.

Kerr, Malcolm H. (1971) *The Arab Cold War: Gamal' Abd al-Nasir and His Rivals, 1958–1970*, Oxford: Oxford University Press.

Kleiman, Ephraim (1998) 'Is There a Secret Arab–Israeli Trade?', *Middle East Quarterly*, Vol. V, No. 2, June.

Kliot, Nurit (1995) 'The Evolution of the Egypt-Israel Boundary: From Colonial Foundations to Peaceful Borders', International Boundaries Research Unit, *Boundary and Territory Briefing*, Vol. 1, No. 8.

Korany, Bahgat and Dessouki, Ali E. Hillal (eds) (2008) *The Foreign Policies of Arab States: The Challenge of Globalization*, Cairo: Cairo University Press.

Landau, Jacob (1993) *The Arab Minority in Israel, 1967–1991*, Oxford: Clarendon Press.

Landau, Jacob (1994) *The Politics of Pan-Islam*, Oxford: Clarendon Press.

Lefebvre, Jeffrey A. (1996) 'Middle East Conflicts and Middle-Level Power Intervention in the Horn of Africa', *Middle East Journal*, Vol. 50, No. 3.

Legum, Colin and Lee, Bill (1977) *Conflict in the Horn of Africa*, New York: Africana Publishing Company.

Le Sage, Andre (2010) 'Africa's Irregular Security Threats: Challenges for U.S. Engagement', *Strategic Forum*, No. 255, May.

Lesch, Ann Mosely (1993) 'External Involvement in the Sudanese Civil War', in David R. Smock (ed.) *Making War and Waging Peace: Foreign Intervention in Africa*, Washington, DC: United States Institute of Peace.

Levran, Aharon (1997) *Israeli Strategy After Desert Storm: Lessons of the Second Gulf War*, London: Frank Cass.

Lewis, Bernard (1996) *The Middle East: Two Thousand Years of History from the Rise of Christianity to the Present Day*, London: Phoenix.

Loescher, Gil (1992) *Refugee Movements and International Security*, Adelphi Paper 268, Summer.

Looney, Robert (ed.) (2009) *Handbook of US-Middle East Relations: Formative Factors and Regional Perspectives*, London: Routledge.

McClintock, David (1980) 'The Yemen Arab Republic', in David Long and Bernard Reick (eds) *The Government and Politics of the Middle East and North Africa*, Boulder, CO: Westview Press.

MacMichael, H.A. (1967) *A History of Arabian Sudan*, London: Frank Cass.

McMurray, David (1999) 'Recent Trends in Middle Eastern Migration', *Middle East Report*, No. 211, Summer.

Makinda, Samuel M. (1992) *Security in the Horn of Africa*, Adelphi Paper 269, London: Brassey's for IISS.

Mason, John W. (1996) *The Cold War, 1945–1991*, London: Routledge.

Meo, Leila (ed.) (1981) *U.S. Strategy in the Gulf: Intervention against Liberation*, Belmont, MA: Association of Arab-American University Graduates.

Mesfin, Berouk (2008) 'The Eritrea-Djibouti Border Dispute', *Situation Report*, 15 September.

Milton-Edwards, Beverley (1996) 'Climate of Change in Jordan's Islamist Movement', in Abdel Salam Sidahmed and Anoushiravan Ehteshami (eds) *Islamic Fundamentalism*, Boulder, CO: Westview Press.

Murphy, Emma C. (1994) 'Structural Inhibitions to Economic Liberalization in Israel', *Middle East Journal*, Vol. 48, No. 1.

Nonneman, Gerd (1997) 'Key Issues in the Yemeni Economy', in E. G. H. Joffé, M. J. Hachemi and E. W. Watkins (eds) *Yemen Today: Crisis and Solutions*, London: Carvel Press.

O'Ballance, Edgar (1988) *The Gulf War*, London: Brassey's.

Ohmae, Kenichi (1995) *The End of the Nation State: The Rise of Regional Economies*, New York: Free Press.

Ottaway, Marina (1982) *Soviet and American Influence in the Horn of Africa*, New York: Praeger.

Owen, Roger (1992) *State, Power and Politics in the Making of the Modern Middle East*, London: Routledge.

Owen, Roger and Sevket, Pamuk (1998) *A History of Middle East Economies in the Twentieth Century*, London: I.B.Tauris.

Paul, Jim (1977) 'Struggle in the Horn', *MERIP Report*, No. 62, Vol. 7.

Peterson, J.E. (1982) *Yemen: The Search for a Modern State*, London: Croom Helm.

Porter, Bruce D. (1984) *The USSR in Third World Conflicts: Soviet Arms and Diplomacy in Local Wars, 1945–1980*, Cambridge: Cambridge University Press.

Prendergast, John (1999) 'Building for Peace in the Horn of Africa: Diplomacy and Beyond', *USIP Special Report*, 28 June.

Record, Jeffrey (1981) *The Rapid Deployment Force and U.S. Military Intervention in the Persian Gulf*, Cambridge, MA: Institute for Foreign Policy Analysis.

Reich, Bernard (1964) 'Israel's Policy in Africa', *Middle East Journal*, Vol. 18, No. 1.

Review of International Studies (2009) 'Globalising the Regional, Regionalising the Global', Special Issue, Vol. 35, February.

Rodinson, Maxime (1968) *Israel and the Arabs*, London: Penguin.

Ronen, Yehudit (1997) 'Sudan', in Bruce Maddy-Weitzman (ed.) *Middle East Contemporary Survey Volume XIX: 1995*, Boulder, CO: Westview Press.

Rothkopf, Carol Zeman (1973) *The Opening of the Suez Canal*, New York: Franklin Watts.

Russet, B. M. (1967) *International Regions and the International System*, Chicago: University of Chicago Press.

Salame, Ghassan (1988) 'Inter-Arab Politics: The Return of Geography', in William B. Quant (ed.) *The Middle East: Ten Years after Camp David*, Washington, DC: Brookings Institution.

Saudi Arabian Monetary Agency (various years) *Annual Report*, Riyadh: SAMA.

Sayigh, Yezid (1997a) 'System Breakdown in the Middle East?', in *Middle Eastern Lectures 2*, Tel Aviv: Tel Aviv University.

Sayigh, Yezid (1997b) *Armed Struggle and the Search for the State: The Palestinian National Movement, 1949–1993*, Oxford: Oxford University Press.

Sayigh, Yezid (1999) 'Globalization Manqué: Regional Fragmentation and Authoritarian-Liberalism in the Middle East', in Louise Fawcett and Yezid Sayigh (eds) *The Third World Beyond the Cold War: Continuity and Change*, Oxford: Oxford University Press.

Schofield, Clive and Pratt, Martin (1996) 'Eritrea and Yemen at Odds in the Red Sea', *Jane's Intelligence Review*, Vol. 8, No. 6.

Schofield, Richard (ed.) (1994) *Territorial Foundations of the Gulf States*, London: University College London.

Schofield, Richard (1997) 'The Last Missing Fence in the Desert: The Saudi–Yemeni Boundary', in E. G. H. Joffé, M. J. Hachemi and E. W. Watkins (eds) *Yemen Today: Crisis and Solutions*, London: Carvel Press.

Schraeder, Peter J. (1994) *United States Foreign Policy toward Africa: Incrementalism, Crisis and Change*, Cambridge: Cambridge University Press.

Schwab, Peter (1985) *Ethiopia: Politics, Economics and Society*, London: Pinter Publishers.

Segev, Samuel (1988) *The Iranian Triangle: The Untold Story of Israel's Role in the Iran-Contra Affair*, New York: Free Press.

Selassie, Bereket Habte (1980) *Conflict and Intervention in the Horn of Africa*, New York: Monthly Review Press.

Shapland, Greg (1997) *Rivers of Discord: International Water Disputes in the Middle East*, London: Hurst.

Shirabi, Hisham (1969) 'The Transformation of Ideology in the Arab World', in Irene L. Gendzier (ed.) *A Middle East Reader*, New York: Pegasus.

Silberman, Leo (1960) 'Ethiopia: Power of Moderation', *Middle East Journal*, Vol. 14, No. 2, Spring.

Soffer, Arnon (1999) *Rivers of Fire*, London: Rowman and Littlefield.

Sokolsky, Joel J. (1987) 'The Superpowers and the Middle East: The Maritime Dimension', in Aurel Braun (ed.) *The Middle East in Global Strategy*, Boulder, CO: Westview Press.

Spears, Ian S. (2009) *Civil War in African States: The Search for Security*, Boulder, CO: First Forum Press.

Suez Canal Report (various years) Cairo: Suez Canal Authority.

Swain, Ashok (1998) 'A New Challenge: Water Scarcity in the Arab World', *Arab Studies Quarterly*, Vol. 20, No. 1.

Taylor, Alan R. (1982) *The Arab Balance of Power*, New York: Syracuse University Press.

Teitelbaum, Joshua (1997) 'Saudi Arabia', in Bruce Maddy-Weitzman (ed.) *Middle East Contemporary Survey Volume XIX: 1995*, Boulder, CO: Westview Press.

Temko, Ned (1973) 'Red Sea Crisis Boosts US', *Christian Science Monitor*, 15 August.

Thompson, William R. (1973) 'The Regional Subsystem: A Conceptual Explication and a Propositional Inventory', *International Studies Quarterly*, Vol. 17, No. 1, March.

Tibi, Bassam (1998) *Conflict and War in the Middle East: From Interstate War to New Security*, London: Macmillan.

Trapmann, A. H. (1915) 'The First Phase of Turkey's Share in the War', *The Great War*, Part 34, Chapter XLVIII, April.

Treverton, Gregory (1981) 'Introduction', in G. Treverton (ed.) *Crisis Management and the Super-powers in the Middle East*, Aldershot: Gower.

Vassiliev, Alexei (1993) *Russian Policy in the Middle East: From Messianism to Pragmatism*, Reading, MA: Ithaca Press.

Waltz, Kenneth (1959) *Man, the State and War*, New York: Columbia University Press.

Waterbury, John (1983) *The Egypt of Nasser and Sadat*, Princeton, NJ: Princeton University Press.

Whelan, Joseph G. and Dixon, Michael J. (1986) *The Soviet Union in the Third World: Threat to World Peace?*, London: Brassey's.

Wilson, Rodney (1995) *Economic Development in the Middle East*, London: Routledge.

Wint, Guy and Calvocoressi, Peter (1957) *Middle East Crisis*, London: Penguin.

Newspapers and magazines

African Security Review
Airforces Monthly
Al-Ahram Weekly
Al-Hayat

Al Quds Al'Arabi
Arab Press Service Diplomat
Asharq al-Awsat
Associated Press
Boundary and Security Bulletin
Christian Science Monitor
Economist Intelligence Unit
Flight International
Guardian Weekly
Gulf States Newsletter
International Herald Tribune
Iraqi News Agency
Jane's Defence Weekly
Jane's Intelligence Review
MENA News Agency
Middle East Economic Digest
Middle East Mirror
Middle East Review
Middle East Security Report
Mid-East Realities
Oil and Gas Journal
Radio France International
Reuters
Reuters Business Briefing
Saudi Gazette
Sudan Focus
Summary of World Broadcasts
The Economist
The Financial Times
The Guardian
The Independent
The Indian Ocean Newsletter
The Jerusalem Post
The New York Times
The Times
The Washington Post
Turkish Daily News
Yemen Times
Yemen Times Business and Economy

Websites

ArabicNews.com
BBC News (online)
CNN.com
Eritrean Network Information Center (online)
http://AddisTribune.EthiopiaOnline.Net/Archives/1999/05/07
http://www.arab.net/arabview/articles/ahmadsalah1.html

http://www.arabfund.org/loans.htm
http://www.arabicnews.com/ansub/Daily/Day/.html
http://www.eritrea.org/EIB/Economy/EconomicProfile.html
http://www.eritrea.org/EIB/News/0998/N091701.html
http://www.milnet.com/milnet/pentagon/centcom/sudan/sudinf.html
http://www.nandotimes.com
Yemen News (online)

Index

Note: page number in **bold** refer to illustrations